Rights-based Direct Practice with Children

Series editor

Child Rights and You, Mumbai, Maharashtra, India

About the Series

This series provides comprehensive source material for teachers, trainers, facilitators and field workers in direct practice with children. It draws linkages among the foundation of life skills of self; psychosocial, sociological and critical theories of child development, childhood and family; the ideology of child rights; the methodology of direct practice with children comprising approaches, methods and skills, drawing from the professions of social work and counselling; and the preventative framework of service delivery systems for children, based on the public health care prevention model.

Each module of the sourcebooks comprises appropriate concepts and theories for developing users' understanding of specific topics, and recommends a range of relevant activities that they can adapt to facilitate participatory learning of different target groups in different contexts. Most of these activities have been piloted in the field by select development support staff of Child Rights and You and their project partners.

This series makes a unique contribution as training and reference sourcebook for professionals and practitioners of child rights across the world, and especially in developing countries.

Series Editor

CRY—Child Rights and You (CRY) is an Indian NGO that believes in every child's right to a childhood—to live, learn, grow, and play. For over four decades, CRY and its 200 partner NGOs have worked with parents and communities to ensure lasting change in the lives of more than 2,000,000 underprivileged children, across 23 states in India.

CRY was founded in 1979—initially the dream of a young 25-year-old airline purser, Rippan Kapur. Rippan had a deep faith that happy, well-cared for children are the basis of a society worth living in, and that every single person or institution has the immense potential to be part of lasting change. Today, it continues to be committed to its vision for a happy, healthy and creative childhood for every child. Its goals and work on the ground include ensuring that children in CRY-supported programmes have access to free and quality education, primary healthcare, reduced rate of child malnutrition and that they are safe from violence, abuse and exploitation. It also works towards making sure children's voices are recognised in issues that affect them. CRY's reason for being is to ensure children can live, learn, play and express themselves, and to bring about lasting change in children's lives.

For more information please visit us at www.cry.org.

More information about this series at http://www.springer.com/series/15428

Murli Desai · Sheetal Goel

Child Rights Education for Inclusion and Protection

Primary Prevention

CHILD RIGHTS AND YOU
www.cry.org
Ensuring lasting change
for children

 Springer

Murli Desai
Former Professor
Tata Institute of Social Sciences
Mumbai, Maharashtra
India

Sheetal Goel
Social Work Practitioner
Surrey County Council
Kingston upon Thames
UK

ISSN 2520-1751   ISSN 2520-176X (electronic)
Rights-based Direct Practice with Children
ISBN 978-981-13-0416-3   ISBN 978-981-13-0417-0   (eBook)
https://doi.org/10.1007/978-981-13-0417-0

Library of Congress Control Number: 2018938644

Printed on acid-free paper

This Springer imprint is published by the registered company Springer Nature Singapore Pte Ltd.
The registered company address is: 152 Beach Road, #21-01/04 Gateway East, Singapore 189721, Singapore

About the Authors

Dr. Murli Desai, M.A. and Ph.D. in social work, and former Professor at the Tata Institute of Social Sciences, was commissioned by CRY to prepare a series of four sourcebooks on rights-based direct practice with children. She has prepared two of the sourcebooks by adapting, updating and adding chapters to her book *A Rights-Based Preventative Approach for Psychosocial Well-Being in Childhood*, published by Springer, in 2010. Other two sourcebooks are newly prepared by her with a co-author. She has drawn from a comprehensive international literature review; curriculum planning and teaching courses on child development, child welfare and child rights in the USA, India and Singapore; consultancy projects with Governments of India, Tamil Nadu and Goa and with international organisations such as UNICEF, Child Protection Working Group and Save the Children; collaboration with voluntary organisations such as Butterflies and Child Rights in Goa; teacher training in schools; and experience of conducting and facilitating workshops for adolescents.

Sheetal Goel has an M.A. in medical and psychiatric social work from the Tata Institute of Social Sciences (TISS), Mumbai. Thereafter, she began her career as a social work practitioner in a Mumbai-based special school for children living with disability. Further, in 1999, she joined the Cell for AIDS Research Action and Training (CARAT), a field-action project of TISS. In 2002, she also worked as a Lecturer at the Medical and Psychiatric Social Work Department in TISS. She has spent a large part of her working life as an HIV counsellor, trainer, activist and researcher in Mumbai. The thrust and focus of her work area are health and sexuality-related issues. She has engaged with children, youth and professionals (that include doctors, nurses, social work students and practitioners and school teachers) through varied training sessions in HIV-related issues and life skills training. She relocated to the UK in 2014 and is currently working as a social work practitioner in the adult social care team of Surrey County Council.

Foreword to the Series

Children are the raison d'être for us at Child Rights and You (CRY), which began work in the late 1970s through the dynamism of its founder, the late Rippan Kapur, who along with seven friends registered this organisation. CRY has nurtured its founder's vision and grown from strength to strength over the decades spanning across a range of rights for children.

Children form approximately one-third of India's population, yet they and the issues they face are not prioritised. Despite having some positive and progressive laws, policies and programmes, the situation still remains grim, with disheartening trends seen in nearly all child rights indicators over the past decade and more. Children have equal fundamental rights as adults and are not lesser or half citizens on the basis of their age. At CRY, we believe that every child has a right to childhood and the right to live, learn, grow and play.

The provisions of the Indian Constitution along with India's ratification of the United Nations Convention on the Rights of the Child (UNCRC) in 1992 give all children the right to life, health, nutrition, name and a nationality; the right to protection from exploitation, abuse and neglect; right to development towards education, care, leisure, recreation and cultural activities; and the right to participation.

Child participation is one of the four core principles of the UNCRC, which asserts that children and young people up to the age of 18 have the right to freely express their views and feelings and that there is an obligation to listen to children's views, enabling their participation in all matters affecting them within the family, schools, public and civic life.

CRY envisions broadening the discourse on child rights to incorporate child development, which entails physical, emotional, social and psychological growth. It also aims to understand the child from the yardsticks of her age-appropriate milestones and the related skills that she needs to achieve to lead an optimally functioning life and thus become more autonomous and responsible.

These sourcebooks on *Rights-Based Direct Practice with Children* endeavour to ensure the assimilation of a multidisciplinary and comprehensive approach to understand the child as a holistic being. They aim to bridge theories with practice using a rights-based perspective. The sourcebooks also aim to bridge the gaps between the adult and the child binary by providing an inclusive and participative approach to working with children; thus, they are aimed not only towards children but also towards adults as receivers of the input. These books will enable the primary duty-bearers to create and facilitate integrated preventive services for children.

CRY's objective in undertaking this work was to see that children undergo transformation such that they are able to exercise their agency based on evolving capacities in matters that affect them and that they are treated with dignity, respect and equity by adults. At CRY, we believe that adults or the primary duty-bearers, including parents, need to be engaged and educated about these rights-based practices in all spaces such as family, school and community at large, resulting in attitudinal shifts, thereby enabling behavioural change both for adults and for children.

The contents of these sourcebooks were pilot tested with children and parents in eight States where CRY has been actively engaged with children and communities. It was observed that after the training, children were much more confident, assertive and empowered with reference to their self and their environment. Some children were instrumental in bringing about relevant changes in their homes and schools and communities, taking responsibility for themselves as well as for their peers, thus strengthening our conviction in these sourcebooks. We urge various development and academic organisations to use this model for creating meaningful change in their fields of learning and practice.

We are sure that this wonderful series in which Dr. Murli Desai has created a practical model for such work will play a role in creating a prevention and protection model for children in different environments and vulnerabilities in an effort to meet CRY's vision of 'a happy, healthy and creative child whose rights are protected and honoured in a society that is built on respect for dignity, justice and equity for all'.

With hope and faith

December 2016

Puja Marwaha
Chief Executive
Child Rights and You

Introduction to the Series

Aims and Target Groups

The series of sourcebooks on *Rights-Based Direct Practice with Children* provides a comprehensive source material to facilitate participatory group workshops and provide reference material for teachers, trainers, facilitators and fieldworkers on direct practice with children. Each sourcebook provides multidisciplinary concepts and theories on the theme and subthemes, and activities and tools based on these. It first aims to facilitate participatory group workshops on the methodology of rights-based direct practice with children for teachers, trainers/facilitators, students and fieldworkers. Those trained can then implement the methodology with children and their primary duty-bearers in the following preventative framework: child empowerment services at the primary prevention level for all children; supplementary childcare and child and family support services at the secondary prevention level for children at risk; and substitute childcare, child protection and justice and child rehabilitation services at the tertiary prevention level for children with socio-legal problems. They can also use it as an ongoing reference material to guide and retrain them and provide feedback for revision of the sourcebooks periodically and use it as a reference material for policy and programme planning for children.

The series comprises all the areas of rights-based direct practice with children: the theories, ideology and methodology of rights-based direct practice with children; life skills development and child rights education for children and their primary duty-bearers for primary prevention; and child rights-based service delivery systems for secondary and tertiary preventions.

This series is prepared for the following institutional and individual target groups, prepared with examples from India, but relevant to all developing countries all over the world: colleges and departments of social work and child development and their teachers and students of the courses on child rights and work with children; colleges and departments of educational psychology, mental health, human rights and teacher education and their teachers and students of courses on children; training institutions run by government organisations that conduct training programmes for work with children and their trainers and trainees for the various schemes for child development and child protection; schools and teachers; and child-centred government and voluntary organisations and their fieldworkers/social workers/development workers and counsellors.

Conceptual Framework

The conceptual framework for the sourcebook series comprises linkages among theories, ideology and self with the methodology of rights-based direct practice with children (Fig. 1).

The theories of child development and childhood mainly comprise psychosocial theories of development in childhood and adolescence; ecological theories of diversity in family and childhood; and critical theories of deconstruction of problems in childhood.

The ideology of child rights (Fig. 2) mainly comprises the values, categories and principles, drawing from the United Nations Convention on the Rights of the Child (1989). The values of child rights are inherent dignity and the equal and inalienable rights of all members of the human family; and peace, dignity, tolerance, freedom, equality and justice. Child rights principles comprise the dignity of the child,

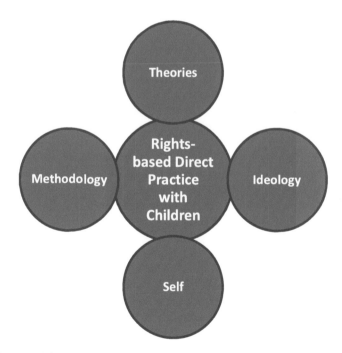

Fig. 1 Conceptual framework of rights-based direct practice with children

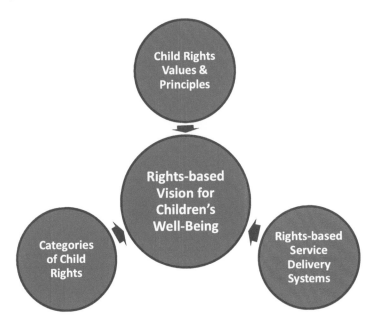

Fig. 2 Ideologies of child rights

primary consideration to the best interests of the child, universality and non-discrimination, and State and societal accountability. The categories of child rights are child's participation rights, development rights, family rights and protection rights. The rights-based service delivery systems comprise the comprehensive integrated systems approach, preventative approach, universal approach, community-based approach and family-based approach.

The rights-based vision for children's well-being comprises growing up with dignity in a democratic family and supportive community; achieving enriched development through health, education and play and recreation; developing self-awareness, proactive thinking skills, emotional intelligence, sensitive inter-personal communication skills and collaborative interpersonal relationship skills; playing a decisive and responsible role in their own life and a participatory role in the family, school, associations and community, and with the State as citizens; and being protected from discrimination, poverty, neglect, parental deprivation, violence, conflict with law and association with armed conflict.

The self-attributes of psychosocial life skills for self-awareness and self-empowerment of the teachers/trainers/facilitators, students/fieldworkers, children and their primary duty-bearers are grouped into self-empowerment, proactive thinking skills, emotional intelligence, sensitive interpersonal communication skills and collaborative interpersonal relationship skills.

Direct practice with children comprises face-to-face work with children and their primary duty-bearers. The methodology of direct practice with children (see Fig. 3) comprises the services, approaches, methods and skills of the professions of social

Fig. 3 Methodology of direct practice with children

work and counselling as applied to work with children. Services for children are divided into primary-, secondary- and tertiary-level services. The primary prevention services for all children comprise child development services and child empowerment services. The secondary prevention services for children at risk comprise supplementary childcare services: day/night/after-school care for children, and child and family support services. The tertiary prevention services for children with socio-legal problems comprise substitute childcare services: foster family care, adoption and institutional care for children, child protection services, services for justice for children and child rehabilitation services.

The approaches of professional engagement with children comprise strength-based approach, person-centred approach, culture-sensitive approach, participatory approach and ethical approach. The methods of practice with children comprise the rights-based method of comprehensive, integrated, systemic, preventative, universal, family and community-based service delivery systems for children; the method of participatory group workshops for empowerment of children and their primary duty-bearers; the method of case management for care and protection of children and their parents at the secondary and tertiary prevention levels; and the method of outcome-based project cycle for service delivery systems for children and their parents.

Methodology of Training

This series recommends the methodology of facilitating participatory group workshops for training of teachers, trainers/facilitators and fieldworkers as well for conducting workshops for children and their primary duty-bearers. The core components of this methodology are experiential learning and group process; facilitating participation and maximising learning instead of teaching, etc. Selection of the methods depends on the type of topics. An assessment of the initial under-standing of or initiation into a topic may be carried out by brainstorming or rounds. Knowledge-focused topics may be learnt through lecturettes/presentations, self-study and small group discussions. Attitude-focused topics may be learnt through reflective self-assessment, and pairing and sharing. Skill-based topics may be learnt through experiential methods such as role-plays and simulations. Field-based topics may be learnt through discussion of video films and case studies, field observations and inviting practitioners. All the methods need to be followed by self-reflection and discussion in small/large groups.

Structure

All the sourcebooks include this introduction to the series. Each sourcebook also includes Preface, Contents, Lists of Summary Charts, Lists of Activities and English–Hindi Glossary of the Sourcebook followed by the modules. Each module chapter starts with the prerequisite modules (to ensure sequencing and linkages) and the module's aim and learner objectives. The first section focuses on the introduction of the module with reference to the overall multidisciplinary concepts and theories for developing the teachers'/trainers'/facilitators' understanding of the module and one or more introductory activities to introduce the module and the units of the module. Each module is divided into units. Each unit is divided into multidisci-plinary concepts and theories for developing the teachers'/trainers'/facilitators' understanding of the unit and a range of relevant activities that they can conduct.

The sourcebook provides one or more activities for each unit. Each activity comprises learner outcome, procedure and tool (if any), questions for discussion and time estimate. When planning the implementation of a module, the teachers/trainers/facilitators will have to use their discretion to select the appropriate activities or adapt them according to the target group (students/fieldworkers/children/primary duty-bearers), their situational context and time available. For facilitating partici-patory workshops, the activities suggested by the fieldworkers/children/parents may be welcome if they meet the learner outcomes. The tools provided for the activities comprise video films, stories, case studies, exercises and charts summarising the concepts and theories in simple words. Local examples, stories and songs can also be invited from the participants, provided they meet the learner outcomes. Every module provides a concluding activity that can be used to ascertain if the participants have achieved the learner objectives and reflect on application of the learning. Each module ends with the references used for writing the chapters.

Previous Books Published in this Series

Sourcebook I: Introduction to Rights-Based Direct Practice with Children in 2018
Sourcebook II: Child Rights Education for Participation and Development: Primary Prevention in 2018

Sourcebook III: Child Rights Education for Inclusion and Protection: Primary Prevention

Preface

This Sourcebook III on "Child Rights Education for Inclusion and Protection: Primary Prevention" requires that the reader is already introduced to and trained in Sourcebook I on "Introduction to Rights-Based Direct Practice with Children" which introduced the multidisciplinary concepts and theories on child development and childhood, the ideology of child rights and methods for direct practice with children and Sourcebook II on "Child Rights Education for Participation and Development: Primary Prevention". Sourcebook III deals with the primary prevention approach of child rights education with specific reference to inclusion and protection.

Conceptual Framework for a Rights-Based Preventative Approach for Children

The preventative approach is an imperative in the rights-based approach as compared to merely dealing with social problems as they arise (a reactive approach). It is the only way to prevent and break the cycle of problems that children face as this approach is grounded in the ecological perspective, oriented to the future, empowerment-focused, developmental (adapted from Downs et al. 2009), cost-effective and prevents labelling of children. To prevent and break the cycle of problems in childhood, the public healthcare prevention model is applied in this Sourcebook Series to a rights-based comprehensive policy approach for children.

Primary Prevention: At the primary prevention level, the goal for rights-based direct practice with children may be prevention of all children's vulnerability through empowerment services, thereby preventing the need for the secondary- and tertiary-level interventions. Sourcebooks II and III focus on primary prevention in rights-based direct practice with children.

Secondary Prevention: At the secondary prevention level, the goal for rights-based direct practice with children may be prevention of exclusion, neglect, separation from parents, abuse and commercial exploitation of children at risk. This goal may be achieved through the systems of supplementary childcare and child supportive services, besides the child development and child empowerment services, thereby preventing the need for the tertiary-level interventions.

Tertiary Prevention: At the tertiary prevention level, the goal for rights-based direct practice with children may be prevention of socio-legal problems of parental deprivation, abuse and commercial exploitation, internal displacement, statelessness and refugee status of children, and conflict with law and association with armed conflict in childhood. This goal may be achieved through the systems of child protection, substitute childcare, rights-based justice and rehabilitation services, besides the systems for child development, child empowerment, supplementary childcare and child supportive services.

Primary Prevention for Empowerment of Children

Universal Primary Prevention of Vulnerability of All Children

At the primary prevention level, the goal may be prevention of all children's vulnerability, through universal child development and integrated child empowerment services, thereby preventing the need for the secondary- and tertiary-level interventions. Child development services include birth registration, health, education, and recreation and cultural activities that need to be ensured by health systems, schools, and recreation and cultural centres, respectively. Integrated child empowerment services include children's associations, life skills development and child rights education for children and their primary duty-bearers and parenting education.

At the primary prevention level, universal services are needed to promote knowledge and skills as well as strengthening the overall capacity of the community and society at large for caring and keeping children safe and protected. Primary prevention services tend to target general populations, although they may be directed towards specific groups. Where some children and families have been identified as needing to make use of those services as part of an individual preventive strategy, then they are classified as secondary. The distinction lies in a referral, a suggestion or the decision of families to use a particular service (Hong, n.d.).

Empowerment of Children

As children's vulnerability mainly takes place due to the adult–child power imbalance due to adultism and patriarchy, this problem can be mainly prevented by empowerment of children. Children's empowerment seeks to activate, support and honour children's ability to know their own knowing (adapted from Weick 1994). Parsons et al. (1994) cite Torre's components of the empowerment process that can be applied to children:

- Positive perceptions of personal worth, efficacy and internal locus of control
- Recognition, by self and others, that some of one's perceptions about one's self and the surrounding world are indeed valid, and therefore legitimate to voice

- The ability to think critically about macrolevel social, political and economic systems as well as about one's position within such systems
- Knowledge and skills necessary to more successfully influence micro-, mediating, and macrosystems

These components can be integrated into the integrated child empowerment services comprising the following:

- Children's associations
- Life skills development for children and their primary duty-bearers
- Child rights education for children and their primary duty-bearers
- Parenting education

Sourcebook I covers children's empowerment through children's associations, life skills development and parenting education, and Sourcebooks III and IV cover the wide range of child rights education.

Systems for Integration of Child Empowerment Workshops

Children's associations and schools are the most important systems to conduct child empowerment workshops at the primary prevention level. These child workshops can also be integrated into the training programmes of the primary prevention government schemes such as the following:

- Rajiv Gandhi Scheme for Empowerment of Adolescent Girls (Sabla Yojana),
- The Kishori Shakti Yojana, known as the Adolescent Girls Scheme and
- The Adolescence Education Programme (AEP) coordinated by the National Council of Educational Research and Training (NCERT) in partnership with the Ministry of Human Resource Development (MHRD) and United Nations Population Fund (UNFPA).

Child Rights Education

Article 42 of the United Nations Convention of the Rights of the Child (UNCRC) states that the 'States Parties undertake to make the principles and provisions of the Convention widely known, by appropriate and active means, to adults and children alike'. According to the UNICEF website (http://www.unicef.org/crc/index_30184.html), child rights education (CRE) is teaching and learning about the provisions and principles of the Convention on the Rights of the Child and the 'child rights approach'—in order to empower both adults and children to take action to advocate for and apply these at the family, school, community, national and global levels. It helps adults and children work together, providing space and encouragement for the meaningful participation and sustained civic engagement of children. Child rights education seeks to:

- Embed the provisions and principles of the Convention and the child rights approach in formal and non-formal learning curricula and learning environments, as well as in the curricula and training of professionals working directly with children, or on issues affecting children.

- Raise awareness of the provisions and principles and the child rights approach through mass media and other channels to reach caregivers, community members and other members of the public.
- Build the capacity of children (as rights-holders) and adults (as duty-bearers) to advocate for and implement these provisions, principles and the child rights approach in daily life and professional practice (http://www.unicef.org/crc/index_ 30184.html).

The aims of child rights education in these sourcebooks are to make children and their primary duty-bearers learn about the ideology, categories, principles and vision of the UNCRC and the Fundamental Rights in the Indian Constitution, so that they both can be empowered to together advocate for and apply them at the family, school and community levels. Its components are divided into Sourcebooks II and III as follows:

1. Sourcebook II: Child Rights Education for Participation and Development: Primary Prevention
2. Sourcebook III: Child Rights Education for Inclusion and Protection: Primary Prevention

Sourcebook Aim and Learner Objectives

Sourcebook III aims at primary prevention for empowerment of children and their primary duty-bearers through child rights education on inclusion and protection with reference to the following topics:

1. Child rights to family life education for acceptance and respect for plurality of family forms, and democratisation of internal family dynamics and family's interactions with its environment;
2. Child rights for non-discrimination and inclusion of girls, children with disability, and Dalit and tribal children;
3. Child's cultural rights to cultural pluralism, intercultural harmony, multiculturalism, interculturality, minority rights and peace;
4. Child rights for financial education comprising knowledge about financial systems, skills for financial management, and financial inclusion; and
5. Child rights to prevention of physical violence such as child abuse, corporal punishment and bullying;
6. Child rights to prevention of commercial exploitation of children such as child labour, trafficking and sale;
7. Child rights to prevention of sexual violence with reference to child sexual abuse and commercial sexual exploitation of children;
8. Child rights to prevention of problems with sexual relationships such as violence, teenage pregnancy, unsafe abortion, unwed motherhood and Sexually Transmitted Infections;

9. Child rights to prevention of child marriage; and

10. Child rights to prevention of conflict with law.

The activities on child rights education given in each module are mainly addressing children. When planning the implementation of a module for children's primary duty-bearers, the facilitators will have to use their discretion to select the appropriate activities or adapt them according to the target group, and their role with reference to child rights.

Module Plan

The Sourcebook comprises 11 modules divided into two parts:

Part 1: Child's Rights Education for Inclusive Family and Society

1. Child Rights in Family Life
2. Rights of Girls and Children with Disability to Non-Discrimination and Inclusion
3. Rights of Dalit and Tribal Children to Non-Discrimination and Inclusion
4. Child Rights to Culture and Inter-Cultural Inclusion
5. Child Rights to Financial Education and Inclusion

Part 2: Child's Rights Education to Prevention of Violence

6. Child Rights to Prevention of Physical Violence
7. Child Rights to Prevention of Commercial Exploitation of Children
8. Child Rights to Prevention of Sexual Violence
9. Adolescent Rights to Prevention of Problems with Sexual Relationships
10. Child Rights to Prevention of Child Marriage
11. Child Rights to Prevention of Conflict with Law

Module Aims and Learner Objectives

Module on Child Rights to Family Life Education: The aim of this module is to learn about child rights to family life through the following learner objectives:

1. Examine the conceptual framework of family, family well-being and child right to family life education;
2. Develop awareness of importance and skills for acceptance and respect for plurality of family forms;
3. Develop awareness of importance and skills for democratisation of family's internal dynamics with scope for the development of individual members and for enriched family relationships; and
4. Develop awareness of importance and skills for democratisation of family's interaction with the environment with scope for the well-being of each family unit and for its harmony with its environment.

Module on Rights of Girls and Children with Disability to Non-Discrimination and Inclusion: The aim of this module is to learn about rights of girls and children with disability for non-discrimination and inclusion through the following learner objectives:

1. Examine the conceptual framework of prejudicing ideologies in self and systems that lead to discrimination and exclusion of children in vulnerable situations and these children's rights to non-discrimination and inclusion;
2. Develop awareness of the prejudicing ideology of sexism that leads to discrimination and exclusion of girls, their rights to non-discrimination, and strategies for their inclusion; and
3. Develop awareness of the prejudicing ideology of ableism that leads to discrimination and exclusion of children with disability, their rights to non-discrimination, and strategies for their inclusion.

Module on Rights of Dalit and Tribal Children to Non-Discrimination and Inclusion: The aim of this module is to learn about rights of Dalits and tribal children to non-discrimination and inclusion through the following learner objectives:

1. Develop awareness of the prejudicing ideology of casteism that leads to discrimination and exclusion of Dalit children who are more vulnerable than other children to casteism, caste-based poverty and stereotypes about their capabilities and roles;
2. Develop awareness of rights of Dalit children to non-discrimination and inclusion;
3. Develop awareness of discrimination and exclusion of tribal children who are significantly affected by tribal displacement for development projects and armed conflicts;
4. Develop awareness of rights of tribal children to non-discrimination and inclusion; and
5. Review the Constitutional and legal rights of Dalits and tribals, including the policy of reservations for Dalits and tribals.

Module on Child Rights to Culture and Inter-Cultural Inclusion: The aim of this module is to learn about child rights to culture and inter-cultural inclusion through the following learner objectives:

1. Examine the conceptual framework of culture and cultural diversity, and threats to cultural diversity due to cultural homogenisation based in Eurocentric development;
2. Review the spread of cultural conflicts rooted in prejudicing ideologies;
3. Examine child's cultural rights to cultural pluralism, intercultural harmony, multiculturalism, interculturality and intercultural inclusion;
4. Develop awareness of religious diversity and religious fundamentalism and learn the skills for protecting child's religious rights and promoting inter-religious inclusion; and

5. Develop awareness of linguistic diversity and learn the skills for protecting child's linguistic rights and promoting inter-linguistic inclusion.

Module on Child Rights to Financial Education and Inclusion: The aim of this module is to learn about child rights to financial education and inclusion through the following learner objectives:

1. Examine the conceptual framework of socio-economic class, poverty, child poverty and child economic citizenship, and child rights to financial education and inclusion for developing financial capability;
2. Develop an understanding of the functioning of banks and learn the skills for savings and asset building through children's accounts;
3. Develop awareness of importance and skills for financial planning and budgeting in children; and
4. Learn to provide consumer education to children and their parents with reference to marketing through mass media and awareness of consumer rights and responsibilities.

Module on Child Rights to Prevention of Physical Violence: The aim of this module is to learn about child rights to prevention of physical violence through the following learner objectives:

1. Examine the conceptual framework of violence against children with reference to physical and psychological violence, commercial exploitation and sexual abuse and sexual harassment which occur in all settings;
2. Understand child rights to prevent violence against them as no violence against children is justifiable and all violence against children is preventable;
3. Develop awareness of causes, child vulnerability and effects of physical abuse/corporal punishment on children, and child rights to its prevention; and
4. Develop awareness of causes, child vulnerability and effects of bullying among children, and child rights to its prevention.

Module on Child Rights to Prevention of Commercial Exploitation: The aim of this module is to learn about child rights to prevention of commercial exploitation through the following learner objectives:

1. Examine the conceptual framework of commercial exploitation of children which comprises abuse by the adult and remuneration in cash or kind to the child or a third person or persons, where the child is treated as a commercial object;
2. Understand child rights to prevention of their commercial exploitation;
3. Develop awareness of child rights to prevention of their exploitation for unpaid/underpaid labour in industries, construction work, restaurant work, domestic work, household-based work, etc.; and
4. Develop awareness of child rights to prevention of their trafficking and sale for begging, labour, prostitution, adoption, entertainment, sale of organs and marriage.

Module on Child Rights to Prevention of Sexual Violence: The aim of this module is to learn about child rights to prevention of sexual violence through the following learner objectives:

1. Examine the conceptual framework of child sexual abuse which is any intentional non-accidental sexual harm done to a child, as an object of gratification, that endangers or impairs the child's health and development
2. Learn about child rights and strategies for prevention of child sexual abuse;
3. Examine the conceptual framework of commercial sexual exploitation of children which comprises sexual abuse by the adult and remuneration in cash or kind to the child or a third person or persons, such as child prostitution, child pornography and child sex tourism; and
4. Learn about child rights and strategies for prevention of commercial sexual exploitation of children.

Module on Adolescent Rights to Prevention of Problems with Sexual Relationships: The aim of this module is to learn about adolescent rights to prevention of problems with sexual relationships through the following learner objectives:

1. Examine the conceptual framework of sexual relationships in adolescence such as romantic and sexual relationships, sexual behaviours and sexual orientation;
2. Develop awareness of problems with sexual relationships, risk and protective factors, and sexual rights and responsibilities to prevent these problems;
3. Develop awareness about violence in sexual relationships with reference to non-consensual sexual experiences and strategies for their prevention;
4. Develop awareness about problems with unprotected sexual relationships, namely, teenage pregnancy, unsafe abortion and unwed motherhood and strategies for their prevention;
5. Develop awareness about transmission of Sexually Transmitted Infections (STIs) and HIV and strategies for their prevention; and
6. Develop awareness about different contraceptive methods, and the strengths and limitations of each, to protect oneself from pregnancy and STIs.

Module on Child Rights to Prevention of Child Marriage: The aim of this module is to learn about child rights to prevention of child marriage through the following learner objectives:

1. Examine the conceptual framework of child marriages with reference to patriarchal norms, family and cultural norms, poverty and end of education;
2. Develop awareness of the effects of child marriages with reference to end of childhood, end of education, forced and unprotected sexual relationships, early pregnancy, maternal mortality, and recycling of malnutrition, gender equality and poverty;
3. Review the Prohibition of Child Marriage Act and the National Strategy for Prevention of Child Marriage and their enforcement in India; and

4. Learn the strategies to prevent child marriages with reference to empowerment of children, mobilisation of families and communities, and promoting girls' education and improving their economic situation.

Module on Child Rights to Prevention of Conflict with Law: The aim of this module is to learn about child rights to prevention of conflict with law through the following learner objectives:

1. Examine the conceptual framework of conflict with law in childhood with reference to its types and causes;
2. Learn the strategies to prevent conflict with law in childhood;
3. Develop awareness of rights of children accused of conflict with law with reference to apprehension and trial; and
4. Review the Juvenile Justice Act of India with reference to role of the police and the Juvenile Justice Board with reference to children accused of conflict with law.

Piloting of the Sourcebooks

I conducted a Training of Trainers (TOT) Workshop II on *The Methodology of Awareness Development on Child Rights and Responsibilities for Child Empowerment* based on the Sourcebooks II and III. The TOT II was held on April 11–22, 2016 to train eight of the Master Trainers from the Development Support Team from the four regions of CRY who had also been trained for the TOT I. This time, I had planned a one-day session on the facilitation method and then the participants facilitated a session each followed by feedback from me and fellow participants. This experience made them experts on the facilitation method as well as on the content of child rights education. The feedback from the CRY Trainers has been useful to revise the nomenclature and sequencing of the modules for Sourcebooks III and IV. In general, the participants felt that they could see a clear link between TOT I which focused on life skills and TOT II which helped them link life skills to children's reality. They were also happy that now they have a structured content on a range of issues to go to the field with.

Some of the feedback received from child participants of workshops of child rights education is listed below in their own words:

- 'We learnt many things from this unique event. We will benefit more from more such events'.
- 'The topics are beyond our school syllabus and interesting'.
- 'The training will help us in our lives'.
- 'I am inspired to work for the rights of the people'.
- My self-confidence has grown after this training'.
- 'The constitution treats us as equal though we quarrel over religion, caste creed, etc. I don't like it'.
- 'We must work for gender equality'.

- 'We should avoid the consumption of alcohol and smoking'.
- 'We should clean our environment for avoiding diseases'.
- 'We can use communication tools such as street plays, posters, slogans, etc. for creating awareness on health and education issues'.
- 'The training was very useful, informative and life transformative'.
- 'The life skills taught in the previous training and the present one are connected and useful'.
- 'Child rights was a very effective new topic and very explorative'.

The parents found the workshops very useful as it delved on issues related to their children, areas which if not made to think and discuss would have remained unspoken. Issues like child marriage, balanced diet, cultural stereotypes and the need for breaking such perceptions, need for facilitating intergenerational dialogue, stating the importance of education and effective communication were areas which were helpful. The parents also shared that they found it extremely interesting that same topics were discussed with them as well as their children. The children encouraged them to attend the workshop despite having the village festival where the entire village is involved. Some of the parents were dropped off to the workshop venue by their children on bicycles as they were fasting for the Puja. This shows that they found the workshop important and significant. Some of the parents felt that the workshop needs to be done once more where they could spend more time and have more fruitful discussions.

At the end of a workshop, a discussion led to develop a plan of action for the parents group to be more sensitive towards the children. The tasks they identified are:

- Conduct a house-to-house campaign for identification of children not in school and aim to enrol all of them in school.
- Emphasise education of girls and women as they are the primary caregivers— with engagement with the men of the villagers.
- Promote awareness of health of girls in the village through ICDS.
- Create awareness of child sexual abuse.
- Work towards pollution-free environment by keeping the village clean and engage with the villagers and Panchayat so that it has an effect on the health of children. Provide dustbins by Panchayat in the village to throw the garbage.

The methods identified by the parents to achieve the above are:

- Use posters and wall writing to create awareness in the village.
- Conduct monthly discussions with VERS and Children Resource Groups (CRG) to come at common points and develop solution to problems.
- Conduct monthly meeting with the children's collectives in the village to get to know the difficulties and develop ways to provide solutions.
- Use the public functions (cultural, religious events) to spread the messages on child rights.

Suggested Workshop Plans for Child Empowerment

Sessions of 2/3 Hours Each	Modules for 10–14 Years Age Group
05	Life Skills Development
21	Child Rights Education
26	**Total**
Sessions of 2/3 Hours Each	**Same Modules with Advanced Activities for 15–18 Years Age Group**
05	Life Skills Development
21	Child Rights Education
26	**Total**

Acknowledgements

I once again congratulate CRY for taking the initiative to prepare sourcebooks on theory and rights-based direct practice with children. I am very grateful to Ms. Puja Marwaha, the Chief Executive of CRY, and her colleague Ms. Vijayalakshmi Arora for giving me the opportunity to carry out this very exciting project of linking theory and rights with practice.

For preparing Sourcebooks II and III, I have drawn from a comprehensive international literature review, curriculum planning and teaching courses on child development, child welfare and child rights in the USA, India and Singapore; consultancy projects with Governments of India, Tamil Nadu and Goa and with international organisations such as UNICEF, Child Protection Working Group and Save the Children; collaboration with voluntary organisations such as Butterflies and Child Rights in Goa; teacher training in schools; and experience of conducting and facilitating workshops for adolescents. I am indebted to each and every one for their inputs into my thinking that has gone into developing and organising knowledge for this book. I am very thankful to Ms. Sheetal Goel, who is an independent social work professional, for co-authoring several modules with me, in Sourcebooks II and III. Her sincere hard work and creativity has made a valuable contribution to the Sourcebooks.

I am grateful to Ms. Sangeeta Kapila, the former In Charge of the Child Centre and Ms. Rakshanda Inam, the new Associate General Manager of the Child Centre of CRY for their prompt cooperation at every stage. The participants of TOT II, Protik Banerjee, Trina Chakrabarti, Ashim Ghosh, Dinesh Kakkoth, Pramod Pradhan, Praveen Singh and Vidya Raman, played multiple roles. They were participants as well as resource persons, role-playing as children as well as adults. Together, we made maximum use of the space that CRY created for us. I gained tremendously from them as they shared important experiences and insights and therefore contributed significantly to the success of the training. I congratulate them and the Child Centre and wish them a very enriched follow-up and institutionalisation of the training on direct practice with children in CRY functioning.

Mumbai, India   Murli Desai
August 2018   Former Professor and Head
                                                              Social Work Education and Practice Cell

References

Parsons, R. J., Jorgensen, J. D. & Hernandez, S. H. (1994). *The Integration of Social Work Practice*. Belmont, CA: Brooks/Cole Publishing Company.
Weick, A. (1994). Reconstructing social work education. In J. Laird (Ed.), *Revisioning social work education: A social reconstructionist approach* (pp. 11–30). New York: The Haworth Press.

Contents

List of Summary Charts

List of Activities

Part I
Child's Rights Education for Inclusive Family and Society

Module 1
Child's Rights in Family Life Education

Prerequisite Modules

The prerequisite Modules for this Module are:
From *Sourcebook I on Introduction to Rights-Based Direct Practice with Children*:

- Modules on Life Skills Development.

From *Sourcebook II on Child Rights Education for Participation and Development: Primary Prevention*:

- Introduction to Child Rights Education,
- Child Rights to Participation and Children's Associations.

Conceptual Framework of Family Life Education

Concepts and Theories

Family and Household

The family may be broadly defined as a unit of two or more persons united by ties of marriage, blood, adoption or consensual unions, generally constituting a single household, and interacting and communicating with each other (Desai, 1994, p. 16). Every individual has a family of orientation or family of origin as it is the family he/she is born into. Most individuals also form a family of procreation, mostly by marriage and childbearing but may be also by consensual relationships, reproductive technologies or adoption (Collins et al., 2007). Family and household are often used synonymously. However, households are places where people live together and share assets. Families and households are related but not all families live in the same households and not all households are families (Leeder, 2003).

© Child Rights and You 2018
M. Desai and S. Goel, *Child Rights Education for Inclusion and Protection: Primary Prevention*, Rights-based Direct Practice with Children, https://doi.org/10.1007/978-981-13-0417-0_1

Importance of Family

Family is considered the most important system for the child as it is an inseparable part of children's birth, identity, name, language, ethnicity, religion and nationality. The family's composition, structure and interaction patterns are major factors in children's survival, health, education, development and protection. Diversity in the environment brings variations in family life, which, in turn, explains differences in children's well-being to a large extent. Similarly, changes in the environment influence the family life, which affects the children (Desai, 1994).

Family as a System and Family Sub-systems

The ecological perspective views family as a social system. As a system, family is a functional unit that is composed of interrelated and interdependent sub-systems. It has a boundary that differentiates it from other systems in the environment and has equilibrium and adaptive propensities that tend to assure its viability as a social system. As a social system, a family comprises of sub-systems. Each member can be considered a sub-system, and its dyad can also be considered a sub-system. Depending on the family form, a family can have the following dyadic sub-systems:

- Conjugal sub-systems,
- Filial sub-systems,
- Fraternal sub-systems
- Grandparent–grandchild sub-systems,
- In-law sub-systems,
- Consensual sub-systems.

Family Well-Being

International Year of the Family: The UN has contributed to discussion of family policy across the world through the proclamation of 1994 as the International Year of the Family (IYF). Its theme was "Family: resources and responsibilities in a changing world", and its motto was "Building the Smallest Democracy at the Heart of Society". The principles of the IYF consider family as the basic unit of society, warranting special attention. The principles of the IYF seek to promote the basic human rights and fundamental freedoms accorded to all individuals by the set of internationally agreed instruments, formulated under the aegis of the UN:

- Universal Declaration of Human Rights,
- The International Covenants on Human Rights,
- The Declaration on Social Progress and Development,

- The Convention on the Elimination of All Forms of Discrimination against Women,
- The Convention on the Rights of the Child,
- The UN Principles for Older Persons.

The IYF recognised the family diversity and addressed the needs of all families (http://social.un.org/index/Family/InternationalObservances/ TwentiethAnniversaryofIYF2014.aspx).

Rights-Based Goals for Family Well-Being: During the IYF, based on the human rights instruments, India's Ministry of Welfare in collaboration with UNICEF India and Tata Institute of Social Sciences (1994) laid down the goals for family well-being. Accordingly, family well-being may be perceived as a combination of gender-aware, child-centred and elderly friendly family rights and responsibilities that cut across the diverse forms of families. Such goals for family well-being were visualised to be threefold:

1. A democratic family with scope for the development of individual members and for enriched family relationships,
2. A democratic environment for the family with scope for the well-being of each family unit and for its harmony with its environment,
3. A family for every individual, unless an adult leaves it by choice.

Family Life Education

Aims: Family life education (FLE) comprises education about family life with the aim to achieve family well-being and prevent problems in family life.

Principles: Following are the principles of FLE:

- FLE is relevant to individuals, couples and families across the lifespan.
- FLE draws on multidisciplinary knowledge.
- FLE is offered in many venues, including community workshops, video and print media, publications, the Internet.
- FLE is educational rather than therapeutic (adapted from Arcus et al., 1993, cited in Duncan & Goddard, 2005).

Learner Objectives of Family Life Education: The learner objectives of FLE workshops may be to develop skills for:

1. Acceptance and respect for plurality of family forms,
2. Democratisation of family's internal dynamics with scope for the development of individual members and for enriched family relationships,
3. Democratisation of family's interaction with its environment with scope for the well-being of each family unit and for its harmony with its environment.

Activities

Introductory Activity 1.1: Brainstorming on Family

Learner Outcome: At the end of this activity, the participants will understand the nuances of the term family and develop awareness of the requirements of family well-being.

Procedure: Use the following procedure to conduct this activity:

1. Conduct a brainstorming session with the participants with the following questions:

   - What do you mean by the word family?
   - Minimally how many persons can make a family?
   - Does a family only mean blood and legal relationships?
   - How is a family by birth different from a family by marriage?
   - Can unrelated persons staying together be considered a family?
   - How is family different from household?
   - What is the importance of family?
   - Do you know of people who do not have a family?
   - Do you know of children who do not have a family?
   - What are the implications of not having a family?

2. Ask the participants what they mean by family well-being and how it can be achieved.
3. Share Summary Chart 1.1 to discuss what leads to family well-being.
4. Introduce the following units of the module:

   - Acceptance and respect for plurality of family forms,
   - Democratisation of family's internal dynamics,
   - Democratisation of family's interaction with its environment.

Time Estimate: 30 min

Acceptance and Respect for Plurality of Family Forms

Concepts and Theories

Family Forms

The family form comprises of its size, age and sex of its members and the relationship among them. Families have plurality of composition that varies with class, ethnicity, geographical location and individual choice (Desai, 2010, pp. 191–192).

The normative or traditional family forms comprise joint and nuclear families:

- The joint family comprises two or more couples and their children, bound together by common movable or immovable property, and may or may not be staying together. Variations in a joint family are lineal joint families, collateral joint families and lineal-cum-collateral joint families. Leslie and Korman (1984) termed extended families as consanguineous families as they focus on blood relations.
- The nuclear family comprises couples and their unmarried children and is generally financially independent of other families. A variation of a nuclear family is the supplemented nuclear family, which comprises a nuclear family with single relatives (Kolenda, 1987). Leslie and Korman (1984) termed nuclear families as conjugal families as a conjugal relation is the core of these families.

According to the National Family Health Survey (NFHS-4) (International Institute for Population Sciences (IIPS) & ICF, 2017), 58% of the households are nuclear in India which are defined as households comprising a married couple or a man or a woman living alone or with unmarried children (biological, adopted, or fostered) with or without unrelated individuals. The proportion of nuclear households is higher in urban areas (61%) than in rural areas (56.2%).

As marriage and children are considered essential elements of a traditional family, the following family forms based in life situations and/or choice face challenges in the traditional society:

- Single-parent families (due to unwed parenthood, death of a spouse, desertion, separation or divorce or migration of a spouse),
- Childless families (due to infertility or out of choice),
- Reconstituted/stepfamily,
- Consensual unions,
- Grandparent–grandchildren families.

There is a need to accept the diversity of family forms and prevent negative perceptions and non-acceptance of these family forms by the traditional society through terms such as "broken families", "marital instability" and "family instability". These families also need acceptance and support through laws.

Activities

Activity 1.2: My Family Genogram and Family Well-Being

Learner Outcome: At the end of this activity, the participants will learn to explore the generational trends in their family life.

Procedure: Use the following procedure to conduct this activity:

1. Explain that a genogram is a multigenerational family tree that plots familial relationships and visually records information about social relationships and biological and psychological issues in the family across three or more generations (Galvin et al. 2008). It goes beyond a traditional family tree by allowing the user to analyse hereditary patterns and psychological factors that punctuate relationships. Genograms allow an individual to quickly identify and understand various patterns in one's family history which may have had an influence on one's current state of mind (Genopro, 2008).
2. Show them how to prepare a genogram by visiting the Genopro website at http://www.genopro.com/genogram/. For example:

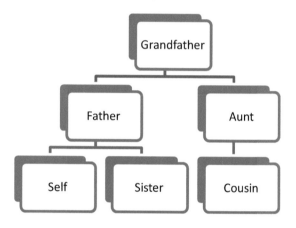

3. Alternately ask the participants to draw their family tree with branches as generations and leaves as people.
4. Ask the participants to draw at least a three-generational family tree or a genogram of their family:

   - Each horizontal line conveys a generation, and generations are joined by vertical lines.
   - They can start with their own generation, including self, siblings and spouses.
   - Their parents' generation can be listed above their own.
   - Their children's generation can be listed below their own.
   - Draw squares for males and circles for females, and place the age of each within. A cross within indicates dead.
   - List siblings/children from the oldest to the youngest, left to right.
   - List husband on the left and wife on the right.
   - Make a circle to include the family members that live together in a household.

5. Ask them to discuss their family genogram with their partner with reference to the following questions:

    a. Do you see any continuities across generations?
    b. Do you see any changes across generations?
    c. Do you see any trends across generations?
    d. Do you see changes in the number of sub-systems in the family?

Time Estimate: 30 min

Activity 1.3: Small Group Discussion on Respecting Plurality of Family Forms

Learner Outcome: At the end of this activity, the participants will learn to understand and respect plurality of family forms.

Procedure: Use the following procedure to conduct this activity:

1. Ask the participants to examine the household composition in their family genogram and form six groups according to their present family form:

    (1) Joint family,
    (2) Nuclear family,
    (3) Single-parent family,
    (4) Childless family,
    (5) Reconstituted/stepfamily,
    (6) Consensual union.

2. Ask each group to discuss the reasons and implications of their family form, and share with the large group.

Questions for Discussion: Use the following questions to discuss this activity:

- What did you learn about the reasons and implications of your own family type?
- What did you learn about the reasons and implications of other types of families?
- Why do we think our household type as "normal" and other family types as "abnormal"?
- Why should we respect plurality of family forms?
- How is it important for family well-being?

Time Estimate: 30 min

Democratisation of Family's Internal Dynamics

Concepts and Theories

Family Internal Dynamics

Family internal dynamics comprises family roles and power, family relationships, family development and family activities. Family internal dynamics is influenced by family ideology.

Family Roles: Family roles are recurring patterns of behaviour developed through the interaction that family members use to fulfil family functions. Roles do not have fixed positions; they are interactive. One cannot be a husband without someone being a wife, and one cannot be a parent without someone being a child. Society provides models and norms for how certain family roles should be assumed, thus creating role expectations. Role performance is the actual interactive role behaviour. Role conflict occurs when role expectations clash or role performance is not satisfactory. Role conflicts also occur between multiple roles of the same person (Galvin et al., 2008).

Power in Family: Power operates transactionally in a family. It does not belong to an individual; it is a property of a relationship between two or more persons. According to McDonald (1980, cited in Galvin et al., 2008), power includes power bases, power processes and power outcomes:

- The bases of family power are resources under the control of family members.
- Power processes are attempts to control others through influence, persuasion and assertiveness.
- Family power outcome is the control over decision-making.

Family Relationships

Family relationships among family dyads comprise the following:

- Management of boundary,
- Perception of the other,
- Feelings for the other,
- Communication patterns,
- Management of differences and conflict.

Family Development

As a family system moves through time, it goes through changes in its composition, as members are added and are lost.

Stages of Family Development: The development stages in a traditional nuclear family may move through the following stages, albeit with variations in the stages depending on the variations in age and life transitions of family members:

- Young persons getting married,
- Young couples bearing and bringing up children,
- Middle-aged couples with children forming their own nuclear families,
- Old couples with children bearing and bringing up their children.

Family Developmental Tasks: A family's developmental task is a growth responsibility that arises at a certain stage in the life of a family, determined by the age and developmental needs of the members of the family. Successful achievement of the developmental tasks leads to satisfaction and success with later tasks, while failure leads to unhappiness in the family, disapproval by society and difficulty with later developmental tasks (Duvall, 1977).

Family Developmental Transitions: Family developmental transitions mean families moving from one developmental stage to another. Examples of family developmental transitions necessary at each stage are adapted below from Carter and McGoldrick (2005):

- Moving to the stage of a couple getting married, the family has to (1) make commitment to a new dyadic sub-system (conjugal), (2) realign with the other sub-systems in the family (filial and fraternal) and with friends and (3) make space for the in-law sub-system.
- Moving to the stage of a couple rearing children, the family has to (1) make readjustments in the conjugal sub-system to (2) make space for a new parenting sub-system with their children and (3) make readjustments in their filial system to make space for their parents' grandparental sub-system.
- Moving to the stage of a couple with adolescent children, the family has to (1) make readjustments in their parenting sub-system to allow the adolescent children for more independence, (2) refocus on their conjugal sub-system and career and (3) make readjustments in their filial system accommodating for care giving of and losing ageing parents.
- Moving to the stage of an elderly couple, the family has to (1) make readjustment to a life of a dependent and (2) readjustment to life with losing the spouse and siblings and preparation of death.

Family Adaptability: Adaptability in interpersonal relationships is the ability of persons to change in response to one another and move towards a state of homoeostasis to manage stability and change. The four levels of adaptability range from rigid (very low), to structured (low to moderate), to flexible (moderate to high), to chaotic (very high). Rigidity characterises relationships that repress change and growth. On the other extreme, relationships that regularly experience extensive change may be considered chaotic. Balanced relationships are generally found at the moderate levels that are structured and flexible (adapted from Galvin et al., 2008).

Family Activities

Family activities include sharing family tasks, having meals together, spending weekends and vacations, celebrating birthdays and festivals and decision-making about these. According to Khavari and Khavari (1989), whenever possible, the entire family should read and discuss the ideas and information together. In this way, each person is provided with a common background from which to learn the necessary skills and attitudes for improving family life.

Traditional Family Ideologies

Patriarchy is an all-pervasive ideology that is manifested by a system of control and distribution of resources by hierarchies of age, gender and generation, leading to strict determination of roles and power. Cohen and Kennedy (2007, p. 152) note that early sociologists defined patriarchy as a system of social organisation in which eldest males in a family exercised more or less unconstrained power both over younger males and women in the preindustrial era. This authority was based in the control over property. Women normally bear all the direct responsibilities for childcare and domestic life—including fetching water and fuel. However, their biological and social reproduction also encompasses playing a key role in food production through agriculture, a role that has often been ignored or misunderstood. Family power has implication for status in the family. Since men and elderly have more power in patriarchal families, they have had a higher status than women and children in these families. However, with changing political economy, the powerless in the family now also includes the elderly who are not considered productive.

Other family ideologies that influence family dynamics are defined by Rogers and Sebald (1962) as:

- Kinship orientation is the degree to which a family fulfils the role expectations of the kinship reference group. Families have traditionally had a strong kinship orientation that influences family norms and subordinates individual interest.
- Familism is the subordination of individual interest to those of the family group.
- Individualism is the primacy of individual interest.

Democratic Family Ideology

According to the Preamble of the UNCRC, children should grow up in a family environment, in an atmosphere of happiness, love and understanding. Such family environment requires family dynamics that comprise family structure influenced by family ideology, family relationships, family development and family activities as discussed below. The first goal for family well-being identified by India's Ministry of Welfare in collaboration with UNICEF India and Tata Institute of Social

Sciences (1994) is a democratic family with scope for the development of individual members and for enriched family relationships. This goal can be achieved by respecting the following rights and responsibilities within the family:

1. Every family member has the responsibility to promote sensitivity and responsiveness, sensitive communication patterns, relationship of companionship instead of hierarchy, democratic decision-making, respect for individual needs and differences, collaborative approaches for resolving conflicts and providing support in crisis situations, thereby promoting enrichment of relationships as well as development of each family member.
2. The vulnerable members of the family need special attention as they lack access to and control over resources and are, therefore, powerless. Children, members with disability and the dependent older persons are vulnerable due to their low capabilities. Women are relatively powerless due to their low socio-economic status in the patriarchal family structure. Every family member is equal in dignity and worth, irrespective of age, gender and abilities so there is a need to promote intra-family equity.
3. Every family member has the right to equal allocation of family resources and division of labour.
4. Both the married partners have the right to gender equality. The concept of man as the head of the family needs to be replaced by the concept of the couple jointly sharing the family responsibilities.
5. Every family member has the right to freedom and choices in opinion, expression and behaviour, in the areas of occupation, marriage and childbearing.
6. There is a need to accept plurality of family forms, especially single-person households, single-parent families and female-headed households, childless couples, mixed marriages and cohabitations.
7. Every family member has the right to life and security of persons, privacy and honour, and protection from mental and physical violence.
8. The society and the State have the responsibility to protect the individual's rights within the family.
9. Violent family practices such as female foeticide and infanticide, child marriage, dowry-related murders, commitment of Sati, family violence against women and children should be urgently halted (adapted from India: Ministry of Welfare, UNICEF India and Tata Institute of Social Sciences, 1994).

In short, a democratic family requires:

- Egalitarian, gender-aware, child-friendly and elderly friendly ideologies,
- Role flexibility and interchangeability,
- Egalitarian power and status allocation,
- Democratic relationships,
- Democratic decision-making.

See Summary Chart 1.2 on Democratic Family.

Democratic Family Relationships

Democratic family relationships require the following:
Semi-open boundary in relationships:

* Interdependence,
* Cohesion,
* Adaptability.

Positive perception of others:

* Egalitarian perception,
* Recognition of strengths,
* Acceptance and respect,
* Celebration of differences.

Positive feelings for others:

* Warmth,
* Humility,
* Genuineness,
* Empathy.

Interpersonal communication skills:

* Open communication skills,
* Body language skills,
* Sensitive listening skills,
* Feedback skills.

Collaborative conflict management skills:

* Win-win goals,
* Attitude adjustment,
* Reducing defensiveness in others,
* Understanding the other person's perception of the conflict.

Democratic Decision-Making

It is important to understand that each member brings unique perspectives, talents and skills to the family, which needs to be valued and fostered. This approach requires significant self-awareness. When a person is aware of one's limitations, it instills humility sufficient to seek another's strengths to compensate for it. Then that weakness becomes strength because it enables complementariness to take place. However, when people are unaware of their weaknesses and act as if their strengths are sufficient, their strengths become their weaknesses—and their very undoing for lack of complementariness (Covey, 1997).

Democratic decision-making is the affirmation of each family member's dignity and contribution to family discussion, no matter how different their contributions might be. All the members should be encouraged to participate in the family decision-making. All members, in turn, have a responsibility to contribute their best for the betterment of the group functioning. It is important to sit in a circle to assure that. When genuine respect is received from others, each person feels comfortable in revealing his or her ideas, confident that no one will ridicule or condemn them (Khavari & Khavari, 1989).

In family decision-making, each member should avoid becoming attached to his or her own ideas or preferences. Once expressed, the idea no longer belongs to an individual, but becomes the property of the family, which means that the contributor can then look at the idea just as objectively as the other members. This leaves the family free to accept or reject the idea without fear of hurting the feelings of the one who suggested it. Even if a solution is not finally adopted as a solution or plan, the one who offered it retains dignity and a sense of worth if given a respectful and courteous hearing. All members should fully understand that rejection of an idea is not a rejection of its originator (Khavari & Khavari, 1989). Sometimes an idea is needed, and sometimes we need to let go an idea. Sometimes we need to lead, and sometimes we need to follow (adapted from Tillman, 2000). Democratic decision-making goes a long way in facilitating greater harmony and better conflict resolution in a family.

Activities

Activity 1.4: Role-Plays to Understanding Family Ideologies

Learner Outcome: At the end of this activity, the participants will understand the traditional and the democratic family ideologies.

Procedure: Use the following procedure to conduct this activity:

1. Ask the participants the following questions:
    a. What do you mean by democracy?
    b. How can the ideology of democracy be applied to a family?
    c. What do you mean by a democratic family, and how it is important for family well-being?

2. Divide the participants into two groups and allocate the following ideologies among them to read:
    a. Traditional family ideologies,
    b. Democratic family ideology.

3. Give a situation of a daughter of the family wanting to marry a man of her choice from her college. Ask each family group to role-play what would happen in their families in this situation.
4. Discuss the pros and cons of traditional versus democratic family.
5. Show Summary Chart 1.2 to summarise the requirements of a democratic family.

Activity 1.5: Exercise on Assessment of Democratic Family Roles and Power

Learner Outcome: At the end of this activity, the participants will learn to make an assessment of roles and power distribution in their family.

Procedure: Use the following procedure to conduct this activity:

1. Ask each participant to fill up the Exercise on Assessment of Family Roles and Power, given at the end of the chapter.
2. Ask them to share it with their partner.

Questions for Discussion: Use the following questions to discuss this activity:

- Are roles determined in your family by sex and/or age?
- How do you assess your family with reference to role flexibility and interchangeability?
- How do you assess your family with reference to power and status allocation? Are roles linked to power and power to status?
- How can you minimise stereotyped gender roles in your family and make roles more flexible and interchangeable?
- How can you make your family more egalitarian, gender-aware, child-friendly and elderly friendly?

Time Estimate: 30 min

Activity 1.6: Role-Play for Democratic Family Decision-Making

Learner Outcome: At the end of this activity, the participants will learn the skills of democratic family decision-making.

Procedure: Use the following procedure to conduct this activity:

1. Form small groups of participants and allot each small group different situations that are pertinent to their daily family life experiences. Examples of such situations are:

    (1) Grandmother coming to stay in a nuclear family,
    (2) Planning a family vacation,
    (3) Budgeting of the bonus income for the family,
    (4) Planning for a sister's wedding,
    (5) Planning for a daughter's career,
    (6) Selection of a new house.

2. The small groups can prepare role-plays on the following steps for democratic decision-making in these situations:

   a. All the members should be relaxed, seated face-to-face in a circle and participate in the decision-making by sharing and listening.
   b. Invite everyone to share the facts of the problem (who, where, when, why and how).
   c. Then invite everyone to share their feelings, opinions and perceptions attached to these facts.
   d. Carry out a brainstorming of suggestions for action and write down on the board without evaluating them.
   e. Discuss each suggestion with reference to its advantages and disadvantages and the resources/capacity that the association has to implement it.
   f. Arrive at a decision that would satisfy all the members.
   g. Allocate roles to implement the decision taken but make a joint commitment and take joint responsibility for its consequences.

3. Ask the small groups to present the role-play to the large group for further inputs and discussion.

Questions for Discussion: Use the following questions to discuss this activity:

- Where was the decision taken?
- When was the decision taken?
- How were the members seated?
- Were the facts shared adequately?
- Were feelings allowed to be expressed?
- What was the level of participation by each member?
- Did members feel free to disagree or express alternate opinions/suggestions?
- How were alternatives weighed and the decision arrived at?
- Were attempts made to take joint responsibility of the decision and allocation of roles for implementing the decision?

Time Estimate: 45 min

Activity 1.7: Activities on Family Relationships

The life skill modules of interpersonal communication and relationships skills from Sourcebook I can be applied to different dyads of family relationships through activities on role-plays on:

- Open Communication with Family Members,
- Body Language with Family Members,
- Sensitive Listening Skills with Family Members,
- Giving and Receiving Negative Feedback with Family Members,

- Giving Positive Feedback to Family Members,
- Warm and Genuine Greetings with Family Members,
- Interdependence, Cohesion and Adaptability with Family Members,
- Collaborative Method to Manage Conflict with Family Members.

See Summary Chart 1.3 for more details.

Activity 1.8: Exercise on Learning Family Adaptability

Learner Outcome: At the end of this activity, the participants will learn the skills of family adaptability to developmental transitions.

Procedure: Use the following procedure to conduct this activity:

1. Ask the participants the following questions:

   a. What are the family development stages?
   b. What are the family developmental transitions?
   c. What do they mean by adaptability to family developmental transitions?
   d. Discuss the need to prevent rigidity and promote structure with flexibility during developmental transitions.

2. Form four small groups and allocate the following case studies to them:

   a. When Radha and Mihir got married, Radha moved to stay with Mihir and his parents. What changes do you think Radha, Mihir and Mihir's family will have to make in the household arrangement and their family life? What would happen if they did not make these changes? How can they promote structure with flexibility during this stage?
   b. While planning for a child, what changes do you think Radha, Mihir and their parents will have to be ready for? What would happen if they do not want to make these changes? How can they promote structure with flexibility during this stage?
   c. When Radha and Mihir's son Amar grows up to be a teenager, what changes do you think Radha, Mihir and their parents and Amar will have to make in their family life? What would happen if they do not want to make these changes? How can they promote structure with flexibility during this stage?
   d. When Radha's and Mihir's parents grow old and dependent, what changes do you think Radha, Mihir and their parents will have to make? What would happen if they do not want to make these changes? How can they promote structure with flexibility during this stage?

3. Ask the small groups to make their presentation to the large group for further inputs.

Time Estimate: 30 min

Activity 1.9: Drawing Family Togetherness

Learner Outcome: At the end of this activity, the participants will learn to value family togetherness.

Procedure: Ask the participants to:

1. Draw a picture of their family, as engaged in the most common activity.
2. List the activities that the family members do together daily, weekly and occasionally.

Questions for Discussion: Use the following questions to discuss this activity:

- Are you happy with your family togetherness? Why?
- Are all the members involved?
- Do members value togetherness or prefer their own activities?
- Is the family seen as an impediment to individual self-fulfilment?
- Who is busier? Men/women? Children/elderly? How can that family member be involved in family togetherness?
- What can you do to improve your family togetherness?

Time Estimate: 30 min

Democratisation of Family's Interaction with Its Environment

Concepts and Theories

Family in the Ecological Perspective

The ecological perspective views an individual in the context of his/her family and the family in the context of its environment as these constantly interact with and, therefore, influence one another. The family's immediate environment comprises of the ethnic/kinship community, neighbourhood, natural environment, workplace, school/college, friends, media and so on. The State, corporate sector and the market influence the family indirectly. The macro-system is the larger international eco-political contexts in which these systems are embedded. Diversity in the environment brings variations in family life, which, in turn, explains differences in individual members' well-being to a large extent. Similarly, changes in the environment influence the family life, which affects its individual members (Desai, 1994). See Summary Chart 1.4.

Community: A community is a collective of people, including individuals, groups, organisations and families that have shared interests; regular interaction to fulfil the shared interests through informal and formally organised means and some degree of mutual identification among members as belonging to the collective (Schriver,

2004, p. 9). Communities are important to children's lives. After the family, the community provides the immediate environment in which children grow and develop. As the domain in which people share common resources (space, natural environment, resources, infrastructure, institutions, agency), a community has an important function in the provision of the immediate protective and developmental environment for children. The community also provides, or has the potential to provide, an environment in which people can group their resources and energies and interact with agents of government, non-State actors or agencies to achieve improvements (Child Protection Working Group Sudan, 2012).

Family Identity: Boundary is the condition that defines the system and sets it apart from its environment. In relation to families, the boundary pertains to patterns of interaction between family and other systems in the environment that are different from patterns of interaction within the family. Family identity is the boundary that separates it from other systems in the environment. It is formed by its structure, ethnic background and financial status. Ethnic background includes race, religion, regional background and mother tongue (Desai, 1994). The boundary affects the flow of inputs and outputs of information and energy between the system and its environment through permeability. Accordingly, boundaries can range on a continuum of closeness to openness. The family as a semi-closed, semi-open system is supposed to open selectively to engage in transactions with other such systems (White & Klein, 2008). A family with highly closed identity can have difficulties adjusting in its environment. For example, a family with religious rigidity in a multireligious neighbourhood or a migrant family with a culture very different from the local families have difficulties adjusting to the environment. A family with very open identity, ready to change every time, can have difficulties maintaining an identity and have no family privacy. A family which is semi-closed and semi-open or open to change selectively can maintain its identity, privacy and harmonious interactions with its environment.

Family Equilibrium: All systems tend towards equilibrium, which is a prerequisite for the continuance of a system achieved by a balance of various forces within and outside of a system. The family is in the position of middle management. On the one hand, it must meet the demands of the larger society, carrying, values and norms of behaviour; on the other hand, it must tend to the needs, performance and morale of its individual members. The requirements from above and below may not always be congruent (Hartman & Laird, 1983). When the family and/or its environment cannot adapt to each other, there exists a state of disequilibrium between the two. Families as systems are vulnerable to disequilibrium because of not only changes internally induced by their members and their own developmental processes but also because of the turbulent and changing nature of their external environment (Zimmerman, 2001).

Democratisation of Family's Interaction with the Environment

The second goal for family well-being identified by India's Ministry of Welfare in collaboration with UNICEF India and Tata Institute of Social Sciences (1994) is a democratic environment for the family with scope for the well-being of each family unit and for its harmony with its environment. This goal can be achieved by promoting the family's following rights and responsibilities with reference to its environment:

1. Every family has a right to freedom of residence in its natural environment. It is the State's responsibility to decentralise development in order to stabilise families in their natural environment. Every family has a responsibility to maintain harmony with nature.
2. The society and the State have the responsibility to protect the individual's rights within the family and plurality of family forms.
3. Every family is equal in dignity and rights, without distinction of family form, ethnicity, religion, language, political opinion or class.
4. The following families require attention and acceptance as they have historically not been accepted as "normal' family forms: single-person households, single-parent families and female-headed households, childless couples, mixed marriages and cohabitations.
5. It is the responsibility of the State and every family to register birth, marriage and death of every family member.
6. Every adult man and woman have the right and responsibility to a livelihood. However, no individual/family should be held in slavery or servitude.
7. Every family has the right to adequate housing, and every family and the State have the responsibility to keep the environment clean and peaceful.
8. Every family and its members have the right to information about and access to public services.
9. Every family has the right to social security/protection in crisis events of the family or its individual members.
10. Every family has the right to consumer protection.
11. There is a need to prioritise attention to the socio-economically vulnerable/at risk families and enhance their inclusion and access public resources and services.
12. It is the responsibility of every family and its members to protect the rights of other families and their members and promote and protect the functioning of the community and the State (adapted from India: Ministry of Welfare, UNICEF India and Tata Institute of Social Sciences, 1994).

Activities

Activity 1.10: My Family Name

Learner Outcome: At the end of this activity, the participants will learn the significance of family name/surname that gives an identity in a socio-cultural environment.

Procedure: Ask the participants to:

1. Think of the meaning of their family name/surname. Some communities do not have family names.
2. Share the following about their family name with their partner:

   - What is the meaning of this family name?
   - What is the history of this family name?
   - Does the family name indicate the race/region/religion/caste/occupation of the family?

Questions for Discussion: Use the following questions to discuss this activity:

- How does family name give a collective identity?
- Does the family name indicate the religion and caste of the person?
- Can family name indicate status in a hierarchy, and therefore exploitative?
- Can the family name create disequilibrium for the family in its environment?
- Can stopping to use family name help prevent such exploitation?

Time Estimate: 15 min

Activity 1.11: My Family Ecomap

Learner Outcome: At the end of this activity, the participants will learn to review their family's interaction with its environment and learn ways to improve it.

Procedure: Use the following procedure to conduct this activity:

1. Explain to the participants that a family ecomap is a family assessment tool that provides a graphic representation of the family's ecological system, that comprises systems with which a family interacts and the nature of these interactions (Kirst-Ashman & Hull, 2006, p. 168).
2. Show Summary Chart 1.4 to discuss family in the ecological perspective.
3. Ask the participants to draw an ecomap of their family as follows:

   (1) Identify your family's environment, that is, the systems with which your family interacts. For each system, identify:
   (2) Whether the relationship of your family with each of these systems is positive (+) or negative (−),
   (3) Whether the relationship of your family with each of these systems is weak (dashed line) or strong (solid line) or stressful (zigzag line),
   (4) Whether the relationship of your family with each of these systems is one-way (dependent) or two-ways (interdependent) (through an arrow) (Hartman, 1995, cited in Poulin, 2005).

4. Use the following questions to discuss the ecomaps:

   - How is the relationship of your family with its environment?
   - With which systems does the family have equilibrium? Why?
   - With which systems does the family have disequilibrium? Why?
   - How can you convert the negative relations to positive ones?
   - How can you convert the weak and stressful relations to strong ones?
   - How can you convert the one-way relations to two-way ones?
   - How can the family be adaptable to its environment?
   - How can the family prevent its exploitation by the environment?

5. Have volunteers read out the requirements of democratisation of family's interaction with the environment and discuss.

Time Estimate: 30 min

Concluding Activity: Achievement of the Learner Objectives

Learner Outcome: By the end of the concluding activity, the participants will ascertain if they have achieved the learner objectives.

Procedure: Use the following procedure to conduct the concluding activity:

1. Show the power points/a chart on the learner objectives, ask the participants to read them one at a time and ask the group if they think they have achieved the objective.
2. The participants may be asked to share their responses in their diary with reference to the following questions:

   - What was a new learning for you in this session?
   - What did you like the best in this session and why?
   - Which activity was most effective?
   - What was not clear/confusing?
   - How can you apply what you have learnt?

Time Estimate: 15 min

Appendix: Summary Charts and Exercises

Summary Chart 1.1 Goals of family well-being
(Adapted from India: Ministry of Welfare, UNICEF India and Tata Institute of Social Sciences 1994)

Summary Chart 1.2 Democratic family

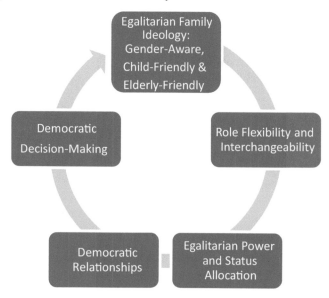

Summary Chart 1.3 Skills for democratic family relationships

Semi-Open Boundary in Relationships: • Interdependence • Cohesion • Adaptability	Positive Perception of Others: • Egalitarian Perception • Recognition of Strengths • Acceptance and Respect • Celebration of Differences
Positive Feelings for Others: • Warmth • Humility • Genuineness • Empathy	Interpersonal Communication Skills: • Open Communication Skills • Body Language Skills • Sensitive Listening Skills • Feedback Skills
Collaborative Conflict Management Skills: • Win-Win Goals • Attitude Adjustment • Reducing Defensiveness in Others • Understanding the Other Person's Perception of the Conflict	

Summary Chart 1.4 Family in the ecological perspective

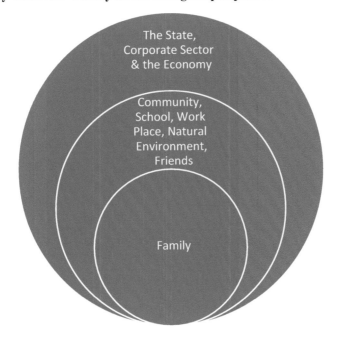

Exercise for Activity 1.5: Assessment of Family Roles and Power

No.	Family Activity	Role: Who Carries it out?	Power: Who has the Final Say?
1	Cooking		
2	Looking after the sick and the old		
3	Shopping		
4	House cleaning		
5	Helping children with studies		
6	Working to earn		
7	Savings and investment		
8	Decision about career/ marriages		

Acknowledgements This chapter is adapted from the author's following chapter from her book: Desai (2010). Chapter 10: Family Life Education. In *A Rights-Based Preventative Approach for Psychosocial Well-Being in Childhood,* Springer, Series on Children's Well-Being: Indicators and Research.

References

Carter, B., & McGoldrick, M. (Eds.). (2005). *The expanded family life cycle: Individual, family and social perspectives* (3rd ed.). New York: Pearson.

Child Protection Working Group Sudan. (2012). *Working with community-based child protection committees and networks: Handbook for facilitators.* Retrieved from http://cpwg.net/wp-content/uploads/2012/09/Working-with-Community-Based-Child-Protection-Committees-and-Netwroks-Child-Frontiers-20110.pdf

Cohen, R., & Kennedy, P. (2007). *Global sociology* (2nd ed.). New York: Palgrave Macmillan.

Collins, D., Jordan, C., & Coleman, H. (2007). *An introduction to family social work* (2nd ed.). Australia: Thomson Brooks Cole.

Covey, S. R. (1997). *The 7 habits of highly effective families.* London: Simon and Schuster.

Desai, M. (1994). Concepts and conceptual frameworks for understanding family. In *Enhancing the role of the family as an agency for social and economic development.* Bombay: Tata Institute of Social Sciences.

Desai, M. (2010). A rights-based preventative approach for psychosocial well-being in childhood. In *Series on children's well-being: Indicators and research.* Heidelberg: Springer.

Duncan, S. F., & Goddard, H. W. (2005). *Family life education: Principles and practices for effective outreach.* Thousand Oaks: Sage.

Duvall, E. M. (1977). *Marriage and family development.* Philadelphia: J.B. Lippincott.

Galvin, K. M., Bylund, C. I., & Brommel, B. J. (2008). *Family communication: Cohesion and change* (7th ed.). Boston: Pearson.

Genopro. (2008). Retrieve from http://www.genopro.com/genogram/

Hartman, A., & Laird, J. (1983). *Family-centered social work practice.* New York: The Free Press.

Heywood, A. (2007). *Political ideologies: An introduction* (4th ed.). New York: Palgrave Macmillan.

India: Ministry of Welfare. (1994). *India's commitment to family well-being: An overview of the national seminar on the international year of the family, 1994.* Bombay: Tata Institute of Social Sciences.

International Institute for Population Sciences & ICF. (2017). *National Family Health Survey (NFHS-4), 2015–16: India.* Mumbai: IIPS.

Khavari, K. A., & Khavari, S. W. (1989). *Creating a successful family.* London: Sterling Publishers.

Kirst-Ashman, K. K., & Hull, G. H., Jr. (2006). *Understanding generalist practice* (4th ed.). Belmont, CA: Brooks/Cole.

Kolenda, P. (1987). *Regional differences in family structure in India.* Jaipur: Rawat Publication.

Leeder, E. J. (2003). *The family in global perspective: A gendered journey.* London: Sage.

Leslie, G. R., & Korman, S. K. (1984). *The family in social context.* New York: Oxford.

Poulin, J. (2005). *Strengths-based generalist practice.* Belmont, CA: Brooks/Cole.

Rogers, E. M., & Sebald, H. (1962). A distinction between familism, family integration and kinship orientation. *Marriage and Family Living, 24,* 25–30.

Schriver, J. M. (2004). *Human behavior and the social environment: Shifting paradigms in essential knowledge for social work practice* (4th ed.). Boston: Pearson Allyn and Bacon.

Tillman, D. (2000). *Living values activities for children ages 8–14*. New Delhi: Sterling Publishers Pvt. Ltd.
White, J. M., & Klein, D. M. (2008). *Family Theories* (3rd ed.). London: Sage.
Zimmerman, S. L. (2001). *Family policy: Constructed solutions to family problems*. London: Sage.

Relevant Child Rights and You Reports and Articles

Kothari, J. (2010–11). The Child's Right to Identity: Do Adopted Children have the Right to know their Parentage? *CRY National Child Rights Fellowship*. Retrieve from https://www.cry.org/resources/pdf/NCRRF/NCRRF_ReportBy_Jayna.pdf.

Module 2
Rights of Girls and Children with Disability to Non-discrimination and Inclusion

Prerequisite Modules

The prerequisite Modules for this Module are:
From *Sourcebook I on Introduction to Rights-Based Direct Practice with Children*:

- Modules on Life Skills Development

From *Sourcebook II on Child Rights Education for Participation and Development: Primary Prevention*:

- Introduction to Child Rights Education
- Child Rights to Participation and Children's Associations

Conceptual Framework of Child Rights and Responsibilities for Inclusion of the Excluded

Concepts and Theories

Social Stratification

Stratification of human beings based on caste, colour, creed, religion, occupation and so on has been a historical phenomenon. It leads to social exclusion in an institutionalised way. It segregates a group of people from the social, political and cultural domains of societal life. It justifies the perception of superiority and inferiority and culminates into a system of domination and subjugation. These processes ultimately lead to oppression and exploitation. Those who benefit out of this social formation do not want to introduce any change in this structure. Significantly, this social system becomes highly resistant to change and transformation (Louis, 2001). The system becomes so strong by systemic exclusion.

© Child Rights and You 2018
M. Desai and S. Goel, *Child Rights Education for Inclusion and Protection: Primary Prevention*, Rights-based Direct Practice with Children, https://doi.org/10.1007/978-981-13-0417-0_2

Systemic Exclusion

Stereotypes: According to Johnson and Johnson (2009, p. 451), a stereotype is defined as a belief that associates a whole group of people with certain traits. In this way, stereotypes function as simplifiers; they reduce the complexity of the social environment and make it more manageable. People form stereotypes in two ways: first, they categorise by sorting single objects into groups rather than thinking of each one as unique. Second, they differentiate between in-groups and out-groups. People commonly assume that the members of out-groups are quite similar but recognise that the members of the in-group they identify with are quite diverse. The failure to notice differences among out-group members results from lack of personal contact with people from these out-groups.

Prejudices: Stereotypes taken to extremes are prejudices that are judgments made about others that establish a superiority/inferiority belief system (Johnson & Johnson, 2009). Prejudice is a judgment or opinion, often negative, of a person or group which is made without careful consideration of accurate relevant information. It normally leads to the view that some people are inferior to others and of less worth and significance. Prejudice involves strong feelings that are difficult to change. For example, prejudice against the capacities of children with disability could cause them to be excluded from regular educational institutions (Griffin, 2008). Prejudices restrict perception of dignity and worth, contribution of each individual in the universe, and make rights and opportunities conditional (Desai, 2002).

According to Save the Children (2008), following are a few causes of prejudices or stereotypes:

- Lack of Factual Information
- **Fear**: Fear of someone different or fear of the unknown.
- **Culture and Religion**: Sometimes, religious and cultural beliefs can perpetuate prejudices. For example, some religions believe disability to be a punishment for past sins.
- **History**: Sometimes, parents or a group of people pass on their own prejudices to their children based on a past experience.
- **Power Differences**: There exist power relations or hierarchies, and people on the lower rung of the ladder are likely to be at the receiving end of prejudices. For example, Dalits in India are often discriminated due to the power equation between the upper and lower castes.
- **Politics**: Some governments or other groups in power benefit if discrimination exists. In such cases, minority populations could be discriminated if the majority thinks that the minority is too insignificant to be treated equally.

Prejudicing Ideologies: Prejudicing ideologies such as adultism, sexism, ableism, casteism and racism are based on perception of inherent physical and mental incapability of persons, based on their age, sex, abilities and ethnicity, respectively. These "isms" justify role stereotypes, hierarchy, discrimination, domination, intolerance, oppression, exploitation and violence. Among children, the prejudicing ideologies have led to exclusion of girls, children with disability, and children of Dalits and tribal communities. Excluded children are more vulnerable to violence, abuse, exploitation and neglect. Family, religion, society, State, and the national and the global systems of market systemically perpetuate such inequality (Desai, 2002).

Discrimination: When prejudice is acted on, it is discrimination which aims at denying members of the targeted groups, treatment and opportunities equal to those afforded to the dominant group (Johnson & Johnson, 2009).

Social Exclusion: Social exclusion has been defined by the Department of International Development (DFID, 2005, p. 3) as "a process by which certain groups are systematically disadvantaged because they are discriminated against on the basis of their ethnicity, race, religion, sexual orientation, caste, descent, gender, age, disability, HIV status, migrant status or where they live". The Child Protection Working Group (2012, p. 155) defines exclusion as the process through which individuals or groups of children are totally or partly marginalised from being able to play a full role in society. While exclusion focuses mainly on social relationships, it feeds into cycles of material deprivation and vulnerability. It is commonly associated with stigmatised social status such as disability, being a member of a group (such as a religious or ethnic minority) that is discriminated against, cultural biases relating to issues such as gender, and economic exclusion. Exclusion fundamentally affects the development of a child's full potential, by blocking his or her access to rights, opportunities and resources.

Kabeer (2005) noted that social exclusion has to be seen as an institutionalised form of inequality, the failure of a society to extend to all sections of its population the economic resources and social recognition which they need in order to participate fully in the collective life of the community. The analysis of social exclusion is thus concerned with institutional rules, relationships and processes through which resources are distributed and value is assigned in a society, focusing particularly on the mechanisms by which access and recognition are granted or denied.

Resources and Power: Prejudicing ideologies determine people's access to resources, justified by role stereotypes. Social status is a derivation of power of control over resources. Groups or systems that have control over resources also have control over the prejudicing ideology that influences role and resource allocation. The vulnerable groups are powerless with reference to control over resources due to the roles that they have historically performed, which are justified by the prejudicing ideologies of the dominant groups. Weber regarded power as the fundamental concept in stratification. Status is a kind of normatively defined social power (Marshall, 1994).

Social Exclusion and Poverty

Socially excluded people are often denied the opportunities available to others to increase their income and escape from poverty by their own efforts. So, although the economy may grow and general income levels may rise, excluded people are likely to be left behind and make up an increasing proportion of those who remain in poverty. Poverty reduction policies often fail to reach them unless they are specifically designed to do so (DFID, 2005). According to Todaro and Smith (2009), perhaps the most valid generalizations about the poor are that they are disproportionately located in rural areas, that they are primarily engaged in agricultural and associated activities, and that they are often concentrated among minority ethnic groups and indigenous peoples.

Child Rights to Non-discrimination

Right to Non-discrimination in Indian Constitution: According to Article 15 of the Indian Constitution, prohibition of discrimination on grounds only of religion, race, caste, sex or place of birth is a Fundamental Right. It further states that nothing in this article shall prevent the State from making any special provision for women and children and any socially and educationally backward classes of citizens or for the Scheduled Castes (SCs) and the Scheduled Tribes (STs), which comprise of historically disadvantaged people recognised in the Constitution of India.

Child Right to Non-discrimination in the UNCRC: Article 2 of the United Nations Convention on the Rights of the Child (UNCRC, 1989) deals with right to non-discrimination as follows:

1. States Parties shall respect and ensure the rights set forth in the present Convention to each child within their jurisdiction without discrimination of any kind, irrespective of the child's or his or her parent's or legal guardian's race, colour, sex, language, religion, political or other opinion, national, ethnic or social origin, property, disability, birth or other status.
2. State Parties shall take all appropriate measures to ensure that the child is protected against all forms of discrimination or punishment on the basis of the status, activities, expressed opinions or beliefs of the child's parents, legal guardians or family members.

Article 29 (d) of the UNCRC states that the education of the child shall be directed to "The preparation of the child for responsible life in a free society, in the spirit of understanding, peace, tolerance, equality of sexes, and friendship among all peoples, ethnic, national and religious groups and persons of indigenous origin".

Inclusion

Inclusion is a process of identifying, understanding and breaking down barriers to participation and belonging. In other words, it means involving everyone and leaving no one out. Everyone can help prevent discrimination by:

- Being aware of discrimination and the way it affects people.
- Avoiding one's own prejudices and stereotypes to avoid discriminating persons.
- Learning about other cultures, religions, castes, gender and disability and so on so that preconceived notions about such groups can be quelled.
- Celebrating diversity where diversity comes from differences between individuals and groups in society arising from gender, ethnic origins, social, cultural or religious background, family structure, disabilities, sexuality and appearance (Griffin, 2008).
- Talking to people who have been discriminated rather than neglecting them.
- Reporting about discrimination to an adult or someone trusted (Save the Children, 2008).

Since the emerging concept of social exclusion contributes to an understanding of the multiple causes of poverty, Kabeer (2005) recommends that policy responses to social exclusion need to use a multipronged approach to address poverty. According to her, a legal framework can help to ensure that discrimination on the grounds of race, ethnicity, disability, gender or age is rendered unacceptable within a society. It can also ensure that rights of excluded groups to land, credit, employment and benefits are secured, given the greater vulnerability of these groups. Policies to address social exclusion may need to incorporate special provisions to address the multiple disadvantages associated with social exclusion and to break the intergenerational transmission of poverty that it has often entailed. Such provisions may entail special attention to geographical or group targeting. It may entail targeting the children of excluded groups to ensure that they do not face the limited life chances which their parents faced. It may also need addressing gender inequalities within excluded groups so that promoting respect for hitherto marginalised cultures does not necessarily promote the internal inequalities which such cultures may embody (Kabeer, 2005).

Inclusion should not be confused with "integration" used generally with reference to children with disabilities (CWDs). Integration implies that CWDs are to be brought into a pre-existing framework of prevailing norms and standards. For example, in the context of education, integration is realised by admitting children with disabilities to "regular" schools. Inclusion, on the other hand, calls for schools to be designed and administered such that all children can experience quality learning and recreation together. This would entail providing students with disabilities with access to Braille, sign language, adapted curricula, physical adjustments like ramps and wide doorways and so on. Hence, inclusion benefits everyone as wide doorways can help teachers, parents and other children apart from those who use a wheelchair. An inclusive curriculum can help all children to better appreciate diversity (UNICEF, 2013).

Activities

Introductory Activity 2.1: Activities to Understand Exclusion

Learner Outcome: At the end of this activity, the participants will develop awareness on the cycle of exclusion and child right to non-discrimination and inclusion.

Procedure: Use the following procedure to conduct this activity:

1. Ask the participants what they mean by exclusion. Then select one of the following two activities.

2. **Planning a Picnic**: Divide the participants into four small groups. Give each group a copy of a list of children given at the end of the chapter. Each group has to select eight children from this list who can be accommodated on an eight-seater boat for a picnic to an island. The group then has to provide reasons for their selection. Ask the small groups to discuss their responses and then make their presentation to the large group.

   Use the following questions to discuss this activity:

   - Which children were selected? Why?
   - Which children were not selected? Why?
   - What is exclusion?
   - Do all children not have the right to recreation?
   - What are the implications for children who are excluded?
   - Show Summary Chart 2.1 and discuss the cycle of exclusion.
   - Explain that our welfare schemes start with the exclusion approach illustrated in this activity.
   - What is inclusion?
   - Show Summary Chart 2.2 and discuss Child Rights to Non-discrimination and Inclusion.
   - How can we convert the exclusion approach to inclusion approach?
   - Can the boat make two trips? Can they look for a bigger boat? Can they go to another place accessible to all the children?

   Source: Adapted from "The Island" in Hope and Timmel (1999, pp. 133–145)

3. **Exercise on One Step Forward**: Keep cut-outs of the Role Cards for Activity on One Step Forward, given at the end of the chapter, that refers to persons of different castes, religion, and linguistics groups, etc. Hand out a card to each participant (there are 16 cards so some participants may receive the same card if there are more than 16 participants). Ask participants to read their cards without showing them to anyone else.

   Ask the participants to imagine they are the person on their card. To help them imbibe their character, ask them a few questions which they will answer in their minds:

   - What is/was your childhood like?
   - Where do you live? Describe the house you live in.
   - What are the games you play or used to play?
   - What are or were your parents like?
   - What do you do during your spare time or holidays?
   - What motivates you and what scares you?
   - Where would you like to be five years from now?

Ask the participants to stand in line facing you. Read a statement from the list below. If participants believe that the statement applies to the person on their card, they take one step forward. Otherwise, they stay where they are. Continue on with the other statements. At the end, some participants will be way out in front, while others will not have moved at all.

Statements:

1. You have never been in serious financial difficulty.
2. You live in an apartment with a telephone and TV.
3. You believe that your language is respected.
4. You believe that your religion and culture are respected.
5. You feel that your views are really listened to.
6. You are not afraid of being arrested by the police.
7. You have never been discriminated against.
8. You are able to go to school.
9. You feel positive about your future as you have received good education.
10. You think you will be able to practice whatever profession you choose.
11. You can celebrate important religious holidays with your family and close friends.
12. You can fall in love with whomever you wish.
13. You can access the Internet and take advantage of what it has to offer.
14. You can access all public places like gardens, temples, community wells.
15. You can access health services.

Questions for Discussion: Use the following questions to discuss this activity:

- How did those of you feel when you stepped forward?
- How did those of you feel when you could not move?
- Have you ever experienced situations where you felt excluded because of some attributes of you?
- What can we do to include everyone and make them feel respected?

Source: Adapted from "Take a step forward" in Compass—A Manual on Human Rights Education with Young People, Council of Europe (2002, cited in Equitas-International Centre for Human Rights Education, 2010)

4. Show Summary Chart 2.1 and discuss the Cycle of Exclusion.
5. Show Summary Chart 2.2 and discuss Child Rights to Non-discrimination and Inclusion.
6. Introduce the following units of the module:

   - Exclusion of girls and their right to inclusion,
   - Exclusion of children with disability and their right to inclusion,
   - Exclusion of Dalit children and their right to inclusion,
   - Exclusion of tribal children and their right to inclusion.

The first two units are covered in this chapter, and the last two are covered in the subsequent chapter.

Time Estimate: 45 min

Exclusion of Girls and Their Right to Inclusion

Concepts and Theories

Concepts of Exclusion of Girls

Sexism: Sexism implies stereotypes of women's physical and mental capabilities, which have led to role stereotypes of earner for the man and housewife for the woman, headship for the man and subordination for women and, therefore, discrimination against women. Sexism consists of attitudes, policies, institutional structures and actions that discriminate against one sex (often but not always, against women), limiting freedom and opportunities (Griffin, 2008).

Gender Roles and Norms: "Sex" is a word that refers to the biological differences between male and female: the visible difference in genitalia, the related difference in procreative function (Connelly, Li, MacDonald, & Parpart, 2000). For ages, it was believed that the different characteristics, roles and status accorded to women and men in society are determined by biology (i.e. sex), that they are natural and, therefore, not changeable. The distinction between sex and gender was introduced to deal with this tendency to attribute women's subordination to their anatomy. Gender is a matter of culture; it refers to the social classification of men and women into "masculine" and "feminine". Gender has no biological origin that the connections between sex and gender are not natural (Bhasin, 2000). Stets and Burke (2000) note that masculinity is often associated with behaviours that are more dominant, competitive and autonomous while femininity is associated with being expressive, emotional, tender and sympathetic. Throughout their life, parents, teachers, peers, culture and society reinforce this. This learned behaviour is what makes up gender identity and determines gender roles (Williams, Seed, & Mwau, 1994).

Gender relations are seen as the key determinant of women's position in society, which can be changed if this is desired. In order to understand and abolish women's subordination, it is essential that the processes by which gender characteristics are defined and gender relations are constructed be examined (Connelly et al., 2000).

Practices of Exclusion of Girls

Son Preference: It has long been observed that as a natural phenomenon, more boys are born than girls. As a result, the normal sex ratio at birth (SRB), calculated as the number of girls born for every 1000 boys born, is usually in the range 943–962. However, early discriminatory behaviour such as gender-biased sex selection before birth or neglect of girls after birth artificially skews SRB as well as child sex ratio (CSR), measured as the number of girls per 1000 boys in the age group 0–6, in favour of boys. Given this context, the CSR remains much below the normal or desirable range of 950 or more girls per 1000 boys. The CSR in India has declined from 927 girls per 1000 boys in 2001 to 918 according to Census 2011 (India: Office of the Registrar General and Census Commissioner, 2014).

While the sex ratio at birth can be affected by sex-selective abortions targeting the female foetus, deliberate discrimination against the girl child can result in higher mortality rates for girls than for boys. According to the National Family Health Survey (NFHS-4) (2015–16), the sex ratio at birth for children born in the last five years was 919 females per 1,000 males only marginally more than 914 of the NFHS-3 (2005–6). According to NFHS-4 (IIPS & ICF, 2017), 63% of currently married women age 15–49 with two living daughters and no sons want no more children, compared with 89 percent with two sons and no daughters and the pattern is similar for men, indicating that son preference is still an important factor in overall fertility preferences in India.

Gender-biased sex selection is a discriminatory practice that is a result of a complex web of factors:

- Deep-seated patriarchal mindsets that lead families to value sons over daughters,
- The need for small families, but with sons, and
- Commercialisation and misuse of medical technology that enables illegal sex selection (India: Office of the Registrar General and Census Commissioner, 2014).

Some of the ill practices that functionaries of the Directorate of Field Publicity (2015) encountered in the villages which were found to be responsible for female foeticide, negligence of education for girl child and their lower status in the society are:

(1) Prevalence of dowry leading to lower preference for girl child,
(2) Treating daughters inferior to sons and they being considered burden,
(3) Delay and negligence in the treatment of baby girls,
(4) Child marriage so as to prevent dishonour of women,
(5) Men in the rural areas do not take much interest in the medical treatment of women,
(6) Lack of separate functional toilets in schools hindering their education,
(7) Lack of transport facilities from villages to colleges hindering higher education for girls,
(8) Domestic violence,
(9) Division in land holding and denial of property rights to women.

The Pre-Natal Diagnostic Techniques (PNDTs) (Regulation and Prevention of Misuse) Act came into force in 1994 to regulate the use of diagnostic techniques capable of sex selection. Subsequently, it was amended in 2003 to regulate pre-conception sex selection as well. The Act is now called the Pre-Conception and Pre-Natal Diagnostics Techniques (Prohibition of Sex Selection) Act. The amended Act not only prohibits determination and disclosure of the sex of the foetus for non-medical reasons but also bans advertisements related to pre-conception and pre-natal determination of sex. The Act has made it mandatory for all ultrasound clinics and other diagnostic facilities capable of sex determination to prominently display a signboard indicating that disclosure of the sex of the foetus is illegal. Further, all such facilities have to be registered with the appropriate authority of the district (usually the Chief Medical Officer or the District Magistrate). The Act requires the manufacturers to provide information to the government about the sale of ultrasound machines and other similar equipment (India: Office of the Registrar General and Census Commissioner, 2014).

Girls' Exclusion in Education: Girls may be denied access or have unequal opportunities to education as compared to boys due to:

- Economic constraints or different priorities of the families,
- Fear that travel to school may expose the girls to sexual abuse which would harm the family honour,
- Concerns about sexual abuse or harassment towards girls from teachers or male students,
- Fear that girls may "find" a boy of different caste or class to marry which would tarnish the family reputation,
- Expectations that girls should help with domestic work,
- Inadequate resources for girls to manage menstruation,
- Local norms about early marriage and childbearing and
- Lack of equal opportunity in the workforce for educated females (The Population Council, 2011).

Limited Agency for Young Women: Findings of a study of 15–29-year-old youth clearly highlight young women's limited agency:

- Just one in four young women (27%) reported independent decision-making on all three issues explored in the survey, namely decisions on choice of friends, spending money and purchase of clothes for oneself.
- Only three-quarters of young women (73%) had the freedom to visit locations within their own village or neighbourhood unescorted.
- Just one-quarter of young women reported freedom to visit at least one place outside the village or neighbourhood unescorted, and 15% could visit a health facility unescorted.
- Fewer than two in five women reported some savings and one in 10 owned a bank or post office savings account.
- Of those who owned an account, just 54% operated it themselves.
- Although young women were more likely than young men to have money saved (36 and 23%, respectively), they were slightly less likely than young men to own a bank or post office savings account (11 and 15%, respectively).
- Young women were much less likely than their male counterparts to operate these accounts themselves (54% vs. 90% of those who had an account) (International Institute for Population Sciences & Population Council, 2010).

Violence Against Girls: The fear of losing the dominant position forces men to find ways of controlling women through violence. From childhood, boys are socialised into patterns of gender identity and related behaviour that give them a sense of superiority over girls and cause some to be violent towards them and most to be ineffective witnesses to this violence (Save the Children, 2009). Women face gender-based violence throughout their life cycle and girls face it throughout their childhood as given in the Summary Chart 2.3.

Rights of the Girl Child

UNCRC: The UNCRC (1989) does not make a mention of girls but mandates non-discrimination and equality by sex in the following articles:

- **Article 2(1)**: States Parties shall respect and ensure the rights set forth in the present Convention to each child within their jurisdiction without discrimination of any kind, irrespective of the child's or his or her parent's or legal guardian's race, colour, sex, language, religion, political or other opinion, national, ethnic or social origin, property, disability, birth or other status.
- **Article 29(1d)**: The preparation of the child for responsible life in a free society, in the spirit of understanding, peace, tolerance, equality of sexes, and friendship among all peoples, ethnic, national and religious groups and persons of indigenous origin.

The following issues of particular relevance to the girl child have been addressed by the Child Rights Committee:

- Legal and de facto equality of girls, and measures taken to ensure to girls equal rights,
- Discriminatory and stereotypical attitudes, prejudices and practices towards girls,
- Marriage age, especially early marriage age of girls, and forced marriage,
- Violence against girls, including traditional practices harmful to girls and women, female genital mutilation, sexual abuse, incest, trafficking, sexual exploitation, girl servants, bride price, female pre-natal sex selection, rape and impunity for rape when followed by marriage,
- Child prostitution, child pornography,
- Girls' health, including family planning education, abortion rates, clandestine abortions, high mortality rates for girls, lack of access to health care and reproductive health care,
- Teenage pregnancy rates,
- Education and literacy rates of girls, school retention and dropout rates,
- Inheritance rights of girls,
- Girl child labour,
- The situation of girls in single parent, female-headed households,
- Maternal health care, including pre-natal services, breastfeeding and paid maternity leave (Goonesekere & De Silva-De Alwis, 2005).

CEDAW: The UN Convention (1979) on the Elimination of All Forms of Discrimination against Women (CEDAW) covers all women, irrespective of age. The CEDAW defines discrimination against women as "any distinction, exclusion or restriction made on the basis of sex which has the effect or purpose of impairing or nullifying the recognition, enjoyment or exercise by women, irrespective of their marital status, on a basis of equality of men and women, of human rights and fundamental freedoms in the political, economic, social, cultural, civil or any other field".

Linkage between Child Rights and Women's Rights: Goonesekere and De Silva-De Alwis (2005) note that there exists a strong link between women's and children's rights especially for girls from a life cycle perspective. Unfortunately, this link has not been thoroughly explored which has given rise to the misconception that women's and children's rights are incompatible. Some of these fears stem from the notion that integrating women's and children's rights will restrict women to the role of caregiver of children. The CEDAW advances girls' human rights by reinforcing certain rights already covered by the UNCRC. They have identified the following measures that illustrate how women's rights and children's rights can intersect and complement:

- Special provisions for girls' education and vocational training enhance employment opportunities for women.
- Legal reform on a child's right to nationality and women's right to inherit property has been critical to the care and development of children. Law reform on nationality and violence against women is an area that clearly links women and children's rights. Support for family law, inheritance and property law reform, birth registration, compulsory education, migrant work and child labour reform impact invariably to prevent exploitation of women and girls.
- Family support services provide protection for women and child victims of gender-based violence.
- The right to access information on sexual and health care will ensure equal access to both adolescent boys and girls to such information.
- Childcare facilities for protecting the best interest of the child and provide support to women's economic participation.
- Alliances with civil society organisations as a cornerstone of the effective private/ public collaboration are essential to both UNCRC and CEDAW implementation. The work of other civil society organizations should also be complementary.

Protecting women's rights protects children's rights as well. Conversely, protecting the rights of children, particularly girls, is the first step in promoting gender equality for women (United Nations Population Fund (UNFPA) & UNICEF, 2011).

Gender Equality and Equity: Gender equality is the long-term consequence of an absence of discrimination based on a person's sex. This can apply to laws, policies or opportunities, or to the allocation of resources or benefits or access to services.

Gender equity is fairness and justice in the distribution of benefits and responsibilities between women and men. The concept recognises that women and men have different needs and power and that these differences should be identified and addressed in a manner that rectifies the imbalance between the sexes (UNFPA & UNICEF, 2011).

Gender-Sensitive Approach: A gender-sensitive approach means identifying major phenomena of inequality and discrimination due to sex and to address such discrimination, if required through affirmative action (giving special benefits to the disadvantaged sex or group). A gender-sensitive approach also means that the same problem may need to be addressed in different ways for boys and girls taking the distinct social roles and domains of males and females into account, and the impact of most programme activities will be different for boys and girls (UNICEF, 2001).

Role of Men and Boys: Save the Children (2009) recommends that men and boys question the narrow definitions and perceptions of gender roles and relations, including different ways of expressing their masculinity. They need to reject the stereotypical portrayal of only an aggressive "macho" man being the "real man" and the culture of violence as proof of masculinity.

Government Schemes for Girls

The Adolescent Girls Scheme: The Adolescent Girls Scheme under the Integrated Child Development Scheme (ICDS) primarily aims at breaking the intergenerational life cycle of nutritional and gender disadvantage and providing a supportive environment for self-development. Under the Scheme, the adolescent girls who are unmarried and belong to families below the poverty line and school dropouts are selected and attached to the local Anganwadi Centres for six-month stints of learning and training activities. The objective of the Scheme is to increase self-confidence, boost morale and give dignity. The adolescent girls scheme has been designed to include 2 sub-schemes, viz. Scheme I (Girl-to-Girl Approach) and Scheme II (Balika Mandal). The Scheme I has been designed for adolescent girls in the age group of 11–15 years belonging to families whose income level is below Rs. 6400/-per annum. The Scheme II is intended to reach to all adolescent girls in the age group of 11–18 years irrespective of income levels of the family.

The Kishori Shakti Yojana: The objectives of the Kishori Shakti Yojana are as follows:

(i) To improve the nutritional and health status of girls in the age group of 11–18 years,
(ii) To provide the required literacy and numeracy skills through the non-formal stream of education, to stimulate a desire for more social exposure and knowledge and to help them improve their decision-making capabilities,
(iii) To train and equip the adolescent girls to improve/upgrade home-based and vocational skills,

(iv) To promote awareness of health, hygiene, nutrition and family welfare, home management and childcare, and to take all measure as to facilitate their marrying only after attaining the age of 18 years and if possible, even later,

(v) To gain a better understanding of their environment-related social issues and the impact on their lives and

(vi) To encourage adolescent girls to initiate various activities to be productive and useful members of the society.

Rajiv Gandhi Scheme for Empowerment of Adolescent Girls (Sabla Yojana): Sabla is a scheme to empower adolescent girls of 11–18 years by improving their nutritional and health status, upgrading various skills like home skills, life skills and vocational skills. The girls will also be equipped with information on health and family welfare, hygiene and guidance on existing public services. The scheme is being implemented in 200 districts across the country on a pilot basis while in the remaining districts Kishori Shakti Yojana (KSY), where operational, will continue as before. The scheme uses the platform of the ICDS wherein Anganwadi Centres (AWC) is the focal point for the delivery of services.

Beti Bachao Beti Padhao: The government has launched the Beti Bachao Beti Padhao programme in 2015 to address the issue of decline in child sex ratio through a mass campaign and multisectoral action plan in 100 gender-critical districts across the country. The objectives of this initiative are:

- Prevention of gender-biased sex-selective elimination,
- Ensuring survival and protection of the girl child,
- Ensuring education and participation of the girl child (India: Directorate of Field Publicity, 2015).

Activities

Activity 2.2: Reflections on Gender Roles

Learner Outcome: At the end of this activity, the participants will 1) develop awareness on their gender role socialisation and its impact on them and 2) learn the skills to reject gender stereotypes in their lives.

Procedure: Use the following procedure to conduct this activity:

1. Ask the participants to reflect upon the advantages and disadvantages of being a girl/boy.
2. Ask each participant individually to complete the sentence: "Sometimes I am glad I am girl/boy because……..". Ask them to enlist as many of the advantages of being a girl/boy as they can and share.

3. Subsequently, ask the participants to complete the following sentence: "Sometimes I wish I were a girl/boy because..........". Again, they should list as many reasons as possible and share.
4. Ask those boys and girls who are into challenging gender role stereotypes in their daily lives to share what contributed to it.

Questions for Discussion: Use the following questions to discuss this activity:

- What are the advantages and disadvantages of being a girl?
- What are the advantages and disadvantages of being a boy?
- How did you feel listening to sentences of others of the same sex? Why?
- How did you feel listening to sentences of the opposite sex? Why?
- How can you reject the gender role stereotypes in your personal life?
- What challenges would you face in rejecting the gender role stereotypes in your personal life?
- How could these challenges be overcome?
- How can you be more respectful and egalitarian to the other sex in your personal life?

Time Estimate: 45 min

Activity 2.3: Game on Gender Based on Facts or Social Constructs?

Learner Outcome: At the end of this activity, the participants will develop awareness of socially constructed gender stereotypes that lead to sexism and deny girls' rights.

Procedure: Use the following procedure for this activity:

1. Take two flipcharts and label one as "Society" and the other as "Biology". Stick these flipcharts on opposite walls of the training room.
2. Ask participants to stand in a straight line at the centre of the room, equidistant from the labelled walls. Read aloud the following list of statements one at a time. After each statement, ask participants to move a step towards the Society wall or Biology wall depending on what they feel regarding the statement, whether it is based on sociocultural factors or has a biological basis.

   List of Statements:

1. Girls are gentle, boys are strong.
2. Boys are better than girls in maths, logical reasoning and analytical thinking.
3. Girls are better than boys in languages or creative work.
4. Girls like to dress up and wear makeup and boys don't care about dressing up.

 5. Girls don't know how to drive well.
 6. Girls/women can give birth to babies.
 7. Boys are good in rough games like football, hockey.
 8. Girls start crying for the smallest of things and boys don't cry.
 9. Girls keep gossiping about other people; they can never keep a secret.
10. Girls love to play with dolls and boys love to play with cars.
11. Boys are messy and keep their belongings untidily and girls are very neat and keep their belonging tidily.
12. Boys don't like to cook food or work in the kitchen and girls like to cook and work in the kitchen.
13. Girls are better at taking care of younger siblings or children and boys don't know how to take care of younger siblings or children.
14. Boys need higher education because they earn money for their family and girls don't need higher education as they get married and stay at home.
 5. Alternately, ask the participants to list the common sexist proverbs on girls and boys or men and women and put up on either of the walls depending on whether these are societal or biological.
 6. Use the following questions to discuss this activity:

  • What are the reasons for gender statements/proverbs being considered biological?
  • What are the reasons for gender statements/proverbs being considered societal?
  • Discuss the difference between "sex" and "gender".
  • What are the assumptions of physical and mental capabilities of men and women reflected in the gender stereotypes?
  • How do gender stereotypes restrict life choices and impact the basic needs of boys as well as girls?
  • How do they lead to justification of abuse and violence against girls and women?
  • How can girls reject gender stereotypes?
  • How can boys reject gender stereotypes?

 7. Ask the participants to make a list of tasks that they would like to undertake to reject the social construction of gender. For example, tasks like "stitch a button", "bake a cake/other cooking action", "fold a shirt", "outdoor session to buy fruits and vegetables" and so on for boys and tasks like "repair a fuse", "write a cheque", "fixing a light bulb" and so on for girls.

Time Estimate: 30 min

Source: Adapted from Module One, Exercise 3: Understanding Gender in Talking About Reproductive & Sexual Health Issues (2006)

Activity 2.4: Video Discussion on Female Foeticide

Learner Outcome: At the end of this activity, the participants will develop awareness about the crime of female foeticide.

Procedure: Show the following video film:

Satyamev Jayate—Female Foeticide

https://www.youtube.com/watch?v=w1ByZCLOvXY

Questions for Discussion: Use the following questions to discuss this activity:

- Why is female foeticide practiced?
- Why are sons preferred to daughters?
- How does the sex of the child get determined?
- What is the time-wise trend of female foeticide? Why?
- Where does it happen prominently?
- Does it happen mostly in villages by uneducated people?
- Why even highly educated people from cities commit female foeticide?
- Why tribals do not ask for preference for sons?
- What are the implications of declining sex ratio? Non-availability of brides for grooms? Sale of brides? Trafficking of women?
- What are the provisions of the Pre-Natal Diagnostic Techniques (PNDTs) (Regulation and Prevention of Misuse) Act?

Time Estimate: Show select portion for 30 min and conduct discussion for 15 min.

Activity 2.5: Video Discussion on Exclusion of the Girl Child
from Education

Learner Outcome: At the end of this activity, the participants will develop awareness about exclusion of girls from education.

Procedure: Show the following video film: Murgiyo Ki Ginti (Hindi)—Meena Unicef

https://www.youtube.com/watch?v=WzLjNeDP-tE

Questions for Discussion: Use the following questions to discuss this activity:

- Why was Meena not being sent to school?
- How does she catch the chicken thief?
- Why should girls be sent to school?
- What are the other ways in which girls are discriminated against? Food? Health care?
- Do girls get as much food as their brothers?

- Do girls get as much health care as their brothers?
- Why are girls generally discriminated against?
- How does it impact the girl child?
- Do girls have rights to equal opportunities and non-discrimination?
- What are the rights of girls?
- How can violation of girls' rights be prevented?
- What is the role of boys in being inclusive about girls?

Time Estimate: 30 min

Activity 2.6: Small Group Discussion on Review of Government Schemes for Girls

Learner Outcome: At the end of this activity, the participants will develop awareness about government schemes for girls.

Procedure: Use the following procedure to conduct this activity:

1. Form four small groups and allocate the following two government schemes for child right-based review and make recommendations. Two groups can review the same set of schemes:

   - The Adolescent Girls/Kishori Shakti/Sabla Scheme,
   - Beti Bachao Beti Padhao Scheme.

2. Ask the small groups to present their review and recommendations to the large group.

Time Estimate: 30 min

Exclusion of Children with Disability and Their Right to Inclusion

Concepts and Theories

Disability

The International Classification of Functioning, Disability and Health (ICF) advanced the understanding and measurement of disability. The ICF emphasises environmental factors in creating disability, which is the main difference between this new classification and the previous International Classification of Impairments, Disabilities, and Handicaps (ICIDH). In the ICF, problems with human functioning are categorised in three interconnected areas:

- Impairments are problems in body function or alterations in body structure—for example, paralysis or blindness,
- Activity limitations are difficulties in executing activities—for example, walking or eating,
- Participation restrictions are problems with involvement in any area of life—for example, facing discrimination in employment or transportation (World Health Organisation & World Bank, 2011).

Disability refers to difficulties encountered in any or all three areas of functioning. The ICF can also be used to understand and measure the positive aspects of functioning such as body functions, activities, participation and environmental facilitation. The ICF adopts neutral language and does not distinguish between the type and cause of disability—for instance, between "physical" and "mental" health. "Health conditions" are diseases, injuries and disorders, while "impairments" are specific decrements in body functions and structures, often identified as symptoms or signs of health conditions (World Health Organisation & World Bank, 2011).

Persons with Disability

Article 1 of the United Nations Convention on the Rights of Persons with Disability (UNCRPD) of 2006 refers to persons with disabilities as those who have long-term physical, mental, intellectual or sensory impairments which in interaction with various barriers may hinder their full and effective participation in society on an equal basis with others. According to the Persons with Disabilities (Equal Opportunities, Protection of Rights and Full Participation) Act, 1995, "person with disability" means a person suffering from not less than forty per cent of any disability as certified by a medical authority.

Ableism and Barriers for Persons with Disability

Ableism describes prejudicial attitudes and discriminatory behaviours towards persons with a disability. It hinges on one's understanding of "normal" ability and the rights and benefits afforded to persons deemed "normal" (Levi, 2006). The abilities of those with disabilities are overlooked, their capacities are underestimated, and their needs are given low priority. The barriers they face are more frequently as a result of the environment in which they live than as a result of their impairment (UNICEF Innocenti Research Centre, 2007). The WHO and the World Bank (2011) documents widespread evidence of barriers for the disabled, including the following:

- Inadequate policies and standards,
- Negative attitudes,
- Lack of provision of services,

- Problems with service delivery,
- Inadequate funding,
- Lack of accessibility,
- Lack of consultation and involvement,
- Lack of data and evidence.

Vulnerability of Children with Disabilities

Children with disabilities (CWDs) are among the most stigmatised and marginalised of all the world's children. While all children are at risk of being victims of violence, these children find themselves at significantly increased risk because of stigma, negative traditional beliefs and ignorance. Lack of social support, limited opportunities for education, employment or participation in the community further isolates them and their families, leading to increased levels of stress and hardship. The CWDs are also often targeted by abusers, who see them as easy victims (Groce, 2005).

Following is a famous quotation by Albert Einstein, "Everybody is a genius. But if you judge a fish by its ability to climb a tree, it will live its whole life believing that it is stupid". CWDs are often like the fish that is expected to climb a tree to prove itself. This is because they are often defined by and judged by what they lack rather than what they have. CWDs get labelled so because of our own construction of what is "normal" and "abnormal", fear of the unknown, media images and so on (UNICEF, 2009).

Rights of Children with Disabilities

Pre-Rights Perception: The persons with disability in India are sometimes perceived to be cursed by God because of bad *karma* in their past lives or of their parents. Then disability was narrowly construed as a medical problem needing health solutions. Persons with disabilities were regarded as objects of pity in need of charity and welfare. This view has now given way to a human rights-based approach to disability, which rejects the idea that obstacles to the participation of persons with disabilities arise primarily from their impairment. It focuses on eliminating social barriers that prevent persons with disabilities from enjoying their human rights on an equal basis with others. Disability is now seen as a socially created problem, and as a matter of removing barriers to the full participation of persons with disabilities (UNICEF, 2009).

UNCRC: Article 23 of the UNCRC requires the States Parties to:

- Recognise that a mentally or physically disabled child should enjoy a full and decent life, in conditions which ensure dignity, promote self-reliance and facilitate the child's active participation in the community.

- Recognise the right of the disabled child to special care and encourage and ensure the extension, subject to available resources, to the eligible child and those responsible for his or her care, of assistance.
- Assistance extended shall be provided free of charge, whenever possible, taking into account the financial resources of the parents or others caring for the child.

UNCRPD: The UN Convention on the Rights of Persons with Disabilities (UNCRPD, 2006) promotes, protects and ensures the human rights for all people with disabilities, including children with disabilities. The principles of this Convention are:

(a) Respect for inherent dignity, individual autonomy including the freedom to make one's own choices, and independence of persons,
(b) Non-discrimination,
(c) Full and effective participation and inclusion in society,
(d) Respect for difference and acceptance of persons with disabilities as part of human diversity and humanity,
(e) Equality of opportunity,
(f) Accessibility,
(g) Equality between men and women,
(h) Respect for the evolving capacities of children with disabilities and respect for the right of children with disabilities to preserve their identities.

Article 7 of the UNCRPD specifically focuses on Children with Disabilities as follows:

1. States Parties shall take all necessary measures to ensure the full enjoyment by children with disabilities of all human rights and fundamental freedoms on an equal basis with other children.
2. In all actions concerning children with disabilities, the best interests of the child shall be a primary consideration.
3. States Parties shall ensure that children with disabilities have the right to express their views freely on all matters affecting them, their views being given due weight in accordance with their age and maturity, on an equal basis with other children, and to be provided with disability and age-appropriate assistance to realise that right.

Indian Constitution: According to Article 41 of the Directive Principles of State Policy of the Indian Constitution, the State shall, within the limits of its economic capacity and development, make effective provision for securing the right to work, to education and to public assistance in cases of disablement among others.

Persons with Disabilities (Equal Opportunities, Protection of Rights and Full Participation) Act

The Persons with Disabilities (Equal Opportunities, Protection of Rights and Full Participation) Act (India: Ministry of Law, Justice and Company Affairs 1995) gives effect to the proclamation on the full participation and equality of the persons with disabilities in the Asian and Pacific Region and provides for their education, employment, creation of barrier-free environment, social security, etc. (http://socialjustice.nic.in/pwdact1995.php)

The Twin-Track Approach for Children with Disabilities

The twin-track approach promotes concurrent action across two broad sets of initiatives. Interventions on either track alone will not provide the breadth of involvement, integration and support needed for people with a disability to fully participate. Genuine inclusion and empowerment can only occur when both tracks are employed together:

1. One set is through disability-specific activities that are targeted directly for people with a disability.
2. The other is through the mainstreaming of disability into broader activities (Christoffel Blindenmission, 2012).

Disability-Specific Initiatives

Depending on the context, a variety of programmes can meet specific needs of people with a disability and remain important aspects of disability-inclusive development:

- **Specific Medical Interventions**: There are many medical programmes that target a specific impairment or causes of impairment.
- **Adaptive Devices**: There is a wide range of adaptive devices such as canes, prosthetics, wheelchairs and hearing aids which enhance the participation and empowerment of people with a disability.
- **Special Education Programmes**: Although debate exists about the pros and cons of "special education", there are situations where this is, in part, the most realistic method to support children with particular disabilities such as deafness. Provision of resources and specialist teacher training can be important here.
- **Disabled Peoples' Organisations**: These organisations are set up and led by people with a disability to represent and support their members.
- **Community-Based Rehabilitation**: Community-based rehabilitation (CBR) is an approach that can address mainstream and disability-specific measures. It is a broad community development approach seeking to empower people with a disability and work in partnership with them (Christoffel Blindenmission, 2012).

Mainstreaming/Inclusion of Children with Disabilities

The UNCRPD has its moorings in the global movement for inclusion of CWD in community life. Inclusion stems from the recognition that all children are full members of society, and that each child is a unique individual who is entitled to be respected and consulted (UNICEF, 2013).

Barriers and Accessibility: Comprehensive accessibility is fundamental for the full inclusion of people with a disability. Removing "disabling" barriers and ensuring comprehensive access play a significant role in creating opportunities for people with a disability to participate in development programmes. Impairments can become less "disabling" if society is accessible and barriers to inclusion are removed. Barriers can be grouped into four categories.

- **Physical or environmental barriers**: Buildings, schools, clinics, water pumps, transport, roads, paths, etc.
- **Communication barriers**: Written and spoken information including media, flyers, Internet, community meetings, etc.
- **Policy barriers**: Including both legislation and policies that discriminates against people with a disability, and/or an absence of legislation that might otherwise provide an enabling framework.
- **Attitudinal barriers**: Including negative stereotyping of people with a disability, social stigma and other forms of overt discrimination. People with a disability often report that attitudes are the most disabling barriers of all (Christoffel Blindenmission, 2012).

Inclusive Approach in Education: Many children and adults with disabilities have historically been excluded from mainstream education opportunities. In most countries, early efforts at providing education or training were generally through separate special schools, usually targeting specific impairments, such as schools for the blind. These institutions reached only a small proportion of those in need and were not cost-effective: usually in urban areas, they tended to isolate individuals from their families and communities. The situation began to change only when legislation started to require including children with disabilities in educational systems. Ensuring that children with disabilities receive good quality education in an inclusive environment should be a priority of all countries. The UNCRPD recognises the right of all children with disabilities both to be included in the general education systems and to receive the individual support they require (World Health Organisation & World Bank, 2011).

Education may take place in a range of settings—such as special schools and centres, special classes in integrated schools or regular classes in mainstream schools—following the principle of "the least restrictive environment". This interpretation assumes that all children can be educated and that regardless of the setting or adaptations required, all students should have access to a curriculum that is relevant and produces meaningful outcomes. A stricter sense of inclusion is that all children with disabilities should be educated in regular classrooms with age-appropriate peers. This approach stresses the need for the whole school system to change. Inclusive education entails identifying and removing barriers and providing reasonable accommodation, enabling every learner to participate and achieve within mainstream settings (World Health Organisation & World Bank, 2011).

Thus, inclusion is different from integration. The latter implies that CWDs are to be brought into a pre-existing framework of prevailing norms and standards. For example, in the context of education, integration is realised by admitting children with disabilities to "regular" schools. Inclusion, on the other hand, calls for schools to be designed and administered such that all children can experience quality learning and recreation together. An inclusive curriculum can help all children to better appreciate diversity (UNICEF, 2013).

Activities

Activity 2.7: Exercise on Attitude to Children with Disabilities

Learner Outcome: At the end of this activity, the participants will develop awareness on common stereotypes against children with disability and how this leads to denial of their rights.

Procedure: Use the following procedure to conduct this activity:

1. Ask the participants the following questions:

    (1) What is disability?
    (2) Which words are generally used for children with disabilities in place of their real names?
    (3) Why does their disability become the major focus for those who are not disabled?

2. Discuss how they deny the child the right to have any other identity except for that linked to the disability.
3. Ask the participants to respond to the Exercise on Attitude to Children with Disability, given at the end of the chapter.
4. Show Summary Chart 2.4 and discuss the interconnected aspects of a disability.

Questions for Discussion: Use the following questions to discuss this activity:

- If you agree with the above statements, why?
- If you disagree with the above statements, why?
- Do you think that our perception of "normal" versus "abnormal" contributes to a negative attitude towards children with disability?
- How do these attitudes affect children with disability?
- How can stereotypes of children with disability be converted into positive perceptions?

Time Estimate: 30 min

Source: The list of common myths and stereotypes is adapted from Human Rights Resource Centre (2007, cited in UNICEF, 2009, p. 29)

Activity 2.8: A Mock Disability Experience

Learner Outcome: At the end of this activity, the participants will get sensitised to the challenges faced by children with disability due to barriers in their social environment.

Procedure: Use the following procedure to conduct this activity:

1. Ask the participants the following questions:

   (1) Do you have a family member (old grandparents included) or a friend living with disability?
   (2) Have you experienced any disability yourself? For example, a short-term disability due to injury? Or language disability when you could not communicate due to difference in language?

2. Divide the participants into three small groups and ask them to undertake the following activities:

   (1) Blindfold Walk: Group members may form pairs and each partner of the pair may take turns getting blindfolded and guided by the partner, while walking through a distance. This brief walk may include taking turns, climbing up or down and so on.
   (2) Hop Walk: In pairs, each partner of the pair may take turns to hopping and guided by the partner, while walking through a distance. The brief walk may include taking turns, climbing up or down and so on.
   (3) Dumb Charade: Form pairs and ask them to communicate through use of signs and gestures.

Questions for Discussion: Use the following questions to discuss this activity:

- What barriers did you face when acting the disabled?
- How did you feel being a disabled?
- How did you manage being a disabled?
- What did you learn about children with visual impairment?
- What did you learn about children with hearing and speech impairment?
- What did you learn about children with orthopaedic impairment?
- Can you generalise the experience of disability?
- How did you feel and cope interacting with the partner who was acting as a disabled?
- Does our society create barriers for children with disability such that they are unable to access resources with ease?
- How can we prevent the barriers for children with disability?

Time Estimate: 45 min

Activity 2.9: Video Discussion on Persons with Disability

Learner Outcome: At the end of this activity, the participants will develop awareness on different issues faced by persons with disabilities.

Procedure: Show the following video film:

Satyamev Jayate (2012): Episode Persons with Disabilities

http://www.satyamevjayate.in/watch-the-episodes/persons-with-disabilities/watch-full-episode.aspx

Questions for Discussion: Use the following questions to discuss this film:

• What are some of the issues and challenges faced by persons with disability in our society? Education-wise? Infrastructure-wise? Transport-wise? Family-wise? Stigma and discrimination in the community?
• Was there any particular person's story that touched you the most? Why?
• How do these challenges impact the lives of persons with disability?
• What helped persons with disability overcome their challenges? Positive attitude to life? Support from family/school/friends/community?

Time Estimate: Show select parts for 30 min followed by discussion for 15 min.

Activity 2.10: Video Discussion on Inclusion of Children with Disability

Learner Outcome: At the end of this activity, the participants will learn the skills of being inclusive about children with disability.

Procedure: Use the following procedure to conduct this activity:

1. Show Summary Chart 2.5 and discuss Rights of Children with Disabilities.
2. Show the following video film:

   Disability: Child Protection—Get Informed Protect Children
   https://www.youtube.com/watch?v=3SzazN2OrsQ

Questions for Discussion: Use the following questions to discuss this activity:

• Why do we tend to exclude the child with disability?
• How does the excluded child with disability feel?
• How can we include the child with disability?
• What are the advantages of inclusion for the child with disability and others?

Time Estimate: 15 min

Activity 2.11: Case Study Discussion on Inclusion of Children with Disability

Learner Outcome: At the end of this activity, the participants will develop skills for inclusion of children with disability.

Procedure: Use the following procedure to conduct this activity:

1. Show Chart 2.6 and discuss the Twin-Track Approach for Children with Disabilities.
2. Form three small groups and allocate the following case studies among them for discussion and recommendations.

   (1) Shaina is a seven-year-old girl with polio who lives in a small town. She cannot move around on her own and is not being sent to school. She is therefore isolated and feels sad all the time. How can her inclusion in the society be facilitated by her family, the local self-government and other children?

   (2) Muhammad is a 16-year-old visually challenged boy who passed his SSC in his town. His family has now moved to a city where his father is looking for a job. How can his inclusion be facilitated by the adults and children in the new neighbourhood?

   (3) Rosy is a ten-year-old girl who cannot hear or speak. She studied in a special school for the hearing impaired until she passed the primary school. Now, efforts are being made to admit her to a regular school. How can her inclusion in a regular school be facilitated by the school management, teachers and other students?

3. Ask the small groups to make their presentation in the form of role-plays to the large group for further inputs.

Time Estimate: 30 min

Concluding Activity: Achievement of the Learner Objectives

Learner Outcome: By the end of the concluding activity, the participants will ascertain if they have achieved the learner objectives.

Procedure: Use the following procedure to conduct the concluding activity:

1. Show the power points/a chart on the learner objectives, ask the participants to read them one at a time and ask the group if they think they have achieved the objective.

2. The participants may be asked to share their responses in their diary with reference to the following questions:

- What was a new learning for you in this session?
- What did you like the best in this session and why?
- Which activity was most effective?
- What was not clear/confusing?
- How can you apply what you have learnt?

Time Estimate: 15 min

Appendix: Summary Charts and Exercises

Summary Chart 2.1 Cycle of exclusion

Summary Chart 2.2 Child rights to non-discrimination for inclusion

Summary Chart 2.3 Gender-based violence in childhood stages
(Adapted from Save the Children (2009))

Stage	Gender-based Violence
Prenatal	Female foeticide
Infancy	Female infanticide, emotional and physical abuse, differential access to food and medical care, negligence
Childhood	Child marriage, genital mutilation, emotional, physical and sexual abuse, differential access to food and medical care, child trafficking, sale and commercial exploitation
Adolescence	Child marriage, dating and courtship violence, sexual harassment and rape, child trafficking, sale and commercial exploitation

Summary Chart 2.4 Interconnected aspects of a disability
(Adapted from World Health Organisation and World Bank 2011)

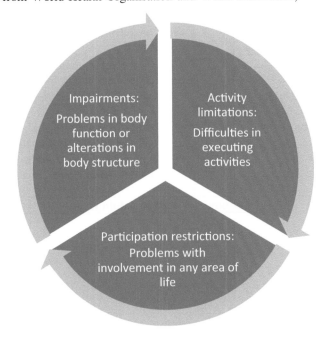

Summary Chart 2.5 Rights of children with disabilities

Children with disability have rights to:
- A full and decent life, in conditions which ensure dignity, promote self-reliance and facilitate the child's active participation in the community.
- Special care and free of charge assistance to the eligible child and those responsible for his or her care.
- Accessibility to education and public assistance.
- Respect for inherent dignity, individual autonomy including the freedom to make one's own choices, and independence of persons.
- Equality of opportunity and non-discrimination.
- Full and effective participation and inclusion in society.
- Respect for difference and acceptance of persons with disabilities as part of human diversity and humanity.
- Respect for the evolving capacities of children with disabilities and respect for the right of children with disabilities to preserve their identities.

Summary Chart 2.6 Twin-track approach for children with disabilities
(Adapted from Christoffel Blindenmission 2012)

Disability-Specific Initiatives	Mainstreaming/ Inclusion of Children with Disabilities
<ul><li>Specific Medical Interventions</li><li>Adaptive Devices</li><li>Special Education Programmes</li><li>Disabled Peoples' Organisations</li></ul>	<ul><li>Prevent Segregation & Adapt the Mainstream Setting for Inclusion</li><li>Remove Physical Barriers & Facilitate Accessibility</li><li>Remove Communication Barriers & Facilitate Right to Information</li><li>Remove Negative Attitudes & Facilitate Acceptance</li></ul>
Community-Based Rehabilitation	

Exercise for Activity 2.1: Planning a Picnic

You have to select eight children from the following list who
can be accommodated on an eight-seater boat for a picnic to an island:

- Varun, 9 years, and visually impaired
- Waman, 13 years, shepherd boy
- Durga, 10 years, belonging to a 'scavenger' family
- John, 11 years, belonging to the Naga tribe of the North-East
- Pranjal, 12 years, a fisherman's daughter
- Pragati, 11 years, child of a divorced parents
- Arijit, 12 years, a street child who works in a tea stall
- Fatima, 10 years, studying in an up-market school
- Kaizad, 15 years, overcoming tobacco use and school dropout
- Shahruk, 6 years, wheelchair bound due to disability
- Abhay, 10 years, coming from the gypsy tribe of Gujarat-Rajasthan belt
- Ashok, 13 years, his parents are scientists of the Indian space Mission
- Panini, 8 years, a sex worker's child
- Surya, 14 years, a mentally challenged boy with speech impairment.

Exercise for Activity 2.1: One Step Forward Role Cards

You are a Muslim girl living with your parents	You are a child from the tribes of Chhattisgarh
Your father is the president of a Multi-National Company	You are an orphaned boy brought up in an orphanage
You are a daughter of a sex worker	You are a Sikh boy
You are a girl from a Brahmin family	Your parents are manual scavengers
You are a street child living on the streets for the past 4 years	You belong to a tanner's family and your parents deal with animal carcass in a tannery
You come from an affluent farmer's family in rural India	You are a Muslim boy from an urban slum
You are a child with hearing impairment	You belong to a middle-class Jain family
You come from a rich Parsi family	You are a child from Khasi tribe of North-east of India.

Exercise for Activity 2.7: Attitude to Children with Disabilities

No.	Attitude to Children with Disability	Agree-1 Disagree-2
1.	• Children with disabilities are cursed as they are made stupid and helpless.	
2.	• Children with disabilities are to be pitied as they have diseases that need to be cured.	
3.	• We all have some or the other disability.	
4.	• Children with disabilities cannot work so are a burden on society.	
5.	• Children with disabilities cannot play sports.	
6.	• Children with disabilities cannot learn or go to school so they are better off going to special schools.	
7.	• Children with disability have many strengths like all of us.	
8.	• Children with disabilities should never get married or have children as they are dependent on others forever.	
9.	• Children with disability can contribute like other children if they are given adequate opportunity and respect.	
10.	• There is no point in investing in resources/opportunities for children with disabilities as there already many other able-bodied marginalised children who need attention.	

References

Bhasin, K. (2000). *Understanding gender.* New Delhi: Kali for Women. Child Protection Working Group. (2012). *Minimum standards for child protection in humanitarian action.* Retrieved from http://cpwg.net/wp-content/uploads/2013/08/CP-Minimum-Standards-English-2013.pdf.

Christoffel Blindenmission. (2012). *Inclusion made easy: A quick program guide to disability in development.* Germany: Author. Retrieved from http://www.cbm.org/Inclusion-Made-Easy-329091.php.

Connelly, P., Li, T. M., MacDonald, M., & Parpart, J. L. (2000). Feminism and development: Theoretical perspectives. In J. L. Parpart, M. P. Connelly, & V. E. Barriteau (Eds.), *Theoretical perspectives on gender and development.* Retrieved from http://www.idrc.ca/es/ev-27444-201-1-DO_TOPIC.html.

Department for International Development. (2005). *Reducing poverty by tackling social exclusion: A DFID policy paper.* Retrieved from http://webarchive.nationalarchives.gov.uk/+/http://www.dfid.gov.uk/Documents/publications/social-exclusion.pdf.

Desai, M. (2002). *Ideologies and social work: Historical and contemporary analyses.* Jaipur: Rawat Publishers.

Equitas-International Centre for Human Rights Education. (2010). *Speaking rights—education toolkit for youth 13 to 17 sample for demonstration.* Montreal: Author. Retrieved from http://equitas.org/wp-content/uploads/2011/01/SpeakingRightsSample.pdf.

Goonesekere, S., & De Silva-De Alwis, R. (2005). *Women's and children's rights in a human rights based approach to development.* New York: UNICEF. Retrieved from http://www.unicef.org/gender/files/WomensAndChildrensRightsInAHumanRightsBasedApproach.pdf.

Griffin, S. (2008). *Inclusion, equality and diversity in working with children.* Malaysia: Pearson Education Limited.

Groce, N. E. (2005). *Violence against disabled children: UN secretary generals report on violence against children thematic group on violence against disabled children.* New York: Convened by UNICEF at the United Nations.

Hope, A., & Timmel, S. (1999). *Training for transformation: A handbook for community workers.* London: Intermediate Technology Publication.

India: Directorate of Field Publicity. (2015). *Beti Bachao Beti Padhao: DFP's Awareness Campaigns in 75 Critical Districts.* Retrieved from http://wcd.nic.in/BBBPScheme/consultation/WCDReportfinal.pdf.

India: Ministry of Law, Justice and Company Affairs. (1995). *The Persons with Disabilities (Equal Opportunities, Protection of Rights and Full Participation) Act, 1995.* Retrieved from http://socialjustice.nic.in/pwdact1995.php.

India: Office of the Registrar General and Census Commissioner. (2014). *Mapping the Adverse Child Sex Ratio in India: Census 2011.* Retrieved from http://www.censusindia.gov.in/2011census/missing.pdf.

International Institute for Population Sciences & ICF. (2017). *National Family Health Survey (NFHS-4), 2015–16: India.* Mumbai: IIPS.

International Institute for Population Sciences & Population Council. (2010). *Youth in India: Situation and needs 2006–2007.* Retrieved from http://iipsindia.org/pdf/India%20Report.pdf.

Johnson, D. W., & Johnson, F. P. (2009). *Joining together: Group theory and group skills* (10th ed.). Columbus, Ohio: Pearson.

Kabeer, N. (2005). *Social exclusion: Concepts, findings and implications for the MDGs, Paper commissioned as background for the Social Exclusion Policy Paper, Department for International Development (DFID), London.* Retrieved from http://www.gsdrc.org/docs/open/SE2.pdf.

Levi, S. J. (2006). Ableism. In G. Albrecht (Ed.), *Encyclopedia of disability* (pp. 2–5). Thousand Oaks, CA: SAGE Publications, Inc. Retrieved from http://knowledge.sagepub.com/view/disability/n2.xml.

Louis, P. (2001). *Casteism is horrendous than Racism: Durban and Dalit discourse*. New Delhi: Indian Social Institute.

Marshall, G. (Ed.). (1994). *The concise Oxford Dictionary of sociology*. New York: Oxford University Press.

Save the Children. (2008). *Equal You and Equal Me*. Sweden: Author. Retrieved from http://resourcecentre.savethechildren.se/library/equal-you-and-equal-me.

Save the Children. (2009). *Allies for change: Together against violence and abuse working with boys and men: A discussion paper for programmers and practitioners*. Sweden.

Stets, J. E., & Burke, P. K. (2000). Femininity/masculinity. In E. F. Borgatta & R. J. V. Montgomery (Eds.), *Encyclopedia of Sociology* (Revised Ed.) (pp. 997–1005). New York: Macmillan. Retrieved from http://wat2142.ucr.edu/Papers/00b.pdf.

Talking About Reproductive & Sexual Health Issues. (2006). *Basics and beyond: Integrating sexuality, sexual and reproductive health and rights—a manual for trainers*. New Delhi: Author.

The Population Council, Inc. (2011). *It's all one curriculum: Guidelines and activities for a unified approach to sexuality, gender, HIV, and human rights education*. New York: Author. Retrieved from http://www.popcouncil.org/uploads/pdfs/2011PGY_ItsAllOneGuidelines_en.pdf.

Todaro, M. P., & Smith, S. C. (2009). *Economic development* (10th ed.). Essex: Pearson Education Ltd.

United Nations. (1979). Convention on the elimination of all forms of discrimination against women. Retrieved from http://www.ohchr.org/en/ProfessionalInterest/pages/cedaw.aspx.

United Nations. (1989). Convention on the Rights of the Child. Retrieved from http://www.ohchr.org/english/law/pdf/crc.pdf.

United Nations. (2006). *Conventions on the Rights of Persons with Disabilities*. Retrieved from http://www.un.org/disabilities/convention/conventionfull.shtml.

United Nations Children's Fund. (2001). *Pocket guide for a rights-based approach to programming for children: Application in South Asia*. Kathmandu: Author.

United Nations Children's Fund. (2009). *It's about ability learning guide on the convention on the rights of persons with disabilities*. New York: Author. Retrieved from http://www.unicef.org/publications/files/Its_About_Ability_Learning_Guide_EN.pdf.

United Nations Children's Fund. (2013). *The state of the World's Children 2013: Children with disabilities*. New York: Author. Retrieved from http://www.unicef.org/sowc2013/files/SWCR2013_ENG_Lo_res_24_Apr_2013.pdf.

United Nations Children's Fund Innocenti Research Centre. (2007). *Promoting the rights of children with disabilities*. Retrieved from http://www.un.org/esa/socdev/unyin/documents/children_disability_rights.pdf.

United Nations Population Fund & United Nations Children's Fund. (2011). *Women's rights and children's rights: Making the connection*. Retrieved from http://www.unfpa.org/webdav/site/global/shared/documents/publications/2011/Women-Children_final.pdf.

Williams, S., Seed, J., & Mwau, A. (1994). *The Oxfam gender training manual*. United Kingdom: Oxfam.

World Health Organisation, & World Bank. (2011). *World report on disability*. Malta: WHO. Retrieved from http://whqlibdoc.who.int/publications/2011/9789240685215_eng.pdf?ua=1.

Relevant Child Rights and You Reports and Articles

Kale, E. (2011). *Normal Childhood's Response to Childhood of Mentally Challenged*: Aspirations and Ground Reality of Mentally Challenged Children. CRY National Child Rights Fellowship. Retrieve from https://www.cry.org/resources/pdf/NCRRF/Eshwar_Kale_2010_Report.pdf.

Module 3
Rights of Dalit and Tribal Children to Non-discrimination and Inclusion

Prerequisite Modules

The prerequisite Modules for this Module are:
From *Sourcebook I on Introduction to Rights-Based Direct Practice with Children*:

- Modules on Life Skills Development.

From *Sourcebook II on Child Rights Education for Participation and Development: Primary Prevention*:

- Introduction to Child Rights Education,
- Child Rights to Participation and Children's Associations.

From *Sourcebook III on Child Rights Education for Inclusion and Protection: Primary Prevention*:

- Rights of Girls and Children with Disability to Non-Discrimination and Inclusion.

Exclusion of Dalit Children and Their Right to Inclusion

Concepts and Theories

Caste System

It is the unique caste system that makes India one of the most unequal societies in the world. According to the Aryan theory of race, when the Aryans first came to India they were divided into three occupational groups: Brahmins, the priests; Kshatriyas, the warriors; and Vaishyas, the traders. The heredity of occupations was not a recognised principle in the early Vedic age. The darker colour of the native inhabitants of India, whom they conquered, seems to have been the cause of the development of the system of *Varna* (colour). As the *Varna* of a person had been

© Child Rights and You 2018
M. Desai and S. Goel, *Child Rights Education for Inclusion and Protection: Primary Prevention*, Rights-based Direct Practice with Children, https://doi.org/10.1007/978-981-13-0417-0_3

assigned to him/ her by virtue of his/ her birth into it, it was also called the *jati* system, which the west translates as caste. Endogamy prevailed as marriages were permitted only within the caste. The hereditary caste system is supposed to have burgeoned in the later Vedic age (Singhal, 1983).

The dark indigenous people and those of mixed descent were casted as *Shudras*, the fourth caste, which is today called Other Backward Classes (OBCs). The *Atishudras* were considered outcastes and untouchables, which are today called Dalits which means the downtrodden. The Shudras were required to do the manual labour jobs but the clean ones. On the other hand, the *Atishudras* were required to deal with human excreta and dead bodies and, therefore, segregated from the society (Stern, 1993). For centuries, the untouchables were not allowed to enter the villages during the daytime or use public utilities such as roads, wells, tanks. They were made to live on the outskirts of the villages and assigned occupations, which were unclean and filthy. They were denied the right to education, of owning land, wearing jewellery and to bargain for a decent wage (Nancharaiah, 2001).

The castes gradually proliferated into sub-castes. While the sub-caste became a source of identity and support for the individual/family, casteism justified hierarchy of castes based on natural and social inferiority of a large number of communities. Sufferings of the lower castes were usually explained by their *karmas*, in this life or the previous lives, and not outside the individuals. No doubts arose about justice in the social arrangement, as though it was God-given (Gore, 1966). Although the caste system is originally linked to Hinduism, it is today a deeply rooted cultural phenomenon that is practised in varying forms within many different religious communities such as Sikhs, Muslims and Christians (International Dalit Solidarity Network (IDSN), 2008).

Concepts of Dalit

According to Dr. B. R. Ambedkar, "Dalithood is a kind of life condition that characterises the exploitation, suppression and marginalization of Dalit people by the social, economic, cultural and political domination of the upper castes' Brahminical ideology". The Dalit Panther, a neo-Buddhist organisation in Bombay, offered a radical definition of Dalit for its hermeneutic ability to recover the revolutionary meaning of the historical past of the Dalit people. The Dalit Panther defines the term Dalit to cover all the lower castes, tribal people, toiling classes and women (cited in Guru, 2005). Social exclusion among the castes is ensured through the practices of endogamy and social separation. Exclusion is, thus, internal to the system and a necessary outcome of its basic features (Thorat & Senapati, 2006).

According to the 2011 Census, Dalits—officially known as "Scheduled Castes"—constitute 201 million people (16.2% of the population). These figures do not include Dalits who have converted or are born and raised within a non-Hindu religious community. It is therefore more than likely that the total Dalit population —including the millions of Dalit Muslims and Christians—by far exceeds the official 201 million. Thorat and Senapati (2007) note that in general the SCs have limited access to ownership of capital assets and employment; they are less educated, suffer from high degree of poverty and are denied full civil, political and cultural rights even today. About 70% of the SCs live in the rural areas. In the year 2000, about 16% of the SCs were self-employed cultivators and another 12% were in non-farm business. Therefore, about 28% had access to capital assets—much lower than the 56% for non-SC/ST group. The per household asset that is reflective of the disparity in wealth worked out to Rs. 49,180 for SCs as against Rs. 134,500 for non-SC/ST. High poverty leads to high infant and child mortality among the SCs (83 and 39%, respectively) as compared to others (61 and 22%, respectively). At least 56% of SC women suffered from anaemia. More than half of the SC children suffered from either malnutrition or undernutrition. The literacy rate among the SC population was 52% as against 63% among others in rural areas in 2001. The corresponding literacy rate for urban area was 68.5 and 81.5%, respectively.

Casteism and Discrimination Against Dalits

Casteism is a prejudicing ideology that justifies hierarchy of castes based on natural and social inferiority. It is a prejudice about superiority or inferiority of other castes with reference to one's own. It justifies intolerance, discrimination and violence against those at the lower rungs of the hierarchy.

According to the Draft *Principles and Guidelines for the Effective Elimination of Discrimination Based on Work and Descent: A Comprehensive Legal Framework to Eliminate Caste Discrimination Globally* by IDSN (2009), the UN terminology for caste-based discrimination is discrimination based on work and descent. They define it as: "any distinction, exclusion, restriction, or preference based on inherited status such as caste, including present or ancestral occupation, family, community or social origin, name, birth place, place of residence, dialect and accent that has the purpose or effect of nullifying or impairing the recognition, enjoyment, or exercise, on an equal footing, of human rights and fundamental freedoms in the political, economic, social, cultural, or any other field of public life. This type of discrimination is typically associated with the notion of purity and pollution and practices of untouchability, and is deeply rooted in societies and cultures where this discrimination is practised."

Dalits face widespread discrimination, which prevents the full attainment of civil, political, economic, social and cultural rights. They are denied access or ownership of land, are forced to work as bonded labourers in degrading conditions and often abused by the State machinery and the upper caste community members (Louis, 2012). Prejudices and discrimination run deep and lead to denial of basic services like education, health, housing and employment. Dalits also suffer violations of their right to life and security of person through State-sponsored or sanctioned acts of violence, including torture. Caste-motivated killings, rapes and other abuses violate Dalit women who face the triple burden of caste, class and gender (Human Rights Watch, 2012).

Discrimination of Dalit Children

Although Dalit families and communities are less patriarchal than the upper caste families, Dalit children are more vulnerable than other children to casteism, caste-based poverty and stereotypes about their capabilities and roles, leading to a restricted childhood, discrimination in education and occupational mobility, resulting in child abuse, child labour, exploitation as Devadasis, etc.

Restricted Childhood: During childhood, Dalit children may not be exposed to the labels like caste or untouchability. However, parents and adults are anxious that the child should not be hurt by transgressing the existing caste boundaries in innocence; hence, the child is fed with many instructions of "Do's and Don'ts"—don't go there, don't enter such house, don't enter the temple, don't play with so and so, don't play in a specific place, don't touch something/someone, don't sit around such a place, don't argue with so and so, don't back answer so and so, don't fight with so and so—a whole lot of protective and preventive instructions. The specific instructions to girls include don't dress like this, don't sit like this, don't come in notice of dominant caste. There are certain do's like—bow before so and so, say *Namaste,* stand when so and so comes, do services when demanded, do physical labour when demanded, do menial work, agree when in conflict, say good things about so and so and praise so and so (Acharya, 2010).

Discrimination in Education: Dalit children are largely segregated from others and restricted to the municipal schools, deficient in basic infrastructure, classrooms, teachers and teaching aids, where they often face abusive, discriminatory treatment at the hands of their teachers and fellow students (Human Rights Watch, 2002). High dropout and lower literacy rates among lower-caste populations have rather simplistically been characterised as the natural consequences of poverty and underdevelopment. Though these rates are partly attributable to the need for low-caste children to supplement their family wages through labour, more insidious and less well documented are the discriminatory and abusive treatment faced by low-caste children who attempt to attend school, at the hands of their teachers and fellow students from upper castes (Human Rights Watch, 2004).

SC children are frequently treated in a humiliating and degrading manner in school and in public places, at times accompanied by severe corporal punishment. Even in government-sponsored schemes like the midday meal scheme, they are made to feel they are children of a lesser God, with segregation in seating arrangements and in eating midday meals, being made to clean the school toilets and carry their footwear in their hands (at times on their heads) while crossing dominant caste areas in the villages and roads, etc. Some of these factors have significantly contributed to the higher dropout rates among Dalit children who face a hostile environment especially at school (National Coalition for Strengthening PoA Act, 2012).

Child Labour: The denial of the right to work and free choice of employment lies at the very heart of the caste system. Dalits are forced to work in "polluting" and degrading occupations such as manual scavenging and are subject to exploitative labour arrangements such as bonded labour, migratory labour and forced prostitution. A majority of child labour comprises Dalits. Dalit children are more likely to end up as child labourers due to their extreme poverty, the discrimination they face in schools, and the need to support their families. Migratory labour is especially pervasive among Dalits, and children are often expected to work alongside their parents in day-labour jobs. Dalit children are also vulnerable to trafficking (Center for Human Rights and Global Justice, 2007). Across social groups, the incidence of child labour was 1.6% for SCs, while it was 0.36% for others. Similarly, in the age group of 10–14 years, the incidence of child labour was the highest, i.e. 15% for SCs compared to others (5%). With respect to gender difference, the incidence is higher for girls than for boys (National Coalition for Strengthening Prevention of Atrocities Act (PoA), 2012).

The caste system is one of the foundations of bonded labour, through which a traditional expectation of free labour, lack of land, and the threat of violence and social and economic boycotts from upper castes conspire to keep many so-called untouchables, or Dalits, in bondage and a perpetual state of poverty. Child labour is an integral part of the bonded labour (Human Rights Watch, 2003).

Manual Scavenging: According to Article 17 of the Constitution of India, "Untouchability" is abolished and its practice in any form is forbidden. The enforcement of any disability arising out of "Untouchability" shall be an offence punishable in accordance with law. The Protection of Civil Rights Act, 1955, prohibits compelling anyone to practise manual scavenging. The Prohibition of Employment as Manual Scavengers and their Rehabilitation Act (2013) prohibits insanitary latrines and engaging or employing persons for manual scavenging and promotes rehabilitation of manual scavengers. However, manual scavengers in India continue to handle human excreta without protection and so they have severe health consequences. They also typically face untouchability practices. Discrimination that extends to all facets of their lives, including access to education for their children, makes it more likely they will have no choice but to continue to work as manual scavengers. Children of manual scavengers also confront discrimination within schools from both teachers and classmates, resulting in particularly high dropout rates (Human Rights Watch, 2014).

Child Abuse: Human Rights Watch has extensively documented police abuse of Dalits, among others. The need for widespread police reform has also been documented by numerous Indian human rights groups and the National Human Rights Commission, and is part of the larger problem of people's inability to access justice (Human Rights Watch, 2003). When Dalits protest against the derogatory caste practices, attacking their women and children is seen by the upper caste elites as the most effective way of teaching them a political lesson (Human Rights Watch, 1999).

Exploitation as Devadasis: The Devadasi system is most prevalent in Karnataka and Andhra Pradesh, in which, Devi means goddess and Dasi means servant. The virginity of dedicated girls was "sacrificed" to ensure that the goddess, and so the land, remained fertile. The belief that when a man has sex with a Devadasi he is actually having sex with the goddess is still perpetuated by some. In the past, Devadasi came from various different social groups, some become courtesans to princes, priests and other high-cast men. This gave them a level of status and autonomy not available to Indian women at that time. However, the Devadasis are now almost exclusively Dalits. As women and Dalits, they are already members of the two most exploited groups in India, and at dedication they are degraded further by the stigma of being a Devadasi and a "fallen woman". Because of this they are extremely vulnerable to exploitation and abuse and will find it even harder to access their legal rights. The Karnataka Devadasi (Prohibition of Dedication) Act, 1982, and the Andhra Pradesh Devadasi (Prohibition of Dedication) Act, 1988, have outlawed the dedication of girls as Devadasi, but the practice still continues (Rolland, 2013).

Activities

Introductory Activity 3.1: Reflections on My Caste Identity

Learner Outcome: At the end of this activity, the participants will develop awareness of how caste is linked to their identity.

Procedure: Use the following procedure to conduct this activity:

1. Ask each participant to complete the following sentence. They could write what their caste means to them that reflect their caste identity.

   Because my caste is _____, I am_____

2. Ask the participants to share what they have written with their partners.

Questions for Discussion: Use the following questions to discuss this activity:

- What does caste mean to you?
- How does it affect your identity?
- How does it affect your behaviour?
- How does it affect other's attitude to you?
- Does caste affect your rights?
- Do you know that India is the only country with a caste system?
- Do we need a caste system? Why?

Time Estimate: 20 min

Activity 3.2: Small Group Discussion on Stereotypes about Castes

Learner Outcome: At the end of this activity, the participants will develop awareness of their stereotypes about different castes, especially the Dalits.

Procedure: Use the following procedure to conduct this activity:

1. Explain the origin of the caste system and how the major five caste groups were formed in India.
2. Form five small groups, and allocate the following castes among them randomly: *Brahmins, Kshatriyas, Baniyas*, OBCs and SCs. If the local caste names are different use the local names.
3. Ask them to discuss the following of the caste given to them:

   - What are the typical characteristics of this caste with reference to cleanliness, housing, abilities, education, occupation and income?
   - How many of these characteristics are stereotypes and how many are real?
   - If these characteristics are very different from other castes, what are the reasons?
   - How many of these characteristics are due to being born into a caste and how many are due to environmental characteristics?

4. Ask the small groups to share their discussion with the large group for further inputs.

Questions for Discussion: Use the following questions to discuss this activity:

- How do our stereotypes about castes lead to the prejudicing ideology of casteism?
- How do our stereotypes about castes lead to perpetuation of the caste system?
- How can we prevent stereotyping about castes?

Time Estimate: 30 min

Activity 3.3: Video Discussion on Awareness Development on Discrimination against Dalits

Learner Outcome: At the end of this activity, the participants will get exposure to the issues of discrimination against Dalits.

Procedure: Show the following video films:
Our Journey—How we know caste
     https://www.youtube.com/watch?v=JC3C2voZjrA

Questions for Discussion: Use the following questions to discuss this film:

- What did the students feel before the project?
- What prejudices are prevalent among non-Dalits against Dalits?
- What did the students find in the village near Delhi?
- In which areas did they find segregation and discrimination?
- How are poverty and caste correlated? Why?
- What does a Dalit mean?
- How can we contribute to dismantle the caste system and prevent discrimination against Dalits?

Time Estimate: 30 min

Activity 3.4: Video Discussion on Untouchability

Learner Outcome: At the end of this activity, the participants will get sensitised to the issue of untouchability.

Procedure: Show the following video film to younger children:

Maina
   https://www.youtube.com/watch?v=Tn5YHXB7Obw&index=7&list=
PL38322753F73B5A71

Questions for Discussion: Use the following questions to discuss this activity:

- What are Maina's questions for her grandmother?
- What are her experiences of exclusion?
- What is the self-image that she has developed?
- What did her friends do?
- How did they interpret casteism as injustice and achieved justice for Maina?

Show the following video film to older children and the primary duty-bearers:
Satyamev Jayate (2012): Episode Untouchability
   http://www.satyamevjayate.in/untouchability/untouchability.aspx

Questions for Discussion: Use the following questions to discuss this activity:

- What is the importance of dignity in our lives?
- Can dignity be taken away from someone because of your birth in a particular caste?
- What identifiers are used for Dalit children in schools?
- What are the discriminatory practices used against children in schools?
- How are Dalit children discouraged from further studies?
- Why educational qualifications do not change the status of Dalits?
- Why some people find no untouchability in cities though there is segregation?
- Why is manual scavenging still being done only by the SCs?
- Why do the non-Hindu religions also observe the caste system?

- Do you think casteism exists all over India and untouchability still exists in many places?
- How can we change our mindsets about casteism and attitude of untouchability?

Time Estimate: Show select parts for 30 min followed by discussion for 15 min

Activity 3.5: Creating Public Awareness on Inclusion of Dalits

Learner Outcome: At the end of this activity, the participants will learn to create public awareness about inclusion of Dalits.

Procedure: Use the following procedure to conduct this activity:

1. Show Summary Chart 3.1 to summarise exclusion of Dalit children.
2. Divide the participants into four groups, and allocate the following topics among them for creating public awareness on inclusion of Dalits:

   (1) Prevention of caste-based stereotypes,
   (2) Prevention of caste-based discrimination in schools,
   (3) Prevention of caste-based discrimination in use of public amenities,
   (4) Prevention of manual scavenging,
   (5) Prevention of the Devadasi system.

2. The small groups may develop charts, poems, street plays, etc., on their topic for creating public awareness and present them to the large group for further inputs.

Questions for Discussion: Use the following questions to discuss this activity:

- How can equality and non-discrimination be achieved across castes?
- How can the environmental characteristics be made favourable for all?
- What are the challenges that we face in doing so?

Time Estimate: 45 min

Exclusion of Tribal Children and Their Right to Inclusion

Concepts and Theories

Concepts of Tribals and Tribal Diversity

The United Nations (UN) adopted the word "indigenous" which includes terms like tribes, first peoples/nations, aboriginals, ethnic groups, *Adivasi* and *Janajati* and other occupational and geographical terms like hunter-gatherers, nomads, that are used in different regions of the world. An official definition of "indigenous" has not been adopted by the UN system due to the diversity of the world's indigenous peoples. Instead, a modern and inclusive understanding of "indigenous" has been developed and includes peoples who:

- Identify themselves and are recognised and accepted by their community as indigenous.
- Demonstrate historical continuity with pre-colonial and/or pre-settler societies.
- Have strong links to territories and surrounding natural resources.
- Have distinct social, economic or political systems.
- Maintain distinct languages, cultures and beliefs.
- Form non-dominant groups of society.
- Resolve to maintain and reproduce their ancestral environments and systems as distinctive peoples and communities (United Nations Permanent Forum on Indigenous Issues, 2006).

India is the nation with the highest concentration of "indigenous peoples" in the world, called Adivasis, which mean indigenous people (Bijoy, 2003). According to the 2011 Census of India, the number of tribals was 84,326,240 (8.2% of the population). The largest concentrations of tribals are found in the seven States of north-east, and the so-called central tribal belt stretching from Rajasthan in the west to West Bengal in the east (India: Ministry of Tribal Affairs, 2012). Sharma (1995) noted that the tribal situation is not the same all over India. Some are still hunters and gatherers, and some are modernised with wide variations between the two extremes. According to him, the common features among the tribal people are the following:

- Their political system is that of self-governance.
- Their economic system comprises of subsistence economy that depends on the entire habitat: land, forest and water.
- The habitat is accepted as the common heritage of the community, and individual ownership is an alien concept.

Tribals in India find themselves targeted as far as misconceptions are concerned. In the eyes of non-tribals, all tribals constitute a homogeneous group. The fact that each tribe is only partly defined by habitat and geography but essentially by social, cultural, linguistic and religious distinctiveness is rarely acknowledged. This ignorance is perpetuated to a large extent by our textbooks. For example, while school history textbooks are replete with histories of other civilisations and societies, there is hardly anything on the history of a large section of our society, especially the north-east. Therefore, it is not surprising that the people of the region feel alienated from the rest of India and the rest of Indians treat them as outsiders (Navani, 2014).

Thorat and Senapati (2007) note that about 46% of the tribals were poor as compared with 20% for the others. The literacy rates among them were much lower,

45% as compared to 62% among others in rural area and 69 and 81% for urban area. The child mortality rates among them were the highest, 46% as against 22% among non-SC/ST.

Race and Racism

Very often, tribal groups are racially different than the non-tribal groups. Race means a group of human beings who are seen (by others or by themselves) as belonging to a separate group, different from other groups. The grouping is mainly based on skin tone and may also relate to colour of eyes and hair, shape of features (such as the nose) or hair texture. Racism consists of attitudes and actions, often based on prejudices and often deriving from stereotypes that discriminate against certain people because they are seen as belonging to a particular race which is seen as inferior to another. Racist attitudes include the view that people of some ethnic origins are less important and valuable than those of other ethnic origins (Griffin, 2008).

Autonomy of Tribal Culture and Disruptions

Tribal communities in India belong to four different language families and several different racial stocks and religious moulds. They have kept themselves apart from the Brahminical hierarchies for thousands of years. In the Hindu caste system, the Adivasis are considered to be Atishudra meaning lower than the untouchable castes. The Adivasis have few food taboos, rather fluid cultural practices and minimal occupational specialisation, while, on the other hand, the mainstream population of the plains has extensive food taboos, more rigid cultural practices and considerable caste-based occupational specialisation. The autonomous existence of the tribals outside the mainstream society HAS led to the preservation of their socio-religious and cultural practices, most of them retaining also their distinctive languages. Widow burning, enslavement, occupational differentiation, hierarchical social ordering, etc., are generally not heard of in these communities. They belong to their territories, which are the essence of their existence: the abode of the spirits and their dead and the source of their science, technology, way of life, their religion and culture (Bijoy, 2003).

Individual tribes have been societies unto themselves with a distinct territory, language, culture and a political and economic demarcation of their own. By virtue of existing as a self-contained unit, they held control over the land and forest in their territory. Traditionally, these resources were either individually or collectively owned and the tribals had usufructuary rights over these. The arrival of the British drastically altered all such relationships (Xaxa, 2011).

The introduction of the alien concept of private property began with the permanent settlement of the British in 1793 and the establishment of the "Zamindari" system that conferred control over vast territories, including Adivasi territories, to designated feudal lords for the purpose of revenue collection by the British. This drastically commenced the forced restructuring of the relationship of Adivasis to their territories as well as the power relationship between Adivasis and "others" (Bijoy, 2003). The invasions of the British to their homelands, particularly the forested region, gave rise to relentless revolts. The hostile terrain, limited economic interests and failure to subdue and control the people led to enactment of special laws to these areas (United Nations Development Programme (UNDP), 2012). However, due to the policies and measures pursued during colonial rule and its continuation in post-independence India, there has been steady erosion in the control and use of these resources by tribes (Xaxa, 2011).

Post-independent Legal Status of Tribal Areas

Indian Constitution: The former colonial arrangement of governance was in effect carried over into the Indian Constitution through Article 244—the Fifth Schedule and Sixth Schedule. An important feature of the Fifth and the Sixth Schedules is that the legal and institutional frame for the tribal areas is expected to be so designed as to be in consonance with the people's institutions in these areas (UNDP, 2012). Article 244 of the Constitution envisages two categories of tribal areas, namely:

1. Fifth Schedule: For the administration and control of the Scheduled Areas and Scheduled Tribes in any State other than the States of Assam, Meghalaya, Tripura and Mizoram,
2. Sixth Schedule: For the administration of tribal areas in the States of Assam, Meghalaya, Tripura and Mizoram.

PESA: The Provisions of the Panchayats (Extension to the Scheduled Areas) Act (PESA) was enacted in 1996, which extended Part IX of the Constitution to the Schedule V Areas and provided for people-centric governance and people's control over community resources and their life, with a central role to the Gram Sabhas. The Gram Sabhas under PESA are deemed to be "competent" to safeguard and preserve the traditions of their people, community resources and customary mode of dispute resolution. The Gram Sabhas further have:

(a) Mandatory executive functions to approve plans of the Village Panchayats, identify beneficiaries for schemes, issue certificates of utilisation of funds,
(b) Right to mandatory consultation in matters of land acquisition, resettlement and rehabilitation, and prospecting licences/mining leases for minor minerals,
(c) Power to prevent alienation of land and restore alienated land,
(d) Power to regulate and restrict sale/consumption of liquor,
(e) Power to manage village markets, control money lending to STs,
(f) Ownership of minor forest produce,
(g) Power to control institutions and functionaries in all social sectors,
(h) Power to control local plans and resources for such plans including Tribal Sub-Plan, etc.

It was expected that PESA would lead to self-governance and empowerment of the people. However, implementation of the Act has not been satisfactory. The rights, livelihood and habitat of the people in these areas, therefore, continue to be under stress, leading to disaffection with the system (India: National Institute of Rural Development, 2013).

Rights of Tribals and Tribal Children

International Labour Organization (ILO) Convention No. 169: According to the International Labour Organization (ILO) Convention No. 169 concerning Indigenous and Tribal Peoples in Independent Countries (1989):

- **Article 8(2)**: These peoples shall have the right to retain their own customs and institutions, where these are not incompatible with fundamental rights defined by the national legal system and with internationally recognised human rights.
- **Article 29**: The imparting of general knowledge and skills that will help children belonging to the peoples concerned to participate fully and on an equal footing in their own community and in the national community shall be an aim of education for these peoples.
- **Article 14(1)**: The rights of ownership and possession of the peoples concerned over the lands which they traditionally occupy shall be recognised.
- **Article 15(1)**: The rights of the peoples concerned to the natural resources pertaining to their lands shall be specially safeguarded. These rights include the right of these peoples to participate in the use, management and conservation of these resources.

The United Nations Declaration on the Rights of Indigenous Peoples: The United Nations Declaration on the Rights of Indigenous Peoples (2007) makes the following provisions:

- **Article 4**: Indigenous peoples, in exercising their right to self-determination, have the right to autonomy or self-government in matters relating to their internal and local affairs, as well as ways and means for financing their autonomous functions.
- **Article 8(1)**: Indigenous peoples and individuals have the right not to be subjected to forced assimilation or destruction of their culture.
- **Article 10**: Indigenous peoples shall not be forcibly removed from their lands or territories. No relocation shall take place without the free, prior and informed consent of the indigenous peoples concerned and after agreement on just and fair compensation and, where possible, with the option of return.

United Nations Convention on the Rights of the Child: Article 30 of the United Nations Convention on the Rights of the Child (UNCRC, 1989) states that "In those States in which ethnic, religious or linguistic minorities or persons of indigenous origin exist, a child belonging to such a minority or who is indigenous shall not be denied the right, in community with other members of his or her group, to enjoy his or her own culture, to profess and practise his or her own religion, or to use his or her own language".

According to Article 29(1d) of the UNCRC, States Parties agree that the education of the child shall be directed to "The preparation of the child for responsible life in a free society, in the spirit of understanding, peace, tolerance, equality of sexes, and friendship among all peoples, ethnic, national and religious groups and persons of indigenous origin".

Universal Declaration on Cultural Diversity: Article 4 of the Universal Declaration on Cultural Diversity (United Nations Educational Scientific and Cultural Organisation (UNESCO), 2002) states that the defence of cultural diversity is an ethical imperative, inseparable from respect for human dignity. It implies a commitment to human rights and fundamental freedoms, in particular the rights of persons belonging to minorities and those of indigenous peoples.

Tribal Displacement

Displacement of Tribals: Unlike the Dalits, the tribals did not face social exploitation but they faced exploitation of their land and forest at the economic level and domination at the political level. In spite of PESA, development projects have led to tribal displacement. The large-scale industrialisation and exploitation of mineral resources and the construction of irrigation dams and power projects in the tribal areas have been the single-most factors that have uprooted more people out of their lands than the transfer of land from tribals to non-tribals on an individual basis (Xaxa, 2011). So far, about 7.5 million ST persons have been displaced, which constitutes 40% of the total person displaced. Out of this, only about 1.85 million are resettled (Thorat & Senapati, 2007). The brutality of displacement due to the building of dams was dramatically highlighted during the agitation over the Sardar Sarovar Dam. The anti-dam movement known as the Narmada Bachao Andolan for the first time systematically revealed how building dams can result in total dislocation of tribal societies. The beneficiaries of the dam are meant to be large landowners; but the tribal people are paying the price. The need to avoid such large-scale displacement, particularly of tribals and in case of unavoidable displacement, their ultimate resettlement and rehabilitation has become central issues of the developmental process itself (Xaxa, 2011).

National Rehabilitation and Resettlement Policy: To address various issues related to land acquisition and rehabilitation and resettlement comprehensively the Department of Land Resources has formulated a National Rehabilitation and Resettlement Policy, 2007. The objectives of this Policy (India: Ministry of Rural Development, 2007) are as follows:

(a) To minimise displacement and to promote, as far as possible, non-displacing or least-displacing alternatives,

(b) To ensure adequate rehabilitation package and expeditious implementation of the rehabilitation process with the active participation of the affected families,

(c) To ensure that special care is taken for protecting the rights of the weaker sections of society, especially members of the Scheduled Castes and Scheduled Tribes, and to create obligations on the State for their treatment with concern and sensitivity,

(d) To provide a better standard of living, making concerted efforts for providing sustainable income to the affected families,

(e) To integrate rehabilitation concerns into the development planning and implementation process,

(f) Where displacement is on account of land acquisition, to facilitate harmonious relationship between the requiring body and affected families through mutual cooperation.

Children of Displaced Tribal Families: Both displacement and denial of access to the forests, especially the former, have impacted tribal children in a significant way. Displacement has invariably led to dislocation of the sources of livelihood, resulting in food insecurity for the family. Even in the face of rehabilitation and resettlement, this problem has persisted. Needless to say, this adversely affected children's nutritional status and their health. Displacement also uprooted them from their traditional habitat and environment and pushed them to an environment they were not only unfamiliar with but often even hostile, resulting in social and psycho-logical adjustment issues. Displacement disrupted the schooling of school-going children and more often than not, acted as the factor of their discontinuation. Even in the case of restriction of access to forest, tribal children are affected though not as severely as in the case of displacement, since tribal life, even if based on settled agriculture, is intricately intertwined with the forest (Xaxa, 2011).

The Scheduled Tribes and Other Traditional Forest Dwellers (Recognition of Forest Rights) Act, 2006: The Scheduled Tribes and Other Traditional Forest Dwellers (Recognition of Forest Rights) Act or the Indian Forest Act in short was enacted in 2006. It has come on the basis that the central factor affecting livelihoods and identity of the forest communities is their lack of access to and control over natural resources in many parts of the country. Its enactment brings in some positive approaches in management of natural resources like:

- Provides an opportunity to democratise the nature of forest management,
- Gives importance to the needs of local communities over forest,
- Mandates that critical wildlife habitats are not diverted subsequently for any other use (Scheduled Castes and Scheduled Tribes Research and Training Institute, 2015).

The Forest Rights Act recognises and vests forest rights in the Scheduled Tribes and other traditional forest dwellers who have been residing in forests for gener-ations but whose rights could not be recorded. It provides for a framework for recording of the forest rights so vested and the nature of evidence required for such recognition and vesting in respect of forest land. Forest Rights Act is a means to address some of the pressing issues affecting livelihood and conservation. By securing tenurial and access rights and providing an empowered authority for conservation, it aims to:

1. Ensure livelihood and food security of the forest-dependent communities.
2. Provide for basic developmental facilities for the forest villages.
3. Provide legal recognition to the community conservation initiatives, thereby strengthening traditional conservation practices that protect some of the critical ecosystems of the country.
4. Protect traditional knowledge and intellectual property relating to biodiversity and cultural diversity.
5. Protect customary rights of the forest communities.
6. Empower communities to protect, conserve and manage forest and biodiversity.
7. Conserve the common forest and biodiversity resources accessed by the community which are threatened by destructive activities.
8. Establish empowered institutions at the community level for conservation and management of natural resources, thereby strengthening conservation governance at the grass roots (Scheduled Castes and Scheduled Tribes Research and Training Institute, 2015).

Tribal Children in Armed Conflict

The problem of poverty, unemployment, deprivation, exploitation and domination experienced in tribal society has led to a movement for liberation from such condition in these societies. In this struggle for liberation, which has at times taken the form of armed conflict between insurgents and State armed forces, common people including children have invariably been drawn either as victims or participants. Children have, however, suffered the most as victims. Not only have they found themselves orphaned due to their parents death but are also physically assaulted, raped, burnt and even impaired by either the security forces or the insurgents. Often they have found their habitat destroyed and are confined to camps without adequate food, water, sanitation and schools (Xaxa, 2011).

In areas of armed conflict, children accused of being members of armed groups were detained, often in violation of national legislation designed to protect children in conflict with the law. In Manipur, it was alleged that the system established under the Juvenile Justice Act 2000 was non-functioning due to inadequate resources; in particular, no juvenile home had been established. As a result, security forces (including police) who detained children in anti-insurgency operations were reportedly claiming that they were over 18 when registering cases against them and sending them to adult detention centres. Human rights organisations attempting to address individual cases of detained children on behalf of parents were hampered by the absence of birth certificates to prove age (Coalition to Stop the Use of Child Soldiers, 2008).

Tribal Children in Armed Conflict in Naxal-affected Areas: The UN Secretary-General's 2013 Annual Report on Children and Armed Conflict notes that recruitment and use of children by Maoist armed groups otherwise known as "Naxalites" are alleged to have continued during the reporting period (i.e. 2012). Reports alleged that the "Naxalites" resorted to large-scale recruitment of children aged between 6 and 12 years into their so-called children's units (Bal Sanghatans) in the affected States. Children were reported to have performed various tasks, including fighting with crude weapons such as sticks or acting as informants. Children as young as 12 years were reported present in Maoist youth groups and allied militia, and handling weapons and improvised explosive devices. Children were reportedly not allowed to leave these associations and faced severe reprisals, including the killing of family members, if they did so (Child Soldiers International, 2013).

According to Human Rights Watch (HRW), "Naxalites organize children between ages six and twelve into Balsangams (village-level children's associations). Depending on their skills and aptitude, children from a Balsangam are 'promoted' to other Naxalite departments: Sangams (village-level associations), Chaitanya Natya Manch (street theatre troupes), Jan militias (armed informers who travel with Dalams), Anddalams (armed squads)". Information gathered by HRW showed that all former Naxalites who served in Sangams, Chaitanya Natya Manch, Jan Militias or Dalams said that they had received weapons training when they were children. In 2013, the Indian Government acknowledged the existence of the practice of "forced recruitment of children from families of poor and marginalized segments of the society by the Maoists" (Child Soldiers International, 2013).

Tribal Children in Armed Conflict in the North-east: The North-east India reports of underage recruitment and use in the North-eastern States of Manipur and Meghalaya with information of children reportedly being used as fighters by armed opposition groups such as the Garo National Liberation Army (GNLA). In January 2013, it was reported that the State Government of Meghalaya had agreed to institute a "high-level inquiry" by an Inspector General of Police to investigate the recruitment and use of children as "child soldiers" by armed groups. In Manipur, children are known to be forcibly recruited and trained as fighters by various armed opposition groups, most notably by the Revolutionary Peoples Front (Child Soldiers International, 2013).

Activities

Activity 3.6: Introduction to Tribal Life

Learner Outcome: At the end of this activity, the participants will develop awareness on the

Procedure: Use the following procedure to conduct this activity:

1. Show the video film: Tribes of India
   https://www.youtube.com/watch?v=oc_rGY0W5Jo
   Ask the following questions to discuss the video:

   • What did you see in the film?
   • What thoughts came to your mind about what you saw?
   • What is a tribe? Is it a homogenous group? What is common across tribes?

2. Make three small groups, and allocate the following topics among them for reading and discussion:

   • Concepts of Tribals and Tribal Diversity,
   • Autonomy of Tribal Culture and Disruptions,
   • Post-Independent Legal Status of Tribal Areas,
   • Rights of Tribals and Tribal Children.

3. Ask the small groups to share their understanding on their topic with the large group.

Time Estimate: 30 min

Activity 3.7: Video Discussion on Displacement of Tribals

Learner Outcome: At the end of this activity, the participants will develop awareness on the problem of displacement of tribals in the name of development.

Procedure: Use the following procedure to conduct this activity:

1. Show the following video film: PESA: Self Rule in Fifth Scheduled Areas in India.wmv
   https://www.youtube.com/watch?v=VtxpoM323C0
   Use the following questions to discuss this video:

   • What is the number of Scheduled Tribes in India?
   • What are tribals known for?
   • What was the status of self-rule of tribals during the Moghul rule?
   • What was the change in the status of self-rule of tribals during the British rule?
   • How did the self-rule of tribals weaken after independence by exploitation of their land, forest and water?
   • What is PESA? What is the role of Gram Sabha under PESA?

2. Show the following video film: Tribal Displacement in India
   https://www.youtube.com/watch?v=BwV3hHRusHg
   Use the following questions to discuss this video:

- Why are tribal being displaced in site of the law of self-governance in tribal areas?
- How many tribals are displaced so far?
- How are they rehabilitated?
- How is their livelihood affected?
- How is their living style affected?
- What are the implications for tribal children?
- How could they be appropriately rehabilitated according to the National Rehabilitation and Resettlement Policy (2007)?

Time Estimate: 45 min

Activity 3.8: Comparison of Life between Not Displaced and Displaced Tribals

Learner Outcome: At the end of this activity, the participants will develop awareness on life of not displaced and displaced tribal peoples.

Procedure: Use the following procedure to conduct this activity:

1. Form two groups of the participants. Ask one group to make a visit to a tribal village that has not been displaced and the other group to make a visit to displaced tribals.
2. Ask them to study the tribal life with reference to the following aspects:

   a. Tribal housing,
   b. Tribal family,
   c. Tribal livelihood,
   d. Relation with natural resources,
   e. Tribal social structure,
   f. Religious practices,
   g. Tribal local self-governance,
   h. Implementation of the reservation policy for STs,
   i. Tribal migration to cities,
   j. Level of modernisation,
   k. Tribal children's rights to health, education and play,
   l. Satisfaction and issues with each of the above from the tribal people's point of view,

3. Each group may allocate the above topics among the members for writing the report which may be presented the next day,
4. Compare the two reports on each aspect to understand tribal life when not displaced and issues when they are displaced.

Time Estimate: One day for the visit and two hours for presentation and discussion

Activity 3.9: Small Group Discussion of Violation of Rights of Tribal Children in Armed Conflict

Learner Outcome: At the end of this activity, the participants will develop awareness of the problems of tribal children in armed conflict.

Procedure: Use the following procedure to conduct this activity:

1. Make two small groups, and allocate the following situations of tribal children in armed conflict for reading and discussion of violation of their rights:

   • Tribal Children in Armed Conflict in Naxal-affected Areas,
   • Tribal Children in Armed Conflict in the North-east.

2. Ask the small groups to discuss the following questions on their topic and present their discussion to the large group:

   • What leads to armed conflicts in these areas?
   • How does the armed conflict affect the tribal children?
   • How can violation of tribal children's rights in these situations be prevented?

Time Estimate: 30 min

Activity 3.10: Street Plays on Public Awareness on Inclusion of Tribals

Learner Outcome: At the end of this activity, the participants will learn to create public awareness about inclusion of tribals.

Procedure: Use the following procedure to conduct this activity:

1. Show Summary Chart 3.2, and summarise exclusion of tribal children.
2. Divide the participants into six groups, and allocate the following topics among them for creating public awareness on inclusion of tribals:

   (1) Restoration of Self-Governance in Tribal Villages,
   (2) Environmental Conservation by Tribals,
   (3) Prevention of Tribal Displacement,
   (4) The Scheduled Tribes and Other Traditional Forest Dwellers (Recognition of Forest Rights) Act, 2006,
   (5) Prevention of Involvement of Tribal Children in Armed Conflict,
   (6) Mainstreaming and Inclusion of Tribal Children.

3. The small groups may develop street plays on their topic for creating public awareness and present them to the large group for further inputs.

Time Estimate: 30 min

Review of the Constitutional and Legal Rights of Dalits and Tribals

Concepts and Theories

The Simon Commission in 1935 first coined the term "Scheduled Castes". All the untouchable castes, which were listed in 1931 Census of India, came to be known as the "Scheduled Castes" (SCs) through the Government of India Act of 1935. In the meantime, the government published a list of Scheduled Castes under the Government of India (Scheduled Castes) Order, 1936 (Jadhav, 2008).

Rights of Dalits and Tribals in the Indian Constitution

After independence, India inherited the term "Scheduled Castes" and committed itself to a socially just and an egalitarian social order. Dalits are legally constituted as Scheduled Castes (SCs) and tribals as Scheduled Tribes (STs). The Constitution, promulgated in 1950, recognised the SCs and the STs as two of the most marginalised social groups needing special protections. A number of provisions, therefore, were specifically incorporated for the two social groups with a view to abolish all forms of discrimination, untouchability and social exclusion emanating from the caste system and to alleviate the peripheral position of these social groups. The government has used a twofold strategy for the empowerment of the SC/STs, which includes firstly the provision of legal safeguards against discrimination and secondly proactive measures in the form of the reservation policy for the public sector and State-supported sectors (Thorat & Senapati, 2006).

Following are the different safeguards provided to them in the Constitution of India:

Fundamental Rights: Following are the relevant articles in the Constitution, under the section on Fundamental Rights:

Article 15: Prohibition of discrimination against any citizen on grounds only of religion, race, caste, sex, place of birth or any of them and prevents any restriction on access to public places.

Article 16(2): No citizen shall, on grounds only of religion, race, caste, sex, descent, place of birth, residence or any of them, be ineligible for, or discriminated against in respect of, any employment or office under the State.

Directive Principles of State Policy: Article 46 of the Directive Principle of State Policy states that "The State shall promote with special care the educational and economic interests of the weaker sections of the people, and, in particular, of the Scheduled Castes and the Scheduled Tribes, and shall protect them from social injustice and all forms of exploitation".

Notification of Scheduled Castes and Scheduled Tribes: According to the Constitution:

- **Article 341(1)**: The President may by public notification, specify the castes, races or tribes or parts of or groups within castes, races or tribes which shall for the purposes of this Constitution be deemed to be Scheduled Castes.
- **Article 342(1)**: The President may by public notification, specify the tribes or tribal communities or parts of or groups within tribes or tribal communities which shall for the purposes of this Constitution be deemed to be Scheduled Tribes.

The 2011 Census notes of India that there are altogether 1,241 individual ethnic groups, etc., notified as the SCs in 31 States/UTs and 705 ST groups in 30 States/UTs (Ministry of Home Affairs, 2013).

The Scheduled Castes and Scheduled Tribes (Prevention of Atrocities) Act: The Scheduled Castes and Scheduled Tribes (Prevention of Atrocities) Act (1989) specifies the offences which are considered as atrocities and provides for deterrent punishments on commission of the same.

Policy of Reservations

Concept of Reservation: Reservation is defined by Chalam (2007, p. 18) as an act through which places or positions are fixed in relation to gender, religion, caste, language or any other nomenclature with an intention to provide the legitimate share to the group so that others cannot appropriate it. Reservation of seats and posts for SCs and STs is social justice measures that aim to bring the disadvantaged groups to the mainstream of the society. These measures follow the universal principles of:

1. Affirmative action which is positive action taken to help the disadvantaged groups,
2. Positive or protective or reverse discrimination means that other things not being equal, the disadvantaged group is granted benefits (Puniyani, 2012).

The Original Intention of Reservations: When reservations were first introduced for the untouchables through the Poona Pact between Ambedkar and Gandhiji, the basic premise was that the untouchables were distinctively the stigmatised community that suffered deep social discrimination in Hindu society. It was agreed that the larger Hindu society could not be relied upon to represent their interests and grant them their dues. Therefore, a kind of mechanism that would ensure they get their due share of representation was needed. Reservation thus became a countervailing mechanism against the social discriminative instinct of Indian society. There was inbuilt motivation for the society to recover from the disease at the earliest and stop the pills. Since the disease basically referred to the caste system, reservations were the catalyst that would hasten its death. Reservations as a policy of positive discrimination need to be exceptional and should be self-destructive. While the self-destructiveness was not expressly provided, it was implicit: if society ceased to discriminate against the Dalits, reservations could be abolished (Teltumbde, 2007).

Thorat and Senapati (2006) noted that the initial vision was to completely negate the deleterious impacts of caste-based discrimination and exclusion. The idea was to create fissures in the hegemonic hold of the immutable status of the higher castes over public services. Therefore, the historicity of reservations included firstly the amelioration in the relative position of the lower castes and secondly restructuring of the institutionalised social relationships in the Indian society on democratic lines.

Reservations Scheduled Castes and Scheduled Tribes in the Indian Constitution: The special provisions relating to reservations for Dalits and tribals in the Indian Constitution are the following:

- **Article 330**: Reservation of seats for Scheduled Castes and Scheduled Tribes in the House of the People.
- **Article 332**: Reservation of seats for Scheduled Castes and Scheduled Tribes in the Legislative Assemblies of the States.
- **Article 334**: Notwithstanding anything in the foregoing provisions of this Part, the provisions of this Constitution relating to (a) the reservation of seats for the Scheduled Castes and the Scheduled Tribes in the House of the People and in the Legislative Assemblies of the States; and (b) the representation of the Anglo-Indian community in the House of the People and in the Legislative Assemblies of the States by nomination, shall cease to have effect on the expiration of a period of seventy years from the commencement of this Constitution.

In 1982, the Constitution specified 15 and 7.5% of vacancies in public sector and government-aided educational institutes as quota reserved for the Scheduled Caste (SC) and Scheduled Tribe (ST) candidates, respectively, based on their proportion in the country. This was to be reviewed after five years. Reservations for the SC/STs in the government services, educational institutions and political bodies like the central and the State legislatures have been incorporated to ensure the proportional participation of the SC/STs in the public domain, the democratic decision-making bodies. It is equally important to understand that the reservation policy is confined to the State-run and supported sectors. The private sector, wherein more than 90% of the SC/ST workers are engaged, is excluded, therefore, remains outside the purview of the reservation policy and opens to possible discrimination (Thorat & Senapati, 2006).

Reservation for Other Backward Classes: "When the first Backward Classes Commission was constituted on 29th January, 1953 under the chairmanship of Kakasaheb Kalelkar, he wanted economic backwardness to be the criterion and not caste in deciding backwardness. But he had to field to the majority of the members who wanted caste to be the criterion, to decide the backwardness" (Dutta, 1991, cited by Jadhav, 2008).

The Mandal Commission's recommendations that were implemented in 1990 comprised 27% reservations for these OBCs in education and jobs. The Mandal Commission was established with a mandate to identify the socially or educationally backward. The Commission identified 54% of the total population (excluding SCs and STs), belonging to 3,743 different castes and communities, as "backward" with reference to the following social, educational and economic criteria:

- Social backwardness: Castes that have to do physical labour as a means of earning and prevalence rate of child marriages,
- Educational backwardness: Proportion of children who have never attended school, school dropouts and matriculates,
- Economic backwardness: Family assets, *kachha* housing, lack of access to drinking water and debts.

In spite of Supreme Court Judgement that reservation should not exceed 50%, States like Tamil Nadu and Rajasthan have reservations for more than 50%. Different political parties are responsible for these figures at different times and in different States.

Filling of the Quota: Xaxa (2001) noted that the filling up of the quota as fixed by the government has been a problem, especially at the upper levels of the government and semi-government services. There are many reasons as to why the quota reserved for the two communities could not be filled up, ranging from apathy and indifference of the government to the unavailability of suitable candidates from the SC and the ST category, on account of their social, economic and educational backgrounds. Contrary to common belief, the percentage of members from weaker sections employed in government services is abysmally low. If one pays attention to their presence in the public sector, one would be shocked by this fact that even the stipulated 15 and 7.5% of the reservation quota fixed for these communities is not filled. Many of these prescribed posts are filled up by the dominant castes (Louis, 2003).

Comparison of Reservations for Dalits versus Tribals: According to Xaxa (2001), the SCs have been able to take better advantage of the reservations than the STs due to various reasons discussed below.

Insiders versus Outsiders: Despite being segregated, discriminated and oppressed, the SCs are invariably a part of the Hindu society. Though divided on the basis of castes, the SCs share language, culture, tradition, etc., of the regional community. However, an average Indian is unable to figure where the tribes fall. Tribes are invariably seen as outsiders, ones who not only do not speak their language but also do not share their customs, tradition and values. Belonging to the tribe, though advantageous at the local level, is hardly so at the regional and national levels. In fact, tribes suffer from all the disadvantages of the community associated with ethnic minorities/communities. They have by and large lived in relatively inaccessible areas and hence have been the last to be exposed to the modern world, especially the State along with its legal-bureaucratic structures and market. The SCs have, therefore, had a greater exposure to the knowledge, information, technology, employment, etc., of the larger society as compared to the STs.

While the SCs have generally been able to fill the jobs earmarked for them at the lower levels, jobs allocated for tribes at such levels remain vacant mainly for two reasons:

1. Either the ST candidates are generally not available or even when available there is a general discrimination or prejudices against them as being outside of their language and religion.
2. Further, to get into these jobs, the tribes also have to learn the language of the dominant community, an advantage that the SCs already possess.

Stigma to Occupations: The industrialisation process did not benefit the STs in the way it did the SCs, mainly because of the nature of their occupation. Tribes more often than not were engaged in agriculture or hunting–food gathering. Tribes have been more interested in acquiring land and start life as agriculturists at the slightest opportunity available to them. Tribes had no dislike for their occupations as were the case with the SCs. There was no stigma attached to their occupation, and there was little inclination to abandon traditional occupation among the tribes.

Pan-India Identity: Because of tribal diversity, there is hardly anything like a tribal identity among tribes at the pan-India level. If at all there is anything like tribal identity, it is confined either to a locality/region or at best to an institution or organisation. Moreover, such identity is at work more at the level of the political or of interest articulation than at social or cultural plane. Even when there has been identity such as this, it has not been assertive and active. Such an identity among the SCs both at the regional and national level is more pronounced in comparison with those of the STs. One of the reasons as to why such identity is much stronger among the SCs is that they have gone through the common historical experience of oppression and discrimination for centuries. This was not the case with the STs.

Collectivism: It is the collectivism and not individualism that dominates the larger part of the life of the tribes. Hence, the principle of individuality and individual performance and excellence is less acceptable as the ethos of the tribal societies. Collectivism is still the central value or ethos among tribes despite existence of certain forms of inequality among them. In view of values such as these, the significance of individual/individualism does not assume the place it assumes in other categories of the population. Hence, performance and achievement that stem from the spirit of individualism are not adequately reflected in the tribal societies. Such a tendency or spirit may be partly responsible for poor performance of tribal students.

Effects of Reservations

A review of the effects of reservations shows that, on one hand, there is no marked improvement in the situations of the marginalised groups. On the other hand, a creamy layer has been created within these groups. A worse outcome is politicisation of caste that has led to backlash from the upper castes, intercaste conflict and solidification of casteism.

No Marked Improvement: An examination of the socio-economic profile of the SCs and STs shows that there has been no marked improvement in their social condition even after five decades of implementation of reservation policies. Literacy rate of these communities indicates that even planned intervention has not improved the educational level of the weaker sections (Louis, 2003). Despite the Constitutional and legal provisions, the SCs still remain and deprived of their adequate due in nation's development and exploited. The reasons observed are:

- These policies are poorly implemented, and welfare schemes remain on paper.
- There is a lack of political will regarding genuine development (social justice) of the SC population.
- The village schools continue to discriminate, preventing them from taking full advantage of these reservations (Desai & Kulkarni, 2008; Kakade, 2008).

Creation of Creamy Layers within the Marginalised Social Groups: According to Teltumbde (2007), reservations in education, employment and politics, instead of strengthening Dalits, have emasculated them politically and caused the creation of a separate class of beneficiaries from among them, which if at all has a very weak linkage with the Dalit masses. Thorat and Senapati (2006) noted that reservations alone are not enough to mainstream the SCs and the STs to the levels of the other sections of the society. The system of reservations meant to uplift the weaker sections has, in fact, succeeded in the creation of creamy layers within the marginalised social groups to the extent that the percolation of the benefits has been marginal and differentially accessed.

Politicisation of Caste: When a part of the recommendations of the Mandal Commission was implemented by instituting reservations for the "backward classes" in 1989, the floodgates were formally opened for politicking on reservation issues. Apart from the considerations of electoral politics, reservations came handy for diverting the attention of people from the deepening unemployment and underemployment problem associated with the liberalisation policies during the 1980s and full-fledged globalisation after 1991. The sway of caste identities in influencing voter groups has intensified with the collapse of the hegemony of the national parties, the emergence of regional parties and the rise of coalition politics. Since explicit caste-based communication is forbidden by the Constitution, reservations become a via media to influence castes. The social justice pedigree of reservations gives this communication a progressive veneer. Reservations-centred politics is played along three main dimensions:

1. Demanding reservations for certain social groups, e.g. Dalit Christians, backward Muslims,
2. Backing demands by certain castes to get included in the reserved categories,
3. Inciting demands for a split in the quota by certain sub-castes in a conglomerate-reserved category (Teltumbde, 2007).

Bhambhri (2005) observed that the Indian politics has been "casteised" because the political class has nurtured and manipulated caste versus caste identities to win an election on the basis of assured caste-based social constituencies. Thus, the policy of reservations might have contributed to the solidification of casteism in India. The caste politics and caste-based social policies as followed in India cannot lead to the erosion of the pernicious caste system.

Backlash from the Upper Castes: While the implementation of affirmative action was being strengthened, the resentment against it was also growing, particularly because the government sought to increase the scope of affirmative action to add quotas for the OBCs besides Dalits. This action followed the report of the Mandal Commission and led to widespread riots in 1990. The resentment flared up again as the government sought to introduce quotas for other backward castes in highly competitive engineering and management schools in 2006. This dissent has unified higher caste Hindus against affirmative action and led to increased sabotage at the local level, where these policies are to be implemented. Upper caste Hindus express their resentment by arguing that while compensatory discrimination seeks to redress the inequities suffered by Dalits and Adivasis, the individuals taking advantage of these benefits belonged to a rich "creamy layer" and were never subject to the severe discrimination faced by their poorer brethren. These critics are highly vocal, and the public discourse is rife with prejudice against Dalit and Adivasi students, whom they view as undeserving and as taking away the privileges of the deserving upper caste Hindus (Desai & Kulkarni, 2008).

Alternatives to Reservation

Louis (2003) noted the following fundamental issues with the policy of reservation, which have continued to haunt the political sociology of India:

(1) Should there be reservation at all for what the Constitution terms as weaker sections, namely the Scheduled Castes, the Scheduled Tribes and the other backward castes?

(2) Should the reservation policy continue as the stipulated time of its implementation has come to an end?

(3) If reservations have to be continued, what should be the criterion to determine backwardness?

(4) Should the provisions of the reservation policy accrue to members from the weaker sections that have attained social mobility?

(5) As there is hierarchy within the SCs and the STs, how can the most backward people within the weaker sections benefit from the provisions of the reservation?

(6) Should not the preferential option be extended to other groups currently handicapped?

(7) Should the reservation policy be extended to the private sector too?

Reservations have created intense debates about individual versus group rights, equality of opportunity versus equality of results, merit versus efficiency and affirmative action versus mandatory reservations (Hasan, 2009). According to Teltumbde (2007), the solution lies in reverting to the original conception of reservations for the SCs and STs as a countervailing force against the disability of Indian society to treat its constituents with equity. Since it is conceived as an antidote to a societal disease, society would strive to recover from it as fast as it can. A proper design of metrics and a monitoring mechanism may record the progress in this direction. The system should be worked as a mechanism to end the caste system itself along with other cultural measures the State ought to take. It is a fundamental duty of the State to support the poor and needy, irrespective of caste and creed, in realisation of their full human potential. This support system can be well devised on secular criteria.

Bhambhri (2005) recommends that the concern for Dalits should be articulated by following secular public policies and not by token policies of reservations. The State should guarantee education, health facilities and employment to every deprived citizen, and this would take care of the genuine interests of the Dalits. The poor should be the real target of secular public policies, and this is the only way to build a new modern casteless secular India.

Activities

Activity 3.11: Posters on Constitutional and Legal Provisions for Scheduled Castes and Scheduled Tribes

Learner Outcome: At the end of this activity, the participants will learn to create awareness on the Constitutional and legal provisions for Scheduled Castes and Scheduled Tribes.

Procedure: Use the following procedure to conduct this activity:

1. Make two small groups, and allocate the following topics among them to read and discuss:

   • The Constitutional Rights of Scheduled Castes and Scheduled Tribes,
   • The Scheduled Castes and Scheduled Tribes (Prevention of Atrocities) Act, 1989,

2. Show the Summary Chart 3.3 to summarise the Rights of Dalits and Tribals in the Indian Constitution,

3. Ask the small groups to make posters on their topic to create public awareness and present them to the large group for further inputs.

Time Estimate: 30 min

Activity 3.12: Small Group Reviews of Caste and Tribe-Based Reservation Policies

Learner Outcome: At the end of this activity, the participants will develop awareness on the strategies and effects of caste and tribe-based reservation policies.

Procedure: Use the following procedure to conduct this activity:

1. Ask the participants what they mean by reservation and why is it necessary.
2. Present a brief history of reservations in India.
3. Form four small groups, and allocate the following topics among them to compare the quota filling of SCs with that of the STs:

   a. Insiders versus Outsiders,
   b. Stigma to Occupations,
   c. Pan-India Identity,
   d. Collectivity.

   Ask the small groups to read and share their understanding with the large group.

4. Ask the same four small groups to discuss the effects of the reservation policy with reference to the following:

   a. No marked improvement in the situations of the marginalised groups,
   b. A creamy layer has been created within these groups,
   c. Politicisation of caste,
   d. Backlash from the upper castes.

   Ask the small groups to read and share their understanding with the large group.

5. Show Summary Chart 3.4 to summarise the Review of the Social Justice Strategies for Dalits and Tribals.

Questions for Discussion: Use the following questions to discuss this activity:

- What did the reservations aim at to start with? Have the aims been achieved? Why?
- What are the effects of reservations for the caste system in India?
- Should the reservations be totally stopped after a stipulated period?
- If reservations have to be continued, what should be the criterion to determine backwardness?
- Should the provisions of the reservation policy accrue to members from the weaker sections that have attained social mobility?
- As there is hierarchy within the SCs and the STs, how can the most backward people within the weaker sections benefit from the provisions of the reservation?
- Should the reservation policy be extended to the private sector too?
- What are the alternatives to reservations?

Time Estimate: 45 min

Concluding Activity: Achievement of the Learner Objectives

Learner Outcome: By the end of the concluding activity, the participants will ascertain if they have achieved the learner objectives.

Procedure: Use the following procedure to conduct the concluding activity:

1. Show the PowerPoints/a chart on the learner objectives, ask the participants to read them one at a time, and ask the group if they think they have achieved the objective.
2. The participants may be asked to share their responses in their diary with reference to the following questions:

   - What was a new learning for you in this session?
   - What did you like the best in this session and why?
   - Which activity was most effective?
   - What was not clear/confusing?
   - How can you apply what you have learnt?

Time Estimate: 15 min

Appendix: Summary Charts

Summary Chart 3.1   Exclusion of Dalit children

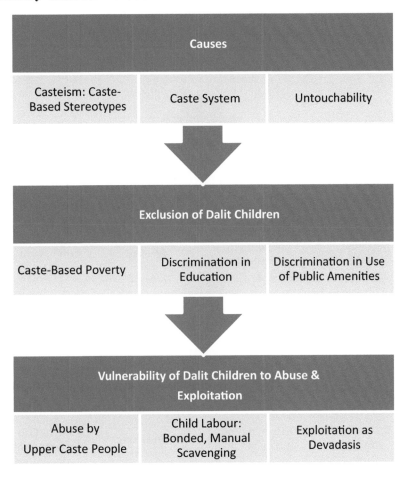

Summary Chart 3.2   Exclusion of tribal children

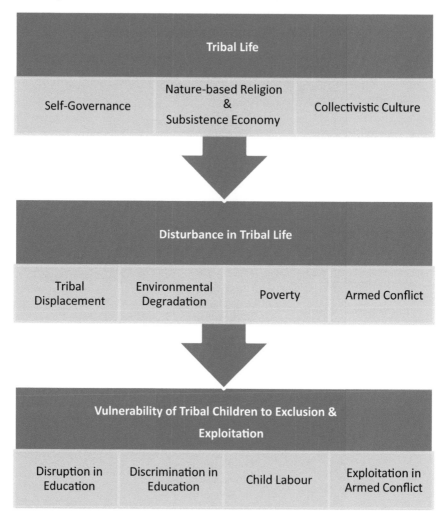

Summary Chart 3.3   Rights of Dalits and Tribals in the Indian Constitution

Fundamental Rights

Article 15: Prohibition of discrimination against any citizen on grounds only of religion, race, caste, sex, place of birth or any of them and prevents any restriction on access to public places.

Article 16 (2): No citizen shall, on grounds only of religion, race, caste, sex, descent, place of birth, residence or any of them, be ineligible for, or discriminated against in respect of, any employment or office under the State.

Article 17: "Untouchability" is abolished and its practice in any form is forbidden. The enforcement of any disability arising out of "Untouchability" shall be an offence punishable in accordance with law.

Article 25 (b): Hindu religious institutions shall remain open to all classes and sections of Hindus.

Directive Principles of State Policy

Article 46: The State shall promote with special care the educational and economic interests of the weaker sections of the people, and, in particular, of the Scheduled Castes and the Scheduled Tribes, and shall protect them from social injustice and all forms of exploitation.

The Scheduled Castes and Scheduled Tribes (Prevention of Atrocities) Act
The Scheduled Castes and Scheduled Tribes (Prevention of Atrocities) Act (1989) specifies the offences which are considered as atrocities and provides for deterrent punishments on commission of the same.

Summary Chart 3.4   Review of the social justice strategies for Dalits and tribals

Aims of Social Justice Measures			
• Bring the historically disadvantaged groups to the mainstream of the society	• Restructure the institutionalised social relationships in the society on democratic lines		
Objectives of Social Justice Measures			
• Negate the hegemonic hold of the immutable status of the dominant groups over public services	• Negate the deleterious impacts of discrimination and exclusion		
Strategies Used			
• Constitutional Rights of Scheduled Castes and Scheduled Tribes	• Reservations: Positive or Reverse Discrimination	• The Scheduled Castes and Scheduled Tribes (Prevention of Atrocities) Act	
Effects of the Strategies Used			
• No Marked Improvement in the Situations of the Marginalized Social Groups	• Creation of Creamy Layers within the Marginalized Social Groups	• Politicisation of Caste, Inter-Caste Conflict, Solidification of Casteism	• Backlash from the Upper Castes

References

Acharya, S. S. (2010). *Access to health care and patterns of discrimination: A study of Dalit children in selected villages of Gujarat and Rajasthan.* New Delhi: Working Paper Series, Indian Institute of Dalit Studies and UNICEF. Retrieved from http://dalitstudies.org.in/wp/wps0103.pdf.

Bhambhri, C. P. (2005). Reservations and casteism. *Economic and Political Weekly*, 806–808.

Bijoy, C. R. (2003). The Adivasis of India: A history of discrimination, conflict, and resistance. *PUCL Bulletin.* Retrieved from http://www.pucl.org/Topics/Dalit-tribal/2003/adivasi.htm.

Center for Human Rights and Global Justice, & Human Rights Watch. (2007). Hidden apartheid: Caste discrimination against India's "untouchables". Shadow Report to the UN Committee on the Elimination of Racial Discrimination. New York: Authors. Retrieved from http://www.hrw.org/sites/default/files/reports/india0207webwcover_0.pdf.

Chalam, K. S. (2007). *Caste-based reservations and human development in India.* Los Angeles: Sage.

Child Soldiers International. (2013). India. Retrieved from file:///C:/Users/HP/Downloads/indiaopacreportjuly20135183846%20(1).pdf.

Coalition to Stop the Use of Child Soldiers. (2008). *Child soldiers: Global report 2008.* Retrieved from http://www.childlineindia.org.in/CP-CR-Downloads/Global%20Report%202008%20child%20soldeirs.pdf.

Dalit Solidarity Network. (2009). *United Nations principles and guidelines for the effective elimination of discrimination based on work and descent. A comprehensive legal framework to eliminate caste discrimination globally.* Retrieved from http://idsn.org/uploads/media/UN_Principles_And_Guidelines_-_IDSN.pdf.

Desai, S., & Kulkarni, V. (2008). Changing educational inequalities in India in the context of affirmative action. *Demography, 45*(2), 245–270.

Gore, M. S. (1966). The cultural perspective in social work in India. *International Social Work, 9*(3), 6–16.

Griffin, S. (2008). *Inclusion, equality and diversity in working with children.* Malaysia: Pearson Education Limited.

Guru, G. (2005). Understanding the category Dalit. In G. Guru (Ed.), *Atrophy in Dalit politics* (pp. 63–76). Mumbai: Vikas Adhyayan Kendra.

Hasan, Z. (2009). *Politics of inclusion: Castes, minorities, and affirmative action.* New Delhi: Oxford University Press.

Human Rights Watch. (1999). *Violence against and exploitation of "untouchable" children.* Retrieved from http://resourcecentre.savethechildren.se/sites/default/files/documents/2213.pdf.

Human Rights Watch. (2002). *Human rights watch report 2002: Children's rights.* Retrieved from www.hrw.org/wr2k2/children.html.

Human Rights Watch. (2003). Small change: Bonded child labour in India's silk industry. *Human Rights Watch, 15*(2). Retrieved from http://idsn.org/fileadmin/user_folder/pdf/New_files/Key_Issues/Bonded_Labour/Small_change-_Child_labour_in_India_s_silk_industry__HRW.pdf.

Human Rights Watch. (2004). *India: Human rights report.* Retrieved from www.hrw.org/reports/2001/globalcaste/caste0801-03.htm.

Human Rights Watch. (2012). *India: UN Members should act to end caste discrimination.* Retrieved from http://www.hrw.org/news/2012/05/14/india-un-members-should-act-end-caste-discrimination.

Human Rights Watch (2014). *Cleaning human waste "manual scavenging", caste and discrimination in India.* Retrieved from https://www.hrw.org/report/2014/08/25/cleaning-human-waste/manual-scavenging-caste-and-discrimination-india.

India: Ministry of Home Affairs. (2013). *Census of India 2011: Release of primary census abstracts data highlights.* Retrieved from http://idsn.org/wp-content/uploads/user_folder/pdf/New_files/India/2013/INDIA_CENSUS_ABSTRACT-2011-Data_on_SC-STs.pdf.

India: Ministry of Rural Development. (2007). *National rehabilitation and resettlement policy*. Retrieved from http://www.dolr.nic.in/NRRP2007.pdf.

India: Ministry of Tribal Affairs. (2012). *State wise tribal population percentage in India*. Retrieved from http://tribal.nic.in/Content/StatewiseTribalPopulationpercentageinIndiaScheduleTribes.aspx.

India: National Institute of Rural Development. (2013). *Training Manual on the Provisions of the PANCHAYATS (Extension to the Scheduled Areas) Act, 1996*. Retrieved from http://www.nird.org.in/NIRD_Docs/PESA%20MANUAL.pdf.

India: The Scheduled Castes and the Scheduled Tribes (Prevention of Atrocities) Act. (1989). Retrieved from http://socialjustice.nic.in/poa-act.php.

International Dalit Solidarity Network. (2008). *Caste discrimination, FAQ*. Retrieved from http://idsn.org/caste-discrimination/faq/?0=International.

International Labour Organization. (1989). *Convention No. 169 concerning Indigenous and Tribal Peoples in Independent Countries*. Retrieved from http://www.ilo.org/dyn/normlex/en/f?p=NORMLEXPUB:12100:0::NO::P12100_ILO_CODE:C169.

Jadhav, P. (2008). Relative disparity in the implementation of reservation policy in india (with respect to scheduled castes). In J. Karade (Ed.), *Development of scheduled castes and scheduled tribes in India* (pp. 1–9). Newcastle: Cambridge Scholars Publishing.

Kakade, S. (2008). Globalisation and scheduled castes. In J. Karade (Ed.), *Development of scheduled castes and scheduled tribes in India* (pp. 1–9). Newcastle: Cambridge Scholars Publishing.

Louis, P. (2003). Scheduled castes and tribes: The reservation debate. *Economic and Political Weekly*, 2475–2478.

Louis, P. (2012). Dalit issues, interventions and movements. In S. Singh (Ed.), *Encyclopaedia of social work in India* (3rd ed., pp. 201–209). Lucknow: New Royal Book Company.

Nancharaiah, G. (2001). Development policy and social change with reference to scheduled castes. In G. S. Bhargava & R. M. Pal (Eds.), *Human rights of Dalits societal violation* (pp. 55–66). New Delhi: Gyan Publishing House.

National Coalition for Strengthening PoA Act. (2012). *Joint stakeholders report on caste based discrimination in India*. New Delhi: National Campaign on Dalit Human Rights. Retrieved from http://www.ncdhr.org.in/resources/publications/ndmj/UPR_Caste_Based_Discrimination,_India_2013.pdf/view.

Navani, D. (2014). North-east Indians and others: Discrimination, Prejudice and textbooks. *Economic and Political Weekly, 49*(24), 19–21.

Puniyani, R. (2012). *Quest for social justice: An illustrated primer*. Mumbai: Vikas Adhyayan Kendra.

Rolland, M. (2013). A light in the darkness: Fighting ritual prostitution in south India. Retrieved from http://www.hart-uk.org/wp-content/uploads/2013/07/A-Light-in-the-Darkness.pdf.

Scheduled Castes and Scheduled Tribes Research and Training Institute. (2015). *Forest Rights Act Training Manual for Government Functionaries and Members of Gram Sabha*. Bhubaneswar. Retrieved from http://www.tribal.nic.in/FRA/data/FRATrainingManual.pdf.

Sharma, B. D. (1995). *Globalisation: The tribal encounter*. New Delhi: Har-Anand Publications.

Singhal, D. P. (1983). *A history of the Indian people*. London: Methuen.

Stern, R. W. (1993). *Changing India*. New Delhi: Cambridge University Press.

Teltumbde, A. (2007). Reverting to the original vision of reservations. *Economic and Political Weekly*, 2383–2385.

Thorat, S. & Senapati, C. (2006). Reservation Policy in India—dimensions and issues. *Working Paper Series, 1*(2). New Delhi: Indian Institute of Dalit Studies. Retrieved from http://www.dalitstudies.org.in/download/wp/0602.pdf.

Thorat, S. & Senapati, C. (2007). Reservation in employment, education and legislature—status and emerging issues. *Working Paper Series, 2*(5). New Delhi: Indian Institute of Dalit Studies. Retrieved from http://www.dalitstudies.org.in/download/wp/0705.pdf.

United Nations. (1989). *Convention on the rights of the child*. Retrieved from http://www.ohchr.org/english/law/pdf/crc.pdf.

United Nations. (2007). Declaration on the rights of indigenous peoples. Retrieved from http://www.un.org/esa/socdev/unpfii/documents/DRIPS_en.pdf.

United Nations Development Program. (2012). *Panchayat Raj (Extension of Scheduled Areas) Act of 1996: Policy Brief.* Retrieved from http://www.in.undp.org/content/dam/india/docs/UNDP-Policy-Brief-on-PESA.pdf.

United Nations Educational, Scientific and Cultural Organisation. (2002). *Universal declaration on cultural diversity: A vision a conceptual platform a pool of ideas for implementation a new paradigm.* Retrieved from http://unesdoc.unesco.org/images/0012/001271/127162e.pdf.

United Nations Permanent Forum on Indigenous Issues. (2006). *United Nations permanent forum on indigenous issues, Fifth Session, Fact Sheet.* Retrieved from http://www.un.org/esa/socdev/unpfii/documents/5session_factsheet1.pdf.

Xaxa, V. (2001). Protective discrimination: Why scheduled castes lag behind scheduled tribes? *Economic and Political Weekly, 36*(29), 2765–2773.

Xaxa, V. (2011). *The status of tribal children in India: A historical perspective.* New Delhi: Institute for Human Development-UNICEF Working Paper Series, Working Paper No. 7, Children of India: Rights and Opportunities. Retrieved from http://www.kcci.org.in/Document%20Repository/virginius_xaxa.pdf, December 8, 2017.

Relevant Child Rights and You Reports and Articles

Kakkoth, S. (2012). Unheard Voices: *A Study on the Perceptions of Tribal School Drop-outs in Kerala*, CRY National Child Rights Fellowship. Retrieve from https://www.cry.org/resources/pdf/NCRRF/NCRRF_ReportBy_Seetha_Kakkoth.pdf.

Mourya, N. (2010–12). *Development Displacement and Childhood in Madhya Pradesh*, CRY National Child Rights Fellowship. Retrieve from https://www.cry.org/resources/pdf/NCRRF/NCRRF_ReportBy_N-Mourya.pdf.

Module 4
Child Rights to Culture
and Intercultural Inclusion

Prerequisite Modules

The prerequisite Modules for this Module are:
From *Sourcebook I on Introduction to Rights-Based Direct Practice with Children*:

- Modules on Life Skills Development.

From *Sourcebook II on Child Rights Education for Participation and Development: Primary Prevention*:

- Introduction to Child Rights Education,
- Child Rights to Participation and Children's Associations,

From *Sourcebook III on Child Rights Education for Inclusion and Protection: Primary Prevention*:

- Rights of Girls and Children with Disability to Non-Discrimination and Inclusion,
- Rights of Dalit and Tribal Children to Non-Discrimination and Inclusion.

Conceptual Framework of Child's Cultural Rights and Rights to Intercultural Inclusion

Concepts and Theories

Culture

Culture: The United Nations Educational Scientific and Cultural Organisation (UNESCO, 2006) noted that culture is defined as the whole set of signs by which the members of a given society recognise one another while distinguishing them

© Child Rights and You 2018
M. Desai and S. Goel, *Child Rights Education for Inclusion and Protection: Primary Prevention*, Rights-based Direct Practice with Children,
https://doi.org/10.1007/978-981-13-0417-0_4

from people not belonging to that society. It has also been viewed as the set of distinctive spiritual, material, intellectual and emotional features of a society or social group encompassing in addition to art and the literature, lifestyles, ways of living together, value systems, traditions and beliefs. It is also important to note that cultures are not static, and they change over time as new generations reject or reformulate some aspect of traditional ways of living (Griffin, 2008). According to Griffin (2008), culture is about the attitudes and values underpinning patterns of tradition and custom which determine everyday aspects of life, such as:

- How the role of men and women is seen in society,
- The way children are brought up,
- The language one speaks, and what, when and how one eats,
- How one dresses, and how one washes and cares for oneself,
- How one decorates and furnishes one's home,
- The religious practices one pursues regularly,
- Drama, music, dance, the literature and art, the manner of celebrating special occasions such as weddings and festivals and attitudes to death and dying.

Ethnicity and Culture: Culture is often linked with ethnicity. According to Max Weber (1978, cited in Law, 2009, p. 63), ethnicity refers to groups of people that not only have a common descent, but also share similarities of physical type, customs, traditions and language. Cohen and Kennedy (2007, p. 162) explain that the social construction of ethnicity is based on social markers, for example those of culture, nationality, language or religion.

Culture and Identity: Culture is at the core of individual and social identity and is a major component in the reconciliation of group identities within a framework of social cohesion (UNESCO, 2006). Cultural identity and a pride in one's culture give people a sense of social and historical rootedness. Culture is different from nature, in that culture encompasses that which is passed on from one generation to the next by learning, rather than through biological inheritance (Heywood, 2007).

Cultural Diversity: According to the United Nations (UN) Convention on the Protection and Promotion of the Diversity of Cultural Expressions (2005), "cultural diversity" refers to the manifold ways in which the cultures of groups and societies find expression. Cultural diversity is made manifest not only through the varied ways in which the cultural heritage of humanity is expressed, augmented and transmitted through the variety of cultural expressions, but also through diverse modes of artistic creation, production, dissemination, distribution and enjoyment, whatever the means and technologies used.

Cultural Expressions: According to the United Nations (UN) Convention on the Protection and Promotion of the Diversity of Cultural Expressions (2005), "cultural expressions" are those expressions that result from the creativity of individuals, groups and societies, and that have cultural content.

There is a tension between universalism and cultural pluralism. There is a need to emphasise the universality of human rights while maintaining cultural difference which may challenge aspects of these rights (UN, 2006). UNESCO (2006) holds firmly to the view that full and unqualified recognition of cultural diversity strengthens the universality of human rights and ensures their effective exercise. It is also important to understand cultural relativity as a practice of evaluating any culture by its own standards and trying not to project your value system onto them. There are reasons that groups of people do what they do, often reasons that make perfectly good sense to them (Leeder, 2003).

Threats to Cultural Diversity

Conventionally, development has been a Eurocentric monocultural project, with modernisation and Westernisation being synonymous (Pieterse, 2010). Cultural homogenisation has led to threats to cultural diversity due to spread of such development. According to Amin (2008), Eurocentrism has created the construct of the "other" as "orientalism" which is inferior to Eurocentrism. It is a cultural prejudice that claims that Western culture is superior to others, and its imitation by all peoples is the only way to progress, justifying colonisation. Not only that, it destroyed the peoples and civilisations who resisted its spread. The ends of the global market economy are served through homogenisation of citizen responses and social tastes (Ahmad, 1998). According to Bhargava (1999), people lose respect for their own cultures and hasten the progress of homogenisation, induced by dominant Eurocentric culture.

Cultural Conflicts

Conflicts between religions, races, castes and linguistic groups have increased in the recent times. Multiculturalists do not perceive any link between cultural diversity and conflict or instability; they hold that such diversity is compatible with political cohesion and cultural recognition underpins political stability. From this perspective, the denial of cultural recognition results in isolation and powerlessness, providing a breeding ground for extremism and the politics of hate (Bhargava, 1999). Prejudicing ideologies and religious fundamentalism play a major role in these conflicts.

Prejudicing Ideologies: While culture is a source of identity, it can also lead to stereotypes about cultures of "others", resulting in tensions, social exclusion, conflicts and even violence within and among societies (UNESCO, 2006). Culture-based prejudicing ideologies comprise ethnocentrism, Eurocentrism, racism and casteism.

Ethnocentrism: Ethnocentrism is judging another culture by the standards of one's own culture, assuming one's own culture to be superior (Leeder, 2003). It often suggests that the way something is done in other ethnic groups is inferior to the way it is done in one's own ethnic group (Marshall, 1994). It blocks recognition of other cultures as good and necessary for others as their own for themselves. Ethnocentrism is applicable to cultural and behavioural practices based on one's own religion, tribe, mother tongue and regional origin. Ethnocentrism leads to ethnic stereotypes, intolerance, discrimination and violence against those with cultural background different than one's own.

Racism: Racism consists of attitudes and actions, often based on prejudices and often deriving from stereotypes that discriminate against certain people because they are seen as belonging to a particular race which is seen as inferior to another. Racist attitudes include the view that people of some ethnic origins are less important and valuable than those of other ethnic origins (Griffin, 2008). Though Indians face racism in white-dominated countries, Indians are racist with reference to non-Whites in the same countries and with non-White and non-Indian foreigners within India.

Casteism: Casteism is a prejudicing ideology that justifies hierarchy of castes based on natural and social inferiority. It is a prejudice about superiority or inferiority of other castes with reference to one's own. It justifies intolerance, discrimination and violence against those at the lower rungs of the hierarchy.

Cultural Diversity and Conflicts in India: India has been a culturally, linguistically, religiously and ethnically diverse country. However, its multicultural flavour has been threatened by different ethnic conflicts based on statehood agitations (for creation of newer States based on cultural and linguistic similarities); regional assertiveness (militant nativist movements); secessionist movements (that demand separation from the Indian State, for example, those in Punjab, Assam and Kashmir); and communal violence (especially between Hindus and Muslims) (Ganguly, 2007).

Protection and Promotion of the Diversity of Cultural Expressions

Objectives: The main objectives of the Convention on the Protection and Promotion of the Diversity of Cultural Expressions (2005) are:

(a) To protect and promote the diversity of cultural expressions,
(b) To create the conditions for cultures to flourish and to freely interact in a mutually beneficial manner,
(c) To encourage dialogue among cultures with a view to ensuring wider and balanced cultural exchanges in the world in favour of intercultural respect and a culture of peace,
(d) To foster interculturality in order to develop cultural interaction in the spirit of building bridges among peoples,
(e) To promote respect for the diversity of cultural expressions and raise awareness of its value at the local, national and international levels,
(f) To give recognition to the distinctive nature of cultural activities, goods and services as vehicles of identity, values and meaning.

Guiding Principles: The main guiding principles of the Convention on the Protection and Promotion of the Diversity of Cultural Expressions (2005) are:

1. **Principle of respect for human rights and fundamental freedoms**: Cultural diversity can be protected and promoted only if human rights and fundamental freedoms, such as freedom of expression, information and communication, as well as the ability of individuals to choose cultural expressions, are guaranteed.
2. **Principle of equal dignity of and respect for all cultures**: The Protection and Promotion of the Diversity of Cultural Expressions presuppose the recognition of equal dignity of and respect for all cultures, including the cultures of persons belonging to minorities and indigenous peoples.
3. **Principle of the complementarity of economic and cultural aspects of development**: Since culture is one of the mainsprings of development, the cultural aspects of development are as important as its economic aspects, which individuals and peoples have the fundamental right to participate in and enjoy.
4. **Principle of equitable access**: Equitable access to a rich and diversified range of cultural expressions from all over the world and access of cultures to the means of expressions and dissemination constitute important elements for enhancing cultural diversity and encouraging mutual understanding.
5. **Principle of openness and balance**: When States adopt measures to support the diversity of cultural expressions, they should seek to promote, in an appropriate manner, openness to other cultures of the world and to ensure that these measures are geared to the objectives pursued under the present Convention.

Promotion of Cultural Rights

Multiculturalism: Multiculturalism as a descriptive term has been taken to refer to cultural diversity that arises from racial, ethnic and language differences (adapted from Heywood, 2007). Multiculturalism opposes cultural imperialism and homogenisation and opposes States whose only objectives are the survival and well-being of the dominant cultural group. A demand to renounce cultural identity as a condition for free and equal citizenship no longer appears to be viable (Bhargava, 1999). As a normative term, multiculturalism implies:

- A positive endorsement, even celebration of communal diversity, based on either the right of different cultural groups to recognition and respect or to the alleged benefits to the larger society,
- Distinctive cultures deserve to be protected and strengthened, particularly when they belong to minority or vulnerable groups (Heywood, 2007).

Interculturality: According to the UN Convention on the Protection and Promotion of the Diversity of Cultural Expressions (2003), "interculturality" refers to the existence and equitable interaction of diverse cultures and the possibility of generating shared cultural expressions through dialogue and mutual respect. Interculturality presupposes multiculturalism and results from "intercultural" exchange and dialogue on the local, regional, national or international level.

A multicultural existence may imply learning about other cultures to produce an acceptance or at least tolerance of different cultures in a society. On the other hand, an intercultural approach aims to go beyond passive coexistence, to achieve a developing and sustainable way of living together in multicultural societies through the creation of understanding of, respect for and dialogue between the different cultural groups (UNESCO, 2006).

Multiculturalism can best flourish when there is an accompanying spirit of interculturality. For example, multiculturalism may suggest official recognition for different languages or religions in a given State but interculturality requires that the majority be encouraged to learn about the minorities and with it the literature and culture of a minority and vice versa, that is, the minority be encouraged to learn about other minorities as well as the majority (Mahajan, 2006).

Minority Cultural Rights: The term "minority culture" generally refers to the culture of "marginalised or vulnerable groups who live in the shadow of majority populations with a different and dominant cultural ideology", the "majority culture". The non-dominant position of minority groups does not always derive from numerical weakness; it often has a qualitative dimension linked to the specific cultural and socio-economic characteristics of the community. Such characteristics can produce value systems and lifestyles that are very different from or even incompatible with those of more dominant groups in society (UNESCO, 2006). Multicultural rights are sometimes called minority rights. These rights are distinct from the liberal conception of rights, in that they belong to groups rather than to individuals. These rights are specific to the groups to which they belong, each cultural group having different needs for recognition based on the specific character of its religion, traditions and way of life (Heywood, 2007, pp. 318–319).

Child's Cultural Rights

To prevent the threats to cultural diversity, it is important to promote child's cultural rights and responsibilities for protection of cultural pluralism, especially for minority cultural groups, as discussed in these sections.

UNCRC: The United Nations Convention on the Rights of the Child (UNCRC) (United Nation, 1989) upholds the right to culture in four main areas, namely access to information, education, cultural identity and participation in cultural life as shown below.

Access to Information:

Article 17 (**a**): States Parties shall "Encourage the mass media to disseminate information and material of social and cultural benefit to the child and in accordance with the spirit of article 29".

Article 17 (**b**): States Parties shall "Encourage international cooperation in the production, exchange and dissemination of such information and material from a diversity of cultural, national and international sources".

Article 17 (d): States Parties shall "Encourage the mass media to have particular regard to the linguistic needs of the child who belongs to a minority group or who is indigenous".

Education:

Article 29 (1c): States Parties agree that the education of the child shall be directed to "The development of respect for the child's parents, his or her own cultural identity, language and values, for the national values of the country in which the child is living, the country from which he or she may originate, and for civilizations different from his or her own".

Cultural Identity:

Article 30: In those States in which ethnic, religious or linguistic minorities or persons of indigenous origin exist, a child belonging to such a minority or who is indigenous shall not be denied the right, in community with other members of his or her group, to enjoy his or her own culture, to profess and practise his or her own religion, or to use his or her own language.

Participation in Cultural Life:

Article 31 (2): States Parties shall respect and promote the right of the child to participate fully in cultural and artistic life and shall encourage the provision of appropriate and equal opportunities for cultural, artistic, recreational and leisure activity.

Cultural Rights in the Indian Constitution: According to Article 29 of the Indian Constitution, protection of interests of minorities is a Fundamental Right:

1. Any section of the citizens residing in the territory of India or any part thereof having a distinct language, script or culture of its own shall have the right to conserve the same.
2. No citizen shall be denied admission into any educational institution maintained by the State or receiving aid out of State funds on grounds only of religion, race, caste, language or any of them.

According to Article 30:

1. All minorities, whether based on religion or language, shall have the right to establish and administer educational institutions of their choice.
2. The State shall not, in granting aid to educational institutions, discriminate against any educational institution on the ground that it is under the management of a minority, whether based on religion or language.

Child's Rights to Intercultural Inclusion

According to Article 29 (1d) of the UNCRC, States Parties agree that the education of the child shall be directed to "The preparation of the child for responsible life in a free society, in the spirit of understanding, peace, tolerance, equality of sexes, and friendship among all peoples, ethnic, national and religious groups and persons of indigenous origin". Besides cultural rights, children have responsibilities to promote intercultural inclusion by protecting and promoting cultural diversity, pluralism, multiculturalism and interculturality.

Activities

Introductory Activity 4.1: Conceptual Framework of Child's Cultural Rights and Rights to Intercultural Inclusion

Learner Outcome: At the end of this activity, the participants will develop awareness of child's cultural rights and rights to intercultural inclusion.

Procedure: Use the following procedure to conduct this activity:

1. Show the following video film: Cultural Diversity of India by Janani Iyer.

   https://www.youtube.com/watch?v=iuUdNN3wll8

2. Form four small groups, and allocate the following topics among them for reading and discussion:

   (1) Concepts of Culture and Cultural Diversity,
   (2) Threats to Cultural Diversity and Cultural Conflicts,
   (3) Child's Cultural Rights,
   (4) Child's Rights to Intercultural Inclusion.

3. Ask the small groups to make their presentation to the large group.
4. Show Summary Charts 4.1, 4.2, 4.3 and 4.4 to summarise the discussion.
5. Introduce the following units of the module:

   - Children's Religious Rights and Rights to Inter-Religious Inclusion,
   - Children's Linguistic Rights and Rights to Interlinguistic Inclusion.

Time Estimate: 30 min

Activity 4.2: Game on Where's My Banana

Learner Outcome: At the end of this activity, the participants will learn to value equality, acceptance and respect for all cultural groups.

Procedure: Use the following procedure to conduct this activity:

1. Ask all the participants to bring a banana from home, or provide one banana per participant.

2. Ask them to "get to know their banana". Ask them not to peel it or eat it. They must closely examine their banana and notice all its characteristics (smell it, touch it, observe it).
3. Put all the bananas in a large bowl. Then, ask the participants to find their banana. Most will recognise their banana. Now, ask the participants to peel their banana before they put it back in the bowl.
4. Ask them once again to find their banana. This time, it will be more difficult and someone may say: "But the bananas are all the same!"

A variation to the activity is using a different fruit (like orange) that can be easily peeled.

Questions for Discussion: Use the following questions to discuss this activity:

- How did you find your banana when it was not peeled?
- How did you find your banana from among all the peeled bananas?
- We saw that the bananas were different on the outside. What about the inside?
- Ethnicity/race/religion/language make people look different from the outside. But how similar are they from the inside?
- Do stereotypes based on the external look help or harm? How?

Time Estimate: 15 min

Source: Banana People, the Woodcraft Folk (2006) cited in Where's My Banana from Equitas—International Centre for Human Rights Education (2008, pp. 103–104)

Children's Religious Rights and Rights to Inter-Religious Inclusion

Concepts and Theories

Concept of Religion

A religion can be defined as a system of faith and belief in the supernatural, omnipotent and omnipresent power, which controls the destiny of humankind, called "God", who is entitled to obedience and worship (Srivastava, 2004). Religious beliefs refer to a social compilation of pre-scientific human wisdom related to the world view. The religious rituals provide an occasion for community sharing of religion and create social bonds. Ethical and moral dimensions in religion set the behavioural norms for human beings (Punyani, 2000). While religions codify behaviour and inspire artistic expressions, including different kinds of artefacts, paintings, songs, attires, music, dances that are used in rituals and sacred ceremonies, they also provide a spiritual recourse to cope with misfortunes of life and address the major passages and transitions in human life (United Nations, 2009,

p. 60). Atheism and agnosticism, both, are forms of religious unbelief. Atheists say that they do not believe in the existence of God or Gods, while agnostics say that they have inadequate knowledge to reach conclusions on the subject (Graves, 1995).

Religious Diversity in India

The religions of the world fall into two well-defined groups, the eastern religions and the Judeo-Christian religions. The eastern religions mainly owe their origin to India: Vedic religion, Buddhism and Jainism in the ancient period, and mysticism and Sikhism in the medieval period. The Judeo-Christian religions owe their origin directly or indirectly to Judaism, an ancient religion of Israel. Judaism gave birth to Christianity and less directly to Islam and Zoroastrianism, in the medieval period (Zaehner, 1959). In India, all these religions have influenced each other and the society at different points of time.

Hinduism: The main source of, what we call today the Hindu religion, lies in the *Vedas*, written during 4000–1000 B.C., by the priestly group of Aryans, namely Brahmins. The original terms of religion in India were Arya Dharma, Vedic Dharma (a religion based in the Vedas) and Sanatan Dharma. The word "Hindu" does not occur at all in any ancient religious literature of India. This term was used by peoples of Western and Central Asia for people living on the other side of River Sindhu, from which the term "Hindu" is derived for the people and "Hindustan" for the country (Nehru, 1945). This religion has the largest number of scriptures, written over a long period of time. According to the Vedic scriptures, Brahman is the ultimate reality, which means that everything in the world is but the manifestation of a part of Brahman. If Brahman is the ultimate reality, and if we are not different from it, birth cannot be our beginning, nor death our end. Samsara means transmigration or the flow of atman (soul) from beyond birth to beyond death. Thus, atman is eternal and birth and death relate to the integration and disintegration of the elements that compose the body (Mahadevan, 1982).

Hindus are diverse within themselves. The liberation of the soul is to be achieved by way of Yoga. The different forms of Yoga are Jnana Yoga (philosophy), *Karma* Yoga (work), Bhakti Yoga (worship) and Raj Yoga (psychic control). Worshipping may be done of different deities. Hindus are also diverse by castes as discussed in the earlier chapter.

Jainism and Buddhism: Around sixth to fifth century B.C., when the Vedic ideology had lost its original purity, giving rise to ritualism, Buddha and Mahavir challenged the authority of the Vedas. Non-Vedic religions Buddhism and Jainism both developed as atheistic creeds. They were against the caste system and admitted into their fold, all peoples, irrespective of their castes. Both these religions promoted equality and non-violence. Both are institutionalised religions, in terms of sanghas (order of monks).

Jainism perceives intrinsic equality among all selves, be they earth bodies, water bodies, vegetable organisms, insects, birds, animals or human beings. The attitude of equality finds expression in non-violence, both, in the domain of religious conduct and in that of philosophical thought. All the Jain religious rites, external or internal, in every field of life, are formulated around non-violence (Sanghvi, 1982).

According to Buddha, there are Four Noble Truths:

- *Dukha* or suffering or pain that seeps at some level into all finite existence on occasions such as birth, sickness, old age, the phobia of death, to be tied to what one abhors and separation from loved ones.
- The cause of the suffering is *tanha* or desire, and is our captivity, in the form of selfish craving.
- Therefore, the cure of suffering lies in being released from the narrow limits of such self-interest into the vast expanse of universal life.
- The overcoming of *tanha* is through the Eightfold Path. The Eightfold Path consists of right knowledge, right aspiration, right speech, right behaviour, right livelihood, right effort, right mindfulness and right absorption (Smith, 1958).

Buddha firmly established the spiritual tradition, making it available to all. It is the notion of truth that occupies the centre in Indian spirituality. Truth need not depend on worship of God, that is a personal God or a deity. Knowing the truth amounts to a resolution of the mystery of human existence. What it demands is an enquiry, a journey into oneself and not towards something outside of human existence—transcendent God or heaven. Search not faith, knowledge not belief, meditation not worship, freedom not heaven, are other contrasting themes which explain the difference between spirituality and religion. A spiritual discourse thus, in its very nature, is secular. It considers any reference to the authority of religion as totally irrelevant to its spiritual enterprise of the search for truth. In the spiritual tradition, truth is, in principle, accessible to all in this very life if the aspirant reaches out directly to it (Agarwal, 1998).

Sikhism: Guru Nanak, who was born in 1469, was greatly influenced by the teachings of Kabir and Indian Sufis. He accepted good things from, both, Hinduism and Islam. Drawing from Nirgun Bhakti (God without a visible form), he preached against image worship, caste system and meaningless religious practices. His teachings are written in the Adi Granth. His followers are called Sikhs (Vas, 1997). Sikhs recognise a single impersonal God, reject Brahminism and acknowledge that all are equal before God (Glossary of Terms, 1998).

Judaism: Judaism can be dated about 1700 B.C., much before the Greek philosophers lived. Christianity was originally a social movement in Judaism (Marshall, 1994). The cornerstone of Judaism is the Hebrew Bible or the Old Testament (Zwi Werblowsky, 1959). Judaism was one of the first foreign religions to arrive in India in the ancient period. Indian Jews are a religious minority of India, but unlike many parts of the world have historically lived in India without any instances of anti-Semitism from the local majority populace, the Hindus. The majority of Indian Jews have migrated to Israel since the creation of the new State in 1947. Of the remaining 5,000, the largest community is concentrated in Mumbai, where 3,500 have stayed over from over 30,000 Jews registered there in the 1940s.

Christianity: Jesus Christ wanted to reform Judaism but ended up launching a new religion called Christianity. Christians believe that salvation from punishment has been made possible by God's mercy in sending a saviour—Jesus Christ—to atone for their sins (Marshall, 1994). Christianity retained the importance of the Hebrew Bible and the essentials of the Jewish ideology as fundamental to its own faith. Jesus Christ used the Ten Commandments as the basis for his moral and ethical teachings (McCasland, Cairns, & Yu, 1969). The church of the Christians of South India, known as the Syrian Christians, was founded by St. Thomas, one of the apostles of Jesus Christ in sixth century A.D. With the arrival of Vasco da Gama in 1498, the influence of the Roman Catholic Church was brought to bear upon this ancient church (Abraham, 1993).

Zoroastrianism: Zoroaster is supposed to have lived in about 1000 B.C. in Persia, whose religion Zoroastrianism was the national religion of the Persian Empire from the third to the seventh century A.D. When Iran had to face Islam, Zoroastrianism could not hold its own and was very nearly wiped out from the land of its birth. A few Zoroastrians clung to the ancient fire of Ahura Mazda and took refuge in India in 936 A.D. (Taraporewala, 1993).

Islam: Islam originated in the seventh-century Arabia with the prophet Mohammed and a holy text called *Koran*. There are five main principles or pillars of Islam: (1) the affirmation that there is no God but God and Mohammed as His prophet, (2) pray five times a day, (3) *zakat* or the giving of 2 1/2% of one's holdings as alms, (4) fasting in the month of Ramadan, during which the *Koran* was revealed and (5) Haj, or pilgrimage to Mecca, where Mohammed was born, at least once in a lifetime (Marshall, 1994). Arabs had been trading with India even before the birth of Islam. Arab merchants had carried back stories of India's riches. From eighth to eleventh centuries, the Arabs and Afghans invaded India and carried back treasures. In the twelfth century, the Turks invaded India and defeated the Rajputs. They decided to set up a kingdom in India, rather than just plundering and going back. For six centuries, Muslim rulers ruled India, first Turks and then Moghuls (Vas, 1997).

The interface of the Indian and the Muslim cultures brought assimilations in the forms of Urdu language, Kathak dance, *sitar* and *tabla* musical instruments, *ghazals* as a form of poetry, *salwar kameez* dresses, food items and so on (Vas, 1997). Islam also promoted non-idol worship in India.

Mysticism of Bhakti and Sufi Movements: Mysticism is the ideology common to the Bhaktas and the Sufis. According to Bose (1964), the mystics believed in the success of love where intellect fails. The mystics are, by nature, tolerant as they see a single truth in all religions (Zaehner, 1994). According to the mystical ideology, the truth or God may be known through spiritual insight, independent of the mind. The mystic ideology is unitive and transcends the subject–object duality. The mystics fostered humaneness, benevolence, charity, tenderness and love, on the basis of realisation of the supreme worth of fellow human beings. In India, Mirabai, Tulsidas, Chaitanya, Surdas and Kabir are the famous Bhaktas. The Sufi sect had originated in Iran. Khwaja Moinuddin Chisti was a renowned philosopher among the Sufi saints, who came to India. The Bhaktas/saints/poets and Sufis strived for communal and caste harmony, for achieving harmony between the two religions and reaching religion to all the people. They rebelled against the caste hierarchy and Brahminism, child marriage, ill-treatment of widows and other such social evils (Vanina, 1996).

Thus, due to its history of invasions, conquests and migration, India has a multireligious social fabric. The religions that did not originate in India also have significantly contributed to the Indian history and culture (Srivastava, 2004). According to the Census of 2011, of the total population, Hindus are 79.80%, Muslims 14.23%, Christians 2.30%, Sikhs 1.72%, Buddhist 0.70%, Jains 0.37%, 0.66% belong to other religions and 0.24% did not state their religion (India, 2015).

Secularism

Secularism refers to the separation of the State/government from the religious institutions for the purpose of governing. The concept of secularism emerged in Europe in the late nineteenth century when they struggled to separate the State from the hegemony of the church or religion. India, on the other hand, did not have to struggle to free itself from the power of the church. Due to its history of invasions, conquests and migration, she had a multireligious social fabric that mutually coexisted. Secularism was therefore conceived as a system to sustain religion and cultural pluralism that had become intrinsic the Indian society (Mallick, 2013). The Preamble of the Indian Constitution States that it is a Secular Democratic Republic. India has no official or established State religion which implies equal treatment of all religions by the State (Mahajan, 2006). Hensman (2004) noted that secularism is a necessary condition for democracy.

Causes of Religious Communalism

Religious Communalism: Communal politics began in India as a result of political mobilisation in the pre-independence period. It culminated in the Partition of India in 1947, a massive religious conflict in her history. Today, communalism has come to pervade in all aspects of life, particularly areas which are the most sensitive, such as education, the media, the forces of law and order and even culture. Communal politics in India has resorted to manipulation or distortion of historical facts to incite religious sentiments and consciousness (Thapar, 1998). The intensification of communal politics in the past couple of decades led to incidents of mass communal violence like the anti-Sikh riots in

1984, bomb blasts in 1993 and terrorists attack in Mumbai in 2008, Gujarat riots against Muslims in 2002 and so on (Punyani, 2012). This has caused loss of life and property, gross violation of fundamental human rights, marginalisation and disenfranchisement of certain sections of people. Such violent religious communalism has their sources in religious ignorance and prejudices and religious fundamentalism.

Religious Ignorance and Prejudices: The causes of religious conflict are complex, deep-seated and multidimensional. Religious communalism assumes that people belonging to one religion have similar interests and that these are opposed to the interests of people belonging to "other" religion (Punyani, 2012). Such ignorance about the "other" provides a fertile ground for breeding sentiments of hatred and animosity. Ignorance also leads to stigmatisation and negative representation of the "other" (most often the minorities) in the cultural history of the nation (Mahajan, 2006). In the context of religious differences and ignorance, prejudices and ethnocentrism flourish which leads to the perception that one's own religion is the only true religion.

Religious Fundamentalism: Fundamentalism refers to a commitment to ideas and values that are seen as basic or foundational which has an enduring and unchanging character. It is therefore seen as opposite of relativism. In the case of religious fundamentalism, the "fundamentals" have usually but not always derived from the content of sacred texts. Fundamental tendencies are identified in all the world's major religions (Heywood, 2007). Religious fundamentalism has arisen as a reaction to secularisation and homogenisation in the context of colonisation and post-colonialism.

Secularisation: Secularism has brought about a distinction between politics and religion. However, secularisation has contributed to a decline of traditional religion and a weakening of what is seen as the "moral" fabric of society. In many parts of the world, religious revivalism has assumed a political form (Heywood, 2007).

Colonisation: Religious fundamentalism arises in deeply troubled societies, particularly societies afflicted by an actual or perceived crisis of identity. The impact of colonialism helps to explain why, although fundamentalism can be found across the globe, its most potent and influential manifestations have been found in the developing world. Colonial rule generally devalued and often suppressed indigenous cultures. As a result, the post-colonial societies inherited a weakened sense of identity and their subordination to Western powers continued. In this context, religious fundamentalism offers a non-Western political identity on the basis of religion (Heywood, 2007).

Militancy: Fundamentalists are usually happy to see themselves as militants, in the sense that militancy implies passionate and robust commitment. Religious fundamentalism has been associated with the existence of a hostile and threatening "other". This demonised "other" may take various guises from secularism and permissiveness to rival religions, Westernisation and Marxism. The consequence of this militancy is a willingness to engage in extra-legal, anti-constitutional political action and sometimes violence and terrorism (Heywood, 2007).

Child's Religious Rights

UNCRC: The UNCRC (1989) upholds the right to culture including religion in four main areas, namely access to information, education, cultural identity and participation.

Indian Constitution: According to the Indian Constitution, right to freedom of religion is a Fundamental Right. The following articles are stated under this fundamental right.

Article 25:

2. Subject to public order, morality and health and to the other provisions of this Part, all persons are equally entitled to freedom of conscience and the right freely to profess, practise and propagate religion.
3. Nothing in this article shall affect the operation of any existing law or prevent the State from making any law:

• Regulating or restricting any economic, financial, political or other secular activity which may be associated with religious practice,
• Providing for social welfare and reform or the throwing open of Hindu religious institutions of a public character to all classes and sections of Hindus.

Article 26: Subject to public order, morality and health, every religious denomination or any section thereof shall have the right:

(a) To establish and maintain institutions for religious and charitable purposes.
(b) To manage its own affairs in matters of religion.

Article 27: No person shall be compelled to pay any taxes, the proceeds of which are specifically appropriated in payment of expenses for the promotion or maintenance of any particular religion or religious denomination.

Article 28:

1. No religious instruction shall be provided in any educational institution wholly maintained out of State funds.
2. Nothing in clause (1) shall apply to an educational institution which is administered by the State but has been established under any endowment or trust which requires that religious instruction shall be imparted in such institution.
3. No person attending any educational institution recognised by the State or receiving aid out of State funds shall be required to take part in any religious instruction that may be imparted in such institution or to attend any religious worship that may be conducted in such institution or in any premises attached thereto unless such person or, if such person is a minor, his guardian has given his consent thereto.

Child's Responsibility to Promote Inter-religious Inclusion

Inter-religious harmony requires promotion of cultural diversity along with a positive acknowledgement of the contribution of minority communities (Mahajan, 2006). Inter-religious harmony also requires inter-religious approach to become an integral part of being a religious person. Children need to know and appreciate not only their own faith but also have an informed understanding of what others believe, and the commonalities they share, both as a human community and in relation to particular challenges (Arigatou Foundation, Interfaith Council on Ethics Education for Children, Global Network of Religions for Children, UNESCO & UNICEF, 2008).

Child rights to intercultural inclusion can be applied to inter-religious inclusion as follows:

- To recognise and respect different religious groups,
- To make a commitment to the religious rights of persons belonging to minorities and those of indigenous peoples,
- To protect and promote the diversity of religious expressions,
- To freely interact in a mutually beneficial manner,
- To ensure harmonious interaction among people and groups with plural and varied religious identities,
- To encourage dialogue among religions with a view to ensuring wider and balanced religious exchanges in the world in favour of inter-religious respect and a culture of peace,
- To celebrate religious diversity,
- To prevent religious domination by a dominant group and homogenisation,
- To promote social cohesion and peace.

Activities

Activity 4.3: Reflections on My Religious Identity

Learner Outcome: At the end of this activity, the participants will review the significance of religion in their life and therefore the need for mutual respect towards everyone's religion.

Procedure: Use the following procedure to conduct this activity:

1. Ask each participant to complete the following sentence:

   Because my religion is _____, I am_____.

2. Ask the participants to share what they have written with their partners.

Questions for Discussion: Use the following questions to discuss this activity:

- What does religion mean to you?
- How do you practise your religion?
- How is it different from other religions?
- How is it similar to other religions?
- How does it affect your identity?
- How does it affect your behaviour?
- What has it taught to you?
- What is secularism? To what extent is it being enforced in India?
- Show the Summary Chart 4.5, and discuss the Religions and Secularism in India.

Time Estimate: 20 min

Activity 4.4: Small Group Discussion on Religion and Peace

Learner Outcome: At the end of this activity, the participants will learn that all religions value peace.

Procedure: Use the following procedure to conduct this activity:

1. Form four small groups, and allocate the following religions among them: Hinduism, Islam, Christianity and tribal religion.
2. Ask the small groups to find out the following about their religion:

   (a) What their religion says about peace.
   (b) What are the stereotypes about this religion and why.

3. Ask the small groups to share their homework with the large group.

Questions for Discussion: Use the following questions to discuss this activity:

- Do all religions value peace?
- If yes, why the major ethnic conflicts have been caused due to religion?
- What is the discourse on peace without reference to any religion?

Time Estimate: 30 min

Activity 4.5: Small Group Discussion on Child's Religious Rights

Learner Outcome: At the end of this activity, the participants will learn about children's religious rights and rights to religious inclusion.

Procedure: Use the following procedure to conduct this activity:

1. Ask the participants what according to them are religious rights?
2. Show Summary Chart 4.7, and discuss Child Right to Freedom.
3. Form five small groups to discuss the religious rights of children from the following religious groups: (1) Muslims, (2) Christians, (3) Sikhs, (4) tribal religions and (5) Hindus.
4. Discuss the following questions related to the religious rights of children in these religions:

   - Can they freely identify themselves with their religion?
   - Can they freely practise their religion?
   - Do you/they have the freedom to change their religion or not follow any religion?
   - Can they participate in religious associations?
   - Are they free to gain religious education?
   - Are they forced to follow a particular religion?
   - Are they being pressured to convert to another religion?
   - How can the religious rights of children be protected?

5. Ask the small groups to share their discussion with the large group.

Time Estimate: 30 min

Activity 4.6: Celebration of Religious Pluralism

Learner Outcome: At the end of this activity, the participants will learn to celebrate religious pluralism in India.

Procedure: Ask the participants to pledge to do anything that celebrates religious diversity. Some suggestions are given below. However, participants may have other ideas too.

- Make charts showcasing positive teachings of different religions.
- Organise a *rangoli* competition with religious harmony as the theme.
- Celebrate different religious festivals.
- Visit places of worship of different religions.

Time Estimate: Depends on the event organised.

Activity 4.7: Role-Plays on Inter-religious Conflicts Versus Harmony

Learner Outcome: At the end of this activity, the participants will develop awareness of the causes and effects of inter-religious conflicts in India and children's and adults' responsibilities to promote inter-religious harmony.

Procedure: Use the following procedure to conduct this activity:

1. Ask the following questions to the participants:

    (a) If every religion teaches peace, why is there so much inter-religious violence?
    (b) How can learning about other religions help to dispel myths about them?
    (c) What is religious fundamentalism? How can it be prevented?

2. Show Summary Chart 4.6 to discuss Causes of Religious Conflicts.
3. Divide the participants into three small groups, and allocate the following topics among them:

    (1) Hindu–Muslim conflicts,
    (2) Hindu–Christian conflicts,
    (3) Hindu–Secularists conflicts.

4. The small groups may discuss their topic with reference to the following questions:

    - What are the major events of this conflict?
    - What are the causes of this conflict?
    - What are the implications of this conflict?
    - How can this conflict be prevented?
    - What are children's responsibilities for promoting understanding, peace, tolerance and friendship among children from all religions?

5. The small groups may prepare role-plays and present them to the large group.
6. Show the Summary Chart 4.4, and apply Child's Rights to Intercultural Inclusion to Inter-religious Inclusion.

Time Estimate: 45 min

Children's Linguistic Rights and Rights to Interlinguistic Inclusion

Concepts and Theories

Language and Culture

Language, defined as a collection of words and rules of syntax and grammar that governs how words are to be arranged in order to convey a particular meaning, may be said to form a core of any culture. All human thoughts are conceptualised through a language, and all human values are pronounced and perceived through it. It is language that introduces us to ourselves (Sengupta, 2009). Each culture has a language that conveys to its members what is important to them. The theory of linguistic determinism says that the way we interpret the world is influenced by our language. We see the world because our language predisposes certain choices of interpretation (Leeder, 2003). According to UNESCO (2006), languages result from a historical and collective experience and express culturally specific world views and value systems. Language is at the heart of issues of identity, memory and transmission of knowledge.

Threats to Linguistic Diversity

Today, increased migration and rapid urbanisation often bring along the loss of traditional ways of life and a strong pressure to speak a dominant language that is, or is perceived to be, necessary for full civic participation and economic advancement. Languages are vulnerable to linguistic erosion and could be rendered endangered when its speakers disappear or when they shift to speaking another language, most often, a larger language used by a more powerful group. Languages are threatened by external forces such as military, economic, religious, cultural or educational subjugation, or by internal forces such as a community's negative attitude towards its own language. The extinction of a language means a loss of traditional knowledge and impoverishment of cultural diversity (UNESCO, n.d.). Estimates which suggest that half the 6,000 languages spoken in the world today are in danger of disappearing are a cause for concern (UNESCO, 2006).

Linguistic Diversity in India

After independence, the reorganisation of Indian States was carried out based on ethnoregional and linguistic lines (except for Punjab in which it was combined with religion). This has been a major instrument for protecting and nurturing linguistic diversity in India. The creation of linguistic identity-based States, each with political rights to govern itself within the framework of the federal system of the Indian Constitution, aided a specific linguistic community to become a majority within a region whereby its language became the official language of that State and the medium of instruction, public examination, communication and media networks. As a consequence, the language of the regional majority grew and flourished (Sengupta, 2009). However, due to interstate migration, some languages which are the majority in one State are a minority in another.

Indian Population by Languages: As per the 2001 Census, India has 122 languages (22 scheduled languages and 100 non-scheduled languages). The scheduled languages include the following with the speakers' strength as percentage to the total population: Hindi (41.03%), Bengali (8.11%), Telugu (7.19%), Marathi (6.99%), Tamil (5.91%), Urdu (5.01%), Gujarati (4.48%), Kannada (4.69%), Malayalam (4.21%), Oriya (4.21%), Punjabi (2.83%), Assamese (1.28%), Maithili (1.18%), Santali (0.63%), Kashmiri (0.54%), Nepali (0.28%), Sindhi (0.25%), Konkani (0.24%), Dogri (0.22%), Manipuri (0.14%), Bodo (0.13%) and Sanskrit (negligible). These 22 scheduled languages have 243 mother tongues embedded in them.

Languages with speakers less than 10,000 have not been accounted for in this Census survey (India: Office of The Registrar General & Census Commissioner, 2011).

The main families of languages spoken in India include the Indo-Aryan family of languages and the Dravidian family of languages.

Indo-Aryan Family of Languages: The Indo-Aryan or Indic languages are the dominant language family of the Indian subcontinent. They constitute a branch of the Indo-Iranian languages, itself a branch of the Indo-European language family. The history of this family of languages is often divided into three main stages:

1. *Old*, comprising Vedic and classical Sanskrit,
2. *Middle* (from about the third century B.C.), which embraces the vernacular dialects of Sanskrit called Prakrits, including Pali,
3. *New or Modern*, (from about the tenth century AD), which comprises the modern languages of the northern and central portions of the Indian subcontinent (History of Indian Languages, 2001).

According to the 2011 Census, Indo-Aryan languages are spoken by 790, 627, 060 Indians.

Dravidian Family of Languages: The Dravidian family of languages has descended from the Proto-Dravidian language. About 23 Dravidian languages are spoken by an estimated 169 million people, mainly in southern India. The four major Dravidian tongues are Tamil, Telugu, Kannada (Kanarese) and Malayalam. They have long literary histories and are written in their own scripts. Telugu is spoken by the largest number of people. Tamil has the richest literature, is thought to be extremely ancient and is spoken over the widest area, including north-Western Sri Lanka. Other Dravidian languages have fewer speakers and are, for the most part, not written. The Dravidian languages have acquired many words from the *Indic* languages, especially from Sanskrit. Conversely, the *Indic* languages have borrowed Dravidian sounds and grammatical structures (History of Indian Languages, 2001).

According to the 2011 Census, the Dravidian languages are spoken by 214, 172, 874 Indians.

Official Languages: After gaining independence from the British in 1947, there was an immediate need to replace English which was seen as "a symbol of slavery". The following five requirements were identified for any language to be accepted as the national language:

1. It should be easy to learn for government officials.
2. It should be capable of serving as a medium of religious, economic and political intercourse throughout India.
3. It should be the speech of the majority of the inhabitants of India.
4. It should be easy to learn for the whole country.
5. In choosing this language, considerations of temporary or passing interests should not count.

However, choosing a national language was not such an easy task for the government due to the following reasons:

1. There were several Indian languages and their dialects with a rich historical and literary background.
2. None of the languages had a clear-cut majority status. This meant that the government would have to choose from one of the Indian languages and accord it special status.
3. It would be difficult to get the public to accept any particular language because they had pride in their own languages.

The final decisions are reflected in the Indian Constitution:

- **Article 343 (1)**: The official language of the Union shall be Hindi in Devanagari script.
- **Article 343 (2)**: Notwithstanding anything in clause (1), for a period of fifteen years from the commencement of this Constitution, the English language shall continue to be used for all the official purposes of the Union for which it was being used immediately before such commencement.
- **Article 346**: The language for the time being authorised for use in the Union for official purposes shall be the official language for communication between one State and another State and between a State and the Union: Provided that if two or more States agree that the Hindi language should be the official language for communication between such States, that language may be used for such communication.
- **Article 347**: On a demand being made in that behalf the President may, if he is satisfied that a substantial proportion of the population of a State desire the use of any language spoken by them to be recognised by that State, direct that such language shall also be officially recognised throughout that State or any part thereof for such purpose as he may specify.

Child's Linguistic Rights

The Indian Constitution provides the following rights and safeguards to preserve linguistic diversity.

Article 29:

1. Any section of the citizens residing in the territory of India or any part thereof having a distinct language, script or culture of its own shall have the right to conserve the same.
2. No citizen shall be denied admission into any educational institution maintained by the State or receiving aid out of State funds on grounds only of religion, race, caste, language or any of them.

Article 30:

1. All minorities, whether based on religion or language, shall have the right to establish and administer educational institutions of their choice.

2. The State shall not, in granting aid to educational institutions, discriminate against any educational institution on the ground that it is under the management of a minority, whether based on religion or language.

Article 350A: It shall be the endeavour of every State and of every local authority within the State to provide adequate facilities for instruction in the mother-tongue at the primary stage of education to children belonging to linguistic minority groups; and the President may issue such directions to any State as he considers necessary or proper for securing the provision of such facilities.

Language and Education in India

The Indian education curriculum follows a three-language formula (adopted in 1957) in which all students with certain exceptions have to study three languages, namely the mother tongue/ home language or the regional language, Hindi and English. Students in the Hindi-speaking areas are required to study one other modern Indian language (National Council for Education Research and Training, 2005, p. 36). This formula assigned importance to the mother tongue for people belonging to linguistic minorities by enabling them to study their mother tongue optionally at the school level (Sengupta, 2009).

Although education in India normally takes place in local, regional or official languages, English is considered prestigious and a preferable medium of instruction as it is perceived to open the doors to higher education in India or abroad. There is an implicit hierarchy with English on the top and the minority languages at the bottom (Priyadarshini, 2012). Pinnock (2009) notes that whether or not a child is taught in their first language, or mother tongue, often has a strong effect on whether or not a child attends school, particularly in rural areas. The language used to deliver the school curriculum pulls down the educational performance of many of those who do not use it at home, particularly those who do not have regular access to it outside school. He notes that these problems can be addressed successfully by providing at least six years of mother tongue education, with gradual introduction of other languages from an early stage. In India, States like Assam and Nagaland who have significant tribal population have made attempts to use tribal languages in education. They have met with reasonable success, while other States, despite problems at the implementation stage, are making newer attempts (UNESCO, 2007, p. 5).

Activities

Activity 4.8: Reflections on My Language Identity

Learner Outcome: At the end of this activity, the participants will develop awareness of the significance of language as a source of identity and the need for respect of every language.

Procedure: Use the following procedure to conduct this activity:

1. If the participant group is cosmopolitan, ask each of them to greet everyone in their mother tongue.
2. Ask each participant to complete the following sentence:

   Because my language(s) is/ are _____, I am_____.

3. Ask them to share what they have written with their partners.

Questions for Discussion: Use the following questions to discuss this activity:

- What does your mother tongue mean to you?
- Do you speak your mother tongue at home?
- Are you studying in your mother tongue? If yes, what are the implications? If no, what are the implications?
- How does it affect your identity?
- How does it affect your behaviour?
- How is it different from other languages?
- How is it similar to other languages?
- Are you bilingual or multilingual? If yes, what is the significance of each language in your life?

Time Estimate: 30 min

Activity 4.9: Small Group Discussion on Cultural Diversity by Regions/ Languages

Learner Outcome: At the end of this activity, the participants will learn to appreciate the regional/ linguistic diversity in India.

Procedure: Use the following procedure to conduct this activity:

1. Ask the participants which languages are spoken in India. Write them down on the board.
2. Ask how much do they know about languages other than their own?
3. Show Summary Chart 4.8, and discuss Indian Population by Scheduled Languages.
4. Form three small groups, and divide the following topics among them for discussion:

   (a) Regional Diversity in Food,
   (b) Regional Diversity in Dresses,
   (c) Regional Diversity in Music and Dance.

5. Ask the small groups to make their presentations to the large group for further inputs.

Questions for Discussion: Use the following questions to discuss this activity:

- What do they enjoy about the linguistic/regional diversity?
- Imagine India without the linguistic/regional diversity?
- Do you know that many languages are getting extinct? What will be the implications of languages becoming extinct? What can be done to prevent their extinction?
- What are the official languages of India? Why?
- What are the official languages of the States?

Time Estimate: 30 min

Activity 4.10: Street Plays to Prevent Stereotypes About Indian States/ Languages

Learner Outcome: At the end of this activity, the participants will review their stereotypes about States/languages other than their own and discuss the solutions to promote interstate/linguistic understanding.

Procedure: Form four small groups, and allocate the following topics among them for discussion:

1. Stereotypes about North Indians by South Indians
2. Stereotypes about South Indians by North Indians
3. Stereotypes about North-Eastern Indians by Indians from Other Regions
4. Stereotypes about Kashmiris by Non-Kashmiri Indians.

Questions for Discussion: Use the following questions to discuss this activity:

1. What are the sources of our stereotypes about States/languages other than their own?
2. What are the implications of our stereotypes about States/languages other than their own?
3. What are children's responsibilities for understanding about States/languages other than their own and inclusion of people from different States?
4. Ask the small groups to prepare street plays for understanding about States/ languages other than their own and inclusion of people from different States and present to the large group for more inputs.

Time Estimate: 45 min

Activity 4.11: Small Group Discussion on Child's Linguistic Rights

Learner Outcome: At the end of this activity, the participants will learn to assess the extent to which the linguistic rights of children are met.

Procedure: Use the following procedure to conduct this activity:

1. Show Summary Chart 4.9, and discuss Child's Linguistic Rights
2. Identify three minority linguistic groups, and form three small groups to discuss the following language rights of children from these minority groups:

   - Can they freely identify themselves with their language?
   - Can they obtain information in their language?
   - Do they get opportunities for expression in their language?
   - Do they have the freedom to use any language?
   - Can they participate in language associations?
   - Can they obtain education in their language?
   - Are they discriminated against because of their language?
   - Is their language respected by others?
   - Can they practise language-based cultural values and practice?
   - Are there stereotypes about their language and culture?
   - How can the language rights of children from minority groups be protected?

3. Ask the small groups to share their discussion with the large group.

Time Estimate: 30 min

Activity 4.12: Celebration of Linguistic Pluralism

Learner Outcome: At the end of this activity, the participants will develop skills to create public awareness on linguistic pluralism.

Procedure: Following are some suggestions for different activities that could be organised to promote interlinguistic group harmony:

- Organise a talent show comprising of popular songs/ poetries in different languages.
- Organise food festivals to showcase cuisine of different regions.
- Screen an award-winning film in a different regional language with subtitles that you understand.
- Organise fashion shows where everyone wears dresses from another State.

Questions for Discussion: Use the following questions to discuss this activity:

- How did you feel carrying out this activity?
- What did you learn about regions other than your own?
- What did you like about regions other than your own?
- What was confusing about regions other than your own?

Time Estimate: Depends on the event organised.

Concluding Activity: Achievement of the Learner Objectives

Learner Outcome: By the end of the concluding activity, the participants will ascertain if they have achieved the learner objectives.

Procedure: Use the following procedure to conduct the concluding activity:

1. Show the PowerPoints/a chart on the learner objectives, ask the participants to read them one at a time, and ask the group if they think they have achieved the objective.
2. The participants may be asked to share their responses in their diary with reference to the following questions:

   - What was a new learning for you in this session?
   - What did you like the best in this session and why?
   - Which activity was most effective?
   - What was not clear/confusing?
   - How can you apply what you have learnt?

Time Estimate: 15 min

Appendix: Summary Charts

Summary Chart 4.1 Understanding culture and cultural diversity

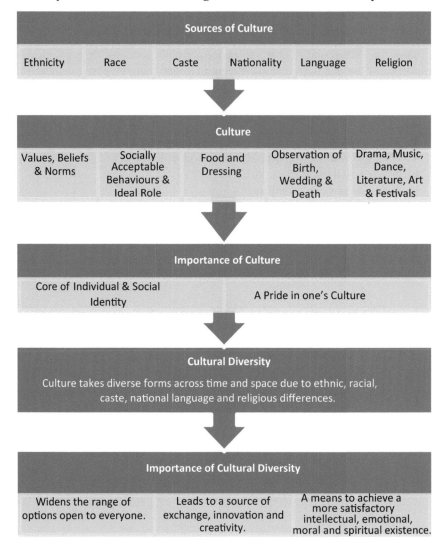

Summary Chart 4.2 Threats to cultural diversity

Prejudicing Ideologies	Colonisation	Post-Colonial Development
↓	↓	↓
Ethnocentrism, Eurocentrism, racism and casteism	Western culture dominates	Homogenisation
↓	↓	↓
Foster stereotypes about 'other' ethnicity, nationality, races and castes	People lose respect for their own cultures	Denial of cultural recognition
	↓	↓
	Denial of cultural recognition	Weakened sense of identity
↓	↓	↓
Culture-based conflicts	Isolation and powerlessness	Religious fundamentalism
	↓	
	Provides a breeding ground for politics of hate	

Summary Chart 4.3 Child's cultural rights

Cultural Right as Human Right: Cultural rights are an integral part of human rights, which are universal, indivisible and interdependent.
Access to Information: Children have right to information and material of social and cultural benefit to the child through the mass media and from a diversity of cultural, national and international sources.
Education: Children have right to education that is directed to the development of respect for the child's parents, his or her own cultural identity, language and values, for the national values of the country in which the child is living, the country from which he or she may originate, and for civilizations different from his or her own.
Cultural Identity: Children belonging to ethnic, religious or linguistic minorities or persons of indigenous origin have the right to enjoy his or her own culture, to profess and practise his or her own religion, or to use his or her own language.
Participation in Cultural Life: Children have right to participate fully in cultural life and to the provision of appropriate and equal opportunities for cultural activity of their choice and conduct their own cultural practices.

Summary Chart 4.4 Child's rights to intercultural inclusion

- To recognise and respect different cultural groups.
- To promote policies for the inclusion and participation of all citizens.
- To make a commitment to the cultural rights of persons belonging to minorities and those of indigenous peoples.
- To protect and promote the diversity of cultural expressions.
- To create the conditions for cultures to flourish and to freely interact in a mutually beneficial manner.
- To ensure harmonious interaction among people and groups with plural, varied and dynamic cultural identities.
- To encourage dialogue among cultures with a view to ensuring wider and balanced cultural exchanges in the world in favour of intercultural respect and a culture of peace.
- To foster interculturality in order to develop cultural interaction in the spirit of building bridges among peoples.
- To celebrate cultural diversity.
- To prevent cultural domination by a dominant group and homogenization.
- To promote social cohesion and peace.

Summary Chart 4.5 Religious diversity and secularism in India
(*Note:* The percentages to the total population are according to the 2001 Census)

Historical Period	Religions of Indian Origin	Religions in India Originated Outside India
Ancient Period	• Vedic religion/ Hinduism (79.80%) • Buddhisim (0.70%) • Jainism (0.37%)	• Judaism (Negligible)
Medieval Period	• Mysticism: Bhakti & Sufi Movements (Negligible) • Sikhism (1.72%)	• Christianity (2.30%) • Islam (14.23%) • Zoroastrianism (Negligible)
Post-Independence Period	**Secularism:** • The Preamble of the Indian Constitution states that it is a Secular State. • It means India has no official or established state religion. • It implies that in India, the state treats all religions equally.	

Summary Chart 4.6 Causes of religious conflicts

Ignorance and Prejudices

- Religious communalists assume that people belonging to one religion have similar interests and that these are opposed to the interests of people belonging to 'other' religion.
- Such ignorance about the 'other' provides a fertile ground for breeding sentiments of hatred and animosity. Ignorance also leads to stigmatisation and negative representation of the 'other' (most often the minorities) in the cultural history of the nation.

Religious Fundamentalism

- Religious fundamentalism has arisen as a reaction to secularisation and homogenisation because of a weakened sense of identity in the context of colonisation and post-colonialism.
- The consequence of this militant religious fundamentalism is a willingness to engage in extra-legal, anti-constitutional political action and sometimes violence and terrorism.

Summary Chart 4.7 Child right to freedom of religion

Freedom of religion or belief should be fully respected and guaranteed and ensures the right to freedom to have a religion or whatever belief of one's choice, and freedom, either individually or in community, with others and in public or private, to manifest one's religion or belief in worship, observance, practice and teaching.
According to the Indian Constitution, right to freedom of religion is a Fundamental Right. Under this fundamental right: • All persons are equally entitled to freedom of conscience and the right freely to profess, practise and propagate religion. • Every religious denomination shall have the right to: (a) Establish and maintain institutions for religious and charitable purposes. (b) Manage its own affairs in matters of religion. • No person shall be compelled to pay any taxes, the proceeds of which are specifically appropriated in payment of expenses for the promotion or maintenance of any particular religion or religious denomination. • Hindu religious institutions of a public character will be thrown open to all classes and sections of Hindus.
The Indian Constitution also states the following: (1) No religious instruction shall be provided in any educational institution wholly maintained out of State funds. (3) No person attending any educational institution recognised by the State or receiving aid out of State funds shall be required to take part in any religious instruction that may be imparted in such institution or to attend any religious worship that may be conducted in such institution or in any premises attached thereto unless such person or, if such person is a minor, his guardian has given his consent thereto.

Summary Chart 4.8 Linguistic diversity in India
(*Note:* The percentages to the total population are according to the 2001 Census)

The Indo-Aryan Family of Scheduled Languages	
Hindi (41.03%), Bengali (8.11%), Marathi (6.99%), Urdu (5.01%), Gujarati (4.48%), Oriya (4.21%), Punjabi (2.83%), Assamese (1.28%), Maithili (1.18%),	Santhali (0.63%), Kashmiri (0.54%), Nepali (0.28%), Sindhi (0.25%), Konkani (0.24%), Dogri (0.22%), Manipuri (0.14%), Bodo (0.13%) and Sanskrit (negligible).
The Dravidian Family of Scheduled Languages	
Telugu (7.19%), Tamil (5.91%), Kannada (4.69%) and Malayalam (4.21%).	

Summary Chart 4.9 Child's linguistic rights

The Indian Constitution provides the following linguistic rights.

Article 29:
1) Any section of the citizens residing in the territory of India or any part thereof having a distinct language, script or culture of its own shall have the right to conserve the same.
2) No citizen shall be denied admission into any educational institution maintained by the State or receiving aid out of State funds on grounds only of religion, race, caste, language or any of them.

Article 30:
(1) All minorities, whether based on religion or language, shall have the right to establish and administer educational institutions of their choice.
(2) The State shall not, in granting aid to educational institutions, discriminate against any educational institution on the ground that it is under the management of a minority, whether based on religion or language.

Article 350A: It shall be the endeavour of every State and of every local authority within the State to provide adequate facilities for instruction in the mother-tongue at the primary stage of education to children belonging to linguistic minority groups; and the President may issue such directions to any State as he considers necessary or proper for securing the provision of such facilities.

References

Abraham, C. E. (1993). The rise and growth of Christianity in India. In H. Bhattacharyya (Ed.), *The cultural heritage of India* (Vol. IV, pp. 547–570). Calcutta: The Ramakrishna Mission.

Agarwal, M. M. (1998). *Ethics and spirituality.* Shimla: Indian Institute of Advanced Study.

Ahmad, I. (1998). Pluralism on trial. In P. R. Ram (Ed.), *Secular challenge to communal politics* (pp. 283–286). Mumbai: Vikas Adhyayan Kendra.

Amin, S. (2008). *Eurocentrism.* Delhi: Aakar Books.

Arigatou Foundation, Interfaith Council on Ethics Education for Children, Global Network of Religions for Children, UNESCO, & UNICEF. (2008). *Learning to live together—An inter-cultural and interfaith programme for ethics education.* Geneva: Arigatou Foundation. Retrieved from http://unesdoc.unesco.org/images/0016/001610/161059e.pdf.

Bhargava, R. (1999). Introducing multiculturalism. In R. Bhargava, A. K. Bagchi, & R. Sudarshan (Eds.), *Multiculturalism, liberalism and democracy* (pp. 1–57). New Delhi: Oxford University Press.

Bose, A. (1964). Philosophy in popular literature. In H. Bhattacharya (Ed.), *The cultural heritage of India* (Vol. III, pp. 458–470). Calcutta: The Ramakrishna Mission.

Cohen, R., & Kennedy, P. (2007). *Global sociology* (2nd ed.). New York: Palgrave Macmillan.

Equitas—International Centre for Human Rights Education (2008). *Play it fair! Human rights education toolkit for children.* Canada: Author. Retrieved from http://www.equitas.org/what-we-do/children-and-youth/play-it-fair-canada/play-it-fair-toolkit/.

Ganguly, R. (2007). Democracy and ethnic conflict. In S. Ganguly, L. Diamond, & M. F. Plattner (Eds.), *The state of India's democracy* (pp. 45–66). USA: JHU Press.

Glossary of Terms. (1998). In P. R. Ram (Ed.), *Secular challenge to communal politics* (pp. 295–301). Mumbai: Vikas Adhyayan Kendra.

Graves, R. N. (1995). Atheism and Agnosticism. In *International encyclopedia of sociology* (pp. 101–104). London: Fitzroy Dearborn Publishers.

Griffin, S. (2008). *Inclusion, equality and diversity in working with children.* Malaysia: Pearson Education Limited.

Hensman, R. (2004). Redefining democracy as a positive alternative to communalism. *Fascism and democracy: The Indian experience* (pp. 75–91). Vikas Adhyayan Kendra: Mumbai.

Heywood, A. (2007). *Political ideologies: An introduction* (4th ed.). New York: Palgrave Macmillan.

History of Indian Languages. (2001). History of Indian languages. Retrieved from http://www.diehardindian.com/demogrph/moredemo/histlang.htm.

India (2015). Census 2011. Retrieved from http://www.census2011.co.in/religion.php.

India: Office of the Registrar General & Census Commissioner. (2011). *Abstract of speaker's strength of languages and mother languages–2001.* Retrieved from http://www.censusindia.gov.in/Census_Data_2001/Census_Data_Online/Language/Statement1.htm.

Law, I. (2009). *Racism and ethnicity: Global debates, dilemmas, directions.* New York: Routledge.

Leeder, E. J. (2003). *The family in global perspective: A gendered journey.* London: Sage.

Mahadevan, T. M. P. (1982). The religio-philosophic culture of India. In The Cultural (Ed.), *Heritage of India* (Vol. I, pp. 163–181). Calcutta: The Ramakrishna Mission Institute of Culture.

Mahajan, G. (2006). Negotiating cultural diversity and minority rights in India. In *Democracy, conflict and human security: Further readings* (pp. 111–122). Sweden: International Institute for Democracy and Electoral Assistance. Retrieved from http://www.idea.int/publications/dchs/upload/dchs_vol2_sec3_4.pdf.

Mallick, M. A. (2013). Multiculturalism, minority rights and democracy in India. *IOSR Journal of Humanities and Social Science, 16*(1), 72–82. Retrieved from www.Iosrjournals.org.

Marshall, G. (Ed.) (1994). *The concise Oxford dictionary of sociology.* New York: OxfordUniversity Press.

McCasland, S. V., Cairns, G. E., & Yu, D. C. (1969). *Religions of the world*. New York: Random House.

National Council for Education Research and Training. (2005). *The national curriculum framework 2005*. Retrieved from http://www.ncert.nic.in/rightside/links/pdf/framework/english/nf2005.pdf.

Nehru, J. (1945). *The discovery of India*. Calcutta: Oxford University Press.

Pieterse, J. N. (2010). *Development theory* (2nd ed.). Los Angeles: Sage.

Pinnock, H. (2009). *Language and education: the missing link. How the language used in schools threatens the achievement of education for all*. London: International Save the Children Alliance & Berkshire: CFBT Education Trust. Retrieved from http://www.unesco.org/education/EFAWG2009/LanguageEducation.pdf.

Priyadarshini, M. (2012). Anglicisation of Hindi. *Economic and Political Weekly, 47*(12), 19–21. Retrieved from http://www.eklavya.in/pdfs/Sandarbh/Sandarbh_83/Anglicisation_Of_Hindi_The_Official_Perspective.pdf.

Punyani, R. (2000). *The other cheek: Minorities under threat*. Delhi: Media House.

Punyani, R. (2012). Communalism and collective violence. In S. Singh (Ed.), *Encyclopaedia of social work in India* (3rd ed., pp. 112–119). Lucknow: New Royal Book Company.

Sanghvi, S. (1982). Some fundamental principles of Jainism. *The cultural heritage of India* (Vol. I, pp. 434–441). Calcutta: The Ramakrishna Mission Institute of Culture.

Sengupta, P. (2009). Linguistic diversity and economic disparity: An issue for multiculturalism in India, *The International Journal of Diversity in Organisations, Communities and Nations, 9*(1), 147–164. Retrieved from https://www.academia.edu/449921/Linguistic_Diversity_and_Economic_DisparityAnIssue_for_Multiculturalism_in_India.

Smith, H. (1958). *The religions of man*. New York: Harper & Row.

Srivastava, H. S. (2004). Indian Core values of peace and harmony. In Z. Nan-Zhao & B. Teasdale (Eds.), *Teaching Asia-Pacific core values of peace and harmony. A sourcebook for teachers* (pp. 229–243). Thailand: UNESCO Asia and Pacific Regional Bureau for Education. Retrieved from http://www.unicef.org/violencestudy/pdf/Teaching%20Asia-Pacific%20core%20values.pdf.

Taraporewala, I. J. S. (1993). Zoroastrianism. In H. Bhattacharyya (Ed.), *The cultural heritage of India* (Vol. IV, pp. 533–546). Calcutta: The Ramakrishna Mission.

Thapar, R. (1998). Communalism and the historical legacy: Some facets. In P. R. Ram (Ed.), *Secular challenge to communal politics a reader* (pp. 6–24). Mumbai: Vikas Adhyayan Kendra.

United Nations. (1989). Convention on the rights of the child. Retrieved from http://www.ohchr.org/english/law/pdf/crc.pdf.

United Nations. (2005). Convention on the protection and promotion of the diversity of cultural expressions. Retrieved from http://unesdoc.unesco.org/images/0022/002253/225383E.pdf.

United Nations. (2009). *State of the world's indigenous peoples*. New York: Author. Retrieved from http://www.un.org/esa/socdev/unpfii/documents/SOWIP_web.pdf.

United Nations Educational, Scientific and Cultural Organisation. (2006). *UNESCO guidelines on intercultural education*. Paris: Author. Retrieved from http://unesdoc.unesco.org/images/0014/001478/147878e.pdf.

United Nations Educational, Scientific and Cultural Organisation. (2007). *Advocacy kit for promoting multilingual education: Including the excluded*. Thailand: Author. Retrieved from http://unesdoc.unesco.org/images/0015/001521/152198e.pdf.

United Nations Educational, Scientific and Cultural Organisation. (n.d.). *Endangered languages (FAQs)*. Retrieved from http://www.unesco.org/new/en/culture/themes/endangered-languages/faq-on-endangered-languages/.

Vanina, E. (1996). *Ideas and society in India from the sixteenth to the eighteenth centuries*. Delhi: Oxford University Press.

Vas, G. (1997). *The story of India for children*. Noida: Blossom Books.

Zaehner, R. C. (1959). Introduction. In R. C. Zaehner (Ed.) *The concise encyclopaedia of living faiths* (pp. 15–22). Boston: Beacon Press.
Zaehner, R. C. (1994). *Hindu and Muslim mysticism*. Oxford: One World Publications.
Zwi Werblowsky, R. J. (1959). Judaism, or the religion of Israel. In R. C. Zaehner (Ed.), *The concise encyclopaedia of living faiths* (pp. 23–50). Boston: Beacon Press.

Relevant Child Rights and You Reports and Articles

Parveen, I. (2010). Exclusion of Muslim Girls from Schools: A participatory analysis in the district of Rampur, CRY National Child Rights Fellowship. Retrieve from https://www.cry.org/resources/pdf/NCRRF/NCRRF_ReportBy_Iram_Praveen.pdf.

Module 5
Child Rights to Financial Education and Inclusion

Prerequisite Modules

The prerequisite Modules for this Module are:
From *Sourcebook I on Introduction to Rights-Based Direct Practice with Children*:

- Modules on Life Skills Development

From *Sourcebook II on Child Rights Education for Participation and Development: Primary Prevention*:

- Introduction to Child Rights Education
- Child Rights to Participation and Children's Associations

From *Sourcebook III on Child Rights Education for Inclusion and Protection: Primary Prevention*:

- Rights of Girls and Children with Disability to Non-discrimination and Inclusion
- Rights of Dalit and Tribal Children to Non-discrimination and Inclusion
- Children's Cultural Rights and Rights to Intercultural Inclusion

Conceptual Framework of Child's Rights to Financial Education

Concepts and Theories

Socio-economic Status

According to the American Psychological Association (APA, 2016), "Socioeconomic status (SES) is often measured as a combination of education, income and occupation. It is commonly conceptualized as the social standing or class of an individual or group. When viewed through a social class lens, privilege, power and control are emphasized. Furthermore, an examination of SES as a gradient or continuous variable reveals inequities in access to and distribution of

© Child Rights and You 2018
M. Desai and S. Goel, *Child Rights Education for Inclusion and Protection: Primary Prevention*, Rights-based Direct Practice with Children, https://doi.org/10.1007/978-981-13-0417-0_5

resources". Socio-economic status is typically broken into three categories (high SES, middle SES and low SES) to describe the three areas a family or an individual may fall into. When placing a family or individual into one of these categories, any or all of the three variables (income, education and occupation) can be assessed.

The structural reproduction of power and privilege is the foundation of social class-based conceptualisations of inequality. From this perspective, social class inequality is treated as a form of social and political dominance that allows some groups (e.g. political elites, corporate owners) to prosper at the expense of others (e.g. workers). Viewed through this lens, inequality is not only conceptualised in terms of differential access to resources but also as the structural recreation of privilege and the fusion of wealth and power, particularly in capitalist societies (APA Task Force, 2006). Social class and classism are coconstructed variables similar to race and racism—that is, race is not meaningful without racism, and social class and classism must operate together, along with SES, to create conditions of inequality, marginalisation and oppression (Liu & Ali, 2005, cited by APA Task Force, 2006).

Social Exclusion and Poverty

Nolan and Whelan (1996, cited in Lister, 2004) defined poverty in terms of the inability to participate in society owing to lack of financial resources, implying low income and low standard of living. According to the Programme of Action of the United Nations World Summit for Social Development (1995), women bear a disproportionate burden of poverty, and children growing up in poverty are often permanently disadvantaged. Older people, people with disabilities, indigenous people, refugees and internally displaced persons are also particularly vulnerable to poverty. Socially excluded people are often denied the opportunities available to others to increase their income and escape from poverty by their own efforts. So, although the economy may grow and general income levels may rise, excluded people are likely to be left behind and make up an increasing proportion of those who remain in poverty. Poverty reduction policies often fail to reach them unless they are specifically designed to do so. According to Todaro and Smith (2009), perhaps the most valid generalisations about the poor are that they are disproportionately located in rural areas, that they are primarily engaged in agricultural and associated activities and that they are often concentrated among minority ethnic groups and indigenous peoples.

Child Poverty

Children are the hardest hit by poverty. Deprivation causes lifelong damage to the mind and body of infants and small children. Child development, especially in the first years of life, is a succession of biological developments for which there is seldom a second chance. Since poor families tend to be larger than non-poor ones, children are also disproportionately represented among the poor. No age group suffers more from human poverty than children (Vandemoortele, 2012). Not only are children more likely to live in poverty and suffer most from poverty than adults, children are also the main link for transmitting poverty to the next generation (Mehrotra & Jolly, 1997, cited in Vandemoortele, 2012). According to Anti-Slavery (2007), most children of poor families work as their labour is necessary for their survival. Many working children do not have the opportunity to go to school and often grow up to be unskilled adults trapped in poorly paid jobs and in turn will look to their own children to supplement the family's income. In this vicious circle, malnourished girls grow up to become malnourished mothers who give birth to underweight babies. Impoverished children become—as parents—transmitters of poverty to the next generation (Vandemoortele, 2012). Financial education is needed for children to understand poverty and wealth in order to break the cycle of poverty.

Economic Dependency of Children

The social construction of adolescence took place when the need for advanced education produced a greater economic dependence on parents between puberty and the time when an individual achieved economic and social independence. Education introduced two important factors: delay in achieving economic self-sufficiency and social experiences separated from adult life (Lesser & Pope, 2007). The implications according to experts are:

- With the increased emphasis on education, the period of social and economic dependency of children on adults became increasingly prolonged (James & James, 2012).
- According to Wyness (2012), childhood is now seen as a period when the real world of sexual, economic and public action is suspended. Children who assume a different position within the generational hierarchy are considered a social and moral threat.
- The prolonged emotional, psychological and economic dependency led to a century-long enduring mythology of adolescence, depicted as a period of "storm and stress" subject to hormonally induced mood swings (Ruddick, 2003).

As a result of the social construction of economic dependency of children, according to most economic models, children have been perceived both as a cost to society and the passive receptacles of benefits and knowledge imparted by adults. In other words, children's integration into society is portrayed, in effect, as a one-way process in which adults give and children receive (Boyden & Levison, 2000). Children's economic rights are generally restricted. Children are unable to sign valid contracts, open bank accounts, borrow money or conduct other financial transactions. They are constrained in their ownership and control over property, and in their right to work and employment (Inter-Agency Working Group on Children's Participation, 2008).

Child's Economic Citizenship

Need for Child's Economic Rights: In order to break the cycle of poverty, Plan (2012) aims to promote the capacities of children and young people to claim and realise their economic rights, the responsibility of households to provide for their development and the responsibility of governments to create the conditions favourable to social and economic environment. Plan recommends that:

- Children, young people and households should have opportunities to accumulate savings.
- Children and youth should develop economic- and employment-related skills and competencies according to their individual development needs and stages in the life cycle.
- Young people should have access to vocational training based on labour market demand and receive support for the transition into work.

The vision of Child and Youth Finance International (CYFI, 2012a) is that all children and youth realise their full potential as economic citizens. For the CYFI, child's economic citizenship or financial engagement is essential to the social and economic well-being of children, families, communities and countries. Three key components of child's economic citizenship they identified are financial capability, financial inclusion and financial education.

Financial Capability: According to the UK Government, financial capability is a broad concept, encompassing people's knowledge and skills to understand their own financial circumstances, along with the motivation to take action. Financially capable consumers plan ahead, find and use information, know when to seek advice and can understand and act on this advice, leading to greater participation in the financial services market (cited by CYFI, 2012a). On the other hand, the CYFI (2012a) perceives financial capability as a combination of a person's ability to act with the assurance of access to the structural opportunity to act. It suggests that children and youth should learn about financial management and the financial world at the same time as they are provided beneficial tools to participate. Thus, financial capability may be dependent on both financial inclusion and financial education.

Financial Inclusion: Financial inclusion means access to basic financial services for children and youth and conveys the provision of quality services that are affordable and convenient. Truly inclusive financial services are delivered in a way that promotes a sense of dignity without regard to age or social and economic status in the larger community, while providing children and youth a secure place to keep money and accumulate assets (CYFI, 2012a). This includes, at a minimum, savings, credit, insurance and payments. Financial inclusion aims to facilitate economic transactions, manage day-to-day resources, improve quality of life, protect against vulnerability, make productivity-enhancing investments, leverage assets and build economic citizenship. For children and youth, basic financial services include, at a minimum, a safe place to keep their money and accumulate savings. Moreover, some groups of children may need access to credit, fixed deposits, insurance, remittances and transfers at various points in their development. For example, children of international migrants may benefit from remittance accounts, especially if their parents or other relatives are abroad. Financial inclusion also includes financial protections to ensure the right to participation and to keep money safe (Sherraden, 2012).

Financial Education: Financial education means the provision of educational instruction and/or materials designed to increase the financial knowledge and skills of children and youth (CYFI, 2012a). Tailoring financial education programming to children and youth becomes an important component in the transition from childhood to adulthood and the development of the next generation of financially responsible, economic citizens (CYFI, 2012b). According to UNICEF (2012), financial education gives children a better understanding of financial matters by teaching them the principles of money management, income generation, saving and spending, investments and credit. This education is often combined with the opportunity to participate in savings schemes, either through an individual savings or checking account or through a group-based savings club. Through financial education, children and youth are exposed to various types of financial systems and learn how to interact effectively with them and various financial service delivery channels, such as online and mobile phone banking.

According to Despard and Hira (2012), three overall trends characterise current global youth financial education efforts:

1. Financial education linked with financial services such as access to child development accounts,
2. A wide variety of interactive delivery mechanisms/media and have opportunities to practise what they have learned,
3. Integration with youth development strategies such as livelihoods, microenterprise, life skills, gender empowerment.

Activities

Introductory Activity 5.1: History of Money

Learner Outcome: At the end of this activity, the participants will develop awareness about the logistics of production of money in India.

Procedure: Use the following procedure to conduct this activity:

1. Show the video film on Learn the History and Measure of Money
   https://www.youtube.com/watch?v=4N79yxPJsJY
2. Ask the following questions to discuss this video:

   a. What were the earlier systems for transactions?
   b. What were their limitations?

3. Plan a visit to a mint or a money museum or conduct a discussion on production of money in India by asking the following questions and examining the Indian coins and currency notes:

   (1) How many of you handle money? When? How is that experience?
   (2) Where are the currency notes and coins produced in India?
   (3) When was the first mint established in India? By whom? Where?
   (4) Who owns the mints in India?
   (5) How many mints are there in India? Where?
   (6) What does a mint do and why?
   (7) What all is printed on the coins?
   (8) What are mint marks? Where are they located? What do they indicate?
   (9) Where are the currency notes printed in India?
  (10) What all is printed on the currency notes?
  (11) The amount is written in how many languages?
  (12) What are the security features on the currency notes? Why are they needed?
  (13) What is the current exchange rate of an Indian rupee with US dollars?
  (14) What is the role of the Reserve Bank of India?

4. Display currency and coins from different countries if possible.

Time Estimate: 2 h for a visit to a mint/30–45 min for discussion

Activity 5.2: Video Discussion on Wealth and Poverty in India

Learner Outcome: At the end of this activity, the participants will develop awareness of the role of citizens versus the State to prevent corruption.

Procedure: Use the following procedure to conduct this activity:

1. Show select parts of the following video film:
   Satyamev Jayate (2014): Episode 4: Kings Everyday
   http://www.satyamevjayate.in/kings-every-day.aspx
   Use the following questions to discuss this video:

   - How wealthy each Indian is with reference to India's total natural wealth?
   - Why is India considered a poor country although it is wealthy?
   - Do children also pay tax? How?
   - Is our government our master or servant?
   - How can we prevent our politicians from being corrupt?
   - What are a citizen's responsibilities for good governance in a democracy?
   - Can we demand accountability from our governments?

2. Discuss causes of poverty with reference to social exclusion of women, Dalits, tribals, persons with disability, older persons and rural people and environmental degradation.

Time Estimate: Show select parts for 30 min followed by discussion for 30 min

Activity 5.3: Brainstorming on Children's Need for Financial Education

Learner Outcome: At the end of this activity, the participants will develop awareness about need for financial education for children.

Procedure: Use the following procedure to conduct this activity:

1. Ask the participants the following questions:

   - What is socio-economic class?
   - Why are some people very rich, some rich and some poor?
   - What do the rich think of the poor?
   - What do the poor think of the rich?
   - What is the significance of money in our lives?
   - Should only adults understand money? Can children also learn about money? Why?
   - Why do children need to get financial education?
   - What should financial education for children comprise?

2. Introduce the following units of the module:

   a. Banking and asset building,
   b. Financial budgeting,
   c. Consumer education.

Time Estimate: 15 min

Banking and Asset Building

Concepts and Theories

Banking

Bank is an institution where people park their surplus money and earn some return called interest. On the other hand, people who need money can borrow from bank for a cost (again interest). Therefore, bank is an institution involved in the business of borrowing and lending money. It charges higher rates of interest while lending and pays lesser interest to depositors. The difference between lending and borrowing rate is called its net interest margin (NIM). For any country, banks play a vital role for the financial needs of individuals and companies, enabling smooth economic activity (Securities and Exchange Board of India (SEBI), 2010).

Types of bank accounts are:

Savings Account: It is useful for depositing your surplus money and withdrawing money needed for expenses. One usually needs to maintain a minimum balance to keep one's bank account active. Banks pay the lowest interest rate on the money kept in this account.

Current Account: This account is basically for business transactions. Banks do not pay any interest on the money kept in this account.

Deposit Account or Fixed Deposit Amount: In this account, money is deposited for a fixed and predetermined term. Interest rate on this account is higher than in the savings account (SEBI, 2010).

Child- and Youth-Friendly Banking Principles

The CYFI has established and distributed a "Child-Friendly Product Prototype" that lists minimum institutional and product requirements. The minimum institutional requirements are:

- The financial institution is licensed under appropriate national laws and regulations. The institution is in good standing with its national regulatory authority.
- The institution is covered by a deposit guarantee scheme, if applicable, in the country.
- The institution has a code of conduct with respect to children including staff training and development programmes on how to interact with children (Sherraden, 2012).

According to the CYFI (2014), the following child- and youth-friendly banking product principles facilitate an international benchmark for safe and reliable banking products for children and youth as well as build awareness among financial institutions of how to contribute to the empowerment and protection of children and youth:

1. **Availability and Accessibility for Children and Youth**: They are widely available and accessible to children and youth despite their economic, social, cultural, or religious situation, gender, age, or ability.
2. **Maximum Control to Children and Youth**: They provide the maximum possible control to children and youth within the boundaries of local jurisdiction and ensure financial ownership.
3. **Positive Financial Incentive for Children and Youth**: To build confidence as children and youth enter the financial system, positive financial incentives (e.g. no overdraft and relatively higher interest rates) are important.
4. **Reaching Unbanked Children and Youth**: The financial institution will proactively reach out to unbanked children and youth in vulnerable communities as part of a larger financial inclusion agenda, within the boundaries of local jurisdiction.
5. **Employing Child- and Youth-Friendly Communication Strategies**: The communication and marketing materials around the product will be child- and

youth-centred, connecting to their needs, interests and level of comprehension. This will be complemented by the ability of all staff within a financial institution to interact in a child- and youth-friendly manner.

6. **A Component of Economic Citizenship Education**: In combination with the product, children and youth are offered a component of economic citizenship education, with elements of financial, life skills and livelihood education.

7. **Monitoring of Child and Youth Satisfaction**: The financial institution monitors the extent to which the product and relating services satisfy the needs and interests of children and youth.

8. **Internal Control**: The financial institution has internal controls in place on all these principles.

Policy for Asset Building

Concept of Asset Building: The asset-building policy approach was developed in the USA in 1991 by Sherraden (1991). It is based on two very simple premises: first that the poor can save and accumulate assets, and second, that assets have positive social, psychological and civic effects independent of the effects of income. He distinguished between assets (identified as the stock of wealth in a household) and income (the flows of resources associated with consumption of goods and series and standard of living). According to him, welfare policy for the poor has been constructed almost exclusively in terms of income and proposed that it needs to be based on the concepts of savings, investment and asset accumulation.

Children's Asset-Building Accounts: Whether known as children's savings accounts (CSAs), SEED accounts, or children's development accounts (CDAs), long-term asset-building accounts are established for children at birth and allowed to grow over their lifetime. Accounts are typically seeded with an initial deposit and built by contributions from family, friends and the children themselves. In addition, accounts are augmented by savings matches and other incentives. Accounts gain meaning as young accountholders and their families engage in age-appropriate financial education (Howard, Humphrey, Rist, Rosen & Tivol, 2010).

According to Beverly, Elliott and Sherraden (2013), the goal of CDAs is to promote saving and asset building for lifelong development. Thus, CDA assets may be used for post-secondary education for youth and homeownership and enterprise development in adulthood. In many cases, public and private entities deposit funds into these accounts to supplement savings for the child. Existing CDA programmes differ in design and features. According to Cramer and Newville (2009, cited in Beverly et al., 2013), the desirable characteristics of CDAs may include the following:

- **Opened Early in a Child's Life**: CDAs may be opened as early as birth. Opening accounts early allows savings to accumulate for a long period of time. Over time, small but regular deposits can result in significant savings amounts, which help make asset accumulation a realistic goal for low- and moderate-income families.

- **Supported by Public Policy**: The government should support asset accumulation and saving in CDAs, particularly for low- and moderate-income households. In this regard, CDAs may be seeded with an initial deposit, and deposits made by children and their parents may be matched up to a certain annual or lifetime limit.
- **Universal**: Ideally, CDAs are universal—available to everyone—in the same way that public education is universal. Universality ensures that all children are included and may benefit. CDAs are universal when accounts are opened automatically for all.
- **Progressive**: Because saving is difficult for low-income households, accounts for lower-income children may be supplemented with additional financial assistance. This assistance may take the form of larger initial deposits, higher matches, additional deposits at milestones (e.g. entering first grade or graduating from high school), and other incentives and subsidies.
- **Restricted**: With few exceptions, savings accumulated in CDAs can be used only for approved purposes. These commonly include post-secondary education (e.g. college or vocational school), down payment on a first home, seed capital to start a small business and retirement.

The UK experience (Blond & Gruescu, 2010) adds that:

- **Managing the Account**: From birth until the age of 12, the account can be managed by the child's parent or legal guardian. From the age of 13 to 17, the child can, if he/she wishes, manage the account and invest his/her savings.
- **Tax Status**: Withdrawal from this account can be tax-exempt.

Asset-Building Schemes in India: In order to improve the survival and welfare of girls and reverse the distorted sex ratio at birth (SRB), the Government of India has launched conditional cash transfers or asset-building schemes for girls. These schemes are administered through the Department of Women and Child Development using the vast network of ICDS and Anganwadi workers.

Dhanalakshmi Scheme: A conditional cash transfer scheme for the girl child with insurance cover called Dhanalakshmi was launched in 2008 by the Ministry of Women and Child Development (MWCD), Government of India, through the State governments in eleven selected backward blocks of seven States. The scheme provides for cash transfers to the family of the girl child (preferably to the mother) on fulfilling certain specific conditions:

- All girls born after 19 November 2008 can get Rs. 5000 after registration of birth.
- Rs. 200 on each immunisation.
- Rs. 1000 on enrolment in primary school and Rs. 500 for each year of retention in school till standard five.
- Rs. 1500 on enrolment in secondary school and Rs. 750 for each year of retention in school till standard eight.

- Each condition like registration of birth, immunisation, school enrolment and retention, insurance (maturity) cover are independent of each other and cannot be applied for retrospective fulfilment of conditionality. For example, if a girl is in Standard 2, she will be eligible for cash transfer from Standard 2 onwards and will not be eligible for cash transfers related to her birth and registration of birth, immunisation, enrolment and retention in Standard 1.
- An insurance maturity cover is taken for the girl child. If the girl child remains unmarried till the age of 18 years, she gets Rs. one lakh.
- The scheme applies to all girl children irrespective of their socio-economic status and the number of girl children in the family.
- The scheme applies only to those girls who have domicile status in the selected blocks.

The responsibilities for implementation of this scheme are allocated as follows:

- On enrolment and retention in school, the MWCD provides cash transfer till Standard 8.
- The Ministry of Human Resources Development provides incentives from Standard 9 to Standard 12.
- The Department of Women and Child Development of the State governments is responsible for implementing the scheme and related cash transfers.
- The Life Insurance Corporation of India (LIC) is responsible for the insurance and maturity components.

Sukanya Samriddhi Account: The Sukanya Samriddhi Account (literally *Girl Child Prosperity Account*) is an asset-building scheme backed by the Government of India targeted at the parents of girl children. The scheme was launched in 2015 as a part of the Beti Bachao Beti Padhao campaign. The scheme encourages parents to build a fund for the future education and marriage expenses for their female child. The account can be opened at any Indian post office or a branch of some authorised commercial banks. The account may be opened by the natural or legal guardian in the name of a girl child from the birth of the girl child till she attains the age of ten years, and any girl child, who had attained the age of ten years, one year prior to the commencement of these rules, shall also be eligible for opening of the account under these rules.

A minimum of ₹1,000 must be deposited in the account annually. The maximum deposit limit is ₹150,000. The scheme currently provides an interest rate of 8.6% (for FY2016–17) and tax benefits. The account shall be opened and operated by the natural or legal guardian of a girl child till the girl child in whose name the account has been opened attains the age of ten years. On attaining age of ten years, the account holder that is the girl child may herself operate the account; however, deposit in the account may be made by the guardian or any other person or authority. The account allows 50% withdrawal at the age of 18 for higher education or marriage purposes. The account reaches maturity at the age of 21. If the account is not closed, then it will continue to earn interest at the prevailing rate. If the girl is over 18 and married, normal closure is allowed.

Review: The United Nations Population Fund (UNFPA)—India (n.d.) carried out a study of these schemes the findings of which point to the need to simplify the eligibility criteria and conditionalities, and also the procedures of registration under each of these schemes. Though year after year substantial financial resources have been directed towards promoting these schemes, there is a lack of field-level monitoring. In the absence of a proper grievance redressal mechanism, the challenges often multiply. In some States, the lack of coordination across different sectors such as health, education and social welfare is adversely affecting the programme implementation. The implementing officers experience the following difficulties:

- They are not receiving the required support from other agencies, resulting in delays and difficulties.
- In some States, the lack of coordination between implementing departments and financial institutions (LIC, UTI, Banks, etc.) also leads to delays in issuing bonds/certificates and opening zero-balance accounts.
- In most of these schemes, the involvement of local PRIs (Panchayati Raj Institutions), NGOs and women's groups is rather limited.
- Some NGO representatives are of the opinion that PRIs may be in a better position to identify the beneficiaries, monitor the progress of implementation and ensure timely transfer of funds.
- Some of the State officials highlighted the fact that in many cases, the guidelines for implementation are not clearly understood and the staff is not oriented towards different aspects of the schemes.

Once these schemes are streamlined, they need to be made universal and extended to boys as well.

Activities

Activity 5.4: History and Functioning of Banks

Learner Outcome: At the end of this activity, the participants will develop awareness of the history and functioning of banks.

Procedure: Use the following procedure to conduct this activity:

1. Show the video film on History of Banking—Bank Bazaar
   https://www.youtube.com/watch?v=4CJsCUwg2Ac

2. Use the following questions to discuss this video:

- Where and when was the first bank initiated?
- Why was there a need for banks?
- What is the history of the word "bank"?

3. Plan a visit of the participants to a bank to learn the following:

- What are the bank's main functions?
- What types of accounts can you open with the banks and for what purpose?
- What interest can you get?
- What does the bank do with this money?
- How does it multiply this money?
- Do your parents have bank accounts? If not, how do they save?
- Do children have bank accounts? Who operates them?
- When can you take a loan from the bank? What should we be cautious about when taking loans?
- What is meant by writing a bank cheque? What is it used for? Have you written one?
- What are safe deposit vaults? Do your parents use safe deposit vaults in the bank? If not, how do they save/take loans?
- What are credit cards? What should we be cautious about when using credit cards?
- What are debit cards? What should we be cautious about when using debit cards?

Time Estimate: 2 h

Activity 5.5: Small Group Discussion on Types of Savings

Learner Outcome: At the end of this activity, the participants will learn the importance of saving and types of saving.

Procedure: Use the following procedure to conduct this activity:

1. Show Summary Chart 5.1 and discuss the basic models of savings systems for children.
2. Form four small groups and allocate the following types of saving systems among them:

   (1) Piggy bank (Saving at Home),
   (2) Children's account in a formal bank,
   (3) School-based savings,
   (4) Children's bank.

3. The small groups should discuss the advantages and disadvantages of each type according to the criteria of safety, ownership and control, liquidity and growth.
4. The small groups may present their discussion to the large group for further inputs.

Time Estimate: 30 min

Activity 5.6: Importance of Children's Accounts for Asset Building

Learner Outcome: At the end of this activity, the participants will develop awareness of the importance of children's accounts for asset building.

Procedure: Use the following procedure to conduct this activity:

1. Ask the participants following questions:

   a. What is an asset?
   b. What are the advantages of having assets?
   c. How can we build assets?
   d. Does your State have an asset-building scheme?
   e. Are you benefiting from it?

2. Form small groups and allocate the Dhanalakshmi scheme and other State-sponsored asset-building schemes for the girl child that they may know of with reference to the following desirable characteristics discussed in this chapter:

   a. Opened early in a child's life,
   b. Supported by public policy,
   c. Universal,
   d. Progressive,
   e. Restricted,
   f. Who manages the account,
   g. Tax exemption.

3. Ask the small groups to present their reviews to the large group for further inputs.

Questions for Discussion: Use the following questions to discuss this activity:

- What is a good asset-building scheme that the government should start?
- Can it be made universal to all the girls without any criteria?
- Can it be extended to boys as well?
- In the absence of a government scheme, can parents open children's accounts and build their assets?

Time Estimate: 30 min

Financial Budgeting

Concepts and Theories

Planning

Proactive planning is a key element of preparing for the future. It includes discussion on financial and non-financial planning in life and discussion of possible unexpected emergencies, in relation to anticipated sources of income and expenses. Comparison of financial planning and non-financial planning, such as planning to prepare for a test, helps students learn by analogy (Amin, Rahman, Ainul, Rob, Zaman, & Akter, 2010). Children's income could be from scholarships, parental remittance, pocket money and cash gifts. They need to plan its use and savings by way of budgeting.

Budgeting

According to the SEBI (2010), budget is a plan for balancing of income and expenditures or a projection of one's income and expenditure. SEBI notes that knowledge of budgeting is an advantage for children as it helps them to develop an economic way of thinking and problem-solving. According to SEBI, budgeting helps to:

- Optimise savings,
- Control spending,
- Save accurately for a particular short-/long-term goal,
- Effectively allot funds to various areas of expenditure in advance.

Budget is a part of planning, and budget helps to redefine one's plan when necessary. A budget helps children to make decisions about how much money they can spend and allows them to take control of their money and serves as a guide to help them to live within the income. If their earnings do not cover their expenses, their budget will make it easier for them to identify which expenses to cut back when all are listed together (Amin et al., 2010).

SEBI (2010) defines the following terms used in budgeting:

Cash Flow Statement: A record of your income and expenses.

Budget Surplus or Deficit: Projected income > Projected Expenditure = Budget Surplus
Projected income < Projected Expenditure = Budget Deficit

Postponing Satisfaction: Let go something now for something better/bigger in the future, for example, giving up the idea to buy a video game now to purchase a bicycle in the future.

Instant Satisfaction: Instantly buy something when you want it. For example, purchase a video game instantly when you want it.

Opportunity Cost: At a point of time, when you give up something to achieve something else, the forgone opportunity is known as "Opportunity Cost". For example, you have an option to either buy a video game or a bicycle and you opt for the bicycle; then, the video game is the opportunity cost for purchasing the bicycle.

Activities

Activity 5.7: Exercise on Assessment of Income and Expenses

Learner Outcome: At the end of this activity, the participants will develop awareness on their self/family patterns of income and expenses.

Procedure: Use the following procedure to conduct this activity:

1. Ask the children if they get scholarships, parental remittance, pocket money and/or cash gifts. If they do, ask them to fill the Exercise on Assessment of Income and Expenses given at the end of the chapter.
2. If children do not have any regular individual income, ask them to assess their family income and expenses in the Exercise on Assessment of Income and Expenses, in consultation with their parents.
3. If the participants are parents, ask them to assess their family income and expenses in the Exercise on Assessment of Income and Expenses.
4. Ask them to share their assessment with their partner.

Questions for Discussion: Use the following questions to discuss this activity:

- Are you happy with your income? Why?
- Are you happy with your expenses? Why?
- Are you being able to save? Where and how?
- Do you feel the need for a household budget?

Time Estimate: 30 min

Activity 5.8: Video Discussion on Budgeting

Learner Outcome: At the end of this activity, the participants will get an exposure to budgeting.

Procedure: Use the following procedure to conduct this activity:

1. Ask the participants what they mean by budgeting and why it is important.
2. Show the following video film:
   CashVille Kidz Episode 23: SMART Budgeting
   https://www.youtube.com/watch?v=58EuubFG9-c

Questions for Discussion: Use the following questions to discuss this film:

- What is a budget?
- What is a SMART budget?
- How does budgeting help?

Time Estimate: 15 min

Activity 5.9: Small Group Discussion on Skills of Budgeting

Learner Outcome: At the end of this activity, the participants will learn the skills of SMART budgeting.

Procedure: Use the following procedure to conduct this activity:

1. Form four small groups and allocate the following topics among them for discussion and budgeting:

   (1) Budgeting of scholarship money,
   (2) Budgeting of pocket money/parental remittance,
   (3) Budgeting of cash gifts that children receive,
   (4) Budgeting for an event in their school/association.

2. The discussion and budgeting may cover the following questions:

   (1) Sources of the money,
   (2) Amount of the money,
   (3) Priority of needs,
   (4) Planning a SMART budget.

2. Ask the small groups to present their discussion and budget to the large group for further inputs.

Questions for Discussion: Use the following questions to conduct discussion:

- How does budgeting help?
- What else did you learn from this activity?

Time Estimate: 45 min

Consumer Education

Concepts and Theories

Consumer

The Consumer Protection Act (CPA) (1986) of India defines a consumer as any person who buys any good or hires or avails any services for a consideration that has been paid or promised or partly paid or partly promised. Goods may include consumable goods (like wheat flour, salt, sugar, fruits) or durable consumer goods (like TV, refrigerator, toaster, mixer, bicycle). Services that one buys may include electric power, telephone, transport service, theatre service.

Consumerism

British economist Paul Elkins (1991) (cited in The WorldWatch Institute, 2010) describes consumerism as a cultural orientation in which "the possession and use of an increasing number and variety of goods and services is the principal cultural aspiration and the surest perceived route to personal happiness, social status, and national success". This takes place in different forms in different cultures, for example commercialisation of different festivals and ceremonies like that of marriage. It has also manifested through change in people's diet as children are exposed to unhealthy foods (like chips, candies) that are nutritionally poor but are much highly advertised in the mass media. Consumerism also affects peoples' values. For example, one of the reasons for juvenile crime (adolescents in conflict with law) is a consumer lifestyle portrayed by the mass media, which creates a desire for products and experiences that are not materially accessible to large sectors of the population unless they resort to illegal activities (UNICEF, 2011, p. 55). Moreover, increased consumption leads to greater exploitation of natural and non-renewable resources like fossil fuels, minerals and metals from the earth and causes more environmental degradation by cutting of trees and more ploughing of land to grow food (often to feed livestock as people at higher-income levels started to eat more meat). Hence, consumerism is not environmentally sustainable (The WorldWatch Institute, 2010).

Child as a Consumer

Over the past two decades, children's participation in consumerism has expanded markedly. Children spend more money, are more likely to be shoppers, devote more time to commercial media, and are more attuned to brands than before (Schor, 2008). Children are believed to be three markets in one: the present market for their current product requirements, future market for all goods and influential market which influences their parents to spend on different products (McNeal, 1987, cited in Sharma, 2011). What makes children a huge potential market in India is the fact that they account for 41% of the population as per Census 2001 data (India: Office of the Registrar General & Census Commissioner, 2011).

Indian families are undergoing a change from the traditional joint family set-up to a nuclear one with more democracy in decision-making regarding purchases. Children now play a significant role, although the amount of influence exerted by them varies by product category and stage of the decision-making process. For certain products, they are instrumental in initiating a purchase, while for others, they make the final selections themselves (Kaur & Singh, 2006). Children also have a "*pester power*" which refers to their ability to nag parents to purchase items (like new toys, comics, magazines, video games, junk food, trendy clothes) which are directly used by them, and the latter would not otherwise buy (Jeevananda & Kumar, 2012). Studies indicate that children also influence decision of buying items that are not exactly of direct use, for example electronic gadgets like the TV, computer, mobile phones, car. (Jain & Kaul, 2014). Apart from family, peers also significantly influence children's knowledge of style, brand and consumption patterns and so on from early in life and continuing through adolescence (Ali, Batra, Ravichandran, Mustafa & Rehman, 2012). Finally, mass media and marketing institutions sell different products and images through different symbols, commercials or other means in a variety of spaces accessed by the children (Schor, 2005).

Marketing and Children

Marketing is the most important tool for stoking consumption in a society. Marketing strategies entail well-researched psychologically targeted persuasive techniques for creating, stimulating, persuading, manipulating and altering con-sumer perceptions through effective media formats. Given that children are an important consumer market and are more vulnerable to manipulations, corporations abuse these persuasive powers of their advertisements to influence children to boost their sales and increase consumption (ANDI—Communication and Rights, 2012). Democratic styles of parenting coupled with an ever-increasing volume of direct-to-child advertisements for food, merchandise, toys, cars, hotel and restaurant chains, tourist destinations, consumer electronics, etc., have proved to be conducive for children to influence household purchases (Schor, 2004 cited in Graboviy, 2011). Schor (2008) however cautions against a simplification of marketing techniques to a stimulus–response model or a direct persuasion effect. She argues that marketing operates by affecting an individual's basic sense of self, relationship to others, perceptions of adequacy and the social context in which consumption takes place.

The TV undoubtedly remains a powerful medium to influence child consumers. However, marketers are moving beyond the TV box to virtually all the spaces and places inhabited by children to attract them (Schor, 2005). Children are bombarded with thousands of consumerist symbols (logos, jingles, slogans, mascots, etc.) each waking hour of their day that they are more likely to recognise these symbols as compared to common wildlife species, birdsong, animal calls or other similar elements! (The WorldWatch Institute, 2010).

Different Arenas for Marketing

The different avenues that are exploited by marketers to target children are discussed below:

Marketing Through the TV: TV channels are filled with commercials directed towards children. Children grow to like many of the products advertised on TV. They may urge parents to buy products they have seen on TV (Kail & Cavanaugh, 2007). At as early as three years of age, children distinguish commercials from programmes. However, preschool children view them as a different form of entertainment, one that is designed to inform viewers. They do not understand their persuasive intent until the analytical phase in life when they realise that commercials are not always truthful (Linn, 2005 cited in Kail & Cavanaugh, 2007). For older children, marketers often use their desire to fit in with their peers and tendency to rebel against authority figures as selling points for their products. Thus, marketers and corporations use their power, money and influence to sculpt society through advertisements and promote value systems that allow them to gain more profit (Graboviy, 2011).

Marketing Through Schools: Marketers tap the school environment to promote their name and products in a number of ways such as sponsored educational materials, advertisement of products by sponsoring sports events or cultural events in schools, and so on (Schor, 2005). Corporations organise competitions to promote their brands. For example, Camel has been conducting drawing competitions in schools for decades where they advertise their products.

Newer Techniques of Marketing: Different newer techniques of marketing include product licensing, product placement, guerilla marketing. These are presented below:

- **Product Licensing**: The act of selling through use of images or logos to promote products other than the ones they were created for referring to product licensing (Campaign for Commercial-Free Childhood, 2005). For example, popular cartoon characters like Chhota Bheem, Ben 10, Spongebob Squarepants are used to sell clothes, accessories candies, cereals, and so on.
- **Product Placement**: It is common to find beverages (like Pepsi, Coke), watches, cars, and so on, being promoted in Bollywood films (Gokhale, 2010).
- **Guerilla Marketing**: Examples of guerilla marketing include corporate naming of stadiums, the growth of advertising in sport, advertising on buses, the airport and hospital channels, advertising in restaurants, and other place-based advertising such as the illumination of sidewalks with ads, street advertising such as product giveaways and "guerrilla teams" doing marketing on the street (Schor, 2005).

Impact of Marketing on Children

Food and Beverage Marketing to Children: Marketers use the different media discussed above to aggressively sell food products like sugary cereals, chips, candies, ice creams, burgers and fries and other snack foods that have poor nutritional value and are associated with childhood obesity and tooth decay (Linn & Novosat, 2008). The promotion of unhealthy food has a significant impact on children's food choices and behaviours which consequently leads to poor health. Moreover, childhood obesity is a leading cause of hypertension and type-2 diabetes in later life (Hannon, Rao, & Arslanian, 2005).

Marketing Beauty Concepts to Children: Female beauty today is defined by "flawless" facial features and "perfect" thin bodies. Glorifications of the thin ideal are everywhere: on TV and film screens, on the Internet, in magazines and on the street billboards. Viewing these glamourised images, which do not represent real girls/women, causes many adolescent girls across the globe to measure their bodies against these unattainable ideals. This leads to a discontentment with body image and is also responsible for eating disorders like anorexia and bulimia in adolescents (UNICEF, 2011, p. 65).

Impact on Values of Children: Exposure to marketing contributes to consumerism in children, and this is a matter of concern. Children are focusing more on materialism and forgetting and discrediting deeper, more intimate aspects of life such as family and friendship. One's sense of self-worth is dependent on the possession of the latest brand or label, and the absence of it leads to low self-esteem (Schor, 2005). Evidence demonstrates a relationship between children's purchase requests and parent–child conflict (Buizen & Valkenburg, 2003).

Conclusion: Children need to be empowered such that they develop a critical lens about being targeted by the marketers. Also, the consumer culture that places value on consumption needs to be addressed through different approaches that include creating better awareness, stricter laws and policies against advertising of harmful products and regular parental involvement and role-modelling.

Consumer Rights

Consumer Protection: Consumers are vulnerable to risk of exploitation and cheating due to unscrupulous and unethical practices of manufacturers or traders some of which are presented below (National Institute of Open Schooling (NIOS), 2012, pp. 267–269):

- Sale of adulterated goods (adding something inferior to the product being sold),
- Sale of spurious goods (selling something of little value instead of the real product),
- Sale of substandard goods (sale of goods which do not confirm to prescribed quality standards),
- Sale of duplicate goods,
- Use of false weights and measures leading to underweight,
- Hoarding and black-marketing leading to scarcity and rise in price,
- Charging more than the maximum retail price (MRP) fixed for the product,

- Supply of defective goods,
- Misleading advertisements (advertisements falsely claiming a product or service to be of superior quality, grade or standard).

Consumer protection refers to safeguarding the interest and rights of consumers including redressal mechanisms for grievances.

Consumer Protection Act, 1986: With an overall objective of providing a medium of redressal to consumer grievances that arise from use of goods or services, the Government of India enacted the Consumer Protection Act, 1986. The consumer rights provided by this Act are listed below.

- **Right to Safety**: This provides a right to be protected against the marketing of goods and services, which are hazardous to life and property. The purchased goods and services availed of should not only meet a consumer's immediate needs, but also fulfil long-term interests.
- **Right to be Informed**: This means a right to be informed about the quality, quantity, potency, purity, standard and price of goods so as to protect the consumer against unfair trade practices.
- **Right to Choose**: This refers to a right to be assured, wherever possible of access to variety of goods and services at competitive price.
- **Right to be Heard**: This means that consumer's interests should receive due consideration at appropriate forums. It also includes right to be represented in various forums formed to consider the consumer's welfare.
- **Right to Seek Redressal**: This means a right to seek redressal against unfair trade practices or unscrupulous exploitation of consumers. It also includes right to fair settlement of the genuine grievances of the consumer.
- **Right to Consumer Education**: This means the right to acquire the knowledge and skill to be an informed consumer throughout life.
- **Redressal of Consumer Grievances**: The Consumer Protection Act makes provision for a semi-judicial system which comprises of District Forum, State Commission and National Commission, which are regarded as consumer courts for redressal of consumer disputes. A written complaint can be filed by an individual consumer or an association of consumers, before the District Consumer Forum for value of up to twenty lakh rupees, State Commission for value up to one crore rupees and the National Commission for value above rupees one crore, in respect of defects in goods and or deficiency in service.

Consumer Responsibilities

Consumer rights and responsibilities are intertwined together, and without sharing consumer responsibility, consumers will find it very difficult to enjoy their rights on a long-term basis. The different consumer responsibilities are discussed as follows (compiled from Advertising Standards Council of India (ASCI), 2014; India: Department of Consumer Affairs, 2009; NIOS, 2012)

- **Be Safety- and Quality-Conscious**: Consumers need to be aware of the quality and safety of the products or services they buy so that they can help curb adulteration and corrupt practices of manufacturers and traders. Consumers should preferably purchase quality-marked products with certification of ISI (Indian Standard Institution), AGMARK (Agricultural Marketing), FPO (Food Process Order), Hallmark (for purity of gold jewellery), Eco-mark (for certification of minimum impact on ecosystem), etc.
- **Don't be Misled by Advertisements**: Advertisements often exaggerate the quality of products. Hence, consumers should not rely on the advertisement entirely and carefully check the product or ask the users before making a purchase. In case of discrepancies, the same should be brought to the notice of the sponsors and the appropriate authority, if need be. The Advertising Standards Council of India (ASCI), a voluntary self-regulatory non-governmental organisation, aims to protect the interests of consumers through self-regulation in advertising. Complaints against misleading or offensive commercials or advertisements selling harmful products can be filed (online too) with the ASCI for relevant changes or pulling out of the commercial altogether.
- **Make an Informed Choice**: A consumer should inspect a variety of goods before buying the goods. For example, a consumer should compare their quality, price, durability, after sales service, etc., before making a purchase decision. This would enable the consumers to make the best choice within the limit of their own resources and also prevent himself/herself from falling prey to high-pressure selling techniques. Making informed choices is preferable to seeking redressal after suffering a loss or injury.
- **Collect Proof of Transaction**: The consumer should insist on a valid documentary evidence (cash memo/invoice) relating to purchase of goods or availing of any services and preserve it carefully. Such proof of purchase is required for filing a complaint, should a situation arise. In case of durable goods, the manufacturers generally provide the warrantee/guarantee card along with the product. It is the duty of consumers to obtain these documents and ensure that these are duly signed, stamped and dated. The consumer must preserve them till the warrantee/guarantee period is over.
- **Be Aware of Consumer Rights**: The consumers must be aware of their rights as consumers (as already discussed above) and exercise them while buying goods and services. For example, it is the responsibility of a consumer to insist on getting all information about the quality of the product and ensure himself/herself that it is free from any kind of defects.
- **Seek Redressal of Grievances**: If a consumer is dissatisfied with the product/services, then he/she can ask for redressal of grievances. A proper claim needs to be filed with the company first. If the manufacturer/company does not respond, then one can approach the consumer forums. One's claim must state actual loss, and the compensation claim must be reasonable. Many a times, a consumer's complaint may be of small value, but its impact on the society as a whole may be very large. Therefore, consumers must make efforts to seek redressal.

- **Proper Use of Products and Services**: It is expected from the consumers that they use and handle the product/services carefully. Sometimes, consumers tend to use the product carelessly during the guarantee period as they expect it to be replaced. This practice should be avoided.
- **Be Environmentally Sensitive**: Consumers must make a conscious effort to reduce consumption and choose environment-friendly alternatives that can be repaired, upgraded, recycled or have a refill package, as far as possible; are efficient in the use of energy; and do not generate unacceptable levels of waste.

Activities

Activity 5.10: Exercise on Intergenerational Variation in Consumption

Learner Outcome: At the end of this activity, the participants will develop awareness on consumerism and its causes and analyse their own consumerist habits.

Procedure: Use the following procedure to conduct this activity:

1. Ask the participants who is a consumer and what is their understanding of consumerism.
2. Ask them to fill the Exercise on Intergenerational Variation in Consumption given at the end of the chapter.
3. Ask them to compare the consumption style of their grandparents, parents and their own to understand how consumerism has evolved over generations.

Questions for Discussion: Use the following questions to discuss this activity:

- What is the intergenerational difference in buying habits?
- Why is consumerism growing?
- Do you think we buy more than what we need?
- Why does buying give us happiness?
- Has the mushrooming of shopping complexes changed the way we shop?
- Does the marketing and advertising industry influence our spending and purchase decisions?
- Do our family members and peers contribute to our consumption habits?
- Do you think brands are important?
- What are the possible consequences of the culture of consumerism? On people, relationships and the environment?
- How can we be more responsible consumers?

Time Estimate: 45 min

Activity 5.11: Identifying the World of Child-Targeted Marketing

Learner Outcome: At the end of this activity, the participants will learn to critically analyse how children are systematically targeted by mass media to sell products.

Procedure: Use the following procedure to conduct this activity:

1. Explain to the participants that you will be reading aloud a slogan (refer list below) and they have to associate it with the right product.

   - Taste The Thunder (*Thums Up*),
   - Fresh N Juicy (*Frooti*),
   - Kuch Meetha Ho Jaaye (*Cadbury*),
   - Jee Lalchaye Raha na jaye (*Alpenliebe*),
   - Bujaaye pyaas, baaki all bakwas (*Sprite*),
   - Dimaag ki batti jalaa de (*Mentos*),
   - No one can eat just one (*Lays*),
   - I'm lovin it (*McDonalds*),
   - Taste Bhi, Health Bhi (*Maggi*),
   - Thodi si pet puja (*Perk*),
   - Tedha Hai Par Mera Hai (*Kurkure*),
   - Haqq se maango (*Priya gold biscuits*).

2. It is very likely that participants are quick to respond with the correct answer. Ask them why is it easy to remember these slogans? Highlight how advertisements pervade our lives that we subconsciously consume them all the time. Therefore, we tend to have a high recall value for these slogans.

3. Next, show few YouTube clippings of advertisements, preferably those targeted at children and adolescents such as Complan, noodles, biscuits. Choose a group of food and beverage products, toiletries and vanity products, stationery products and toys while selecting the advertisements. After viewing the advertisements, have a guided discussion using the following questions.

Questions for Discussion: Use the following questions to discuss this activity:

- Do you think some advertisements are targeted at children and adolescents?
- What are some of the common products targeted at children and adolescents?
- Do you like them? Why?
- What are some of the different techniques used? (Like use of animation, use of a celebrity, music, bright colours, catchy jingles, filming techniques)
- How do you feel convinced about the product?
- Do these advertisements play a role in your or your family's purchase decisions? How?
- Do you think that you as children push your parents for new products advertised on the TV?
- Who do you think pays for these expensive advertisements?

Time Estimate: 45 min

Source: Adapted from "Looking at Food Advertising" in MediaSmarts (2012)

Activity 5.12: Small Group Debates on Marketing

Learner Outcome: At the end of this activity, the participants will learn to critically debate about aspects of child-targeted marketing and advertising.

Procedure: Use the following procedure to conduct this activity:

1. Divide participants into four small groups and allot each one of the following topics of debate (suggestions for topics can be invited from the participants as well).

   - TV commercials: A Boon or Bane,
   - Children's Channels Need to be Commercials Free—Agree or Disagree,
   - Ban Fast Food Marketing—Agree or Disagree.

2. Within each small group, participants may divide themselves equally to represent both sides of the debate topic. Allow them 15 min to prepare the relevant points.
3. Finally, have each group present their debate to the large group.

Time Estimate: 45 min

Activity 5.13: Video Discussion on Buying Habits

Learner Outcome: At the end of the activity, the participants will learn the skill to plan their expenses so that they get the best for their money.

Procedure: Show the following video film:

CashVille Kidz Episode 3: Smart Buying Habits

https://www.youtube.com/watch?v=8vlJw0ary5Y

Questions for Discussion: Use the following questions to discuss this activity:

- What homework is needed before you buy anything?
- How can you compare the quality of products and the prices?
- How can you save money when you go shopping?

Time Estimate: 15 min

Activity 5.14: Exercise on Consumer Rights and Responsibilities

Learner Outcome: At the end of this activity, the participants will develop awareness of consumer rights and responsibilities.

Procedure: Use the following procedure to conduct this activity:

1. Show the video film on Rights and Duties of the Consumers
   https://www.youtube.com/watch?v=aTcDO_sjMM4
2. Alternately, show Summary Chart 5.2 and discuss consumer rights provided by the Consumer Protection Rights and Consumer Responsibilities.
3. Distribute copies of the question cards and the answer cards on Consumer Rights and Responsibilities, given at the end of the chapter.
4. Explain that this activity contains a series of 26 cards. Each card is a consumer right or a consumer responsibility question with a corresponding answer card.
5. Distribute one card to each participant. Each participant will read his/her own card which is either a question card (Q) or answer card (A). Subsequently, they will write in their workbook what they think their matching card will say. For example, if a participant has an answer card, then he/she will write a matching question card for the same and vice versa.
6. Having written their responses, participants should be asked to move around the classroom until they match their card with a coparticipant's card.
7. Finally, one by one, each pair can present their question and answer cards to the large group.

Time Estimate: 45 min

Source: Adapted from "Consumer Match-Up Cards" in Consumer Affairs Victoria (2011, pp. 1–13).

Activity 5.15: Video Discussion on National Consumer Helpline

Learner Outcome: At the end of the activity, the participants will learn to use the National Consumer Helpline to protect themselves as consumers.

Procedure: Use the following procedure to conduct this activity:

1. Ask the participants if they have heard, read or experienced situations of consumer fraud. If yes, ask if they would like to share it with the large group.
2. Show the video film on Economics—Class 10—Consumer Protection
   https://www.youtube.com/watch?v=7asg2nTRVKY
   Use the following questions to discuss this film:

   - What are the factors leading to consumer exploitation?
   - What are the effects of consumer exploitation?

3. Show the video film on Jago grahak jago ad 5
   https://www.youtube.com/watch?v=A64j5o-6ix4

Use the following questions to discuss this film:

- What is the National Consumer Helpline?
- When can you call them? How do they help?

Time Estimate: 15 min

Activity 5.16: Visit to a Consumer Court

Learner Outcome: At the end of this activity, the participants will understand the procedure of consumer protection through consumer courts.

Procedure: Plan a visit to the local consumer court to understand how this system helps in consumer protection.

Time Estimate: Half day

Concluding Activity: Achievement of the Learner Objectives

Learner Outcome: By the end of the concluding activity, the participants will ascertain if they have achieved the learner objectives.

Procedure: Use the following procedure to conduct the concluding activity:

1. Show the power points/a chart on the learner objectives, ask the participants to read them one at a time, and ask the group if they think they have achieved the objective.
2. The participants may be asked to share their responses in their diary with reference to the following questions:

- What was a new learning for you in this session?
- What did you like the best in this session and why?
- Which activity was most effective?
- What was not clear/confusing?
- How can you apply what you have learnt?

Time Estimate: 15 min

Appendix: Summary Charts and Exercise

Summary Chart 5.1 Basic models of savings systems for children
(Adapted from UNICEF, 2012)

Basic Models of Savings Systems	Advantages	Disadvantages	Concerns
Personal Savings (children use traditional methods of saving)	• Children have constant control and access to their savings box	• Higher risk of loss or theft	• Need to develop relevant method of tracking the financial transaction through a simple ledger
School-based Savings (a systematized way of saving is organized at the school level)	• Children's savings easily accessible to them • Lesser risk than personal savings bank • Use of financial ledgers become systematic and relevant	• Burden of risk is on the school, with a particularly higher level of responsibility on the teachers	• Need to determine ways to secure savings through regulated financial service providers
Savings in a Bank	• Savings are secure • Children learn about and interact with formal institution • Use of financial ledgers become systematic and relevant	• Savings can be less accessible • May need to negotiate favourable terms and conditions with banks	• Decide on individual or group accounts • Decide on collection and withdrawal

Summary Chart 5.2 Consumer rights and responsibilities

Consumer Rights	Consumer Responsibilities
• Right to Safety	• Be Safety and Quality Conscious
• Right to be Informed	• Don't be Misled by Advertisements
• Right to Choose	• Make an Informed Choice
• Right to be Heard	• Collect Proof of Transaction
• Right to Seek Redressal	• Be aware of Consumer Rights
• Right to Consumer Education	• Proper use of Products and Services
• Redressal of Consumer Grievances	• Seek Redressal of Grievances
	• Be Environmentally Sensitive
Source: The Consumer Protection Act, 1986	**Sources:** Advertising Standards Council of India (2014; India: Department of Consumer Affairs (2009); & NIOS (2012)

Exercise for Activity 5.7: Assessment of Income and Expenses

Assessment of Income

Source of Income	Income		
	Daily	Monthly	Yearly

Assessment of Expenses

Items	Daily	Monthly	Yearly
Food			
Transportation			
Clothes			
School related Expenses etc.			
Recreation			
Housing			
Payment of Loan/ Debt			
Other (Specify)			

Exercise for Activity 5.10: Inter-Generational Variation in Consumption

	Buying Habits of Grandparents	Buying Habits of Parents	Buying Habits of Myself
Food			
Clothes			
Housing			
Electronic Gadgets			
Toys/ Games			

Exercise for Activity 5.14: Consumer Rights and Responsibilities

Questions on Consumer Rights and Responsibilities	Answers on Consumer Rights and Responsibilities
Q: What does the consumer right to redress mean?	**A:** Redress means the right to be compensated for faulty goods or unsatisfactory services.
Q: How can I ascertain the quality of a product?	**A:** To ascertain quality, it is preferable to buy products with certification of ISI, AGMARK, FPO, Hallmark, (for purity of gold jewellery), Eco-mark (for certification of minimum impact on ecosystem) etc.
Q: Do advertisements mislead buyers?	**A:** Advertisements make different claims about their products. For example, processed food like jams, jellies, cereals, canned food, etc. are projected as healthy food to children when the reality is that these foods have poor nutritive value.
Q: When can I get a refund?	**A:** Consumers have a right to a refund, replacement or repair if, at the time of purchase, the goods were faulty, not suitable for the purpose intended, or different from the samples shown in the shop. You may be offered a repair, exchange or credit note rather than a refund. You will need the receipt.
Q: What does it mean to have a Consumer Right to Quality?	**A:** We have a consumer right to quality so the goods we purchase are of decent quality, that is, goods are fit for the purpose for which they were made.

Q: When I am not entitled to a refund?	**A:** You may have no right to a refund when: • You cannot provide proof of purchase, such as a receipt. • The goods are fine, but you changed your mind. • The goods were bought for someone who doesn't want them. • The goods were damaged after you bought them.
Q: What does it mean to have a Consumer Right to Safety?	**A:** A Consumer Right to Safety means consumers have a right to be protected from dangerous goods and services. For example, some medicines are banned by the government because they are found harmful to body.
Q: What if I buy goods that are faulty?	**A:** If you believe the goods you bought are faulty you should stop using them, report the fault and return them as soon as possible. You may need to convince the trader that there is a fault and the goods were not damaged after you bought them.
Q: Do consumers have rights?	**A:** Yes, consumers have rights. These include the right to be heard, the right to choice and the right to information.
Q: What should consumers do before they buy?	**A:** Before buying, consumers should be clear about what they want (for example the size, style and colour), how much they can afford; consumers should check for faults and compare prices.

Q: How can you make a consumer complaint?	**A**: Consumer complaints can be made individually or through a consumer forum. A written complaint, can be filed before the District Consumer Forum for value of up to 20 lakh rupees, State Commission for value up to 1 crore rupees, and the National Commission for value above rupees 1 crore, in respect of defects in goods and or deficiency in service.
Q: When I buy something, why should I keep the receipt?	**A**: A receipt is your proof of purchase. It is an important record of where and when you bought something and how much it cost. You need the receipt if something goes wrong and you want an exchange or a refund.
Q: How do I make an informed choice while making a purchase?	**A**: Consumers must always read labels of products for the maximum retail price (MRP), date of manufacture and expiry (for food items and medicines), different nutrients (for food products) and presence of chemical agents like artificial colours or flavours. If the product packaging is tampered with, then such products should be completed avoided.

References

Advertising Standards Council of India. (2014). *About ASCI mission.* Retrieved from http://www.ascionline.org/index.php/mission.html.

American Psychological Association. (2016). *Children, youth, families and socioeconomic status.* Washington: Author. Retrieved from http://www.apa.org/pi/ses/resources/publications/factsheet-cyf.aspx.

Ali, A., Batra, D. K., Ravichandran, N., Mustafa, Z., & Rehman, S. U. (2012). Consumer socialisation of children: A conceptual framework. *International Journal of Scientific and Research Publications, 2*(1), 1–5. Retrieved from http://www.ijsrp.org/research_paper_jan2012/ijsrp-jan-2012-23.pdf.

Amin, S., Rahman, L., Ainul, S., Rob, U., Zaman, B., & Akter, R. (2010). *White paper: Enhancing adolescent financial capabilities through financial education in Bangladesh.* Population Council. Retrieved from http://www.popcouncil.org/uploads/pdfs/2010PGY_WhitePaperBanglaFinancialEd.pdf.

ANDI—Communication and Rights. (2012). *The rights of children and right to media strengthening convergences in legal frameworks and public policies.* Brazil: Author. Retrieved from http://www.andi.org.br/infancia-e-juventude/publicacao/the-rights-of-children-and-the-right-to-media.

Anti-Slavery. (2007). *Child labour.* Geneva: Author. Retrieved from http://www.antislavery.org/homepage/antislavery/childlabour.htm#what.

APA Task Force. (2006). *Report of the APA task force on socioeconomic status.* Washington, DC. Retrieved from http://www.apa.org/pi/ses/resources/publications/task-force-2006.pdf.

Beverly, S. G., Elliott, W., & Sherraden, M. (2013). Child development accounts and college success: Accounts, assets, expectations, and achievements. *CSD Perspective*, 13–27.

Blond, P., & Gruescu, S. (2010). *Asset building for children: Creating a new civic savings platform for young people.* London: Res Publica.

Boyden, J., & Levison, D. (2000). *Children as economic and social actors in the development process.* Sweden: Ministry of Foreign Affairs.

Buizen, M., & Valkenburg, P. M. (2003). The unintended effects of television advertising a parent-child survey. *Communication Research, 30*(5), 483–503. https://doi.org/10.1177/0093650203256361.

Campaign for Commercial Free-Childhood. (2005). *The facts about marketing to kids.* Retrieved from http://nepc.colorado.edu/publication/the-facts-about-marketing-kids.

Child and Youth Finance International (2012a). *Children and youth as economic citizens: Review of research on financial capability, financial inclusion, and financial education.* Amsterdam: Author. Retrieved from http://childfinanceinternational.org/index.php?option=com_mtree&task=att_download&link_id=374&cf_id=200.

Child and Youth Finance International. (2012b). *An introduction to child and youth finance education: Developing quality financial, social and livelihoods education for children and youth.* Retrieved from http://childfinanceinternational.org/index.php?option=com_mtree&task=att_download&link_id=376&cf_id=200.

Child and Youth Finance International. (2014). *Developing responsible retail banking products for children and youth: Banking a new generation.* Retrieved from http://www.childfinanceinternational.org/resources/publications/2014-banking-a-new-generation.pdf.

Consumer Affairs Victoria. (2011). *Consumer stuff for kids a teaching and learning resource.* Victoria: Author. Retrieved from http://www.consumer.vic.gov.au/library/publications/resources-and-education/teacher-resources/consumer-stuff-for-kids-a-teaching-and-learning-resource.pdf.

Despard, M., & Hira, T. (2012). Financial education for children and youth. In Child and Youth Finance International. *Children and youth as economic citizens: Review of research on financial capability, financial inclusion, and financial education.* Amsterdam: Author. Retrieved from http://childfinanceinternational.org/index.php?option=com_mtree&task=att_downloa.

Gokhale, S. V. (2010). *Comparative study of the practice of product placement in bollywood and hollywood movies* (Master's theses). Paper 3860. Retrieved from http://scholarworks.sjsu.edu/etd_theses/3860.

Graboviy, A. (2011). Consumerism and its dangers to children: A call for regulation in advertising. *Gatton Student Research Publication, 3*(1), 2–11. Retrieved from http://gatton.uky.edu/gsrp/downloads/issues/spring2011/consumerism%20and%20its%20dangers%20to%20children%20a%20call%20for%20regulation%20in%20advertising.pdf.

Hannon, T. S., Rao, G., & Arslanian, S. A. (2005). Childhood obesity and type 2 diabetes mellitus. *Pediatrics, 116*(2), 473–80. Retrieved from http://pediatrics.aappublications.org/content/116/2/473.long.

Howard, R., Humphrey, L., Rist, C., Rosen, B., & Tivol, L. (2010). *From piggy banks to prosperity: A guide to implementing children's savings accounts.* SEED. Retrieved from http://cfed.org/assets/pdfs/Piggy_Banks_to_Prosperity.pdf.

India. (1986). *Consumer protection act.* Retrieved from http://www.cccindia.co/corecentre/Database/Docs/DocFiles/Consumer-Protection-Act-No.-68.pdf.

India: Department of Consumer Affairs. (2009). *Consumer rights.* Retrieved from http://consumeraffairs.nic.in/consumer/?q=node/6.

India: Ministry of Law and Justice. (1986). *The consumer protection act, 1986.* Retrieved from http://www.ncdrc.nic.in/1_1.html.

India: National Institute of Open Schooling. (2012). *Business studies (215) syllabus.* Retrieved from http://www.nios.ac.in/media/documents/Secbuscour/English/chapter-17.pdf.

India: Office of the Registrar General & Census Commissioner. (2011). *Census of India 2011 houses household amenities and assets figures at a glance.* New Delhi: Author. Retrieved from http://www.censusindia.gov.in/2011census/hlo/Data_sheet/India/Figures_Glance.pdf.

Inter-Agency Working Group on Children's Participation. (2008). *Children as active citizens: Commitments and obligations for children's civil rights and civic engagement in East Asia and the Pacific: A policy and programme guide.* Retrieved from http://www.unicef.org/eapro/Children_as_Active_Citizens_A4_book.pdf.

Jain, N., & Kaul, R. (2014). A study of impact of pester power on family buying decision in electronic & digital products in Indore City. *Indian Journal of Research in Management, Business and Social Sciences, 2*(1), 21–26. Retrieved from http://www.ijrmbss.com/assets/pdf/Vol2Iss1/5.pdf.

James, A., & James, A. (2012). *Key concepts in childhood studies* (2nd ed.). London: Sage.

Jeevananda, S., & Kumar, S. (2012). Degree of children influence on parents buying decisions. *European Journal of Business and Management, 4*(14), 49–57.

Kail, R. V., & Cavanaugh, J. C. (2007). *Human development: A life span view* (4th ed.). Canada: Thomson Learning Inc.

Kaur, P., & Singh, R. (2006). Children in family purchase decision making in India and the west: A review. *Academy of Marketing Science Review, 8,* 1–30. Retrieved from http://www.amsreview.org/article/kaur08-2006.pdf.

Lesser, J. G., & Pope, D. S. (2007). *Human behavior and the social environment: Theory and practice.* Boston: Pearson Allyn and Bacon.

Linn, S., & Novosat, C. L. (2008). Calories for sale: Food marketing to children in the twenty-first century. *Annals of the American Academy of Political and Social Science, 615,* 133–155. https://doi.org/10.1177/0002716207308487.

Lister, R. (2004). *Poverty.* Malden, MA: Polity Press.

Plan. (2012). *Economic security strategy 2010–2015: Promoting the economic rights of children and young people.* Retrieved from https://plan-international.org/about-plan/resources/publications/economic-security/plans-economic-security-strategy-2010-2015/.

Ruddick, S. (2003). The politics of aging: Globalization and the restructuring of youth and childhood. *Antipode: A Radical Journal of Geography, 35*(2), 334–362.

Schor, J. B. (2005). *When childhood gets commercialized, can children be protected?* Paper prepared for Yale Legal Theory Workshop, March 31, 2005. Retrieved from http://www.yale.edu/law/leo/052005/papers/schor.pdf.

Schor, J. B. (2008). Understanding the child consumer. *Journal of the American Academy of Child and Adolescent Psychiatry, 47*(5), 486–490. https://doi.org/10.1097/CHI.0b013e318167660d.

Securities and Exchange Board of India. (2010). *Financial education for school children.* Retrieved from http://www.sebi.gov.in/cms/sebi_data/investors/financial_literacy/Financial%20Education%20for%20School%20Children.pdf.

Sharma, A. (2011). Role of family in consumer socialisation of children: Literature review. *Researchers World—International Refereed Journal of Arts Science & Commerce Research, II* (3), 161–167. Retrieved from http://www.researchersworld.com/vol2/issue3/Paper_18.pdf.

Sherraden, M. (1991). *Assets and the poor: A new American welfare policy.* Armonk, New York: M. E. Sharpe.

Sherraden, M. (2012). Financial inclusion among children and youth. In Child and Youth Finance International. *Children and youth as economic citizens: Review of research on financial capability, financial inclusion, and financial education.* Amsterdam: Author. Retrieved from http://childfinanceinternational.org/index.php?option=com_mtree&task=att_download.

The World Watch Institute. (2010). *State of the world transforming cultures from consumerism to sustainability.* Retrieved from http://blogs.worldwatch.org/transformingcultures/wp-content/uploads/2009/11/SOW2010-PreviewVersion.pdf.

Todaro, M. P., & Smith, S. C. (2009). *Economic development* (10th ed.). Essex: Pearson Education Ltd.

United Nations. (1995). *World summit for social development programme of action.* Retrieved from http://www.un.org/esa/socdev/wssd/text-version/agreements/poach2.htm.

United Nations Children's Fund. (2011). *The state of the world's children 2011: Adolescence an age of opportunity.* New York: Author. Retrieved from http://www.unicef.org/adolescence/files/SOWC_2011_Main_Report_EN_02092011.pdf.

United Nations Children's Fund. (2012). *Child social and financial education.* Retrieved from http://www.unicef.org/publications/files/CSFE_module_low_res_FINAL.pdf.

United Nations Population Fund—India. (n.d.). *Special financial incentive schemes for the girl child in India a review of select schemes.* New Delhi. Retrieved from http://countryoffice.unfpa.org/india/drive/SPECIALFINANCIALINCENTIVESCHEMES.pdf.

Vandemoortele, J. (2012). *Equity begins with children.* UNICEF, Social and Economic Policy Working Paper. Retrieved from https://docs.google.com/viewer?url=http%3A%2F%2Fwww.unicef.org%2Fsocialpolicy%2Ffiles%2FEquity_Begins_with_Children_Vandemoortele_JAN2012.pdf.

Wyness, M. (2012). *Childhood and society* (2nd ed.). New York: Palgrave Macmillan.

Part II
Child's Rights Education to Prevention of Violence

Module 6
Child Rights to Prevention of Physical Violence

Prerequisite Modules

The prerequisite Modules for this Module are:
From *Sourcebook I on Introduction to Rights-Based Direct Practice with Children*:

- Modules on Life Skills Development

From *Sourcebook II on Child Rights Education for Participation and Development: Primary Prevention*:

- Introduction to Child Rights Education;
- Child Rights to Participation and Children's Associations;

Conceptual Framework of Child Rights to Prevention of Violence

Concepts and Theories

Concepts of Child Abuse

Violence against Children: The World Report on Violence against Children by, the independent expert for the United Nations (UN), Pinheiro (2006), identified violence against children in the home and family, schools and educational settings, care and justice institutions, places of work and the community. Physical and psychological violence, sexual abuse and sexual harassment are forms of violence which occur in all settings.

Child Abuse: Child abuse is:

- Any intentional non-accidental physical, emotional and psychological or sexual harm done to a child that endangers or impairs the child's physical, emotional and psychological or sexual health and development.

© Child Rights and You 2018
M. Desai and S. Goel, *Child Rights Education for Inclusion and Protection: Primary Prevention*, Rights-based Direct Practice with Children, https://doi.org/10.1007/978-981-13-0417-0_6

- By older children, parents, relatives, caretakers, neighbours, teachers, employ-ers, police or strangers; in family, neighbourhood, street, school, institutions, workplace or police/judicial custody.
- Because of adult–child power imbalance due to adultism and patriarchy, psychosocial problems or socio-economic problems, and cycle of abuse (Desai, 2010).

Physical Child Abuse: The World Health Organisation (WHO) and International Society for Prevention of Child Abuse and Neglect (ISPCAN) (2006) define physical abuse of a child as the intentional use of physical force against a child that results in—or has a high likelihood of resulting in—harm for the child's health, survival, development or dignity. This includes hitting, beating, kicking, shaking, biting, strangling, scalding, burning, poisoning and suffocating. Much physical violence against children in the home is inflicted with an object of punishing.

Child Sexual Abuse: The WHO and ISPCAN (2006) define child sexual abuse (CSA) as the involvement of a child in a sexual activity that he or she does not fully comprehend, is unable to give informed consent to, or for which the child is not developmentally prepared, or else that violates the laws or social taboos of society. Children can be sexually abused by both adults and other children who are—by virtue of their age or stage of development—in a position of responsibility, trust or power over the victim.

Emotional and Psychological Child Abuse: The WHO and ISPCAN (2006) define emotional and psychological abuse of children as one that involves both isolated incidents, as well as a pattern of failure over time on the part of a parent or caregiver to provide a developmentally appropriate and supportive environment. Acts in this category may have a high probability of damaging the child's physical or mental health, or its physical, mental, spiritual, moral or social development. Abuse of this type includes the restriction of movement; patterns of belittling, blaming, threatening, frightening, discriminating against or ridiculing; and other non-physical forms of rejection or hostile treatment.

Cultural Determinism of Child Abuse

Cultural Variation in Perception of Child Abuse: As child abuse and neglect first came to public and professional attention in the Western world, using a framework drawn from Western-based conceptions of child abuse and neglect, a Western view of "abuse" has been privileged. Questions arose as to whether child maltreatment was limited to the Western world or whether it occurred throughout the world (Rosado, 1994). While Korbin (1981) identified child abuse and neglect cross-culturally, he found that some child-rearing practices are viewed as acceptable by one culture but as abusive and neglectful by another. While cultures vary in their definitions of child abuse and neglect, each group nevertheless has criteria for identifying behaviours that are outside the realm of acceptable child training.

Comparative cultural studies indicate wide variations in what is thought to be either beneficial or harmful treatment in childrearing; few actions can be taken for granted as intrinsically good or bad. For example, in some societies a swift, quickly forgotten slap may be regarded as less disruptive to the bonds between parents and children than a scolding would be. The Western practices of putting babies to sleep alone in their own bedrooms are seen as uncaring or even abusive by people in other cultures (Korbin, 1981).

Cultural Relativity: Cultural relativity recommends the practice of evaluating any culture by its own standards and trying not to project your value system onto them. There are reasons that groups of people do what they do, often reasons that make perfectly good sense to them (Leeder, 2003). However, Zechenter (1997) notes that cultural relativism has the potential of undermining the modern human rights law developed during the last fifty years.

Cultural Identity versus Child Abuse: Anthropologists have gone to great efforts to explain how culturally sanctioned rites that may cause children pain, suffering, or harm, fall outside the rubric of "abuse" in that they are collective expressions of cultural values, for example female circumcision and child marriages. As such, not only adults who perform and perpetuate the rites, but also children who are subjected to them, view these rites, however painful and terrifying, as having a positive long-term value. The child's view of his or her experience and treatment has long been recognised as an important consideration in differentiating cultural practices from idiosyncratic abuse (Korbin, 2003).

Koramoa, Lynch and Kinnair (2002) distinguish between traditional cultural practices that enhance a child's cultural identity and those that cause harm. The problem, of course, is that some practices like female circumcision and child marriage do both. Cultural identity is so central to group membership, and thus, personal identity that any suggestion of negative effects or inappropriateness of any practice is likely to be sensitive, particularly if any pressure for change comes from outside the culture condoning the practice. Thus, change is far more likely to occur where a campaign is led within the same or a similar culture.

Causes of Child Abuse

Structural Causes: Critical theorists opine that child abuse is systemic or structural (Burman, 2008) due to adultism, patriarchy and vulnerability of marginalised children.

Adultism: Adultism implies assumptions about physical and mental incapability of children, which lead to role stereotypes of dependency, hierarchy, intolerance, discrimination and also justifies violence against them. Thus from an adultist perspective, child abuse is not an anomaly, and it is built into the way in which we define childhood (Mason & Steadman, 1996). When adults are given the authority to control their children for disciplining them, child abuse gets institutionalised in the family, schools and society.

Patriarchy: The feminist theorisation identifies male power, hegemony and socialisation as the key causal factors of child abuse, not only within the family but also outside of it, in a wide range of settings (Corby, 2002).

Vulnerability of Marginalised Children: Some groups or categories of children are especially vulnerable to different forms of violence: children with disabilities, orphaned children (including those orphaned by AIDS), indigenous children, children from ethnic minorities and other marginalised groups, children living or working on the streets, children in institutions and detention, children living in communities in which inequality, unemployment and poverty are highly concentrated, child refugees and other displaced children (Pinheiro, 2006). Of course, abuse takes place across classes but the upper classes may be able to conceal it because of access to greater resources and less scrutiny by social services (Downs, Moore, & McFadden, 2009). Pinheiro (2006) noted that:

- Young children are at greatest risk of physical abuse while adolescents are at greater risk of sexual abuse.
- Boys are more at risk of physical abuse than girls, and girls are at greater risk of neglect and sexual violence.

Family Level Causes: Faller and Ziefert (1981, cited in Downs et al., 2009) have identified the following family dynamics in maltreating parents:

- Parental collusion: One or both parents may be the active abusers, but in most instances, there is a passive parent who gives covert permission for the other parent to abuse the child.
- Scapegoating: When there is a marital discord, the antagonism between husband and wife may be displaced on the child.
- Reorganised families: The resentment between members of the reconstituted households may result in the physical or sexual abuse of children.
- Single-parent status: Single-parenting in itself does not place children at risk of abuse or neglect, but poor single-parent families are overrepresented in child protection services.
- Adolescent parents.
- Lack of extended family/kinship support.

Individual Level Causes: Faller and Ziefert (1981, cited in Downs et al., 2009) have identified the following as the most common personality characteristics found in maltreating parents, most of which can be applied to other abusers also:

- Low self-esteem;
- Excessive dependency;
- Poor impulse control;
- Rigid superego structures;
- Deficient superego development/weak conscience;
- Social isolation;
- Serious difficulty coping with the demands of parenting;
- Lack of parenting skills and knowledge of child development.

Cycle of Abuse: Children learn how to parent from their parents. Abused children develop low self-esteem, poor management of negative emotions and problem-solving, and weak communication and social skills. These traits further make them abusers of children as adults, unless they can break the intergenerational transmission of abuse or the cycle of abuse.

Under Reporting of Violence Against Children

According to Pinheiro (2006):

- Much violence against children is often hidden, unreported or under-recorded for various reasons like fear and stigma related to reporting, societal or cultural acceptance of violence in the guise of disciplining of children or the lack of safe and trusted ways for children or adults to report the violence.
- Very young children who suffer violence in their homes lack the capacity to report.
- Many children are afraid to report incidents of violence against them for fear of reprisals by perpetrators or of interventions by authorities which may worsen their overall situation.
- In many cases parents, who should protect their children, are silent if the violence is perpetrated by a spouse or other family member, or a more powerful member of society such as an employer, a police officer, or a community leader.
- Fear is closely related to the stigma frequently attached to reporting violence. In societies where patriarchal notions of family "honour" are valued above girls' human rights and well-being, an incident of rape or sexual violence can lead to ostracism of the victim, further violence and even death at the hands of her family.
- Persistent social acceptance of some types of violence against children is a major factor in its perpetuation in almost every State. Children the perpetrators of violence against them and the public at large may accept physical, sexual and psychological violence as an inevitable part of childhood.
- Corporal punishment and other forms of cruel or degrading punishment, bullying and sexual harassment, and a range of violent traditional practices may be perceived as normal, particularly when no lasting visible physical injury results.

Child Right to Protection from Abuse

According to Article 19(1) of the UNCRC (United Nations, 1989), "States Parties shall take all appropriate legislative, administrative, social and educational measures to protect the child from all forms of physical or mental violence, injury or abuse, neglect or negligent treatment, maltreatment or exploitation, including sexual abuse, while in the care of parent(s), legal guardian(s) or any other person who has the care of the child".

The Directive Principles of State Policy of the Indian Constitution include "Protection of children and youth from neglect and abuse".

Pinheiro (2006) identified the following among the key principles which are reflected in his recommendations:

- No violence against children is justifiable.
- All violence against children is preventable.

Child Responsibility for Protection from Abuse

It is essential that children in difficult situations should not be conceptualised merely as susceptible victims. Representing children as passive victims rather than active survivors undermines the possibility of them acting on their situation and thereby further threatens their self-esteem and self-efficacy. The view of children as resourceful suggests that children may be better served by assuming an active role in their own protection and at least some degree of responsibility for their own safety, insofar as this is possible (Boyden & Levison, 2000).

Child Right to Protection in the National Policy for Children

According to the National Policy for Children (2013):

- The State shall create a caring, protective and safe environment for all children, to reduce their vulnerability in all situations and to keep them safe at all places, especially public spaces.
- The State shall protect all children from all forms of violence and abuse, harm, neglect, stigma, discrimination, deprivation, exploitation including economic exploitation and sexual exploitation, abandonment, separation, abduction, sale or trafficking for any purpose or in any form, pornography, alcohol and substance abuse, or any other activity that takes undue advantage of them, or harms their personhood or affects their development.
- The State commits to taking special protection measures to secure the rights and entitlements of children in need of special protection, characterised by their specific social, economic and geopolitical situations, including their need for rehabilitation and reintegration, in particular but not limited to, children affected by migration, displacement, communal or sectarian violence, civil unrest, disasters and calamities, street children, children of sex workers, children forced into commercial sexual exploitation, abused and exploited children, children forced into begging, children in conflict and contact with the law, children in situations of labour, children of prisoners, children infected/affected by HIV/AIDS, children with disabilities, children affected by alcohol and substance abuse, children of manual scavengers and children from any other socially excluded group, children affected by armed conflict and any other category of children requiring care and protection.

- The State shall promote and strengthen legislative, administrative and institutional redressal mechanisms at the national and State level for the protection of child rights. For local grievances, effective and accessible grievance redressal mechanisms shall be developed at the programme level.

Child Protection Through Childline

Childline was launched in 1998 as a national 24×7 free emergency outreach service for children in need of care and protection. Any child or concerned adult can dial the toll-free number 1098 and access emergency services any time of the day or night. Childline links them to services for their long-term care and rehabilitation. Childline India Foundation (CIF) provides vital support to the Childline service across the country. It is responsible for expansion of Childline, ensuring quality standards, research, documentation and child protection advocacy.

Activities

Introductory Activity 6.1: Understanding and Attitude to Child Abuse

Learner Outcome: At the end of this activity, the participants will develop awareness on what is child abuse.

Procedure: Use the following procedure to conduct this activity:

1. Ask the participants to fill up the Exercise on Attitude to Child Abuse, given at the end of the chapter.
2. Use the following questions to conduct discussion:
   1. What is child abuse and what is not abuse?
   2. How is abuse different from disciplining?
   3. Do children need beating and punishments sometimes? When?
   4. How will children develop discipline if not beaten up?
3. Form seven small groups and allocate the following topics among them for reading the relevant notes and discussion:
   (1) Cultural Determinism of Child Abuse;
   (2) Structural Causes of Child Abuse;
   (3) Family Level Causes of Child Abuse;
   (4) Individual Level Causes of Child Abuse;
   (5) Child Right to Protection from Abuse;
   (6) Child Responsibility for Protection from Abuse;
   (7) Child Right to Protection in the National Policy for Children.

4. Ask the small groups to make their presentation to the large group.
5. Use the following questions to conduct discussion:

    a. Why is child abuse not considered a big issue in our country?
    b. How is child abuse being recycled?
    c. What is child right to protection?
    d. What is parents' responsibility to prevent their abuse?
    e. What is other adults' responsibility to prevent their abuse?
    f. What is child responsibility to prevent their abuse?

6. Show and discuss Summary Chart 6.1 on understanding child abuse.
7. Introduce the following units of the module:

    a. Prevention of Physical Abuse of Children;
    b. Prevention of Sexual Abuse of Children.

Time Estimate: 45 min

Activity 6.2: Visit to Childline Office

Learner Outcome: At the end of this activity, the participants will learn about the procedure of Childline for protection of children from abuse.

Procedure: Plan a visit to a local Childline office and learn how it helps children facing abuse.

Time Estimate: half a day

Prevention of Physical Abuse/Corporal Punishment of Children

Concepts and Theories

Concept of Physical Abuse of Children

Physical abuse of children is the most commonly known and widely prevalent form of child abuse which is:

- Any intentional non-accidental physical harm done to a child that endangers or impairs the child's physical, emotional and psychological health and development;
- By older children, parents, relatives, caretakers, neighbours, teachers, employers, police or strangers; in family, neighbourhood, street, school, institutions, site of occupation or police custody;

- Because of adult–child power imbalance due to adultism and patriarchy, psychosocial problems or socio-economic problems, and cycle of abuse (Desai, 2010).

Physical abuse is often used for disciplining the child and results in physical injuries as well as psychological damage (Winton & Mara, 2001).

Physical Abuse of Children in Different Settings

According to Pinheiro's (2006) report, corporal punishment and other forms of cruel or degrading punishment are used by parents and other family members at home, by those responsible for their care in institutions, by teachers in schools and are also inflicted on children in conflict with the law. In the community, a child who is labelled vagrant or antisocial may be assaulted or otherwise ill-treated, with impunity, by figures in authority, including police. Children forced into prostitution frequently describe their violent treatment by clients as if it were something they deserved.

Physical Abuse in Family: In what we call a paradox, the home, a natural environment for children to promote their growth and provide safety, is a site of violence against children where protectors or caregivers (that include the parents, step-parents, foster parents, siblings or significant others) are often the perpetrators of violence. Violence at home frequently takes place in the context of discipline and manifest in the form of physical, cruel or humiliating punishment. Physical violence is often accompanied by psychological violence like insulting, name-calling, isolation, rejection and so on. The home is considered to be a "private" sphere thereby making elimination of violence very challenging (Pinheiro, 2006).

Physical Abuse in Schools: School going children across the world spend a considerable part of their day in the educational settings. Therefore, schools need to provide a safe environment to children. However, global data indicate that educational settings expose children to physical abuse through corporal punishment, playground fighting or aggression, bullying by other children, gang violence and assault with weapons (Pinheiro, 2006).

Physical Abuse of Children in Institutions: Children in institutions are at risk of violence from staff and officials responsible for their well-being. Corporal punishment in institutions is not explicitly prohibited in many countries. Overcrowding and squalid conditions, societal stigmatisation and discrimination, and poorly trained staff heighten the risk of violence. Lack of effective complaints, monitoring and inspection mechanisms coupled with inadequate government regulation to hold perpetrators accountable create a culture of impunity and tolerance of violence against children (Pinheiro, 2006)

Physical Abuse in Work Settings: Despite the International Labour Organisation's Convention concerning Minimum Age for Admission to Employment that precludes children under the minimum age of employment from being in the workplace, millions of children work legally or illegally, especially in the informal sector. Children are physically abused to coerce them to work or to punish or control them in the workplace setting. Perpetrators of abuse at the workplace are largely the "employers" but could also include coworkers, clients, foremen, customers, police and criminal gangs and, in the case of sexual exploitation, pimps (Pinheiro, 2006).

Physical Abuse on the Street: According to a study by Butterflies (2004), the children who live on the streets, both girls and boys, are relatively more susceptible to violence and abuse as they lack the protection of an adult guardian and shelter. They are exposed to abuse by:

- The older street boys, who bully them, beat them and forcibly take away their earnings or belongings.
- Employers who make them work under exploitative working conditions besides thrashing them for not doing the work properly.
- Police who round them mostly in the nights to clear the streets of "vagrants".
- Public who verbally and physically abuse them, as they perceive them as deviants and delinquents.

Concept of Corporal Punishment

The UN Committee on the Rights of the Child (2006, p. 4) defines "corporal" or "physical" punishment as any punishment in which physical force is used and intended to cause some degree of pain or discomfort, however light. Most involves hitting ("smacking", "slapping", "spanking") children, with the hand or with an implement—a whip, stick, belt, shoe, wooden spoon, etc. But it can also involve, for example, kicking, shaking or throwing children, scratching, pinching, biting, pulling hair or boxing ears, forcing children to stay in uncomfortable positions, burning, scalding or forced ingestion. In the view of the Committee, corporal punishment is invariably degrading. In addition, there are other non-physical forms of punishment that are also cruel and degrading and thus incompatible with the Convention. These include, for example, punishment which belittles, humiliates, denigrates, scapegoats, threatens, scares or ridicules the child.

According to the Juvenile Justice Act of India (India: Ministry of Law and Justice, 2016), "corporal punishment" means the subjecting of a child by any person to physical punishment that involves the deliberate infliction of pain as retribution for an offence, or for the purpose of disciplining or reforming the child.

Causes of Corporal Punishment

According to the Save the Children (n.d.), the use of corporal punishment is strongly rooted in our society and is passed on through generations; however, this does not mean that corporal punishment is justified. UNICEF ROSA (2001) noted that the phenomenon of corporal punishment clearly reflects and manifests children's lack of power and their low social status within society and the family as well as in the classroom. Children are generally seen as not "mature", and the assumption is made that adults know best and thus must make decisions about children's lives. The teacher is considered a figure of authority that must be obeyed while the students should adjust and comply. Parents resort to corporal punishment for different reasons:

- Because they consider it appropriate to children's education.
- Because it relieves tension.
- Because they lack sufficient resources to tackle a situation or do not have strategies for achieving what they want.
- Because they are not skilled at interpreting the social situations in which they are using corporal punishment.
- Because they cannot control their emotions (Save the Children, n.d.).

Effects of Corporal Punishment on Children

Save the Children (n.d.) noted the following effects of corporal punishment on children:

- It lowers their self-esteem.
- It teaches them to be victims.
- It interferes with the learning process.
- It hampers the capacity to understand the relationship between behaviour and its consequences.
- It makes children feel lonely, sad and abandoned.
- It promotes a negative view of other people and of society as a threatening place.
- It creates barriers that impede parent–child communication and damages the emotional links established between them.
- It stimulates anger and a desire to run away from home.
- It teaches that violence is an acceptable way of solving problems.
- It does not teach children to cooperate with authority; it teaches them to comply with the rules or to infringe them.
- Children can suffer from accidental physical injuries.

Save the Children (n.d.) noted the following effects of corporal punishment on parents:

- Corporal punishment can produce feelings of anxiety and guilt, even when the use of this kind of punishment is considered appropriate.
- Violence tends to escalate. The use of corporal punishment increases the probability that parents will show aggressive behaviour in the future with growing frequency and intensity and also in other contexts.

- Corporal punishment inhibits communication and damages the relationship between parents and their children.
- When parents use corporal punishment because they lack alternative resources, they feel the need to justify their behaviour to themselves and to society. So the unease derived from using corporal punishment on children is exacerbated by confused feelings arising from an incoherent and unfounded rationale.

Save the Children (n.d.) noted the following effects of corporal punishment on society:

- Corporal punishment increases the use of violence in society and legitimizes it in the eyes of succeeding generations.
- It promotes a double standard: there are two categories of citizens—children and adults. It is acceptable to assault children, but not adults.
- Corporal punishment contributes to broken family patterns:
- Families where there is no communication between members become divided into assailants and the assaulted.
- Families that are not integrated into society are in conflict with the equality advocated by democracy.
- Corporal punishment makes protection of the child difficult. Because the practice of corporal punishment is tolerated, children lose faith in society as a protective environment.
- Corporal punishment contributes to a society characterised by submissive citizenship, where individuals have learned from their earliest years that being a victim is a natural condition.

Child Right to Protection from Corporal Punishment

According to Article 28(2) of the UNCRC, States Parties shall take all appropriate measures to ensure that school discipline is administered in a manner consistent with the child's human dignity and in conformity with the present Convention. According to Article 17 of the Right of Children to Free and Compulsory Education Act (RTE), 2009, "No child shall be subjected to physical punishment or mental harassment".

The UN Committee on the Rights of the Child (2006) believes that implementation of the prohibition of all corporal punishment requires awareness-raising, guidance and training for all those involved. This must ensure that the law operates in the best interests of the affected children—in particular when parents or other close family members are the perpetrators. The first purpose of law reform to prohibit corporal punishment of children within the family is prevention: to prevent violence against children by changing attitudes and practice, underlining children's right to equal protection and providing an unambiguous foundation for child protection and for the promotion of positive, non-violent and participatory forms of child rearing.

According to the Global Initiative to End All Corporal Punishment of Children and Save the Children Sweden (2010), the human rights imperative to end corporal punishment of children is supported by the following reasons for eliminating it:

- Children have a right to respect for their human dignity and physical and mental integrity and a right to protection from all forms of violence, including equal protection from assault under the law.
- Children also have basic human rights to education, development, health and survival, which can be threatened when they are subjected to corporal punishment.
- Corporal punishment has negative short- and long-term effects on children and their development.
- Responding to unacceptable behaviour by using corporal punishment teaches children that violence is an appropriate strategy for resolving conflict or getting people to do what you want.
- Corporal punishment is ineffective as a means of discipline. Any change in behaviour is likely to be due to fear of punishment rather than to understanding right from wrong. There are positive ways to teach, correct and discipline children which are better for the child's development and relationships with parents and others, without using corporal punishment.
- The legality of corporal punishment undermines child protection because it reinforces and perpetuates the idea that a certain degree of violence against children is acceptable and that children should not have the same respect for their human dignity as adults.

Prevention of Violence in Schools

School going children across the world spend a considerable part of their day in the educational settings. Therefore, schools need to provide a safe environment to children. However, global data indicate that educational settings expose children to physical abuse through corporal punishment, playground fighting or aggression, bullying by other children, gang violence and assault with weapons (Pinheiro, 2006).

The National Commission for Protection of Child Rights (2008) direct the education departments of all the States to ensure the following:

1. All children are to be informed through campaigns and publicity drives that they have a right to speak against corporal punishment and bring it to the notice of the authorities. They must be given confidence to make complaints and not accept punishment as a "normal" activity of the school.
2. Every school, including hostels, Juvenile Justice Homes, shelter homes and other public institutions meant for children must have a forum where children can express their views. Such institutions could take the help of an NGO for facilitating such an exercise.
3. A box where children can drop their complaints, even if anonymous has to be provided for in each school.

4. There has to be a monthly meeting of the Parent–Teacher Associations (PTAs) or any other body such as the School Education Committees and Village Education Committees to review the complaints and take action.
5. The PTAs are to be encouraged to act immediately on any complaints made by children without postponement of the issue and wait for a more grave injury to be caused. In other words, the PTAs need not use their discretion to decide on the grievousness of the complaint.
6. Parents as well as children are to be empowered to speak out against corporal punishment without any fear that it would have adverse effect on children's participation in schools.
7. The education department at all levels block, district and State are to establish procedures for reviewing the responses to the complaints of children and monitoring the action taken on the same.

Activities

Activity 6.3: Video Discussion on Protection of Children from Physical Abuse

Learner Outcome: At the end of this activity, the participants will develop awareness on the causes and effects of physical abuse of children.

Procedure: Use the following procedure to conduct this activity:

1. Show the video film: Raghu (right to protection from family abuse) http://www.youtube.com/watch?v=Ix8yGYk3nKA&list= PL38322753F73B5A71
2. Use the following questions to discuss this activity:

   - Why do parents beat up their children frequently?
   - What are the effects of physical abuse on children?
   - How can physical abuse be prevented?
   - What should the child who is abused do?
   - What should his friends do?
   - What should the parents do?
   - What adultist attitude of society needs to change?

3. Form small groups and allocate the following topics among them to read the relevant notes and discuss with examples:

   a. Causes of corporal punishment;
   b. Effects of corporal punishment;
   c. Child right to protection from corporal punishment.

4. Ask the small groups to make a presentation of their discussion to the large group.

Time Estimate: 45 min

Activity 6.4: Video Discussion on Prevention of Corporal Punishment in Schools

Learner Outcome: At the end of this activity, the participants will develop awareness about

Procedure: Use the following procedure to conduct this activity:

1. Show the video film The Rose: Short film on Corporal Punishment by Childline
   https://www.youtube.com/watch?v=3kN60wTiLk8
2. Use the following questions to conduct discussion on the video:

   - Why was the teacher physically harassing the child? What was she telling the child? What was she expecting the child to do? Why?
   - How were the other children behaving with this child?
   - What was its effect on the child?
   - What was the rose project?
   - How did the child carry it out?
   - What are child rights against corporal punishment?
   - What did the Childline worker tell the teacher?
   - How does the teacher react?
   - What is the role of parents of the child who receives corporal punishment?
   - Should corporal punishment be stopped? Why?

3. Ask the participants to list the different types of corporal punishment they have experienced or heard of and their effects.
4. Show Summary Chart 6.2 to understand the causes and prevention of corporal punishment.

Time Estimate: 25 min

Activity 6.5: Street Plays on Protection of Children from Physical Abuse

Learner Outcome: At the end of this activity, the participants will learn the skills to protect children from physical abuse.

Procedure: Use the following procedure to conduct this activity:

1. Divide the participants into five small groups and give each a case situation from the following. Ask them to analyse their case situation and prepare street plays for creating public awareness on the following points:

   - What makes the child vulnerable to physical abuse?
   - What are the effects of physical abuse on children?
   - What are the effects of physical abuse on society?
   - How can children be protected from abuse?

Case Situations:

(1) Farzeen (age 14 years) works as a full-time domestic maid in Mumbai. While working, she mistakenly broke a piece of chinaware in her employer's house. She was inflicted with cigarette burns on her hands, and part of her salary was deducted for this mistake. She works all through the day and is given very less food to eat. Her family who is very poor stays very far off in the village. She continues to endure this ill-treatment as she has nowhere to go.

(2) Shekhar (age 8 years) studies in class III in a municipal school. His maths teacher makes them regularly narrate tables in class. Whoever makes a mistake is spanked with a ruler on the knuckles. One day, Shekhar was hit on his knuckles for not remembering his tables well. He was in pain for two days. Now he is so petrified of this teacher that he does not want to go to school on the days of math periods. He is too scared to even talk about it to anyone.

(3) Rajiv (age 13 years) was asked by his father to buy a packet of cigarette. As Rajiv was feeling unwell, he politely expressed his inability to buy the cigarettes. On being refused, his father got very angry and did not allow him food or water for the whole day.

(4) David (age 10 years) is being beaten by the Railway Police as he was sleeping at the railway station. He says that this is a daily occurrence, and often the boys paid money to the Railway Police to be allowed to sleep at the station.

(5) Aditi (age 8 years) lives in a State-run shelter home for street children. The older girls in shelter home expect her to do their chores like washing clothes. If she tries to refuse, she is beaten up by them. Aditi is scared to complain to the authorities for fear of being beaten for going against them.

2. Have the small groups present their street plays to the large group for feedback.

Time Estimate: 45 min

Prevention of Bullying Among Children

Concepts and Theories

Concept of Bullying: According to Sampson (2002, cited in Hess & Drowns, 2004, p. 184), "Bullying has two key components: repeated harmful acts and an imbalance of power. It involves repeated physical, verbal or psychological attacks or intimidation directed against a victim who cannot properly defend him or herself because of size or strength, or because the victim is outnumbered or less psychologically resilient". Bullying can cover teasing, staring, calling names, threatening, blocking path, hitting, hurting, stealing, talking nastily or ignoring. Bullying can take place in schools, playgrounds or even at home (Mehtani, 2012). Verbal bullying comprises calling children names such as stupid, idiot, *thingu* (shortie), *motu* (fatty), *kalia* (blackie), *langda* (lame), *totda* (stammerer) and so on depending upon their behaviour or physical appearance or disability. It conveys inferiority which can be humiliating and emotionally abusive.

Causes of Bullying: Bully victims are examples of passiveness; they are depressed and lonely, physically weaker, have lower social status and are less popular. They have low self-esteem and are generally anxious, cautious and fit into the withdrawn category of rejected children. Bullying is an example of aggressiveness. Bullies are typically physically stronger than their peers. They have strong needs for power and enjoy being in control. They have been reared in a family environment characterised by indifference, low involvement and lack of warmth. This context results in little sense of personal empathy and a high degree of hostility towards others (Newman & Newman, 2006).

Effects of Bullying: According to Ericson (2001, cited in Hess & Drowns, 2004, p. 184), "Bullying can affect the social environment of a school, creating a climate of fear among students, inhibiting their ability to learn and leading to other antisocial behaviour…".

UNICEF Malaysia (2007) discusses the following effects of bullying:

- **The Effect on the Victim**: Students who are the victims of bullying suffer behavioural consequences, including:

    - Loss of an interest in schoolwork.
    - Reluctance to attend school, poor attendance, lower grades.
    - Limited social contact with peers.
    - Mood swings, especially towards depression, irritability, unhappiness, outbursts of anger.
    - Report headaches, stomach pains (frequently in the morning before leaving for school), poor appetite and loss of sleep.
    - Visible cuts, scratches, bruises.
    - Loss of personal property because of theft or extortion.

- **The Effect on the Bully**: Students who bully others also suffer behavioural consequences, including:

    - Lower grades.
    - Antisocial behaviours, including use of drugs, alcohol and tobacco, and engaging in vandalism.
    - Be truant from school.
    - Dropout of school.
    - Oppositional behaviour and defiance directed at adults, including adult authority figures.
    - More likely to be convicted of criminal behaviour in a court of law.

- **The Effect on the Bystander/Witness**: Students who witness bullying may also suffer behavioural consequences, including:

    - Feelings of anger and helplessness for not knowing what to do;
    - Nightmares about being the next target;

- Guilt for not taking action;
- Fear of certain areas in school (UNICEF Malaysia, 2007).

Equitas (2008) notes that even if meant as a "joke", words can have a negative impact on the children and on the overall group dynamic:

- Verbal abuse lowers self-esteem and causes anxiety and stress in those children who suffer it.
- Name-calling and jeering that are used "just for fun" often escalate to bullying and physical violence.
- A bullying incident often lasts less than one minute, but can leave emotional scars that last a lifetime.
- Verbal abuse makes children feel unsafe and limits their capacity and will to participate and speak freely.

Zero Tolerance: Equitas (2008) recommends that a "zero tolerance" approach should be taken to maintain an environment in which children feel respected and safe. Equitas proposes two steps in effective intervention:

1. Put a stop to the behaviour.
2. Educate the children involved, choosing the right time and place.

Depending on the circumstances, children may choose to intervene immediately with the group, or wait and deal with the issue privately as given below by Equitas (2008).

Educating on the Spot:

- Allows for immediate action and support.
- Provides the opportunity to remind the children that there is a zero tolerance policy for verbal abuse.
- Reassures the children and makes them feel safer.
- Shows that there are consequences to using offensive language.
- Provides the opportunity to explain to all the children that using offensive language is unacceptable and that everyone has the right to be respected.

Educating at a Later Time:

- Allows the people involved (offenders, victims, staff) time to calm down.
- Gives offenders the opportunity to save face.
- Avoids putting the victims in an embarrassing situation.
- Allows more time to explore and explain the consequences of verbal abuse.

Possible forms of group intervention:
  Explain to the child in a clear and firm, but respectful tone:

- What you just said is unacceptable…
- Respect is very important in our group. What you just said was not respectful to…
- Please apologise to…

Possible forms of private intervention:

- What did you mean by saying "You're an idiot"?
- How do you think (name of the child) felt when you said that?
- Why is it unacceptable to say what you said?
- What you said is a stereotype. Stereotypes are like lies, and they hurt other people's feelings.
- What could you do next time to show more respect?

Reparation: The Society for Safe and Caring Schools and Communities (2007) recommend that an effective reparation agreement must be logical and healing, and it must include the following criteria:

- **It must be related to the offence**: This means that the reparation has something to do with the negative behaviour and ideally aims to reverse the negative impact. For example, damage to a personal belonging could involve repairing the belonging. Bullying could involve, among other things, the person responsible for the harm "looking out" for the harmed in the future, ensuring that he or she is not bullied by someone else.
- **It must be reasonable**: There is no sense setting consequences that the person responsible for the harm is not capable of fulfilling. This increases the likelihood of failure and rejection of the process, leading to alienation rather than reintegration. There is also no benefit in creating consequences that are too lenient. Consequences that encourage learning must require some amount of effort or sacrifice to have impact.
- **It must be respectful**: It must not harm anyone involved. Reparation that enhances rather than transforms feelings of guilt, increase feelings of alienation and resentment. An example might be forcing the person responsible for the harm to wear a tag saying "I am a bully". Everyone involved should retain his/her dignity.
- **It must be responsible**: The person responsible for the harm must take responsibility for completing the reparation and not let it fall to someone else.

Activities

Activity 6.6: Video Discussion on Protection from Bullying

Learner Outcome: At the end of this activity, the participants will develop awareness about bullying and learn the skills to stop bullying and being bullied.

Procedure: Use the following procedure to conduct this activity:

1. Show the video film by Save the Children: Ek Naya Suraj Hindi
   https://www.youtube.com/watch?v=veo2kIo2LFk&list=
   PL38322753F73B5A71

2. Use the following questions to discuss this video:

- Why do some children bully?
- What are its effects on others?
- How can a group of children stop the one who bullies?
- How can talking to adults help stop the one who bullies?
- How can the bullies be made less aggressive?
- Why do some children allow others to bully them? How can they become more assertive?
- What is the role of parents of the child who bully?
- What is the role of parents of the child who is bullied?
- What is the role of school authorities to prevent bullying in schools?
- How can reparation be carried out?

3. Show Summary Chart 6.3 to summarise on bullying.

Time Estimate: 20 min

Activity 6.7: Role-Plays on Protection from Verbal Bullying

Learner Outcome: At the end of this activity, the participants will learn the skills to protect themselves from verbal abuse.

Procedure: Use the following procedure to conduct this activity:

1. Ask the participants what they mean by verbal abuse? List the responses on the board.
2. Make a list of abusive words that they are called or they have heard some children being called. For example, stupid, idiot, *thingu* (shortie), *motu* (fatty), *kalia* (blackie), *langda* (lame), *totda* (stammerer), etc. Discuss the following questions:

   (1) Why do children verbally abuse other children?
   (2) What are the effects of verbal abuse on children?
   (3) How can we convey zero tolerance to verbal abuse?

3. Identify any one situation and form four small groups to prepare role-plays on three ways to put a stop to bullying:

   (1) How the child can respond to the one who abuses immediately,
   (2) How the child can go and talk to the one who abuses after he/she calms down,
   (3) How a group of children can respond to verbal abuse of one child and
   (4) How the school/community leader can plan reparation.

4. Present the role-plays to the large group for further inputs.

Time Estimate: 30 min

Activity 6.8: Small Group Discussion on Zero Tolerance to Violence in Schools

Learner Outcome: At the end of this activity, the participants will learn how to prevent and deal with violence in schools at the policy level.

Procedure: Use the following procedure to conduct this activity:

1. Form three small groups and allocate the roles of students, parents and teachers to them. Ask each group to prepare a draft of "Zero Tolerance to Violence in School" policy to include preventive and responding approaches to corporal punishment and bullying.
2. Ask the groups to make their presentations to the large group and discuss how these inputs may be used to make a "no violence in school" policy for the school.

Time Estimate: 30 min

Concluding Activity: Achievement of the Learner Objectives

Learner Outcome: By the end of the concluding activity, the participants will ascertain if they have achieved the learner objectives.

Procedure: Use the following procedure to conduct the concluding activity:

1. Show the power points/a chart on the learner objectives, ask the participants to read them one at a time and ask the group if they think they have achieved the objective.
2. The participants may be asked to share their responses in their diary with reference to the following questions:

   - What was a new learning for you in this session?
   - What did you like the best in this session and why?
   - Which activity was most effective?
   - What was not clear/confusing?
   - How can you apply what you have learnt?

Time Estimate: 15 min

Appendix: Summary Charts and Exercises

Summary Chart 6.1 Understanding child abuse

Causes of Child Abuse		
Structural Causes	**Family Level Causes**	**Individual Level Causes**
• Poverty • Patriarchy • Adultism • Vulnerability of marginalised children ↓	• Parental collusion • Scapegoating • Reorganised families • Single-parent status • Adolescent parents • Lack of extended family ↓	• Low self-esteem • Excessive dependency • Poor impulse control • Rigid superego structures • Deficient superego development • Social isolation • Serious difficulty coping with the demands of parenting • Lack of parenting skills and knowledge of child development ↓
Child Abuse		
• Intentional non-accidental physical, emotional and psychological or sexual harm done to a child, that endangers or impairs the child's physical, emotional and psychological or sexual health and development; • By older children, parents, relatives, caretakers, neighbours, teachers, employers, police or strangers; in family, neighbourhood, street, school, institutions, workplace, or police/ judicial custody. • Because of adult-child power imbalance due to adultism and patriarchy, psycho-social problems or socio-economic problems, and cycle of abuse.		
Cycle of Abuse		
• Abused children develop low self-esteem, poor management of negative emotions and problem solving, and weak communication and social skills. • Children learn how to parent from their parents. • These traits further make them abusers of children as adults.		

Summary Chart 6.2 Prevention of corporal punishment

Causes of Corporal Punishment: Adultism		
• Children's lack of power and their low social status • Children generally seen as not 'mature' ↓	• The assumption made that adults know best and thus must make decisions about children's lives ↓	• The teacher is considered a figure of authority that must be obeyed while the students should adjust and comply ↓

Concept of Corporal Punishment
Physical and Non-Physical Punishment Intended to Cause some degree of Pain or Discomfort   ↓

Effects of Corporal Punishment on Children
• It lowers their self-esteem. • It teaches them to be victims. • It interferes with the learning process. • It hampers the capacity to understand the relationship between behaviour and its consequences. • It makes children feel lonely, sad and abandoned. • It promotes a negative view of other people and of society as a threatening place. • It creates barriers that impede parent-child communication and damages the emotional links established between them. • It stimulates anger and a desire to run away from home. • It teaches that violence is an acceptable way of solving problems. • It doesn't teach children to cooperate with authority; it teaches them to comply with the rules or to infringe them.

Child Right to Protection from Corporal Punishment	
UNCRC: School discipline should be administered in a manner consistent with the child's human dignity	**Right of Children to Free and Compulsory Education Act:** No child shall be subjected to physical punishment or mental harassment.

Prevention of Corporal Punishment

1. Children have a right to speak against corporal punishment and bring it to the notice of the authorities. They must be given confidence to make complaints and not accept punishment as a 'normal' activity of the school.
2. Every school, including hostels, JJ Homes, shelter homes and other public institutions meant for children must have a forum where children can express their views.
3. Every school must provide for a box where children can drop their anonymous complaints.
4. PTAs, School Education Committees and Village Education Committees need to review the complaints in monthly meetings and take action.

Summary Chart 6.3 Prevention of bullying

Bullies	Bully-Victims
• Directs attacks or intimidation against a victim	• Cannot properly defend himself or herself
• Are aggressive, have strong needs for power and enjoy being in control	• Are passive, blame themselves for their problems
• Are physically bigger/ stronger	• Are physically weaker
• Have low self-esteem	• Have low self-esteem
• Enjoy temporary popularity	• Are lonely and less popular
• Lack personal empathy	• Are generally anxious and cautious

Bullying
Repeated physical, verbal, or psychological attacks or intimidation against a victim in schools, playgrounds, or even at home ↓

Effects of Bullying
Affects the social environment of a school Creates a climate of fear among students Inhibits their ability to learn Leads to other antisocial behaviour ↑

Prevention of Bullying		
Schools need to formulate and strictly implement a policy of no violence in school	Bullies need life skills of self-esteem, emotional intelligence and relationship skills	Victims need life skills of self-esteem, emotional intelligence and relationship skills

Exercise for Activity 6.1: Understanding and Attitude to Child Abuse

No.	Which of the following situations can be considered child abuse?	Is it child abuse? Yes-1 No-2
1)	When the parents deprive a seven year old child of food as punishment for watching more TV.	
2)	When the widowed mother locks a three year old child at home with arrangement for food, because she has to go to work.	
3)	When the parents lock up an adolescent daughter in a room, because she has an affair with a boy in the neighbourhood.	
4)	When two children fight, and harm one another.	
5)	When an elder child bullies a younger child.	
6)	When the parents constantly compare their child with that of the neighbour.	
7)	When the teacher makes the child kneel and touch his toes for two hours for not doing his homework.	
8)	When the police beat up a street child who is begging.	
9)	When a 12 year old girl who looks after her four year old brother gets tired by the evening, so gets beaten up by the mother.	
10)	When a male relative shares with a girl the pleasures of his sex life.	
11)	When the parents hug their child before he or she goes to sleep.	

Acknowledgements This chapter is partly adapted from the following chapter by the author: Desai, M. (2010). Chapter 17: Abuse in Childhood and Tertiary Prevention. In *A Rights-Based Preventative Approach for Psychosocial Well-Being in Childhood*. Heidelberg: Springer, Series on Children's Well-Being: Indicators and Research.

References

Boyden, J., & Levison, D. (2000). *Children as economic and social actors in the development process*. Sweden: Ministry of Foreign Affairs.

Burman, E. (2008). *Deconstructing developmental psychology* (2nd ed.). London: Routledge Taylor and Frances Group.

Butterflies. (2004). *Summary of major findings of a field based study on child abuse*. New Delhi: Butterflies.

Corby, B. (2002). Child abuse and child protection. In B. Goldson, M. Lavalette, & J. McKechnie (Eds.), *Children, welfare and the state* (pp. 136–151). London: Sage Publications.

Desai, M. (2010). *A rights-based preventative approach for psychosocial well-being in childhood*. Heidelberg: Springer, Series on Children's Well-Being: Indicators and Research.

Downs, S. W., Moore, E., & McFadden, E. J. (2009). *Child welfare and family services: Policies and practice* (8th ed.). Boston: Pearson A and B.

Equitas—International Centre for Human Rights Education. (2008). *Play it fair!: Human rights education toolkit for children*. Montreal. Retrieved from http://equitas.org/wp-content/uploads/2011/01/SpeakingRightsSample.pdf.

Global Initiative to End All Corporal Punishment of Children & Save the Children Sweden. (2010). *Ending corporal punishment and other cruel and degrading punishment of children through law reform and social change: Campaign manual*. Retrieved from http://www.acabarcastigo.org/wp-content/uploads/2011/10/Ending-corporal-punishment-and-other-cruel-and-degrading-punishment-of-children.pdf.

Hess, K. M., & Drowns, R. W. (2004). *Juvenile justice*. Australia: Thomson Wadsworth.

India: Ministry of Law and Justice. (2016). *Juvenile justice (care and protection of children) amendment act, 2015*. New Delhi. Retrieved from http://wcd.nic.in/sites/default/files/JJ%20Act,%202015%20_0.pdf.

Koramoa, J., Lynch, M. A., & Kinnair, D. (2002). A continuum of child-rearing: Responding to traditional practices. *Child Abuse Review, 11*(6), 415–421.

Korbin, J. E. (1981). Introduction. In J. E. Korbin (Ed.), *Child abuse and neglect: Cross-cultural perspectives* (pp. 1–12). Los Angeles: University of California Press.

Korbin, J. E. (2003). Children, childhoods, and violence. *Annual Review of Anthropology, 32*, 431–446.

Leeder, E. J. (2003). *The family in global perspective: A gendered journey*. London: Sage Publications.

Mason, J., & Steadman, B. (1996). *The significance of the conceptualisation of childhood for promoting children's contributions to child protection policy*. Paper presented at the Fifth Australian Family Research Conference, organised by the Australian Institute of Family Studies, Brisbane.

Mehtani, H. (2012). *Happiness: A treasure within: Book 3*. New Delhi: Sultan Chand.

National Commission for the Protection of Child Rights. (2008). *Protection of children against corporal punishment in schools and institutions: Summary discussions by the working group on corporal punishment*. Delhi. Retrieved from http://harprathmik.gov.in/pdf/rte/corporal%20punishment%20ncpcr.pdf.

Newman, B. M., & Newman, P. R. (2006). *Development through life: A psychosocial approach* (10th ed.). Belmont: Brooks/Cole.

Pinheiro, S. (2006). *World report on violence against children.* Geneva. Retrieved from http://www.unicef.org/lac/full_tex(3).pdf.

Rosado, C. (1994).*Understanding cultural relativism in a multicultural world.* Retrieved from http://www.rosado.net/pdf/Cultural_Relativism.pdf.

Save the Children. (n.d.). *Educate, don't punish!: Awareness campaign against corporal punishment of children in families.* Retrieved from http://www.unicef.org/lac/spbarbados/Implementation/CP/Global/Educate_donthit_SaveManual.pdf.

The Society for Safe and Caring Schools and Communities. (2007). *Restorative justice community/classroom conferencing: A guide for parents and teachers.* Edmonton: Author. Retrieved from http://safeandcaring.ca/wp-content/uploads/2013/08/Restorative-Justice-booklet-Web-version.pdf.

United Nations. (1989). *Convention on the rights of the child.* Retrieved from http://www.ohchr.org/english/law/pdf/crc.pdf.

United Nations Committee on the Rights of the Child. (2006). *General Comment No. 6. The right of the child to protection from corporal punishment and other cruel or degrading forms of punishment (articles 19, 28(2) and 37, inter alia), CRC/C/GC/6.* Geneva: Author.

United Nations International Children's Fund ROSA. (2001). *Corporal punishment in schools in South Asia.* Kathmandu. Retrieved from http://www.crin.org/docs/resources/treaties/crc.28/UNICEF-SAsia-Subm.pdf.

United Nations International Children's Fund: Malaysia. (2007). Stop violence in schools! The scope and impact of bullying. Malaysia: Author. Retrieved from http://www.unicef.org/malaysia/UNICEF_-_Fact_Sheet_-_Impact_and_Scope_of_Bullying.pdf.

Winton, M. A., & Mara, B. A. (2001). *Child abuse and neglect: Multidisciplinary approaches.* Boston: Allyn and Bacon.

World Health Organization & International Society for Prevention of Child Abuse and Neglect. (2006). *Preventing child maltreatment: A guide to taking action and generating evidence.* Retrieved from http://apps.who.int/iris/bitstream/10665/43499/1/9241594365_eng.pdf.

Zechenter, E. M. (1997). In the name of culture: Cultural relativism and the abuse of the individual. *Journal of Anthropological Research, 53*(3), 319–347. Retrieved from http://www.class.uh.edu/faculty/tsommers/moral%20diversity/cultural%20relativism%20abuse%20of%20individual.pdf.

Module 7
Child Rights to Prevention of Commercial Exploitation

Prerequisite Modules

The prerequisite Modules for this Module are:
From *Sourcebook I on Introduction to Rights-Based Direct Practice with Children*:

- Modules on Life Skills Development

From *Sourcebook II on Child Rights Education for Participation and Development: Primary Prevention*:

- Introduction to Child Rights Education;
- Child Rights to Participation and Children's Associations;
- Child Rights to Sexual Health Education.

From *Sourcebook III on Child Rights Education for Inclusion and Protection: Primary Prevention*:

- Child Rights to Prevention of Violence

Conceptual Framework of Child Rights to Prevention of Commercial Exploitation of Children

Concepts and Theories

Concept of Child Commercial Exploitation

Commercial exploitation of children comprises abuse by the adult and remuneration in cash or kind to the child or a third person or persons, where the child is treated as a commercial object. The commercial exploitation of children constitutes a form of coercion and violence against children and amounts to a contemporary form of slavery (Adapted from the Stockholm Declaration and Agenda for Action adopted at the First World Congress against Commercial Sexual Exploitation of Children, 1996). Article 3 of the United Nations (UN) Protocol to Prevent, Suppress and

© Child Rights and You 2018
M. Desai and S. Goel, *Child Rights Education for Inclusion and Protection: Primary Prevention*, Rights-based Direct Practice with Children, https://doi.org/10.1007/978-981-13-0417-0_7

Punish Trafficking in Persons, especially Women and Children, Supplementing the UN Convention against Transnational Organised Crime (2000) states that exploitation shall include, at a minimum, the exploitation of the prostitution of others or other forms of sexual exploitation, forced labour or services, slavery or practices similar to slavery, servitude or the removal of organs.

By this definition, commercial exploitation of children comprises:

1. Exploitation of children for unpaid/underpaid labour in industries, construction work, restaurant work, domestic work, household-based work, etc.
2. Trafficking and sale of children: are gender and age-specific, rural to urban, interstate and international, for begging, labour, prostitution, adoption, entertainment, sale of organs and marriage.
3. Commercial sexual exploitation of children: takes the forms of child marriage, child prostitution, sex tourism and pornography (Desai, 2010).

Causes of Commercial Exploitation of Children

Changing Economy: The unregulated global market forces have unleashed social and economic changes in last two decades that have irreversibly impacted the lives of even those who survive in marginal informal economies of remote South Asian rural villages and low-income urban peripheries. Globalisation has stimulated urbanisation, expanded trade across national borders, increased mobility of capital and labour and challenged subsistence economies. Dominated by international competition, production has been dissociated from its place of origin and workers have lost the social function of contributing to the development of their own communities. Work has progressively turned into a commodity and workers into slaves, now being exploited at an industrial level, to a degree never seen before—not even during the transatlantic slave trade (ECPAT, 2014). The drive for rising profits too often trumps ethics, resulting in children being exploited in factories and sweatshops (UNICEF, 2005b).

According to a United Nations Development Programme Report (1999), factors contributing to the increase in trafficking of women include globalisation, and economic liberalisation, increased demand and supply of trafficked persons, professionalisation of the traffickers and syndicates, modern transport, technology and the Internet, growth of sex tourism, feminisation of poverty, trading in human organs, changing nature of prostitution and erosion of social capital.

Vulnerability of the Poor: The vulnerability that accompanies economic poverty among around half of South Asia's population is compounded by the presence and tolerance of inequality and marginalisation based on age, gender, class, caste, ethnicity and religion. These factors combine in harmful ways to push entire social groups to the margins, leaving them with inadequate economic assets, limited opportunities, low social status and, generally, an inability to generate the resources necessary to satisfy their basic needs. Such circumstances put families under severe strain as increasing instability erodes their capacity to act as the frontline of protection for their children. At the same time, shifts in the economy have weakened the social structures that ordinarily serve as a safety net to help meet basic needs, such as public health, education and other social services, pushing them further and further beyond the reach of those most in need. As more families drift towards the social and economic margins of society, their children's vulnerability to all forms of violence, abuse and exploitation is exacerbated (ECPAT, 2014).

Child Right to Protection from Commercial Exploitation

The United Nations Convention on the Rights of the Child (UNCRC, 1989) does not use the word "commercial" but makes the following provisions for protection of children from exploitation:

- Article 36 states that "States Parties shall protect the child against all other forms of exploitation prejudicial to any aspects of the child's welfare".
- Article 39 states that "States Parties shall take all appropriate measures to promote physical and psychological recovery and social reintegration of a child victim of any form of neglect, exploitation, or abuse; torture or any other form of cruel, inhuman or degrading treatment or punishment; or armed conflicts. Such recovery and reintegration shall take place in an environment, which fosters the health, self-respect and dignity of the child".

The Fundamental Rights provided by the Indian Constitution include "Right against Exploitation: Prohibition of traffic in human beings and forced and child labour".

Activities

Introductory Activity 7.1: Brainstorming on Understanding Commercial Exploitation of Children

Learner Outcome: At the end of this activity, the participants will develop awareness on concept, causes and effects of commercial exploitation of children.

Procedure: Use the following procedure to conduct this activity:

1. Ask the participants the following questions:

    a. What do you know of commercial exploitation of children?
    b. How is it different from child abuse?
    c. What are its causes?
    d. What are its effects?
    e. How can it be prevented?

2. Show Summary Chart 7.1 and discuss the stakeholders/causes, types, effects and prevention of commercial exploitation of children.
3. Introduce the following units of the module:

   • Prevention of Exploitation of Children for Labour;
   • Prevention of Trafficking and Sale of Children.

Time Estimate: 15 min

Prevention of Exploitation of Children for Labour

Concepts and Theories

Concepts of Child Labour

Child Work: In the pre-industrialised period, work was a natural part of life for children. Industrialisation was not responsible for children's entry into the work-force, but it extended children's employment opportunities out of domestic industries and in the factories, mills and mines (Stack & McKechnie, 2002).

Extension of childhood up to 18 years of age sometimes isolates adolescents from productive activities that once conferred on them social standing and acceptance. Prolonged schooling does not assure employment that would have come more easily to them if they joined work early. In fact, prolonged schooling without vocational training may increase unemployment in young adults, who would then drift into idleness, substance use or crime. Work experience entails understanding how the adult labour market works, learning how to negotiate with adults other than parents, appreciating the value of money, developing a sense of responsibility and other good work habits. In situations where the quality of education is questionable, it is commonly thought as preferable for children to leave school, so that they can focus their attention on work, which seems like a more fruitful way of spending their time and brings immediate economic returns (Boyden & Levison, 2000).

According to the International Labour Organisation (ILO) (http://www.ilo.org/ipec/facts/lang–en/index.htm), not all work done by children should be classified as child labour that is to be targeted for elimination. Children's or adolescents' participation in work that does not affect their health and personal development or interfere with their schooling is generally regarded as being something positive. This includes activities such as helping their parents around the home, assisting in a family business or earning pocket money outside school hours and during school holidays. These kinds of activities contribute to children's development and to the welfare of their families; they provide them with skills and experience and help to prepare them to be productive members of society during their adult life.

Child Labour: Due to industrialisation, home and work got separated, so children were no longer employed by the parents but by strangers and in conditions that were not healthy (Stack & McKechnie, 2002), giving rise to the issue of child labour.

According to ILO (http://www.ilo.org/ipec/facts/lang–en/index.htm), the term "child labour" is often defined as work that deprives children of their childhood, their potential and their dignity, and that is harmful to their physical and mental development. It refers to work that:

- Is mentally, physically, socially or morally dangerous and harmful to children; and
- Interferes with their schooling by:
    - Depriving them of the opportunity to attend school;
    - Obliging them to leave school prematurely; or
    - Requiring them to attempt to combine school attendance with excessively long and heavy work.

ILO further affirms that whether or not particular forms of "work" can be called "child labour" depends on the child's age, the type and hours of work performed, the conditions under which it is performed, etc. In its most extreme forms, child labour involves children being enslaved, separated from their families, exposed to serious hazards and illnesses and/or left to fend for themselves on the streets of large cities— often at a very early age (http://www.ilo.org/ipec/facts/lang–en/index.htm).

The Invisible Child Labour: Many working children are virtually "invisible". They work in private homes, either as domestic servants (reputedly the largest single type of employment for girls under 18 working outside their own homes), or as part of a household which takes on sub-contracted work as "homeworkers": stitching footballs, for example or weaving carpets. Most of these children are girls. Others are invisible because they work away from towns and cities in agriculture, fishing, hunting and forestry. While children working in their own homes and for their own families are in an environment which ought to protect them, some are still subjected to exploitation or work in hazardous conditions. The informal economy draws in large numbers of children. Almost by definition, it is unregulated: labour laws are not observed and governments generally make little or no attempt to enforce them. Child domestic workers, for example, are rarely given a formal contract and are routinely subjected to abuse (UNICEF, 2005a).

Domestic Work: Since domestic labour is usually unregulated, this type of work is often hidden from the public eye. Children, particularly girls, are often exposed to cruel treatment, forced to work excessive hours and prohibited from attending school. Sometimes, they have been trafficked into the situation. Most child domestic workers are girls, although the proportion of girls and boys varies from place to place. Children are constantly on call and deprived of sleep. They may get inadequate food and may perform hazardous jobs for which they are unprepared. In many cultures, sexual favours are seen as simply part of the job. Girls who dropout of domestic work often run a high risk of ending up in prostitution or other forms of commercial sexual exploitation (ILO, 2004).

The Worst Forms of Child Labour: While child labour takes many different forms, a priority is to eliminate without delay the worst forms of child labour as defined by Article 3 of ILO Convention No. 182:

(a) All forms of slavery or practices similar to slavery, such as the sale and trafficking of children, debt bondage and serfdom and forced or compulsory labour, including forced or compulsory recruitment of children for use in armed conflict;
(b) The use, procuring or offering of a child for prostitution, for the production of pornography or for pornographic performances;
(c) The use, procuring or offering of a child for illicit activities, in particular for the production and trafficking of drugs as defined in the relevant international treaties;
(d) Work which, by its nature or the circumstances in which it is carried out, is likely to harm the health, safety or morals of children.

Debt Bondage: According to ILO (2004), debt bondage to a landlord is a particular kind of forced labour that can entrap children from poor families in agriculture without land or with too little of it to meet their subsistence needs. If the parents become indebted, they may have little choice but to bond their children into agricultural or domestic labour to repay the debt. Debt bondage places children ultimately at the mercy of the landowner (or a contractor or money-lender), where they suffer economic hardship and are deprived of education.

Causes of Child Labour

Supply of Child Labour: Anti-Slavery (2007) identified the following causes of child labour:

- **Poverty**: Most children work because their families are poor, and their labour is necessary for their survival. Being a result of poverty, child labour also perpetuates poverty. Many working children do not have the opportunity to go to school and often grow up to be unskilled adults trapped in poorly paid jobs and in turn will look to their own children to supplement the family's income.
- **Discrimination**: Discrimination on grounds of gender, race, caste/tribe or religion also comprises reasons for child labour.
- **Lack of Access to Education**: For many children, school is not an option. Education can be expensive and some parents feel that what their children will learn is irrelevant to the realities of their everyday lives and futures. In many cases, school is also physically inaccessible or lessons are not taught in the child's mother tongue, or both.
- **Profitability**: Children are often employed and exploited because, compared to adults, they are more vulnerable, cheaper to hire and are less likely to demand higher wages or better working conditions. Some employers argue that children

are particularly suited to certain types of work because of their small size and "nimble fingers".

Demand for Child Labour: The relatively low wages paid to children are often a reason why employers prefer them to adult workers. Some children work unpaid, particularly as domestic workers, in conditions that would be denounced as "slavery" if they involved adults. Employers find children more obedient and easier to control. Unlike older workers, they are unlikely to initiate protests or form trade unions. It is also easy for adults to intimidate children. Employers can force child workers into submission when the children are dependent on them for food, lodging and even emotional support. Employers take advantage of the public's acceptance of corporal punishment to beat their child workers as a means of controlling them (UNICEF, 2005c).

Child Right to Protection from Exploitation for Labour

UNCRC: The UNCRC makes the following provisions to protect children from exploitation for labour:

- Articles 28 and 29 state that primary education should be free and compulsory for all children. Different forms of secondary, general and vocational education should be made available and accessible to every child, free or with financial assistance to those who need it. Children also have the right to educational and vocational information and guidance.
- According to Article 31, children have the right to rest and leisure, to engage in play and recreational activities appropriate to their age and to participate freely in cultural life and the arts.
- According to Article 32, the child has the right to be protected from economic exploitation and from performing any work that is likely to be hazardous to or interfere with the child's education, or to be harmful to the child's health or physical, mental, spiritual moral or social development.

When the Indian Government ratified the UNCRC, in 1992, it made a declaration that it will undertake measures to progressively implement the provisions of Article 32, due to lack of resources and the practical problems associated with prescribing minimum ages for employment. According to the *Alternate Report on the Status of Child Labour in India* by the Campaign Against Child Labour (1998), the rationale given for the declaration is not substantive, lacks the political will and is inconsistent and meaningless in the light of the CRC as a whole.

The ILO Convention: The ILO Convention No. 138 establishes three age limits:

- 18 for hazardous work;
- 15 for full-time employment in non-hazardous work;
- 13 for "light" work that does not interfere with education.

Convention on the Abolition of Slavery: According to Article 1 of the Supplementary Convention on the Abolition of Slavery, the Slave Trade, and Institutions and Practices Similar to Slavery, "Each of the States Parties to this Convention shall take all practicable and necessary legislative and other measures to bring about progressively and as soon as possible the complete abolition or abandonment of the following institutions and practices...:

(a) Debt bondage, that is to say, the status or condition arising from a pledge by a debtor of his personal services or of those of a person under his control as security for a debt, if the value of those services as reasonably assessed is not applied towards the liquidation of the debt or the length and nature of those services are not respectively limited and defined;

(b) Serfdom, that is to say, the condition or status of a tenant who is by law, custom or agreement bound to live and labour on land belonging to another person and to render some determinate service to such other person, whether for reward or not, and is not free to change his status;...

(d) Any institution or practice whereby a child or young person under the age of 18 years delivered by either or both of his natural parents or by his guardian to another person, whether for reward or not, with a view to the exploitation of the child or young person or of his labour" (United Nations, 1956).

Indian Policy and Laws for Protection of Children from Exploitation for Labour

Fundamental Right in Indian Constitution: According to Article 23 of the Indian Constitution, prohibition of traffic in human beings and forced labour is a Fundamental Right. Traffic in human beings and *beggar* and other similar forms of forced labour are prohibited and any contravention of this provision shall be an offence punishable in accordance with law. Article 24 of the Indian Constitution states that prohibition of employment of children in factories, etc., is a Fundamental Right. No child below the age of fourteen years shall be employed to work in any factory or mine or engaged in any other hazardous employment.

Child Labour (Prohibition and Regulation) Act: The government has not imposed a total ban on child labour, thinking that the survival of the poor depends on it. On the other hand, there is little success in alleviating poverty so that it impacts on the prevalence of child labour or even in regulating child labour. There is a plethora of legislation, of which the Child Labour (Prohibition and Regulation) Act, 1986 is the main one. As per this Act, "child" means a person who has not completed his fourteen year of age. The Act prohibits employment of children in 18 occupations and 65 processes. The Act regulates the condition of employment in all occupations and processes not prohibited under the Act. Any person, who employs any child in contravention of the provisions of the Act, is liable for punishment with imprisonment for a term which shall not be less than three months but which may extend to one year or with fine which shall not be less than Rs. 10,000 but which may extend to Rs. 20,000 or both. To date, there has not been a single conviction under this Act. Cases have been registered but result in small fines or remain languishing in the court of law. Many State governments have not created even the rules or the regulatory infrastructure visualised by the act. Prosecution is complex and complicated as without hard evidence and witnesses it is impossible to convict the offenders. Lack of proof of age is another impediment in the enforcement of the law (Sekar, 2001).

Policy for Child Labour: The Child Labour Prohibition and Regulation Act, 1986, was followed by the adoption of a National Policy on Child Labour in 1988. It contains the action plan for tackling the problem of child labour. It envisages:

- A legislative action plan: The government has enacted the Child Labour (Prohibition & Regulation) Act, 1986, to prohibit the engagement of children in certain employments and to regulate the conditions of work of children in certain other employments.
- Focusing and convergence of general development programmes for benefiting children wherever possible, A core group on convergence of various welfare schemes of the government has been constituted in the Ministry of Labour and Employment to ensure that, the families of the child labour are given priority for their upliftment.
- Project-based action plan of action for launching of projects for the welfare of working children in areas of high concentration of Child Labour.

Bonded Labour Act: In India, bonded labour is specifically outlawed under the Bonded Labour System (Abolition) Act of 1976, and the Scheduled Castes and the Scheduled Tribes (Prevention of Atrocities) Act of 1989. However, many millions of Dalits, indigenous people and other minority groups continue to be enslaved under this system. Anti-Slavery International (2003) believes this is because the discrimination which underpins this system is also helping to maintain it. Many local officials continue to show a reluctance to implement this legislation. This may be because they are afraid of the power of local landowners or contractors, but it may also be because the individuals and institutions themselves are inherently discriminatory and sympathise with the idea that Dalits, indigenous people and other minority groups owe a duty of labour to landlords for little or no pay.

Profile of Child Labour in India

According to the statistical report of Government of India (2012):

- The Census found an increase in the number of child labourers from 11.28 million in 1991 to 12.66 million in 2001.
- In addition, nearly 85% of child labourers in India are hard-to-reach, invisible and excluded, as they work largely in the unorganised sector, both rural and urban, within the family or in household-based units.

- As per Census of India 2001, the major occupations engaging child labour are paan, bidi and cigarettes (21%), construction (17%), domestic workers (15%) and spinning and weaving.
- Although the Child Labour (Prohibition and Regulation) Act, 1986, aims to prohibit the entry of children into hazardous occupations and to regulate the services of children in non-hazardous occupations, a significant portion of children in the country are engaged in such activities. For example, the firecrackers industry in India is known to employ children in their factories who are not only exposed to hazardous chemicals, but are also to unsafe working conditions.

Activities

Activity 7.2: Video Discussion on Child Domestic Labour

Learner Outcome: At the end of this activity, the participants will develop awareness on violation of rights of domestic child labour.

Procedure: Show any of the following video films:
Meena Sheher Mein (Hindi)—Meena Unicef
https://www.youtube.com/watch?v=mrd0FbRL6Sg
Save the Children. Nandu
https://www.youtube.com/watch?v=ASJd5AFCNeM&list=
PL38322753F73B5A71

Questions for Discussion: Use the following questions to discuss this film:

- Why do children work?
- What kinds of work do they engage in?
- What problems do child workers face?
- Why are they vulnerable to exploitation?
- Why is domestic work invisible?
- What are the effects of working as a child and being exploited?
- What happens to these children's right to education and recreation?
- Do any labour laws apply to them?
- How can ban on child labour and compulsory education be enforced?

Time Estimate: 15 min

Activity 7.3: Small Group Discussion on Child Labour

Learner Outcome: At the end of this activity, the participants will develop awareness on different aspects of child labour.

Procedure: Use the following procedure to conduct this activity:

1. Form four small groups of participants and allocate the following topics among them:

    a. Concepts of Child Labour
    b. Causes of Child Labour
    c. Child Right to Protection from Exploitation for Labour
    d. Indian Policy and Laws for Protection of Children from Exploitation for Labour

2. Ask the small groups to read the relevant notes, discuss and make a presentation to the large group.

Questions for Discussion: Use the following questions to discuss this activity:

- How can children protect themselves from exploitation for labour?
- What is the role of children's associations to prevent child labour?
- What is the role of parents to prevent child labour?
- What is the role of the State to prevent child labour?

Time Estimate: 30 min

Activity 7.4: Street Plays for Creating Public Awareness on Child Labour

Learner Outcome: At the end of this activity, the participants will learn to create public awareness on the exploitation of children's labour in different occupations and its prevention.

Procedure: Use the following procedure to conduct this activity:

1. Form six small groups and ask each group to interview one of the following working children:

    (1) Child waiter in a restaurant/tea stalls
    (2) Child selling toys at traffic signals/in trains
    (3) Child rag-picker
    (4) Child as babysitter in someone's home
    (5) Child worker in an industry
    (6) Children on railway stations with their shoe polish kit

2. Ask the following questions in the interview:

    - Why does the child work in this occupation?
    - Why does this child not go to school?
    - What are his/her working hours and days?
    - What are his/her rest hours and off-duty days?

- Does the child get time to play?
- Does the child get enough food to eat?
- What salary does the child get?
- Who takes the child's salary?

3. Ask each small group to plan a street play based on the interview with the following aims:

    a. How can we help this child go to school instead of work?
    b. How can exploitation of children for labour be prevented?

Time Estimate: 45 min for presentation and discussion

Prevention of Trafficking and Sale of Children

Concepts and Theories

Concepts of Trafficking

According to Article 3 (a) of the UN Protocol to Prevent, Suppress and Punish Trafficking in Persons, especially Women and Children, Supplementing the UN Convention against Transnational Crime (2000), "Trafficking in persons" shall mean the recruitment, transportation, transfer, harbouring or receipt of persons; by means of threat or use of force or other forms of coercion, abduction, fraud, deception, abuse of power or a position of vulnerability or the giving or receiving of payments or benefits to achieve the consent of a person having control over another person; for the purpose of exploitation. Exploitation shall include, at a minimum, the exploitation of the prostitution of others or other forms of sexual exploitation, forced labour or services, slavery or practices similar to slavery, servitude or the removal of organs". Trafficking in human beings is the third-largest form of organised crime globally, after trafficking in arms and drugs. Globalising trends have transformed national contours and eroded social norms and sexual mores rooted in centuries-old culture and tradition (ECPAT, 2014).

Population Council (2002) clarifies the distinction between trafficking and migration and smuggling, all of which refer to movements within or across border:

- Migration is free, with consent, for the purpose of improvement of livelihood, and legal.
- Smuggling is also with consent and for the purpose of improvement of livelihood, but illegal, with a brokerage fee.
- On the other hand, trafficking is slavery because traffickers use violence, threats and other forms of coercion to force their victims to work against their will.

Concepts of Child Trafficking

Article 3 (c) of the UN Protocol to Prevent, Suppress and Punish Trafficking in Persons, especially Women and Children (2000) states that "The recruitment, transportation, transfer, harbouring or receipt of a child for the purpose of exploitation shall be considered 'trafficking in persons' even if this does not involve any of the means set forth in subparagraph (a) of this article". This means even if trafficking of a child is not by means of threat or use of force or other forms of coercion, abduction, fraud, deception, abuse of power or a position of vulnerability or the giving or receiving of payments or benefits to achieve the consent of a person having control over another person, it is still trafficking.

Children are trafficked for begging, labour, prostitution, adoption, entertainment, sale of organs and marriage.

Concept of Sale of Children

According to Article 2 of the Optional Protocol to the Convention on the Rights of the Child on the Sale of Children, Child Prostitution and Child Pornography (2000a, cited in United Nations Children's Fund Innocenti Research Centre, 2009), sale of children means "any act or transaction whereby a child is transferred by any person or group of persons to another for remuneration or any other consideration". Article 3 states that sale of children is offering, delivering or accepting, by whatever means, a child for the purpose of sexual exploitation, transfer of organs for profit, engagement of the child in forced labour or the adoption of a child.

Children can be sold at each stage of the trafficking process (UNICEF Innocenti Research Centre, 2009).

Modus Operandi of Child Trafficking

Recruitment: Child trafficking begins when a child is recruited by someone or, in some cases, approaches a recruiter to find out about how to move to find work or in the hope of being able to leave the place where they are for opportunities elsewhere. Recruiters may be the person who actually employs the child, or an intermediary, part of a chain of people involved in the trafficking (ILO, 2009). They are, therefore, active participants in their own trafficking, as far as recruitment and transportation are concerned. This dimension adds to the difficulty of developing methodologies to ascertain the actual number of trafficked persons and creating effective protections against the phenomenon (UNICEF, 2001).

Movement: Generally, internal trafficking uses various landforms of transport—train, truck, taxi, bus or private car—and sometimes people are also taken on foot. Where national borders are relatively open, people may move by road or on foot across the border using routes that have been known to local people for many years.

These may be relatively easy crossings but they may also involve hazardous and tortuous routes through deserts and mountains or across a river. Air routes are also used to move people for trafficking, although not in large numbers. Once children are on the move, they are of course at increased risk in a number of ways. Often the transport used to move them may be substandard (unregistered fishing boats or adapted road vehicles, for example). Their general welfare may be at risk—they may not have adequate food or water or may get sick. Children's vulnerability increases as they move further away from the safety nets of their own communities, especially if they do not speak the language of the place they are moved through or to (ILO, 2009).

Exploitation: Regardless of the initial purpose, all child victims of trafficking are highly vulnerable to sexual abuse and exploitation because they are removed from support structures such as their families and communities. During the process of trafficking, children can be sold several times for various purposes—they are commodities in a business that generates billions of dollars and operates with impunity (ECPAT International, 2008). Children who have been trafficked are by definition exploited when they arrive at their destination. This exploitation can take many forms, depending on the sex of the child, their age, the nature of the labour market into which they have been trafficked, and the level of their skills, as well as their vulnerability. Trafficking victims are exploited in a wide range of different sectors: they may end up in agricultural work, on plantations, mining, factories of various kinds, prostitution, entertainment outlets like bars or clubs, street-based activities such as hawking or organised begging, adoption or armed conflict. Many children are trafficked to become household servants. The babies that are sometimes trafficked for adoption may find themselves being raised for a specific exploitative purpose, for example to work on the family farm or in the family business (ILO, 2009).

Strategies to Keep the Victims Submissive: ECPAT International (2006) notes that following are the common ways in which traffickers keep young people submissive:

- Confiscation of their identity documents;
- Threats of reporting them to the authorities;
- Violence/threats of violence towards the child/members of the child's family;
- Social isolation, keeping the young person locked up or limiting their freedom in another way;
- Claiming that the young person owes money and depriving the young person of money.

Children at Risk of Trafficking

UNICEF (2005b) notes the following factors that make children vulnerable to trafficking:

Poverty: Victims of trafficking often come from poor families and lack economic opportunities. Children who have minimal education, lack vocational skills, or have few prospects for job opportunities are most at risk. With promises of employment opportunities abroad, families in extreme poverty may send their children away to work.

Gender Inequality: Where women and girls are objectified and seen as commodities, a climate is created in which girls can be bought and sold. Girls are frequently abused within their families, making the lure of traffickers seem like an escape from domestic exploitation and violence.

Low School Enrolment: Children who are not in school can easily fall prey to traffickers. Uneducated children have few opportunities for their future and are therefore more vulnerable to traffickers' promises of money and a "better life".

Children without Caregivers: Children without parental protection, or those placed in institutions, are targets for traffickers. Without guidance, a sense of belonging or opportunities, they may be at an increased risk of trafficking.

Lack of Birth Registration: Children who are not registered are more susceptible to trafficking. When children are without a legal identity, it is easier for traffickers to "hide" them.

Humanitarian Disasters and Armed Conflict: During conflicts, children may be abducted by armed groups and forced to participate in hostilities. Cataclysmic events that disrupt livelihoods or result in the death of one or both parents make children vulnerable to trafficking.

Specifically, children at risk of trafficking are:

- Street children and those living in slums;
- The orphaned and the disabled;
- Children living in brothels or in communities practicing religious and cultural prostitution;
- Children who have been stigmatised by abuse or molestation;
- Children born to victims of AIDS;
- Children in custodial and educational institutions away from families; and
- Children of bonded labourers and those working as domestic help (India: Department of Women and Child Development, 1996 cited by National Human Rights Commission (NHRC), UNIFEM and Institute of Social Sciences, 2003).

Profile of Traffickers

Traffickers are people who contribute to child trafficking with the intent to exploit. They include recruiters, intermediaries, document providers, transporters, corrupt officials, service providers and employers of trafficked children, even though most of these people take part in only one element of the whole trafficking process. Trafficking intermediaries include the following:

- People who specialise in providing information to traffickers about which border crossings are open and when;
- People who give advice on the best times to move people;
- People who take responsibility for identifying and bribing corrupt border guards or immigration officers;
- At the place of destination, there may be people whose job is to keep watch over the trafficked children as perverse guardians, and sometimes bodyguards who are there not so much to protect the children but the investment of the trafficker;
- Institutional players such as corrupt police, government officers and consular staff may be involved in trafficking (ILO, 2009).

Governments have a responsibility to exercise due diligence in ensuring that all those who work in the various arms of government, no matter how far removed they may seem from the centre of power, are held accountable for their actions (ILO, 2009).

Impact of Trafficking on Children

UNICEF (2005b) notes that child trafficking victims are subjugated and physically abused by the perpetrators: traffickers, employers, pimps, madams and customers. The report describes the following physical, emotional and social impact of trafficking on children.

Emotional Impact: Children who have been trafficked have reported feelings of shame, guilt and low self-esteem and are frequently stigmatised. They often feel betrayed, especially if the perpetrator was someone they had trusted. These factors as well as the experience itself can cause nightmares, sleeplessness, feelings of hopelessness and depression. Some children who have been trafficked turn to substance abuse to numb their psychic pain and others attempt suicide.

Social Impact: Children who are trafficked typically suffer adverse effects to their social and educational development. Many have no family life and are forced to work at young ages. Without access to school or family support, and cut off from normal social activities, they fail to develop their potential. Also, under constant surveillance and restriction, they have little contact with the outside world and often do not have the possibility to seek help.

Sexually Transmitted Infections: Children trafficked into the sex industry are susceptible to contracting sexually transmitted infections, including HIV/AIDS. Many women and girls report that "customers" pay more for sex without a condom, and they—especially girls—are rarely in a position to insist upon condom use. Domestic workers, street children, child labourers and children in detention are vulnerable to rape and sexual exploitation and are at high risk of contracting HIV/AIDS.

Revictimisation: For children who have been trafficked and "rescued", the repatriation process can be traumatic. Children are often treated as criminals and even sometimes imprisoned, either in the country to which they have been trafficked or subsequently in their home country on return. They may also be vulnerable to revictimisation or retrafficking if appropriate care and protection is not available (ECPAT International, 2006).

Child Right to Protection from Trafficking

UNCRC: According to Article 35 of the UNCRC (1989), "States Parties shall take all appropriate national, bilateral and multilateral measures to prevent the abduction of the sale of or traffic in children for any purpose or in any form". The Optional Protocol to the UNCRC on the Sale of Children, Child Prostitution and Child Pornography of 2000 prohibits the sale of children, child prostitution and child pornography.

The 2000 UN Protocol to Prevent, Suppress and Punish Trafficking in Persons, especially Women and Children aims at preventing and combating trafficking in persons, paying particular attention to women and children; protecting and assisting the victims of such trafficking, with full respect for their human rights; and promoting cooperation among State Parties in order to meet those objectives. It protects and promotes the following rights to the trafficked persons: right against exploitation, rights to non-discrimination, privacy and confidentiality, information, be represented and heard, assistance, safety, compensation and voluntary repatriation and right against forceful deportation.

ILO: The ILO C182, the Worst Forms of Child Labour Convention, 1999, includes sale and trafficking of children; and the use, procuring or offering of a child for prostitution, for the production of pornography or for pornographic performances, in the term "worst forms of child labour", to be eliminated as a priority.

Indian Constitution: According to Article 23 of the Indian Constitution, prohibition of traffic in human beings and forced labour is a Fundamental Right. Traffic in human beings and *beggar,* and other similar forms of forced labour are prohibited and any contravention of this provision shall be an offence punishable in accordance with law.

Indian Penal Code: Under Article 363A (1) of the Indian Penal Code (1860), "Whoever kidnaps any minor (boys under 16 years and girls under 18 years of age) or, not being the lawful guardian of a minor, obtains the custody of the minor, in order that such minor may be employed or used for the purpose of begging shall be punishable with imprisonment of either description for a term which may extend to ten years, and shall also be liable to fine". In 2011, an increase of a massive 43% was registered in kidnapping and abduction in India. A total of 15,282 cases of kidnapping and abduction of children were reported during this year as compared to 10,670 cases in the previous year (India: Ministry of Statistics and Programme Implementation, 2012).

Prevention of Child Trafficking

Nair (2007) recommends that addressing vulnerable persons/areas is an important strategy in the prevention of trafficking. Police should develop synergy with the concerned governmental and non-governmental organisations and undertake the following steps:

(1) Identify the vulnerable persons/areas and focus attention on them.
(2) Pay special attention to the most vulnerable persons (e.g. children in brothels).
(3) Mount surveillance for suspects and look-out for victims at possible transit/ transfer points like bus stands, railway stations, wayside hotels (Dhaba), beach resorts.
(4) Facilitate empowerment programmes for them by networking with government departments, etc.
(5) Involve multiple agencies to provide sustainable livelihood options.
(6) Adopt a "human rights approach" in all activities and programmes and discard the "welfare act" orientation.

The research report of NHRC et al. on trafficking (2003) indicates a strong linkage between missing persons and trafficking. In one year, more than 30,000 children were reported missing and one-third of them remain untraced. This study has established with examples that many of these "missing children" are, in fact, trafficked. Based on this observation, Nair (2007) notes that prevention of trafficking requires the following:

• Understand the linkage between "missing" persons and "trafficked" persons, because many who are "reported missing" have been, in fact, trafficked.
• Follow-up missing women and children till a logical conclusion is arrived at.
• Follow-up all the leads in this process to ensure that those responsible for making the person missing are brought to book.
• Provide the details of missing children to the police agencies and NGOs who are working with the rescue of trafficked persons so that they could also follow up.

Activities

Activity 7.5: Video Discussion on Child Trafficking

Learner Outcome: At the end of this activity, the participants will develop awareness about child trafficking.

Procedure: Show the following video selectively and conduct discussion:
Save the Children: Child Trafficking in Bihar, India
https://www.youtube.com/watch?v=-hzl4vw0-zs

Questions for Discussion: Use the following questions to discuss this activity:

- In which situations are children vulnerable to trafficking? Why?
- What are they trafficked for?
- How is trafficking carried out?
- What are the effects of being trafficked?
- What are the child rights violated by trafficking?
- What is trafficking?
- How can trafficking of children be prevented?

Time Estimate: 30 min

Activity 7.6: Role-Plays on Prevention of Trafficking and Sale of Children

Learner Outcome: By the end of this activity, the participants will learn to create public awareness on how trafficking and sale of children can be prevented.

Procedure: Form five small groups and allocate the following case studies among them for preparing the street plays for presentation to the large group:

Case 1: Lalit grew up in a very poor family with four other siblings. His father was the sole breadwinner of the family, earning a small income as an agricultural labourer. As the eldest child, Lalit was expected to help his father. As a result, he dropped out of school at the age of 13 to work as a field hand. One day, a neighbour told him that he should migrate to Delhi where he could find a job and earn more money. He agreed, and shortly thereafter, his neighbour accompanied him to a bus that would take him to Delhi. However, once he reached Delhi, the driver handed him over to another man who sold him to a beggars' gang. Whenever he tried to escape, he was caught and beaten.

Case 2: A village agent visited Deepti's family and promised her mother 5,000 rupees ($79) a month if she sent Deepti to work in Delhi. Once she reached the capital she was sold off to a family. "It was only after a few years I realised I had been sold", she recalls. "I was extremely hurt and was in tears. My life was tough. I worked from six in the morning until midnight. I had to cook meals, clean the house, take care of the children and massage the legs of my employers before going to bed. If I didn't do my job well, they used to scold me". (http://www.theguardian.com/global-development/2015/apr/28/child-trafficking-india-domestic-labour-chhattisgarh).

Case 3: When Nafisa turned 13, the man she loved told her that he wanted to marry her and that he could make her into a famous singer one day. She agreed and ran away with him to a big city. When they arrived, he told her that he wanted to keep her safe with his aunt until her parents stopped looking for them. In a few days, he would return for her. She was reluctant to see him go, but she trusted his decision. That night, she was told that she had been sold by the man she loved and that she would have to work off her debt by selling her body each night.

Case 4: With very few unmarried women of marriageable age in his town in Haryana, Tomy was told of a couple who could get him a bride. When he visited them, they asked him questions about what type of bride he would like such as from which State, what age, for permanent or temporary marriage. When he gave his expectations of a young girl, he was asked for an amount of Rs. 50,000, and a trip was planned for him to visit Bihar and get married to a teenage girl from a poor family.

Case 5: After her husband's death, Malti was visited by an elderly woman Mrs. Pandey running a charitable organisation. Mrs. Pandey told Malti that since she remained the only earner in the family, she should give up one of her two daughters to the charitable organisation where she will be looked after better. After much persuasion, Malti agreed and gave away her daughter and was given Rs. 10,000 in return. After a couple of months, the organisation sold her daughter to Nancy, who desperately wanted a child, for Rs. 25,000.

Questions for Discussion: The small groups can use the following questions for preparing the role-plays:

- Which children are vulnerable to trafficking?
- What are they trafficked for?
- What are the effects of being trafficked?
- How can trafficking of children be prevented?
- How can children protect themselves from trafficking?
- What is the role of children's associations to prevent child trafficking?
- What is the role of parents to prevent child trafficking?
- What is the role of the State to prevent child trafficking?

Time Estimate: 45 min

Activity 7.7: Charts on Protection of Children from Kidnapping

Learner Outcome: At the end of this activity, children will learn the skills to protect oneself from kidnapping when alone at home or when with strangers and parents will learn how to reinforce such skills in children.

Procedure: Use the following procedure to conduct this activity:

1. Ask the children the following questions:

    a. What do you mean by stranger danger?
    b. How would you look after yourselves to prevent danger?
    c. Do you know your parents' full names and your full address?

2. Form four small groups and ask them to conduct discussion on what they would be cautious about at home/in public places/in school/on the internet. At the end of the activity, participants can be asked to prepare charts on dos and don'ts of tackling stranger danger and put up in their classrooms.

3. When alone at home:

   a. What would you do if you are alone at home and the doorbell rings?
   b. What would you do if you are alone at home and a stranger calls for your parents? Would you tell them that you are alone at home?

4. When alone in a public place:

   a. What would you do if you are walking on the road and a stranger tries to walk closer to you?
   b. What would you do if a stranger gives you food or gifts?
   c. If you are playing outside their home, would you play in a lonely place or where there are more people?

5. When in School:

   a. What would you do if you are in school and a stranger tells you that your parents have sent him/her to fetch you?

6. On the Internet:

   a. What would you do if

With parents, you can conduct this activity by asking them how they would reinforce the safety skills in children.

Time Estimate: 15 min

Concluding Activity: Achievement of the Learner Objectives

Learner Outcome: By the end of the concluding activity, the participants will ascertain if they have achieved the learner objectives.

Procedure: Use the following procedure to conduct the concluding activity:

1. Show the power points/a chart on the learner objectives, ask the participants to read them one at a time and ask the group if they think they have achieved the objective.
2. The participants may be asked to share their responses in their diary with reference to the following questions:

   • What was a new learning for you in this session?
   • What did you like the best in this session and why?
   • Which activity was most effective?
   • What was not clear/confusing?
   • How can you apply what you have learnt?

Time Estimate: 15 min

Appendix: Summary Charts

Summary Chart 7.1 Commercial Exploitation of Children

Stakeholders of Commercial Exploitation of Children		
Victims: Supply of Children at Risk	**Exploiters: Demand for Cheap Products by Adults & Increased Consumerism**	**Profit-Makers: Network of Crime**
• Children in Poverty • Neglected Children • Abused Children • Out of School Children • Street Children • Children in Institutions • Children in Emergency Situations	• Consumers • Customers • Clients	• Traffickers • Employers • Agents • Pimps • Intermediaries • Supportive Corrupt Officers

↓

Commercial Exploitation of Children		
Exploitation of Children for Unpaid/ Underpaid Labour	**Trafficking and Sale of Children**	**Commercial Sexual Exploitation of Children**
• Work in Industries • Construction Work • Restaurant Work • Domestic Work • Household-based Work	• Rural to Urban, Inter-State & International • For Begging, Labour, Prostitution, Adoption, Entertainment, Sale of Organs & Marriage • Sale of Children	• Child Prostitution • Child Sex Tourism • Child Pornography

↓

Effects			
No Participation, No Education & No Recreation	Ill-Health	Physical, Sexual & Emotional Abuse	Revictimisation by the Police & Other State Systems
Prevention Strategies			
Compulsory and Free Education	Jobs/Livelihood for Adults	Enforcement of Legal Bans	Creating Public Awareness

References

Anti-Slavery. (2007). *Child labour*. Geneva: Author. Retrieved from http://www.antislavery.org/homepage/antislavery/childlabour.htm#what.

Anti-Slavery International. (2003). *Contemporary forms of slavery related to and generated by discrimination: Forced and bonded labour in India, Nepal and Pakistan*. Retrieved from www.antislavery.org/archive/submission/submission2003-discrimBL.htm).

Boyden, J., & Levison, D. (2000). *Children as economic and social actors in the development process*. Sweden: Ministry of Foreign Affairs.

Campaign Against Child Labour. (1998). *An alternate report on the status of child labour in India, A response to the first India country report on the convention of the rights of the child*. Mumbai.

Desai, M. (2010). A rights-based preventative approach for psychosocial well-being in childhood. In *Series on children's well-being: Indicators and research*. Heidelberg: Springer.

ECPAT. (2014). *The commercial sexual exploitation of children in South Asia: Developments, progress, challenges and recommended strategies for civil society*. Retrieved from http://www.ecpat.org/wp-content/uploads/2016/04/Regional%20CSEC%20Overview_South%20Asia.pdf.

ECPAT International. (2006). *Combating the trafficking in children for sexual purposes: Questions and answers*. Bangkok: Author. Retrieved from http://www.ecpat.net/EI/Publications/Trafficking/Trafficking_FAQ_ENG.pdf.

ECPAT International. (2008). *Questions and answers about the commercial sexual exploitation of children*. Bangkok: Author. Retrieved July 4, 2006 from http://www.ecpatusa.org/EcpatUSA_PDF/faq%20update%20from%20ecpat%20international.pdf.

India: Ministry of Statistics and Programme Implementation. (2012). *Children in India 2012: A statistical appraisal*. Retrieved from http://mospi.nic.in/mospi_new/upload/Children_in_India_2012.pdf.

International Labour Organization. (2004). *Child labour: A textbook for university students*. Geneva. Retrieved from http://www.ilo.org/wcmsp5/groups/public/—ed_norm/documents/publication/wcms_067258.pdf.

International Labour Organization. (2009). *Training manual to fight trafficking in children for labour, sexual and other forms of exploitation*. Retrieved from http://www.unicef.org/protection/Textbook_1.pdf.

Nair, P. M. (2007). *Trafficking women and children for sexual exploitation: Handbook for law enforcement agencies for law enforcement agencies in India* (2nd ed.). New Delhi: UNODC.

National Human Rights Commission, UNIFEM and Institute of Social Sciences. (2003). *A report on trafficking in women and children in India: 2002–3*. New Delhi. Retrieved from http://nhrc.nic.in/Documents/ReportonTrafficking.pdf.

Population Council. (2002). *Anti-trafficking programs in South Asia: Appropriate activities, indicators and evaluation methodologies*. New Delhi.

Sekar, H. R. (2001). Child labour: A perspective. In *Child labour in India: An overview* (pp. 16–19). New Delhi: V.V. Giri National Labour Institute.

Stack, N., & McKechnie, J. (2002). Working Children. In B. Goldson, M. Lavalette, & J. McKechnie (Eds.), *Children, welfare and the state* (pp. 87–101). London: Sage.

The Stockholm Declaration and Agenda for Action. (1996). *Adopted at the first world congress against commercial sexual exploitation of children*. Sweden: Stockholm.

United Nations. (1956). *Supplementary convention on the abolition of slavery, the slave trade, and institutions and practices similar to slavery*. Retrieved from http://www.ohchr.org/EN/ProfessionalInterest/Pages/SupplementaryConventionAbolitionOfSlavery.aspx.

United Nations. (1989). *Convention on the rights of the child*. Retrieved from http://www.ohchr.org/english/law/pdf/crc.pdf.

United Nations. (2000). *Protocol to prevent, suppress and punish trafficking in persons, especially women and children*. Retrieved from http://www.osce.org/odihr/19223?download=true.

United Nations Children's Fund. (2001). *Summary report on commercial sexual exploitation of children and child sexual abuse in South Asia.* Kathmandu.

United Nations Children's Fund. (2005a). *Child labour resource guide.* http://www.unicef.org/csr/css/Child_labour_resource_Guide_UK_NatCom.pdf.

United Nations Children's Fund. (2005b). *Combating child trafficking: Handbook for parliamentarians.* Retrieved from http://www.unicef.org/ceecis/IPU_combattingchildtrafficking_GB.pdf.

United Nations Children's Fund. (2005c). *End child exploitation.* Retrieved from http://www.unicef.org.uk/Documents/Publications/ecechild2_a4.pdf.

United Nations Children's Fund Innocent Research Centre. (2009). *Handbook on the optional protocol on the sale of children, child prostitution and child pornography.* Retrieved from http://www.unicef-irc.org/publications/pdf/optional_protocol_eng.pdf.

United Nations Development Programme. (1999). *AIDS in Southwest Asia: A development challenge.* New Delhi.

Relevant Child Rights and You Reports and Articles

Child Rights and You. (2016). *Crime Against Children in India, CRY Media release*: Crime against Children.Retrieve from https://www.cry.org/wp-content/uploads/2018/01/CRY-Media-release-Crime-against-Children-2017.pdf.

Child Rights and You. (2017). *How can You Help Prevent Child Exploitation.* Retrieve from https://www.cry.org/blog/can-help-prevent-child-exploitation.

Module 8
Child Rights to Prevention of Sexual Violence

Prevention of Sexual Abuse of Children

Concepts and Theories

Concepts of Child Sexual Abuse

According to ECPAT (2008b, p. 18), sexual abuse of a child can be defined as contacts or interactions between a child and an older or more knowledgeable child or adult, such as a stranger, sibling or parent, when the child is being used as an object of gratification for the abuser's sexual needs. These actions are carried out using force, threats, bribes, trickery or pressure. The World Health Organization and International Society for Prevention of Child Abuse and Neglect (ISPCAN) (2006) define child sexual abuse (CSA) as the involvement of a child in sexual activity that he or she does not fully comprehend, is unable to give informed consent to, or for which the child is not developmentally prepared, or else that violates the laws or social taboos of society. Children can be sexually abused by both adults and other children who are—by virtue of their age or stage of development—in a position of responsibility, trust or power over the victim.

According to the Pinheiro (2006) Report, in most societies, sexual abuse of girls and boys is most common within the home or is committed by a person known to the family. But sexual violence also occurs in schools and other educational settings, by both peers and teachers. It is rife against children in closed workplaces, such as domestic labourers employed in private households. It also takes place in institutions and in the community, at the hands of people known to the victim and others. Girls suffer considerably more sexual violence than boys, and their greater vulnerability to violence in many settings is in large part a product of the influence of gender-based power relations within society.

Thus CSA is:

- Any intentional non-accidental sexual harm done to a child, as an object of gratification, that endangers or impairs the child's physical, sexual, emotional and psychological health and development;
- By older children, parents, relatives, caretakers, neighbours, teachers, employers, police or strangers; in family, neighbourhood, street, school, institutions, site of occupation or police custody;
- Because of adult–child power imbalance due to adultism and male–female power imbalance due to patriarchy or psychosocial problems, and cycle of abuse (Desai, 2010).

Types of Child Sexual Abuse in the Order of Severity

Faller (1993) lists the types of CSA behaviour as follows, in the order of increasing severity:

- Non-Contact Acts: Sexual comments, exposing one's sex organs and persuading the child to do the same, voyeurism (peeping), showing pornographic material and masturbating self in the presence of the child.
- Sexual Contact: Touching the child's sex organs and inducing the child to do the same to one's own, and frottage or rubbing one's sex organs against the child's body or clothing.
- Digital or Object Penetration: Placing finger or an object in the child's vagina or anus and asking the child to do the same for self.

- Oral Sex: Tongue kissing, breast sucking, kissing, licking, biting, cunnilingus (licking, kissing, sucking, biting the vagina or placing the tongue in the vaginal opening), fellatio (licking, kissing, sucking, biting the penis) and anilingus (licking, kissing the anal opening).
- Penile Penetration: Vaginal and anal intercourse.

Types of Sex Offenders of Children

According to ECPAT (2008b), child sex offenders come from all walks of life and social backgrounds. They can be found in any profession and in any country. They may be heterosexual or homosexual, and although the vast majority is male, there are also female offenders. Child sex offenders are generally divided into situational, preferential and incestual/others.

Preferential Child Sex Offenders: Preferential child sex offenders have a definite sexual preference for children. They are fewer in numbers than situational offenders, but potentially can abuse larger numbers of children as this is their desire and intention. Their behavioural patterns have been identified:

- Seducers use affection, attention or gifts to lure children and are often willing to spend long periods of time grooming their victims in preparation for the abuse. They may also use threats, blackmail and physical violence to discourage disclosure.
- Introverted offenders have a preference for children but lack the ability to interact with them. They engage in a minimum amount of communication with victims and tend to abuse unknown or very young children.
- Least common are sadistic offenders, who in addition to a sexual interest in children, also derive sexual pleasure from inflicting pain. This type of offender is most likely to use force to gain access to the child and is also likely to abduct or even murder the victim (ECPAT, 2008b).

Paedophiles: The *Diagnostic and Statistical Manual of Mental Disorders* (American Psychiatric Association, 1994) describes paedophilia as "the act or fantasy of engaging in sexual activity with prepubertal children as a repeatedly preferred or exclusive method of achieving sexual excitement … Isolated sexual acts with children do not warrant the [clinical] diagnosis of paedophilia". The manual adds that a person who fits this diagnosis would have to be at least 16 years old and five years older than the child to whom their sexual fantasies are directed. Paedophiles may focus on either boys or girls or have no gender preference. Not all paedophiles sexually abuse or harass children. Some may have fantasies about sex with children but they do not act them out with a child (although they may use child pornography). Others may abuse children in different ways, including non-physical sexual abuse and exploitation. Most clinically definable paedophiles are male; female paedophiles exist but are rare.

The paedophile may not view sexual contact with children as harmful (ECPAT International, 2008a).

Situational Child Sex Offenders: The situational child sex offender does not have a true sexual preference for children, but engages in sex with children because the opportunity arises. Such offenders may exploit children because they have entered into situations in which a child is easily accessible to them, or certain disinhibiting factors are present which cause them to delude themselves about the child's age or consent to the sexual activity. Sexual exploitation of children may be an act committed while on holiday or it may develop into a long-term pattern of abuse (ECPAT, 2008b).

Other Child Sex Offenders: United Nations High Commissioner for Refugees (UNHCR, 2003) noted that perpetrators of sexual and gender-based violence are sometimes the very people upon whom survivors depend to assist and protect them as listed below.

Intimate partners (husbands, boyfriends): In most societies, the accepted gender role for male intimate partners is one of decision-making and power over the female partner. Unfortunately, this power and influence are often exerted through discrimination, violence and abuse.

Family members, close relatives and friends: Girls are far more likely to suffer sexual and gender-based violence within the domestic sphere. From neglect to incest, these human rights violations are not always reported, since they involve fathers, stepfathers, grandfathers, father-in-laws, brothers and/or uncles as perpetrators.

Influential community members (teachers, leaders, politicians): Leaders and other community members in positions of authority can abuse that power through acts of sexual and gender-based violence. The victim/survivor in these situations is even more reluctant to report the violence because of the perpetrator's position of trust and power within the community.

Vulnerability of Children to Sexual Abuse

Gender Differences in Child Sexual Abuse: Both girls and boys can be victimised through sexual exploitation and sexual violence although the nature of the risks and the types of abuse may differ. For girls, sexual violence is a form of gender-based violence and is often centred around their comparatively powerless position in society. For boys, sexual violence is more typically, especially in conflict situations, used as a method of intimidation. Additionally, cultural and societal norms, particularly around the issues of masculinity and sexuality, contribute to making it difficult for boys to speak out about their experiences and for adults to recognise that boys are also in need of protection (ECPAT, 2006b). The majority of children are being sexually abused by adult males. However, there are also cases of adult females sexually abusing boys (International Rescue Committee, 2012).

Children at Risk: According to ECPAT (2006b), children in the following situations are vulnerable to sexual exploitation and sexual violence:

- **Children without parental care**: Children without parental care including orphans, unaccompanied and separated children, children living on their own, in foster families or in institutions face greater hazards given their lack of normal parental and community support and protection.
- **Mentally and physically disabled children**: Mentally and physically disabled children and those with other "special needs", frequently have a reduced ability to either evade abuses or understand what might be happening to them and to be able to speak out. This might be compounded by a perceived lack of "worth" of the life of the child by the community and hence a consequent lack of care, attention and protection.
- **Children from marginalised groups**: Children from marginalised groups such as those from minority ethnic, tribal and religious communities often suffer more adverse economic consequences due to discrimination, making them vulnerable to exploitation or may be left unprotected by weak legal and policy frameworks. Children from some communities may be actively targeted for sexual exploitation due to disadvantageous beliefs about them, for example, children of Dalit communities in India.
- **Children in armed conflict**: Sexual violence and exploitation are closely associated with child soldiers as such abuses often occur within the context of children being forcibly recruited into armed forces. Girls especially may be forcibly recruited and used as "sex slaves", though this may be considered as a way of protecting themselves and their families against further physical and sexual abuse in conflict situations.

Effects of Sexual Abuse on Children

In General: The harm done to children through the abusive experiences of sexual violence is varied, having long-lasting and dramatic implications for the child. Harms may include, but are not limited to:

- **Physical Consequences**: Physical injury, death, pregnancy, unsafe abortions, higher levels of infant and maternal mortality, sexually transmitted diseases and infections and the contraction of HIV/AIDS
- **Emotional Consequences**: Depression a sense of shame at being violated, post-traumatic stress disorder, loss of confidence and self-esteem, self-harm and suicidal thoughts and acts
- **Social Consequences**: Ostracism and rejection by family and community, social stigma and longer-term consequences including lost educational, skills training and employment opportunities, and reduced chances of marriage, social acceptance and integration. The effect of these harms can be increased risk and vulnerability to further incidences of sexual violence and sexual exploitation (ECPAT, 2006b).

On Boys: Many facts and information related to sexual abuse are applicable to both boys and girls; however, there are specific issues related to boy child survivors. Current research on male experiences of sexual abuse finds that beliefs impact how boys, particularly adolescents, experience and externalise sexual abuse:

- A boy may see himself as less of a male (emasculation).
- He may see himself as being powerless and thus flawed.
- He may see himself as being labelled as sexually interested in males (homosexual).
- Adolescent boys may also believe that no matter what, all sexual activity is appropriate for males (International Rescue Committee, 2012).

It is important to understand that sexual abuse does not cause homosexuality. Service providers are responsible for educating child survivors, caregivers and community members about the effects of sexual abuse. Homosexuality carries an additional stigma across communities and mistaken beliefs about the effects of sexual abuse may make it more difficult for a male adolescent sexually abused by an adult male to disclose (International Rescue Committee, 2012).

Reasons for Child's Hesitation for Communication of Disclosure

According to the International Rescue Committee (2012), following are common reasons why children do not disclose sexual abuse:

- **Fear of consequences**: Many children are afraid to tell an adult about abuse because they feel physically threatened, or because they believe they will be taken away from their families or blamed for shaming the family or involving outside authorities. The fear of the consequences may be greater than fear of the abuse itself.
- **Fear of dismissal by the adults**: Children are often afraid that adults will not believe them. They are afraid that their parents, community leaders, clan members, religious leaders and others will dismiss their claims and refuse to help. The perpetrator may compound this fear by convincing the child that no one will believe them, or that they will get into trouble if they speak out, etc.
- **Manipulation by the perpetrator**: The perpetrator may trick or bribe the child (for example, give the child a gift in exchange for non-disclosure). The perpetrator will often make the child feel embarrassed or guilty about the abuse. Sometimes the perpetrator will blame the child, saying he or she invited the abuse.
- **Self-blame**: Children may believe the sexual abuse is their fault or they may think the abuse is deserved. A child may feel that they allowed the abuse and should have stopped it. In no case is a child ever responsible for the sexual abuse they experience.

- **Protection of the perpetrator**: The child may want to protect the perpetrator and/or family in some way, especially if the perpetrator is close to the child and his/her family.
- **Very young age**: Children who are very young may be unaware they have experienced sexual abuse. They may think that the abuse is normal: particularly if the abuser is someone the child knows and trusts. Younger children may also have linguistic or developmental limitations that prevent disclosure.
- **Physical or mental disability**: Children may be unable to disclose the abuse if they are unable to speak to or otherwise reach out to a service provider.

Gender Difference in Disclosure: In general, males, especially adolescent males, may be much less likely to disclose and/or speak about their abuse experiences because being a victim can be seen as a countercultural experience for an adult male and/or male child/adolescent. Boys do not always prefer to speak with male service providers. In fact, the opposite may be true. Never assume that a boy or girl will feel more comfortable speaking with a service provider of his or her own gender. Rather, children should ideally be offered a choice of male or female service provider (International Rescue Committee, 2012).

Facilitate Disclosure: According to the National Human Rights Commission and Prasar Bharati (n.d.), if a child discloses that he/she has been sexually abused or exploited:

- Do support the child and explain that he/she is not responsible for what happened.
- Do believe the child.
- Do be empathetic, understanding and supportive.
- Do consult a doctor and consider the need for counselling or therapy for the child.
- Don't panic or overreact. With your help and support, the child can make it through this difficult time.
- Do not criticise the child.
- Do not get angry with the child.
- Do not make the child feel guilty about the abuse.
- Do not ignore the abuse. Lodge a complaint with the police and ensure that the abuse stops immediately. Your first responsibility is to the child to protect him/her and to ensure that there is no breach of privacy or confidentiality.

Child Rights to Protection from Sexual Abuse

Article 34 of the United Nations Convention on the Rights of the Child (UNCRC) (United Nations, 1989) states that the States Parties shall undertake to protect the child from all forms of sexual exploitation and sexual abuse.

The Protection of Children from Sexual Offences Act in India

Aim: The Protection of Children from Sexual Offences (POCSO) Act, 2012, aims to strengthen the legal provisions for the protection of children from sexual abuse and exploitation. It defines a child as any person below the age of 18 years and provides protection to all children from the offences of sexual assault, sexual harassment and pornography (India: Ministry of Law and Justice, 2012).

Offences and Punishment: The POCSO Act provides for stringent punishments, which have been graded as per the gravity of the offence. The punishments range from simple to rigorous imprisonment of varying periods. There is also provision for fine, which is to be decided by the court. An offence is treated as "aggravated" when committed by a person in a position of trust or authority of child such as a member of security forces, police officer, public servant, etc. The punishments for offences covered in the Act are:

- Penetrative Sexual Assault (Section 3)—Not less than seven years which may extend to imprisonment for life, and fine (Section 4)
- Aggravated Penetrative Sexual Assault (Section 5)—Not less than ten years which may extend to imprisonment for life, and fine (Section 6)
- Sexual Assault (Section 7)—Not less than three years which may extend to five years, and fine (Section 8)
- Aggravated Sexual Assault (Section 9)—Not less than five years which may extend to seven years, and fine (Section 10)
- Sexual Harassment of the Child (Section 11)—Three years and fine (Section 12) (India: Ministry of Law and Justice, 2012)

It is surprising that the POCSO Act does not include commercial sexual exploitation of children discussed in the next section.

Prevention of Sexual Abuse of Children

Be Cautious and Prepared: As part of overall safety education, there is a need to talk with children about what to do if/when they feel unsafe. Have children practice proper responses to danger or potential violence through role playing, etc. This can help increase the child's self-confidence and efficacy in handling a potential threat. When teaching a child about safety planning, caseworkers should discuss the following:

- Help the child name some adults that make him/her feel safe. Once the safe people are identified, the caseworker can encourage the child to tell them if they feel worried or unsafe.
- Help the child name places that make them feel safe, especially those places they would go if they didn't feel safe at home.

- Map out a plan with the child and practice how the child would respond if he/ she felt unsafe. What would he/she do? What would he/she say? It is important to have children practice saying "No!" to an adult who is doing anything to make them feel uncomfortable. Role playing is very useful to help children practice saying "No". (The International Rescue Committee, 2012).

Practice Assertiveness: Children should practice what they would do if they experience NOT okay touching. It is helpful to explain to the child the following points:

- Nobody should touch your private parts in a sexual way; even if it is someone you know and love.
- If you feel funny, strange or uncomfortable about the way someone's touching you, you should tell that person, "NO!"
- Give children techniques (run, hide, ask for help, call out, scream) to use in response to inappropriate touching or behaviours. Make sure to help the child identify a trusted adult whom he/she can confide in if anyone threatens them again (The International Rescue Committee, 2012).

Working with Men and Boys: Save the Children (2003) recommends working with men and boys to prevent CSA through the following ways:

- Calling on and organising boys and men in the society to protest against violence and CSA and to take initiatives for more equal gender roles and relationships.
- Promoting programmes for young men on parenting and stressing the benefits for all members in society of men playing a more active role in nurturing their children and abandoning the culture of violence and abuse as a proof of masculinity. Fathers should encourage both girls and boys to express and participate in decisions that affect them.
- Identifying boys and men who break with traditional stereotyped behaviour and internalise gender equality, and engaging them to support programmes that address violence and child abuse as good role models.

Activities

Introductory Activity 8.1: Video Discussion on Good Touch Bad Touch

Learner Outcome: At the end of this activity, the participants will know the difference between good touch and bad touch and develop skills to protect one's body from bad touch.

Procedure: Use the following procedure to conduct this activity:

1. Show one of the following video films, to initiate discussion on how to protect oneself from child sexual abuse:

- Komal: A Film on CSA by Childline
  https://www.youtube.com/watch?v=VkY0xqtw6W8
- Choti si asha Hindi
  https://www.youtube.com/watch?v=ooSZZ705Cn4&list=
  PL38322753F73B5A71&index=2
- Plan India NGO. Chuppi Todo.
  https://www.youtube.com/watch?v=BR1xQULU-TQ
- Child Abuse animation (anime pro)-2
  https://www.youtube.com/watch?v=Z9yYNz76a-o
- Child Abuse—Neighbour Ad
  https://www.youtube.com/watch?v=3iLYmEUdTjA
- Child Abuse within Family—Prevention Ad
  https://www.youtube.com/watch?v=zhFRLBWt2aQ

2. Use the following questions to discuss this film:

- Why did these adults try to sexually abuse the children?
- In what situations are children vulnerable to sexual abuse?
- What are the effects of sexual abuse on the children?
- How can children protect themselves from sexual abuse?

Activity 8.2: Video Discussion on Prevention of Child Sexual Abuse

Learner Outcomes: At the end of this activity the participants will learn the strategies for prevention of sexual violence against children.

Procedure: Use the following procedure to conduct this activity:

1. Show the video film: Child Sexual Abuse in Pakistan: Animated
   https://www.youtube.com/watch?v=xGXoQXGTzhA
   Use the following questions to discuss this video:

- What should the child do to protect himself or herself from sexual abuse?
- What should the families and community do to protect children from sexual abuse?

2. Show Summary Chart 8.1 and discuss the guidelines for children for protection from Sexual Abuse.

- Is it difficult to say no to a family member if he/she is an abuser? If yes, why?
- Who can be a trusted person (in home, school or community) to talk to/run to in case of abuse?
- If a friend tells you about someone abusing him/her, what would you advise him/her?

Time Estimate: 30 min

Activity 8.3: Video Discussion on Child Sexual Abuse

Learner Outcome: At the end of this activity, the participants will develop awareness on different aspects of child sexual abuse.

Procedure: Use the following procedure to conduct this activity:

1. Show the Summary Chart 8.2 and discuss the types of sex offenders of children.
2. Show the video on Satyamev Jayate (2012): Episode Child Sexual Abuse
   http://www.satyamevjayate.in/child-sexual-abuse/childsexualabuse.aspx

Questions for Discussion: Use the following questions to discuss this activity:

- Who are generally the sexual abusers of children?
- What is the effect of sexual abuse on children?
- Why children do not share about sexual abuse?
- In what ways the child sexual abusers make sure that children do not disclose the abuse?
- How can child sexual abuse be prevented?

Time Estimate: Show select parts for 30 min followed by discussion for 15 min

Activity 8.4: Exercise on Myths and Facts About Child Sexual Abuse

Learner Outcome: At the end of this activity, the participants will learn to dispel common myths associated with child sexual abuse.

Procedure: Use the following procedure to conduct this activity:

1. Make copies of the Exercise on Beliefs on Child Sexual Abuse, given at the end of the chapter and circulate a copy each among all participants. Ask them to read all the statements and respond agree/disagree against each statement. Allow them 10 min for this.
2. Read each statement aloud and ask participants for their response.
3. Use the following facilitator's answer keys to bust these myths commonly associated with sexual abuse.

No.	Facilitator's answer keys
1	Myth. Danger from strangers is only a small part of the problem. Research evidence world over indicates that in a majority of cases, the child's relatives, family, friends or someone known and trusted by the child is involved
2	Myth. An overwhelming majority of those who sexually abuse children are men although women are the ones who spend most time with children. Only a small minority of women report to have abused children

3	Myth. Depending on the definition used for child sexual abuse, there is a much higher prevalence of child sexual abuse in any society than mental illness. Unfortunately, the men who sexually abuse children are often ordinary, respectable men holding positions of responsibility in the family, society and workplace and fulfilling their duties as per the demand of their role
4	Myth. Sexual abuse cuts across classes, caste, religious and educational barriers and occurs irrespective of what the background of the abuser and the child is
5	Myth. Most times, children are unable to disclose or talk about abuse. In rare instances, when they do talk, it is not their imagination or fantasy but very real; children need to be believed and supported if they talk about any sexual touching or if they express any reservations about interacting with particular adults
6	Myth. All children, irrespective of their age, colour, family background, sexual knowledge are vulnerable to abuse. They are perceived as easy targets because of the power the abuser has and the inability of children to speak up or stop abuse
7	Myth. Children do not report abuse for several reasons: They are afraid no one will believe them; they are afraid that the abuser may harm or kill them or their loved ones; they are afraid they will lose the love of their parents and near and dear ones; they do not have a language to disclose abuse
8	Myth. Children are experts at hiding their pain. It is difficult to say from external appearance if the child is sexually abused. However, adults need to be alert to any changes in the child's behaviour, performance at school, emotionality, fear of certain places or people, resistance to go or meet some people and sleeping and eating patterns. A traumatic experience in a child's life is often expressed through indirect means
9	Myth. Most children are abused by persons known to them; relatives, family friends, neighbours, drivers, watchmen, doctors, religious leaders. Such abuse often takes place in one's home which is considered as a safe haven. The abuser enjoys the trust of the family members and has easy access to the child
10	Myth. Boys are as much prone to sexual abuse as girls

Source Maitra (n.d.)

Questions for Discussion: use the following questions to discuss this activity:

- Why are there so many myths around child sexual abuse?
- Did any myth related to child sexual abuse evoke specific emotion like surprise or shock or something similar? Why?
- What kind of impact does child sexual abuse have on the abuse survivor?
- How can the child sexual abuse survivor be helped?

Time Estimate: 45 min

Activity 8.5: Role-Plays of Helping a Child Who Is Sexually Abused

Learner Outcome: At the end of this activity, the participants who are parents or teachers will learn the skills to help a child who gets sexually abused.

Procedure: Use the following procedure to conduct this activity:

1. Show Summary Chart 8.3 and discuss the core child-friendly beliefs about child sexual abuse.
2. Ask for volunteers to role-play what they would do if a child tells them about his or her experience with sexual abuse:

   - Would they believe the child?
   - Would they blame the child?
   - Would they shame or ridicule the child?
   - Would they ask the child to keep it a secret?
   - Would they believe the child and provide support and give him/her confidence to talk?

Time Estimate: 30 min

Prevention of Commercial Sexual Exploitation of Children

Concepts and Theories

Concepts of Commercial Sexual Exploitation of Children

According to the Stockholm Declaration and Agenda for Action adopted at the First World Congress against Commercial Sexual Exploitation of Children, in Stockholm, Sweden, in 1996, "The commercial sexual exploitation of children is a fundamental violation of children's rights. It comprises sexual abuse by the adult and remuneration in cash or kind to the child or a third person or persons. The child is treated as a sexual object and as a commercial object. The commercial sexual exploitation of children constitutes a form of coercion and violence against children, and amounts to forced labour and a contemporary form of slavery".

According to ECPAT (2008b), "The primary, interrelated forms of commercial sexual exploitation of children—often referred to as CSEC—are prostitution of children, child pornography and trafficking of children for sexual purposes. Other forms include child-sex tourism, and in some cases, child marriage. Children can also be commercially sexually exploited in other, less obvious ways, such as through domestic servitude or bonded labour. In these cases, a child is contracted to provide work but the employer believes that the child can also be used for sexual purposes". As the profit factor is an important characteristic of CSEC, child marriages do not always fit into CSEC. A separate chapter is presented on child marriage in this sourcebook. As trafficking of children is carried out not only for commercial sex, it has been discussed in another chapter. The forms of CSEC discussed in this chapter are child prostitution, child pornography and child sex tourism (CST).

The UN Optional Protocol to the UNCRC on the Sale of Children, Child Prostitution and Child Pornography (2000a) noted the significant increase in international traffic in children for the purpose of sale of children, child prostitution and child pornography, and the widespread and continuing practice of sex tourism, to which children are especially vulnerable, as it directly promotes the sale of children, child prostitution and child pornography.

The ECPAT International (2005, p. 21) differentiates CSEC from CSA as follows:

• In CSA, child is inside the system—often still in school, whereas in CSEC the child is outside the system—not in school.
• In CSA, the wider community is sympathetic and supportive of the child victim, but in CSEC the wider community views such children's behaviour in a negative way.

Causes of Commercial Sexual Exploitation of Children

Causes of commercial sexual exploitation of children can be seen as increase in the combination of the demand and the vulnerability of children. Hughes (2004) divides the demand for victims to be used for commercial sex acts into the following three components:

1. The primary level of the demand is the men (and occasionally women) who seek out women, children and sometimes men, for the purpose of purchasing sexual acts. Men who solicit and buy sex acts are often called "customers", "clients" and "consumers", terms that normalise men's behaviour.
2. The second level of demand is the profiteers in the sex industries. They include the traffickers, pimps, brothel owners and supporting corrupt officials who make money from sex trafficking and prostitution. They are criminals and often members of transnational organised crime networks.
3. The third factor is the culture that indirectly creates a demand for victims by normalising prostitution. Media depictions of prostitution and other commercial sex acts suggest that prostitution is a victimless crime. In places where women and girls, or certain ethnicities or classes of women and girls are devalued, there is more acceptance of prostitution and the exploitation of a female relative in prostitution to financially support the family.

ECPAT International (2008b) lists the following factors leading to vulnerability of children to CSEC:

• Societal acceptance/harmful traditions and customs
• Discrimination/ethnicity
• Irresponsible sexual behaviour and myths regarding benefits of having sex with virgin young girls
• Poverty
• Family abuse and neglect of children

- Emergency situations such as natural disaster or armed conflict situations
- Living and working in the streets
- HIV/AIDS
- Consumerism in the middle class
- Guise of adoption
- Inadequate laws and corruption
- Information and communication technologies

Trafficking for Commercial Sexual Exploitation of Children in India

India is a significant source, destination and transit country for trafficking of children for commercial sexual exploitation. Children are trafficked into India from Bangladesh and Nepal, and through India to Pakistan and the Middle East. Ongoing conflicts and lack of livelihood options, combined with the high profit of brothel owners fuelled by the demand for young girls (possibly resulting from the fear of contracting HIV/AIDS from older and more experienced girls), have contributed to the increase in trafficking over the years. However, the majority of trafficking in underage girls for sexual exploitation happens within the country. Children are trafficked to and from states such as Andhra Pradesh, Bihar, Karnataka, Uttar Pradesh, Maharashtra, Madhya Pradesh, Rajasthan and West Bengal (ECPAT International, 2006a).

Almost half of the children trafficked within India are between the ages of 11 and 14; they are subjected to physical and sexual abuse and kept in conditions similar to slavery and bondage. Debt bondage is one of many strategies used by exploiters to keep children in constant servitude. Girls are forced to serve an average of seven "clients" per day and have no say in the choice of the customer or the use of contraceptives. Interviews with the trafficked girls showed severe impacts on their health, with 32.3% of respondents suffering from diseases such as HIV/AIDS, sexually transmitted infections (STIs) and other gynaecological problems. Having no legal documents/identity makes the victims highly vulnerable to threats of apprehension by authorities, extortion, detention, prosecution and deportation (ECPAT International, 2006a).

Child Rights to Protection from Commercial Sexual Exploitation

Article 34 of the UNCRC states that the States Parties shall undertake to protect the child from all forms of sexual exploitation and sexual abuse. For these purposes, States Parties shall in particular take all appropriate national, bilateral and multilateral measures to prevent:

(a) The inducement or coercion of a child to engage in any unlawful sexual activity;
(b) The exploitative use of children in prostitution or other unlawful sexual practices;
(c) The exploitative use of children in pornographic performances and materials.

The Optional Protocol to the UNCRC on the Sale of Children, Child Prostitution and Child Pornography (2000a) guarantees various rights to children: Right against exploitation and rights to information, be represented and heard, assistance, privacy and confidentiality, protection, speedy trial, rehabilitation and compensation. The ILO C182, the Worst Forms of Child Labour Convention, 1999, includes sale and trafficking of children; and the use, procuring or offering of a child for prostitution, for the production of pornography or for pornographic performances, in the term "worst forms of child labour", to be eliminated as a priority.

Policy and Legislation for Combating Trafficking and Commercial Sexual Exploitation of Women and Children

Immoral Traffic (Prevention) Act: To deal with the problem of commercialised prostitution, in 1956, the Suppression of Immoral Traffic Act was enacted, which was amended in 1986. According to this Act, any person who keeps or manages, or acts or assists in the keeping or management of a brothel, shall be punishable. The ITPA has provision for prosecuting brothel keepers, those knowingly living on the earnings of prostitution or procuring, inducing or forcing persons into prostitution, or detaining a person in premises where prostitution is carried on as well as those carrying on prostitution in the vicinity of public places. Even so, the sections of the Act relating to brothel keepers, procurers and pimps are seldom enforced by the law enforcing agencies. Men mostly go scot-free and the hapless person exploited for prostitution gets further victimised by the law. The law thus criminalises the victims.

India is a signatory to the UN Protocol to Prevent, Suppress and Punish Trafficking in Persons Especially Women and Children (2000b), which covers trafficking for situations other than prostitution. However, the ITPA only penalises the offence of trafficking if the victim is used for the purpose of prostitution.

The Indian Penal Code: Following actions amounting CSEC are punishable under the Indian Penal Code (1860).

Section 366A: Whoever, by any means whatsoever, induces any minor girl under the age of eighteen years to go from any place or to do any act with intent that such girl may be, or knowing that it is likely that she will be, forced or seduced to illicit intercourse with another person shall be punishable with imprisonment which may extend to ten years, and shall also be liable to fine.

Section 372: Whoever sells, lets to hire or otherwise disposes of any person under the age of eighteen years with intent that such person shall at any age be employed or used for the purpose of prostitution or illicit intercourse with any person or for any unlawful and immoral purpose, or knowing it to be likely that such person will at any age be employed or used for any such purpose, shall be punished with imprisonment of either description for a term which may extend to ten years, and shall be liable to fine.

Section 373: Whoever buys, hires or otherwise obtains possession of any person under the age of eighteen years with intent that such person shall at any age be employed or used for the purpose of prostitution or illicit intercourse with any person or for any unlawful and immoral purpose, of knowing it to be likely that such person will at any age be employed or used for any purpose, shall be punished with imprisonment of either description for a term which may extend to ten years and shall also be liable to fine.

Scheme for Prevention of Trafficking and Commercial Sexual Exploitation of Women and Children: The Ministry of Women and Child Development has formulated a Central Scheme called "Comprehensive Scheme for Prevention of Trafficking for Rescue, Rehabilitation and Reintegration of Victims of Trafficking for Commercial Sexual Exploitation-Ujjawala". The scheme has been conceived primarily for the purpose of preventing trafficking on the one hand and rescue and rehabilitation of victims on the other. The prevention component of the scheme includes:

(1) Formation and functioning of Community Vigilance Groups.
(2) Sensitisation Workshops/Seminars.
(3) Awareness generation through mass media including *kalajathas*, street plays, puppetry or through any other art forms, preferably traditional.
(4) Development and printing of awareness generation material such as pamphlets, leaflets and posters (in local language).

Child Prostitutes

Concept: The Optional Protocol to the UNCRC *on the Sale of Children, Child Prostitution and Child Pornography* (2000a) defines child prostitution as "the use of a child in sexual activities for remuneration or any other form of consideration".

The term "prostitution" is conventionally understood as an act of selling of sex, by a woman, against payment. According to Patkar and Patkar (n.d.), this term inaccurately depicts the woman as an independent actor acting on her own accord, for her own profits. They prefer the term "victims of commercial sexual exploitation", as it is sexual exploitation, carried out for the profit of the exploiter, by providing access to the victim's sexual faculties, to any customer who is ready to pay for it. According to Mehta (2002), adults in prostitution may be seen as victims or consenting parties, but there exists no two opinions that in child prostitution children are victims as they are powerless, innocent and dependent on adults for their well-being.

Child prostitution occurs when someone benefits from a commercial transaction in which a child is used for sexual purposes. Some of those who may benefit from such transactions include pimps, other intermediaries, parents or certain business sectors, such as hotels. A child is also a victim of prostitution when he/she engages in sex in return for basic needs such as food, shelter or safety, or for favours such as higher grades at school or extra pocket money to purchase consumer goods (ECPAT, 2006b).

Locations: Based on his work with child prostitutes in Goa, Pandey (2006) categorised the phenomenon of child prostitution into brothel-based, hotel- and lodge-based, street-based and mobile nature:

Brothel-based Child Prostitution: In the brothel-based phenomenon, the minor girls are housed in rooms and the perpetrators include brothel keepers and pimps who solicit the customers. They are mostly caged and do not have access to anyone other than the customers. The girls in this situation have to entertain all kind of customers brought by the traffickers. They do not have any choice as if they refuse they are physically abused. They are no different from bonded slaves (Pandey, 2006).

Hotel- and Lodge-based Child Prostitution: In the hotel and lodge-based phenomenon, minor girls are mostly locked in the rooms of a hotel/lodge and soliciting of the customers is done by the pimps, hotel staff, taxi drivers and traffickers. The girls are paraded before the customers for selection. Once the girl is selected by the customer, she is sexually exploited by the customer in the same hotel. A large amount of earning from this kind of prostitution is taken by the hotel and lodge staff/owners (Pandey, 2006).

Street-based Child Prostitution: In the street-based phenomenon, the traffickers/perpetrators force the minor girls to solicit customers on their own and then take the customers to a hotel/lodge with whom they already have an understanding. Sometimes, they are even sexually exploited in isolated places such as jungles, vehicles. A large amount of the earnings goes to the perpetrators and for renting rooms in hotels and lodges (Pandey, 2006).

Mobile Child Prostitution: In the "mobile" phenomenon, victims are carried in vehicles by the traffickers and soliciting is done by the trafficker's agents. Most of the times, the victims are kept in the vehicle and the vehicle is parked in tourist areas. Once the traffickers' agents fix the deal with the customers, they inform the traffickers sitting in the vehicle and the vehicle comes and drops the victim at the destination given by the agent. Once the job is over the vehicle comes back and collects the girl/s. It is found that this kind of exploitation is done in a very organised manner with the involvement of the traffickers who have control over the victims, taxi drivers and hotel and lodge staff. In this kind of phenomenon, the customers also directly contact the traffickers by mobile phones and girls are delivered to their desired location (Pandey, 2006).

Culturally Sanctioned Child Prostitution: The prostitution of children is culturally sanctioned in some communities in India through the practice of Devadasi or Jogini, whereby young girls who are offered in sacrifice to the gods to fulfil religious obligations go to live in temples and are used in prostitution. Although these practices were banned by the Prohibition of Dedication Act 1982, there are reportedly still many Devadasis in the States of Bihar, Andhra Pradesh and Tamil Nadu. Similarly, women and children of certain tribes (such as Bhil, Garasatya, Kulbeliya, Banjara and Jogi) and certain castes (Nayak, Baori, Damami, Sikhlingar and Mazhbi) in the State of Rajasthan are involved in culturally sanctioned prostitution (ECPAT International, 2006b).

Child Pornography

Concepts of Child Pornography: According to the Optional Protocol to the UNCRC on the Sale of Children, Child Prostitution and Child Pornography (2000a), child pornography is "any representation, by whatever means, of a child engaged in real or simulated explicit sexual activities or any representation of the sexual parts of a child for primarily sexual purposes".

Modus Operandi: Child pornography includes photographs, visual and audio representations and writing and can be distributed through magazines, books, drawings, movies, videotapes, mobile phones and computer discs or files. Child pornography exploits children in many different ways:

1. Children may be tricked or coerced into engaging in sexual acts for the production of pornography, or images may be made in the process of sexually exploiting a child without the child's knowledge. These images are then distributed, sold or traded.
2. Those who "consume" and/or possess pornographic depictions of children are also exploiting the children, especially as the demand for such materials maintains the incentive to their production and consequently to the sexual abuse of the child.
3. The makers of pornography commonly use their products to coerce, intimidate or blackmail the children used in the making of such material (ECPAT International, 2008b).

In certain parts of the world, there is a marked involvement of organised crime networks in the production and distribution of child pornography. The most obvious use of child pornography is sexual arousal and gratification. However, it is also used to validate certain beliefs and behaviour (e.g. the notion that it is okay to have sex with children), establish trust among others interested in abusing children, gain entrance to private clubs and to make a profit. At a societal level, child pornography, whether of real or simulated images of children, continues to cultivate a demand that involves sexual abuse and exploitation of children and is linked to prostitution of children, child sex tourism and trafficking of children for sexual purposes (ECPAT International, 2008b).

The digital age has facilitated the production and dissemination of child pornography. Advances in computer technology have made the creation and distribution of child pornography easier, cheaper and more difficult to detect. It should be noted, however, that those who make and access child pornography are not only paedophiles or preferential abusers. It has developed into a multimillion-dollar industry that can be run from within the exploiter's home. It is virtually impossible to ensure the physical destruction of child pornography once it has been posted on the Internet. The International Conference on Combating Child Pornography on the Internet, held in Vienna in 1999, called for the worldwide criminalisation of the production, distribution, exportation, transmission, importation, intentional possession and advertising of child pornography and stressing the importance of closer cooperation and partnership between governments and the Internet industry (UNICEF, 2004).

The Protection of Children from Sexual Offences Act in India: The Protection of Children from Sexual Offences (POCSO) Act, 2012, aims to strengthen the legal provisions for the protection of children from sexual abuse and exploitation. It defines a child as any person below the age of 18 years and provides protection to all children from the offences of sexual assault, sexual harassment and pornography. Sections 13 and 14 of the Act deals with "Use of Child for Pornographic Purposes" punishment for which is five years and fine and in the event of subsequent conviction, seven years and fine (India: Ministry of Law and Justice, 2012).

Child Sex Tourism

Concept of Child Sex Tourism: CST is the commercial sexual exploitation of children by people who travel from one location to another to engage in sexual acts with minors. Child sex tourists often travel from a richer country to one that is less developed. However, child sex tourists may also be travellers within their own countries or regions. Sex tourism preys on sexual and economic inequality, and fosters other forms of commercial sexual exploitation of children such as child trafficking for sexual exploitation. Child sex exploiters may try to rationalise their actions by claiming that sex with a child is culturally acceptable in the place they are visiting, or that the money or goods exchanged benefit the child and his or her community (ECPAT International, 2008b).

Sex tourism is an expression of massive and obscene economic inequalities between affluent and poor counties, as well as between affluent individuals in poor countries and the mass of poor people. Westerners' desire for sexual contact with local adults and children is often structured by their racist constructions of the exotic and erotic "primitive", while their racist assumptions about cultural difference are used to justify and defend their sexually exploitative acts (Davidson & Taylor, 1996). Inadequate laws and inefficient judicial systems are among the main causes of child sex tourism in developing countries; because they lead paedophiles to believe that they can go to these countries and abuse children without the risk of prosecution (UNICEF, 2004).

Child Sex Tourists: According to ECPAT International (2008a), child sex tourists may be married or single, male or female (though the majority are male), foreign or local, wealthy or budget tourists and from a high socio-economic or a disadvantaged background. Although they have no distinguishing physical features, patterns of social behaviour or particular mannerisms, it is possible to separate them into three distinct categories: The preferential child sex tourist, the paedophile and the majority being the situational child sex tourists.

Victims of Child Sex Tourism: Victims of CST often come from socio-economically disadvantaged backgrounds. However, this is not their only characteristic: many come from ethnic minorities, displaced communities and other marginalised social groups. Victims are both girls and boys, some of whom may also have been victims of domestic abuse and neglect. Working children, especially those involved in the tourism industry and who are dependent on seasonal income, can easily fall victim to CST. Sometimes, simply being born in a tourism destination characterised by major wealth discrepancies between incoming tourists and local inhabitants can be enough for a child to become exploited in CST (ECPAT International, 2008a).

Consequences of Child Sex Tourism: Regardless of the background of child victims of sex tourism, they all experience severe emotional, psychological and physical consequences as a result of their exploitation:

- The physical violence involved in the sexual exploitation of a child results in injury, pain and fear, while the acute psychological distress of sexual exploitation results in guilt, low self-esteem, depression and, in some instances, suicide.
- Children are also more vulnerable to sexually transmitted infections (STI), including HIV/AIDS.
- Child victims of CST are often stigmatised by their communities and have difficulty obtaining formal or informal education.
- They do not receive community support, nor do they experience the same social interaction, or develop as members of the community in the same way as other children do.
- For these reasons, it is more difficult for victims of CSEC to support themselves financially or to live independently as adults later in life.
- The consequences of CST on children are severe and their health, well-being and future opportunities are all jeopardised by the exploitation to which they have been subjected ECPAT International, 2008a).

No tourist should ever think that sexual contact of any kind with a child does not gravely affect the child or that it is acceptable if money or some other form of consideration is exchanged with the child (ECPAT International, 2008a).

Child Right to Protection from Commercial Sexual Exploitation

United Nations Convention on the Rights of the Child: Article 34 of the UN Convention on Rights of the child states that the child has the right to protection from all forms of sexual exploitation and sexual abuse that include the inducement or coercion of a child to engage in any unlawful sexual activity; the exploitative use of children in prostitution or other unlawful sexual practices and the exploitative use of children in pornographic performances and materials.

Optional Protocol to the UNCRC on the Sale of Children, Child Prostitution and Child Pornography: According to Article 8 of the Optional Protocol on the Sale of Children, Child Prostitution and Child Pornography (2000a), States Parties shall adopt appropriate measures to protect the rights and interests of child victims of the practices prohibited under the present protocol at all stages of the criminal justice process.

Worst Forms of Child Labour Convention: The ILO C182, the Worst Forms of Child Labour Convention, 1999, includes sale and trafficking of children, and the use, procuring or offering of a child for prostitution, for the production of pornography or for pornographic performances, in the term "worst forms of child labour", to be eliminated as a priority.

Prevention of Commercial Sexual Exploitation of Children

Most prevention programmes focus on children at risk of sexual exploitation in the context of prostitution, and on their families. Prevention should also focus on reducing demand through advocacy with clients and potential clients, in particular men. According to the Special Rapporteur, this approach is based on the belief that "the majority of men who purchase sex from child prostitutes are probably 'situational offenders' who do not have a distinct preference for children but may use a situation or opportunity to sexually exploit an accessible child" (UNICEF Innocenti Research Centre, 2009).

Activities

Activity 8.6: Small Group Discussion on Commercial Sexual Exploitation of Children

Learner Outcome: At the end of this activity, the participants will develop awareness about violation of rights of children being sexually exploited for profit.

Procedure: Use the following procedure to conduct this activity:

1. Ask the participants what they mean by commercial sexual exploitation of children.
2. Make three small groups for discussion of children being commercially sexually exploited in the following ways:

   (1) Child prostitution
   (2) Child pornography
   (3) Child sex tourism

3. Ask the small groups to read the relevant section, discuss and make a presentation to the large group.
4. Show Summary Chart 8.4 to summarise on Commercial Sexual Exploitation of Children.

Questions for Discussion: Use the following questions to discuss this activity:

1. What are the causes of this problem?
2. Which children are vulnerable to this problem?
3. What are the effects of this problem on children?
4. What rights of these children are violated?
5. How can this exploitation be prevented?

Time Estimate: 45 min

Activity 8.7: Posters for Creating Public Awareness on Commercial Sexual Exploitation of Children

Learner Outcome: At the end of this activity, the participants will learn to raise public awareness on prevention of commercial sexual exploitation of children.

Procedure: Use the following procedure to conduct this activity:

1. Use the same three small groups for discussion of children being commercially sexually exploited in the following ways:

   (1) Child prostitution,
   (2) Child pornography,
   (3) Child sex tourism,

2. Ask the small groups to prepare posters and role-plays to raise awareness on their topic and present to the large group.

Time Estimate: 30 min

Concluding Activity: Achievement of the Learner Objectives

Learner Outcome: By the end of the concluding activity, the participants will ascertain if they have achieved the learner objectives.

Procedure: Use the following procedure to conduct the concluding activity:

1. Show the power points/a chart on the learner objectives, ask the participants to read them one at a time and ask the group if they think they have achieved the objective.

2. The participants may be asked to share their responses in their diary with reference to the following questions:

   • What was a new learning for you in this session?
   • What did you like the best in this session and why?
   • Which activity was most effective?
   • What was not clear/confusing?
   • How can you apply what you have learnt?

Time Estimate: 15 min

Appendix: Summary Charts and Exercises

Summary Chart 8.1 Guidelines for children for protection from sexual abuse

What is Good Touch	
• If people who love you touch you to show their warmth or affection for you, it is good touch as it makes us feel good. • A doctor can touch any part of your body if there is a problem there. But he/she should do that only in presence of your parents/ trusted adults.	

What is Bad Touch	What you Should do to Protect Yourself from Bad Touch
• Anyone who touches your sexual organs. • Anyone who makes you feel uncomfortable. • It could be a known person or an unknown person.	• Stop the person. • Say "NO". • Even if the abuser offers you sweets or your favourite thing as a gift, you should not get carried away. • Even if the abuser asks you to keep it a secret, you must talk to a trusted adult about it. • If the abuser blackmails or scares you, you should try to run away to a trusted adult.

Talk to Yourself	
• Your body is yours and you have a responsibility to keep it healthy and safe. • You are your best friend. • It is your responsibility to protect your dignity. • If someone abuses you it is not your fault.	

Summary Chart 8.2 Types of sex offenders of children

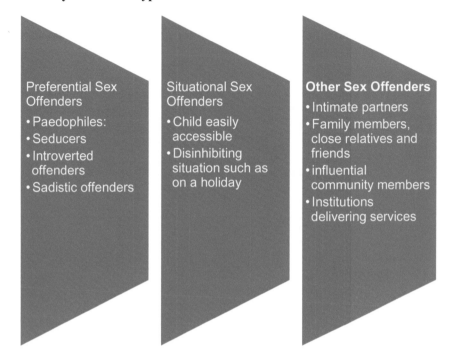

Preferential Sex Offenders
• Paedophiles:
• Seducers
• Introverted offenders
• Sadistic offenders

Situational Sex Offenders
• Child easily accessible
• Disinhibiting situation such as on a holiday

Other Sex Offenders
• Intimate partners
• Family members, close relatives and friends
• influential community members
• Institutions delivering services

Summary Chart 8.3 Core child-friendly beliefs about child sexual abuse
(Adapted from International Rescue Committee, 2012)

- Children tell the truth about sexual abuse.
- Children are not at fault for being sexually abused.
- Children can recover and heal from sexual abuse.
- Children should not be stigmatized, shamed, or ridiculed for being sexually abused.
- Adults, including caregivers and service providers, have the responsibility for helping a child heal by believing them and not blaming them for sexual abuse.

Summary Chart 8.4 Commercial sexual exploitation of children

Stakeholders of Commercial Sexual Exploitation of Children		
Victims: **Supply of** **Children at Risk**	**Exploiters:** **Demand for Sex by** **Adults**	**Profit-Makers:** **Network of Crime**
• Children in Poverty • Neglected Children • Abused Children • Out of School Children • Street Children • Children in Institutions • Children in Emergency Situations	• Consumers/ Customers/ Clients who can be • Situational Sex Offender • Paedophile • Preferential Sex Offender	• Traffickers • Brothel-Owners • Pimps • Intermediaries • Supportive Corrupt Officers

↓

Commercial Sexual Exploitation of Children

- Trafficking and Sale of Children for:
  - Child Prostitution
  - Child Sex Tourism
  - Child Pornography

↓
Effects

Physical, Sexual & Emotional Abuse	Injury/ Ill-Health/ STI/HIV/ Psychological Distress	No Participation, No Education & No Recreation	Stigmatisation No Community Support	Criminalisation by the Police & Other State Systems

Prevention Strategies

Compulsory and Free Education	Jobs/ Livelihood for Adults	Enforcement of Legal Bans	Creating Public Awareness

Exercise for Activity 8.3: Myths and Facts about Child Sexual Abuse

No	Beliefs on Child Sexual Abuse	Agree/ Disagree
1.	Only strangers abuse children sexually.	
2.	Both women and men sexually abuse children.	
3.	Men who sexually abuse children are mentally sick or perverted.	
4.	Child sexual abuse happens only in poor or problem families.	
5.	When children say they have been abused, it is often a figment of their imagination or fantasy.	
6.	Only beautiful or sexually precocious children are abused.	
7.	Children enjoy being touched sexually, that is the reason they do not report sexual abuse.	
8.	We can tell if a child is sexually abused.	
9.	Child sexual abuse can never happen in one's home.	
10.	Boys cannot be sexually abused.	

Acknowledgements   This chapter is partly adapted from the following chapter by the author: Desai, M. (2010). Chapter 18: Commercial Exploitation in Childhood and Tertiary Prevention. In *A Rights-Based Preventative Approach for Psychosocial Well-Being in Childhood.* Heidelberg: Springer, Series on Children's Well-Being: Indicators and Research.

References

American Psychiatric Association. (1994). *Diagnostic and statistical manual of mental disorders* (4th ed.). Washington, DC: Author. Retrieved from https://www.partners.org/assets/ documents/graduate-medical-education/substanceb.pdf.

Davidson, J. O., & Taylor, J. S. (1996). *Child prostitution and sex tourism in Goa.* Bangkok: ECPAT International.

Desai, M. (2010). *A rights-based preventative approach for psychosocial well-being in childhood.* Heidelberg: Springer, Series on Children's Well-Being: Indicators and Research.

ECPAT International. (2005). *The psychosocial rehabilitation of children who have been commercially sexually exploited: A training guide.* Bangkok: Author. Retrieved from http:// www.ecpat.net/sites/default/files/rehab_trainingmanual_eng.pdf.

ECPAT International. (2006a). *Combating the trafficking in children for sexual purposes: Questions and answers.* Bangkok: Author. Retrieved from http://www.ecpat.net/EI/ Publications/Trafficking/Trafficking_FAQ_ENG.pdf.

ECPAT International. (2006b). *Global monitoring report on the status of action against commercial sexual exploitation of children: India.* http://www.ecpat.net/sites/default/files/India %201st.pdf.

ECPAT International. (2008a). *Combating child sex tourism: Questions & answers.* Bangkok: Author. Retrieved from http://www.ecpat.net/sites/default/files/cst_faq_eng.pdf.

ECPAT International. (2008b). *Questions and answers about the commercial sexual exploitation of children.* Bangkok: Author. Retrieved from http://www.ecpatusa.org/EcpatUSA_PDF/faq% 20update%20from%20ecpat%20international.pdf.

Faller, K. C. (1993). *Child sexual abuse: Intervention and treatment issues.* Washington, D.C.: US Department of Health and Human Services.

Hughes, D. M. (2004). *Best practices to address the demand side of sex trafficking.* Retrieved from http://www.uri.edu/artsci/wms/hughes/demand_sex_trafficking.pdf.

India: Ministry of Law and Justice. (2012). *The protection of children from sexual offences act, 2012.* Retrieved from http://wcd.nic.in/sites/default/files/childprotection31072012.pdf.

International Rescue Committee. (2012). *Caring for child survivors of sexual abuse: Guidelines for health and psychosocial service providers in humanitarian settings.* New York: Author. Retrieved from http://www.unicef.org/pacificislands/IRC_CCSGuide_FullGuide_lowres.pdf.

Maitra, S. (n.d.). *Understanding child sexual abuse.* Childline. Retrieved from http://www. childlineindia.org.in/Understanding-Child-Sexual-Abuse.htm.

Mehta, L. (2002). Social profile of child sex workers. *Social Welfare, 3–7.*

National Human Rights Commission & Prasar Bharati. (n.d.). *Child abuse: A guidebook for the media on sexual violence write media against children.* Retrieved from http://www.nhrc.nic.in/ Documents/Publications/MedGuideChild.pdf.

Pandey, A. (2006). *Trafficking and sale of children and child prostitution.* Paper submitted for the Assessment and Recommendations for Mainstreaming Child Rights in Goa, by the Goa Initiative for Mainstreaming Child Rights. Panjim.

Patkar, P., & Patkar, P. (n.d.). *Frequently asked questions on commercial sexual exploitation and trafficking.* Mumbai: Prerana.

Pinheiro, S. (2006). *World report on violence against children.* Geneva. Retrieved from http:// www.unicef.org/lac/full_tex(3).pdf.

Save the Children. (2003). *Working with boys and men to end gender discrimination and sexual abuse of girls and boys*. Dhaka: Author.

The Stockholm Declaration and Agenda for Action. (1996). *Adopted At the first world congress against commercial sexual exploitation of children*, Stockholm, Sweden.

United Nations. (1989). *Convention on the rights of the child*. Retrieved from http://www.ohchr.org/english/law/pdf/crc.pdf.

United Nations. (2000a). *Optional protocol on the sale of children, child prostitution and child pornography*. Retrieved from http://www.ohchr.org/EN/ProfessionalInterest/Pages/OPSCCRC.aspx.

United Nations. (2000b). *Protocol to prevent, suppress and punish trafficking in persons, especially women and children*. Retrieved from http://www.osce.org/odihr/19223?download=true.

United Nations Children's Fund. (2004). *Child protection: A handbook for parliamentarians*. Retrieved from http://www.unicef.org/publications/index_21134.html.

United Nations Children's Fund Innocenti Research Centre. (2009). *Handbook on the optional protocol on the sale of children, child prostitution and child pornography*. Retrieved from http://www.unicef-irc.org/publications/pdf/optional_protocol_eng.pdf.

United Nations High Commissioner for Refugees. (2003). *Sexual and gender-based violence against refugees, returnees, and internally displaced persons: Guidelines for prevention and response*. Retrieved from http://www.unicef.org/violencestudy/pdf/UNHCR%20-%20SGBV.pdf.

World Health Organization & International Society for Prevention of Child Abuse and Neglect. (2006). *Preventing child maltreatment: A guide to taking action and generating evidence*. Retrieved from http://apps.who.int/iris/bitstream/10665/43499/1/9241594365_eng.pdf.

Module 9
Adolescent Rights to Prevention of Problems with Sexual Relationships

Prerequisites Modules

The prerequisite Modules for this Module are:
From *Sourcebook I on Introduction to Rights-Based Direct Practice with Children*:

- Modules on Life Skills Development

From *Sourcebook II on Child Rights Education for Participation and Development: Primary Prevention*:

- Introduction to Child Rights Education
- Child Rights to Participation and Children's Associations
- Child Rights to Physical Health and Hygiene
- Child Rights to Sexual Health Education

Conceptual Framework of Adolescent Rights to Prevention of Problems with Sexual Relationships

Concepts and Theories

Romantic and Sexual Relationships in Adolescence

The declining age at menarche and schooling have prolonged the period of adolescence. Together with a growing independence from parents and families, this has led in recent decades to more premarital sexual relations (World Health Organization (WHO), 2004a).

© Child Rights and You 2018
M. Desai and S. Goel, *Child Rights Education for Inclusion and Protection: Primary Prevention*, Rights-based Direct Practice with Children,
https://doi.org/10.1007/978-981-13-0417-0_9

Types of Romantic and Sexual Relationships: Abraham's (2002) study with older adolescents and youth in a low-income community in Mumbai showed three types of relationships with the opposite-sex peers:

- *Bhai-behen*: a platonic relationship,
- 'True love': a romantic one with intention to marry, and
- 'Time-pass': a transitory sexual relationship.

She noted that the extent of physical intimacy varies between each type of relationship from minimal physical intimacy (like shaking hands) in *bhai-behen* to sexual intercourse in "time-pass" relationships. In general, "true love" relations may not involve intercourse but include holding hands, touching, kissing and hugging.

Romantic Relationships: Despite strict social norms prohibiting premarital opposite-sex mixing, opportunities do exist for the formation of premarital romantic relationships in India. The findings of a national study of youth (15–29 years old) by the International Institute of Population Sciences (IIPS) and Population Council (2010) confirm the following:

- Significant minorities of young men and women had made or received a "proposal" for a romantic relationship (21–23%).
- A smaller percentage reported that they had been involved in a romantic partnership (19 and 9% of young men and women, respectively).
- Patterns of premarital romantic partnerships suggest that where partnerships occurred, they were initiated at an early age and were usually hidden from parents but not from peers.
- The majority of youth who engaged in a premarital romantic partnership had expectations of a longer-term commitment; young women were considerably more likely than young men to have expected a romantic relationship to lead to marriage (87 and 57%, respectively).
- The experiences of the married suggest, moreover, a disconnection between intentions and reality: while 64 and 92% of married young men and women who reported a premarital romantic partner, respectively, had intended to marry their premarital partner, far fewer (23 and 64%, respectively) had done so.

Sexual Behaviours

Range of Sexual Behaviours: People, regardless of their sexual identity, gender or physical ability, can express and experience their sexuality through a variety of sexual behaviours. One sexual behaviour is not better (or worse) than another, as long as the partners respect each other, no one is harmed, and both partners fully consent to it. Sexual behaviours among adolescents fall along a continuum—from non-penetrative activities to intercourse:

- Masturbation refers to touching oneself or genitals to achieve sexual arousal.
- Caressing, kissing, sharing erotic fantasies, stimulating a partner's genitals with one's hand and rubbing against each other are practices that may lead to orgasm and do not involve penetration.

- Oral sex is mouth-to-genital contact.
- Intercourse is sexual activity in which the penis enters the vagina or anus. Other forms of penetrative sex may involve using the fingers or an object (The Population Council, 2011).

Sexual arousal may reach a peak or climax, called orgasm. Along with a feeling of euphoria, orgasm involves involuntary contraction and release of muscles and secretion of fluid (ejaculate, with semen, in males; genital lubrication in females.). Many females reach orgasm only through stimulation of the clitoris.

Premarital Sex: According to the youth study carried out by IIPS & Population Council (2010):

- Eleven per cent of young men and five per cent of young women aged 15–24 had engaged in premarital sex in adolescence, that is, before age 20.
- There was a clear progression in reported physical intimacy and sexual experience with romantic partners: while 88% of young men had held hands with a romantic partner, just 42% had sex with their partner. Among young women, while three quarters had held hands with a romantic partner, just one in four (26%) had engaged in sexual relations.
- Young men tended to initiate premarital sex earlier than young women; moreover, youth in rural areas tended to initiate premarital sexual activity earlier than their urban counterparts.

Age at First Sexual Intercourse: According to NFHS-4 (IIPS & ICF, 2017), in India, the median age at first sexual intercourse is 19.1 years for women age 25–49. Ten percent of women age 25–49 had sex before age 15, and 38 percent before age 18. By age 20, 58 percent of women age 25–49 have had sexual intercourse. On an average, men age 25–49 in India initiate sexual intercourse at age 24.3, five years older than women. One percent of men age 25–49 first had sexual intercourse before age 15 and 7 percent had sexual intercourse before age 18. By age 25, 55 percent of men have had sexual intercourse.

Gender Differences: Boys are often permitted, or even pressured, to be sexually active, as long as their sexual desires are directed towards females. For example, some boys are encouraged to and may wish to delay sexual activity. However, they often feel significant pressures to "prove their manhood" through early, repeated and sometimes aggressive heterosexual experiences. Taking risks (including sexual ones) is commonly expected of boys and men in many settings. Girls, on the other hand, often receive negative or contradictory messages about sex. Many girls are taught that they should not be sexually active prior to marriage. They may even be punished for being sexually active. At the same time, girls are expected to be sexually appealing. Media images may sexualise girls at a young age. Girls are often socialised to be submissive to their boyfriends and husband and to men in general (The Population Council, 2011).

Sexual Orientation

The following definitions of sexual orientation are taken from the American Psychological Association (APA, 2008):

- **Sexual orientation** refers to the sex of those to whom one is sexually and romantically attracted.
- **Heterosexual**: It refers to attraction to members of the other sex, that is, boys or men feel attraction to girls or women and vice versa. In common parlance, they are called 'straight'.
- **Homosexual**: It refers to men or women who have preferential sexual attraction to people of their same sex over a significant period of time. It includes both gays (men who feel attracted to other men) and lesbians (women who feel attracted to other women).
- **Bisexuals**: It refers to people who feel attracted to members of both sexes.
- **Transgenders**: Transgender people may be attracted to people of the same sex, the other sex, or both.

Sexual orientation can be understood along a continuum from completely heterosexual to bisexual to completely homosexual preferences. For most adolescents, romance involves members of the opposite sex. However, in early and mid-adolescence, some may experience a period of sexual questioning during which they sometimes report emotional and sexual attractions to members of the same sex. While these experiences could simply be a part of the larger process of sexual identity formation, there are adolescents who identify themselves clearly as homosexuals (Kail & Cavanaugh, 2007). This identification occurs in mid-adolescence but not until young adulthood do most homosexuals express their sexual orientation publicly (D'Augelli, 1996 cited in Kail & Cavanaugh, 2007). Because of the negative societal attitudes against homosexuality, adolescents take time to gather the courage to "come out". In contrast, as heterosexuality is believed to be the norm, adolescents establish a heterosexual orientation without much soul searching (Savin-Willams, 1995 cited in Sigelman & Rider, 2006). What causes or determines one's sexual orientation is not well understood though (The Population Council, 2011).

Prevention of Problems with Sexual Relationships

Problems with Sexual Relationships: Adolescents experiment with sexual behaviour, sometimes making informed decisions about protection from pregnancy and sexually transmittable infections (STIs) and at other times without such planning or consent too (Sigelman & Rider, 2006, p. 344). Studies that have explored adolescent sexual behaviours point out that adolescents are vulnerable to unsafe, unwanted or forced sexual relations, unplanned pregnancy and abortion, adolescent childbearing, and the risk of reproductive tract infections (RTIs), HIV and other sexually transmitted infections (STIs). Malnutrition, particularly among young women, is widespread and deprives adolescents of the extra nutritional requirements to support their rapid growth during adolescence and places young women at risk of adverse reproductive health consequences (Santhya & Jejeebhoy, 2012).

Thus if the adolescents have entered sexualised relationships, an understanding of rights and responsibilities in sexual relationships is very important to prevent problems such as

- Violence in sexual relationships,
- Teenage pregnancy, problems with unsafe abortion and unwed motherhood and
- Sexually transmitted infections (STIs) and HIV.

Risk Factors: Increased chances of risky premarital sexual relations among adolescents include:

- Poor academic performance,
- Abuse of substances such as drugs, alcohol and tobacco,
- Access to pornographic films and other X-rated materials,
- Having peers who are sexually active,
- Family instability and
- Being part of the workforce, especially for males as it brings financial independence (Santhya & Jejeebhoy, 2012).

Additionally, misconceptions or myths about sexual behaviours, STIs and HIV, inadequate knowledge about contraception, lack of availability or accessibility to reproductive and sexual health services, an environment of secrecy shrouded around sex, gender imbalance and a general sense of invulnerability also contribute to risky adolescent sexual behaviours (Jejeebhoy & Sebastian, 2003).

Protective Factors: Research suggests protective factors for adolescents against risky premarital sexual relations include:

- Being in school and having academic goals,
- Living in a stable family environment where parents or significant other act as "gatekeepers",
- Having knowledge about sex and sexuality and having self-efficacy to refuse unsafe or unwanted sex (Santhya & Jejeebhoy, 2012).

Sexual Rights: According to WHO (2006, p. 5), sexual rights include the right of all persons, free of coercion, discrimination and violence, to:

- The highest attainable standard of sexual health, including access to sexual and reproductive healthcare services,
- Seek, receive and impart information related to sexuality,
- Sexuality education,
- Respect for bodily integrity,
- Choose their partner,
- Decide to be sexually active or not,
- Consensual sexual relations,

- Consensual marriage,
- Decide whether or not, and when, to have children and
- Pursue a satisfying, safe and pleasurable sexual life.

Sexual Responsibilities: According to the Population Council (2011), following are the factors that contribute to having mutually satisfying, responsible and safe sexual experiences:

- Knowing that you and your partner both have the same rights and cooperating to ensure mutual respect, consent and responsibility,
- Treating each other as equals, and as people, not just as bodies,
- Feeling comfortable in communicating what each partner wants or does not want,
- Respecting a partner's right not to do anything that feels uncomfortable or unsafe,
- Being honest with each other,
- Feeling intimacy,
- Feeling cared for,
- Using safe and effective ways to protect yourself and your partner from unwanted pregnancy and sexually transmitted infections (STIs), including HIV,
- Working to protect yourself and your partner from emotional harm,
- Being aware of your own desires and comfort level and those of your partner and
- Being able to give and to accept pleasure.

Role of the State

Adolescence Education Programme: India as a society has been known to have conservative stand on boy–girl relationships. Moreover, sexuality education of adolescents tends to get opposed in India on the ground that it would encourage adolescents and youth to engage in sexual activities. But the studies discussed in this module show that sexual behaviours and relationships are a reality in urban and rural India and therefore adolescents need to be provided with the knowledge and skills to make the right and safer choices for themselves. Recognising the need to provide sexuality education, the Adolescence Education Programme (AEP) was initiated as early as 1993 as an introduction to sex education. It was repeated in the National Curriculum Framework in 2005 and was subsequently launched in 2005 by the Ministry of Human Resource Development and the National AIDS Control Organisation. The curriculum for AEP has been revised, from mainly HIV to a broader framework to enable young people not only to gain information on sexual and reproductive health matters but also to understand the risks they face and ways to address these. However, there has been no consensus in the State governments and a majority of them have not been willing to include sex education as part of the curriculum (Santhya & Jejeebhoy, 2012).

ARSH: The Adolescent Reproductive and Sexual Health (ARSH) strategy addresses the needs of adolescents under Reproductive and Child Health (RCH) II by setting up clinics, particularly in the existing public healthcare facilities.

However, evaluations of the functioning of these programmes suggest that the strategy has not succeeded in either increasing services for the adolescents or in improving the quality of services received by them (Santhya & Jejeebhoy, 2012).

Lack of Focus on Boys and Men: It has been noted that most of the programmes focus on young girls, neglecting the role of young boys in maintaining sexual and reproductive health for themselves and their partners. It is, nonetheless, essential to include boys in the group in order to develop equitable gender attitudes among them. It is also important to acknowledge the vulnerabilities faced by this group, be it substance misuse or experience of unsafe premarital sex (Santhya & Jejeebhoy, 2012).

RKSK: Following are the strategies of the Rashtriya Kishor Swasthya Karyakram (RKSK) to improve knowledge, attitudes and behaviour in relation to sexual and reproductive health (India: Ministry of Health & Family Welfare, 2013):

Promotion:

- Information about changes during adolescence, process of growing up (with focus on the 10–14 age group), safe sex and reproduction,
- Genital health and hygiene,
- Counselling on concerns related to growing up, sexuality, relationships, body image and identity (with focus on the 10–14 age group),
- Promotion of responsible sexual behaviour,
- Information on management of unwanted pregnancy,
- Legality of abortion and consequences of unsafe abortion,
- Information on causation, transmission and prevention of RTIs/STIs and HIV.

Prevention:

- Counselling on concerns related to nocturnal emission and menstrual problems,
- Access to non-clinical contraceptives such as condoms, oral contraceptive pills (OCPs) and emergency contraceptives,
- Screening for RTIs and STIs,
- Access to Integrated and Counselling and Testing Centre (ICTC).

Management:

- Management of menstrual disorders,
- Management of RTIs/STIs,
- Safe abortion services,

Activities

Introductory Activity 9.1: Exercise on Myths and Facts About Sexual Behaviours and Gender Norms

Learner Outcome: At the end of this activity, the participants will review different types of sexual behaviours and gender norms for the same.

Procedure: Use the following procedure for this activity:

1. Divide the participants into pairs and provide a copy of the Exercise on Myths and Facts about Sexual Behaviours and Gender Norms (given at the end of the chapter) to each pair.
2. Ask the pairs to write their responses against each statement after briefly discussing the answers among them.
3. Ask the pairs to share their responses for each statement and discuss using the following answer keys.

No	Facilitator answer keys
1.	False: There is no problem with masturbating frequently. The only time masturbation can be considered a problem is if it gets in the way of other things the person should be doing or if the person is disturbing other people or otherwise causing harm to themselves
2.	False: Being good does not mean not having sexual feelings and emotions. Girls can also masturbate to release sexual tension
3.	False: Boys are socialised to believe that they have to perform on their first night to prove their masculinity. There is an implied social sanction to practice for the big day by engaging in sexual acts prior to marriage. However, lack of complete knowledge about safe sexual behaviours could potentially pose risk for sexually transmitted infections and HIV
4.	False: It is normal for both adolescent girls and boys to be curious about sexual behaviours. Hence, girls who see erotic magazines do not cease to be good as it is a natural expression of their curiosity
5.	False: Having knowledge makes a girl better prepared for sexual acts and also better protected herself against unwanted pregnancy and STIs. It does not indicate loss of character
6.	False: Boys are socialised to believe that they have uncontrollable sexual desires and therefore they cannot stop themselves from touching and feelings girls. But, doing this against a girl's wish amounts to sexual abuse and must not be continued
7.	False: Girls live in fear about their "family honour" or are often scared to report such sexual advances, and therefore, they do not protest. It does not mean they are enjoying it
8.	True: Having accurate and complete knowledge can help girls to make responsible and safe decisions
9.	False: Girls are socialised to believe that if they have knowledge about sex or are not passive, then her character will be doubted upon. Also, boys/men are supposed to awaken their sexuality, that too only after marriage. In reality, girls also have sexual desires and should not be judged for expressing the same

10.	False: Boys and girls are equal in relationships. Boys do not own their girlfriends' body. Girls should be in full control of their body
11.	False: Some boys and men feel sexually attracted to boys and men, and some girls and women feel sexually attracted to girls and women. This is called homosexuality. Some are bisexuals that is they feel sexually attracted to persons from the same as well as the opposite sex

Questions for Discussion: Use the following questions to discuss this activity:

- Were you surprised that the commonly held perceptions about sexual behaviours and gender norms are mythical? Which ones?
- Why do you think that misconceptions surround sexual behaviours and gender norms?
- How do these misconceptions impact sexuality of girls and boys?
- Do these misconceptions lead to unnecessary anxiety and stress related to sexual behaviours?
- Do you think that these commonly held perceptions about sexual behaviours perpetuate a submissive for girls/women in their sexual relationships? Do they prevent them from being able to access sexuality-related information? How?
- How can about sexual behaviours and gender norms be prevented?

Time Estimate : 45 min

Sources: This activity has been adapted from Activity 22, Unit 3 in The Population Council (2011, pp. 66–69.) Some attitude statements are based on a research report by Abraham (2002).

Activity 9.2: Case Discussion on Sexual Rights and Responsibilities in Adolescence

Learner Outcome: At the end of this activity, the participants will understand the sexual rights and responsibilities and their application in adolescence.

Procedure: Use the following procedure to conduct this activity:

1. Ask the participants:
   a. Do sexual behaviours lead to certain vulnerabilities in adolescents? If yes, what are they?
   b. What are sexual rights?
   c. What are sexual responsibilities?
2. Show Summary Charts 9.1 and 9.2, and discuss sexual rights and responsibilities.
3. Divide the participants into three small groups, and allot each a case situation from below. Following are the questions for discussion:
   - What are the different issues that emerge in your case situation?
   - What would you do in place of the protagonists in your case situation?

- How would you prevent getting hurt emotionally or physically?
- How would you mutually respect each other's sexual rights?

Case Situation 1: Shahana and Tejas are 17-year-olds, studying in the same coaching classes. They have known each other for years as they live in the same neighbourhood. They both "like" each other and hold hands in privacy. Tejas wants to do more than just holding hands, while Shahana is undecided and scared.

Case Situation 2: Deepti and Sukhdeep are tenth graders and are good friends. They often get teased by their friends as boyfriend–girlfriend. One day Sukhdeep happened to kiss Deepti. They are not sure if they want to be in a serious relationship.

Case Situation 3: Sheena and Peter are twelfth graders. Their families know each other well. Peter feels that they will get married to each other once they graduate. So he insists that Sheena has a sexual relationship with him. Sheena has said no so far but fears that she might lose Peter.

Ask the small groups to present their discussions to the large group.

4. Use the following questions to discuss this activity:

- Why do teenagers want to have a boyfriend or girlfriend? Is it because everyone has a romantic partner?
- What type of a person do teenagers want to have as a boyfriend or girlfriend? Why?
- How can premature sexual debut be prevented?
- How can chances of getting hurt emotionally or physically are minimised?
- How can mutual respect for each other's sexual and reproductive rights remain non-negotiable?
- Should the teenagers wait until they are married or more mature emotionally?
- Should they wait for the relationship to have more commitment?

5. Introduce the following units of the module:

a. Prevention of violence in adolescent sexual relationships,
b. Prevention of teenage pregnancy, abortion and unwed Motherhood,
c. Prevention of sexually transmitted infections and HIV,
d. Use of contraceptives.

Time Estimate: 30 min

Prevention of Violence in Adolescent Sexual Relationships

Concepts and Theories

Concept of Sexual Consent: According to the Criminal Law (Amendment) Ordinance, 2013, consent means an "unequivocal voluntary agreement when the woman by words, gestures or any form of verbal or non-verbal communication, communicates willingness to participate in the specific sexual act, provided that the woman who does not physically resist the act of penetration shall not by the reason only of that fact, be regarding as consenting to the sexual activity". The Ordinance raised the age of consent to 18 years from the earlier age bar of 16 years. Age of consent is the age below which consent is irrelevant in law, and this sets the benchmark for "statutory rape". In other words, a person below 18 years is considered to lack legal capacity to consent to the sexual act. Therefore, all sexual acts among adolescents could be tried under the existing rape laws of India. Although the intention of the amendment was to secure the children and adolescents against sexual abuse, this raise in age of statutory rape has been criticised by both academicians and activists as it seems to taint adolescents with criminality of rape for sexual behaviours that are consensual; not forced, abusive or violent. It is feared that in the context of India, where the parental and community policing of intercaste and intercommunity relationships and marriages is so deeply entrenched, this provision may get used for retribution against romantic relationships that break the caste–class boundaries (Mehra, 2013).

Non-Consensual Sexual Experiences: All people have the right to give or withhold sexual consent. All people have the responsibility to respect their partners' right to give or withhold such consent. Sexual coercion occurs when someone forces (or attempts to force) another individual to engage in sexual activity against her/his will. In a coercive situation, a person may be physically forced to have sex. Or he or she may fear social or physical consequences for refusing unwanted sex (The Population Council, 2011).

The gender imbalance in sexual relationships often increases the risks faced by young females. The need to conform to these double standards may cause young females to fear disclosing their sexual activity and may result in reluctance among them to report sexual experience. This fear may also inhibit sexually active female adolescents from seeking contraceptive services. The fear of losing her partner or incurring his anger appear to be important factors inhibiting young females from exercising choice in the timing of sexual activity or negotiating the use of condoms or other contraceptives (Jejeebhoy et al., 1999, cited by WHO, 2004a). Such gender inequality can lead to sexual violence in the form of control, jealousy, lust and rape against girls and women.

Prevalence of Violence in Adolescent Sexual Relationships: According to the youth study by IIPS and Population Council (2010), the non-consensual sexual experiences reported by the youth are as follows:

Verbal Harassment:

- As many as 33% of young men admitted that they had verbally harassed a girl. More urban than rural young men reported the perpetration of verbal harassment (39% vs. 30%).
- Verbal harassment was experienced by substantial minorities of young women (11%) and fewer young men (6%).

- Rural–urban differences suggest, moreover, that young women in urban settings were somewhat more likely than their rural counterparts to have experienced verbal harassment (14% vs. 10%).

Non-Consensual Sexual Touch:

- More than a fifth (21%) of young men admitted touching a girl's private parts, brushing past a girl or making physical contact with her in a sexual way without her consent.
- Few youths (three to four per cent) admitted the experience of unwanted sexual touch. Surprisingly, gender differences were not observed.

Unwanted and Forced Sex:

- One in seven young women who had sex with an opposite-sex romantic partner reported that their partner had forced them to have sex the first time.
- Very few (0.4%) of young men reported that they had forced sex on a girl.

Activities

Activity 9.3: Small Group Discussion on Sexual Consent and Violence

Learner Outcome: At the end of this activity, the participants will develop awareness on importance of sexual consent and prevention of violence in sexual relationships.

Procedure: Use the following procedure to conduct this activity:

1. Form three small groups, and allocate the following topics among them for reading the notes and presentation to the large group:

   a. Concept of sexual consent,
   b. Non-consensual sexual experiences,
   c. Prevalence of violence in adolescent sexual relationships.

2. Show clips from movies that have focused on sexual consent such as *Pink* and *Anarkali of Arah*.
3. Use the following questions to conduct a discussion:

   a. Why is sexual consent important?
   b. Who is generally the perpetrator and who is generally the victim in violence in sexual relationships? Why?
   c. How can violence in sexual relationships be prevented?

Time Estimate: 30 min

Prevention of Teenage Pregnancy, Abortion and Unwed Motherhood

Concepts and Theories

Use of Contraceptives

According to NFHS-4 (IIPS & ICF, 2017), among sexually active unmarried female adolescents between 15 and 19 years of age, 40.5% of the urban population use condom and 59.5% do not use any contraceptives. On the other hand, among sexually active adolescents between 15 and 19 years of age, 11.9% of the rural population use any one contraceptive, mainly condom and 88.1% do not use any contraceptives. As far as sexually active married female adolescents between 15 and 19 years of age are concerned, 16.8% of the urban population use any one method and 83.2% do not use any contraceptives. On the other hand, among sexually active married female adolescents between 15 and 19 years of age, 14.4% of the rural population use any one contraceptive, and 85.6% do not use any contraceptives.

According to the analyses presented by Santhya and Jejeebhoy (2012), communication prior to a sexual relation often consisted of boys or young men convincing the girl to have sex. Generally, there is no communication about protection from pregnancy. Although the large majority of young people have heard of contraception and HIV/AIDS, few had in-depth awareness about contraceptive methods or modes of HIV transmission. Moreover, socio-demographic differentials in current contraceptive practice are notable: adolescent girls and rural, poorly educated and economically disadvantaged young women are less likely than others to have used contraception within marriage (Santhya & Jejeebhoy, 2012). If adolescents go to family planning services, they are often unwelcome, and the providers of contraceptives are frequently unsupportive of adolescents and refuse to provide them with contraceptives (Kaufman et al., 2001, cited by WHO, 2004a).

Thus, different barriers to contraceptive use among adolescents (whether married or unmarried) are:

- Lack of knowledge about contraceptives,
- Girls' inability to negotiate contraceptive use with their male sexual partners,
- Lack of access to contraceptives and information about their use and
- Unsupportive service providers.

Teenage Pregnancy

According to NFHS-4 (IIPS & ICF, 2017), in India, 28% of women age 15–19 have begun childbearing; five percent of women have had a live birth and three percent are pregnant with their first child.

- Teenage pregnancy is relatively high in rural areas. Nearly one in every 10 women in rural areas in the age group 15–19 have begun childbearing.
- The level of teenage pregnancy decreases with an increasing level of schooling.

- Twenty percent of women age 15–19 with no schooling have already begun childbearing, compared with only 4 percent of women who had 12 or more years of schooling.
- Childbearing among women age 15–19 decreases with the level of wealth. Only 3 percent of teenage women in the highest wealth quintile have begun childbearing, compared with 11 percent of teenage women in the lowest two wealth quintiles.
- Teenage childbearing is higher among scheduled tribe women age 15–19 years (11%) than the other three caste/tribe groups.
- More than half (52%) of currently married women age 15–19 have already begun childbearing.

Abortion

Abortion Law: According to the Medical Termination of Pregnancy Act, 1971 (amended in 2002), a pregnancy may be terminated by a registered medical practitioner:

(a) Where the length of the pregnancy does not exceed twelve weeks if such medical practitioner is, or
(b) Where the length of the pregnancy exceeds twelve weeks but does not exceed twenty weeks, if not less than two registered medical practitioner are, of opinion, formed in good faith, that

  i. The continuance of the pregnancy would involve a risk to the life of the pregnant woman or of grave injury to her physical or mental health or
  ii. There is a substantial risk that if the child were born, it would suffer from such physical or mental abnormalities to be seriously handicapped.

Unsafe Abortion: Although abortion was legalised in 1972, the number of illegal providers of abortion services is very high, and among unmarried adolescents, the number of abortions in unhygienic conditions by unlicensed practitioners is estimated to be considerable (United Nations Population Fund (UNFPA), 2001, cited by WHO, 2004a). Among the women who are exposed to these dangerous interventions, pregnant adolescents are an important group. There are four major areas of difference between adolescents and adults: a longer delay in seeking abortion; resorting to less-skilled providers, the use of more dangerous methods; and a longer delay in seeking help for complications. Because of all these factors, pregnant adolescents, particularly the unmarried, are more likely to suffer serious complications than other women (WHO, 2004a).

According to the youth study by the IIPS and Population Council (2010):

- A major factor delaying timely access to safe abortion services in adolescence is the lack of awareness among the young about the legality of abortion as well as information on facilities providing safe and legal abortion or providers of legal abortion services.

- Just seven per cent of both young men and women aged 15–24 years were aware that it is legal for married and unmarried women to seek abortion, that it is illegal to seek abortion for pregnancies beyond 20 weeks and that it is illegal to terminate a pregnancy because the foetus is a female and the couple wants a son.

Effects of Teenage Pregnancy

According to the State of the World Population by the UNFPA (2013, p. 4), adolescent pregnancy often alters the course of a girl's entire life. The risk of maternal morbidity and mortality, preterm delivery, low birth weight or stillbirth is higher in the case of adolescent mothers, especially those from low-income households, than that of older females, as they are already nutritionally depleted. Early childbearing leads to denial of basic rights to health, nutrition, education and freedom from violence and exploitation, reinforces existing gender divisions and can lead to a spiral of low self-esteem, helplessness and poverty.

One of the determinants of poverty may be the fact that in many countries adolescent childbearing is associated with premature termination of education. Comparable problems are apparent for the children of adolescent mothers; in the long run, they have a significantly poorer nutritional status than the children of older mothers and lower scores on a language development test; their mothers also more frequently reported behavioural problems (WHO, 2004a).

Government Strategies to Reduce Teenage Pregnancies

Following are the RKSK strategies to reduce teenage pregnancies in India:

Promotion:

- Information about risks of early conception and use of contraceptives,
- Address social pressure and concerns related to early marriage, conception and contraception.

Prevention:

- Counselling for contraceptive use and method choices,
- Access to quality contraceptive services, including emergency contraception,
- Referral for clinical contraceptives such intra-uterine contraceptive devices (IUCDs), as per the protocol.

Management:

- Management of adverse events, following use of contraceptive methods (India: Ministry of Health & Family Welfare, 2013).

Activities

Activity 9.4: Case Discussion on Adolescent Pregnancy, Contraceptive Use and Abortion

Learner Outcome: At the end of this activity, the participants will develop awareness about the implications of pregnancy in adolescence and discuss the way to avoid the same.

Procedure: Use the following procedure to conduct this activity:

1. Divide participants into three small groups, and allot each a case study from below. Allow them 10 min to read the testimonial, and discuss the questions. Then, have the groups present their responses to the large group.

Case Study 1: "I was 16 and never missed school. I liked studying. I dreamt of going to college and then getting a good job. But one day, I was told that I had to leave it all, as my parents bartered me for a girl my elder brother was to marry. Such exchange marriages are called *atta-satta* in my community. I pleaded with my mother, but my father had made up his mind. My only hope was that my husband would let me complete my studies. But he got me pregnant even before I turned 17. Since then, I have hardly ever been allowed to step out of the house. Everyone goes out shopping and for movies and neighbourhood functions, but not me. Sometimes, when the others are not at home, I hold my baby and cry. She is such an adorable little girl, but I am blamed for not having a son. Hopefully, customs like *atta-satta* and child marriage will be totally gone by the time my daughter grows up, and she will get to complete her education and marry only when she wants to"—Komal, 18, India (UNFPA, 2013, p. 2).

Questions:

- What makes girls vulnerable to pregnancy in adolescence?
- How does pregnancy in adolescence impact the girls?
- Why are adolescent girls unable to avoid an unwanted pregnancy or plan a pregnancy? Lack of knowledge about contraception? Lack of health services to access contraceptives? Lack of decision-making power? Societal pressure to conceive? Others?
- What could help girls to prevent an early or unwanted pregnancy?

Case Study 2: "A very young girl approached me for an abortion. She said her partner had refused to use a condom, and she didn't want to get onto oral contraceptive pills because she feared they would lead to weight gain, and affect her chances of pregnancy later. Her choice of contraception was the emergency pill which she popped each time she had sex. Sometimes, she had taken as many as six pills a month. Over the next few months, she experienced severe menstrual irregularity, weight gain, mood swings and water retention. She also developed polycystic ovarian syndrome. On one occasion, the pill did not do its job; hence she came to me for the termination of pregnancy"—A Mumbai-based gynaecologist (Rathod, 2014).

Questions:

- Identify the different issues faced by adolescent girls with regard to protection from pregnancy and choice of contraceptive use.
- What could help girls to prevent pregnancy in adolescence?

Case Study 3: Manju was 17 years old, in her first year of junior college. Her boyfriend had stopped taking her calls after she told him the pregnancy test was positive. She had heard of acquaintances and friends undergoing abortions and had researched abortion pills online. Armed with that knowledge, she went to a pharmacy and bought an abortion-inducing drug sold for Rs. 32 which cannot be legally sold without a doctor's prescription, but it can be easily bought over the counter, as was done by Manju. She dutifully followed the instructions to keep the tablets under her tongue for 30 min. She started bleeding within two hours. Over the next two days, she missed college due to heavy bleeding and nausea, and later experienced morning sickness. She thought that it was an after-effect. She couldn't sleep on her right side as it hurt. Her friend spoke to some girls in her PG accommodation and suggested an abortion clinic where no one will know she had gone. An ultrasound and a pelvic examination later, the doctor confirmed that she had an incomplete abortion because of pills she had taken before, and that infection had set in. He recommended surgical evacuation. "He said the only option to get rid of it was through some vacuum aspiration method which would cost Rs. 10,000". (adapted from http://www.firstpost.com/living/shamed-and-scarred-stories-of-legal-abortions-in-india-1179659.html).

Questions:

- What makes girls vulnerable to pregnancy in adolescence?
- Why do adolescent boys often do not cooperate when their girlfriends become pregnant?
- What do pregnant girls do when they are not aware that abortion is legal in India and they can go to any good hospital or health centre?
- How is unsafe abortion harmful? How can it be prevented?

Time Estimate: 30 min

Prevention of Sexually Transmitted Infections and HIV

Concepts and Theories

Concept: STIs are infections that spread primarily from person to person through a sexual contact. Some STIs can spread from mother to child during pregnancy and childbirth and through blood products and tissue transfer. STIs cause discomfort and pain to people who have them (WHO, 2014b). Some common STIs include syphilis, gonorrhoea, hepatitis, herpes, HIV. While most of the STIs can be treated with relevant medications, HIV is a STI with no cure currently, and hence, preventing the spread of HIV is very significant in controlling the epidemic. HIV is an acronym for human immunodeficiency virus. Once in the body, HIV gradually destroys the white blood cells so that their number/count decreases to such an extent that the immune system becomes too weak to fight infections. The most advanced stage of HIV infection is acquired immunodeficiency syndrome (AIDS), which can take from two to 15 years to develop depending on the individual. AIDS is defined by the development of certain cancers, infections or other severe clinical manifestations (WHO, 2014a).

Signs and Symptoms: Common symptoms of STIs include vaginal discharge, urethral discharge in men, genital ulcers and abdominal pain (WHO, 2014b). Common signs of an HIV infection include unexplained weight loss, unexplained and prolonged fever, cough or diarrhoea, white blotches in the mouth. An individual's HIV status cannot be determined by merely looking at the person, but only by certain specific blood tests that should be performed with the informed consent of the individual along with adequate counselling before and after the test (WHO, 2014a).

Prevalence: Unprotected sexual relations make young girls extremely susceptible to STIs, in particular infections with HIV in regions with a high prevalence of the virus. The fact that older and experienced men seek sexual relations with young girls without using barrier contraceptives leads to the dissemination of these diseases. In countries with a high prevalence of HIV, some men even purposely have sex with young girls in an attempt to avoid becoming infected with HIV. Unprotected sexual intercourse is the risk behaviour common to both unintended pregnancy and HIV infection. Under these circumstances, young girls at the beginning of their reproductive lives are at highest risk of HIV infection and relatively often a pregnancy in a young adolescent could be combined with a recent infection and high viral load (WHO, 2004a).

According to NFHS-4 (IIPS & ICF, 2017), in India, only 22 percent of young women and 32 percent of young men age 15–24 have comprehensive knowledge of HIV, which includes knowing that consistent use of condoms during sexual intercourse and having just one uninfected faithful partner can reduce the chance of getting HIV, knowing that a healthy-looking person can have HIV, and rejecting two common misconceptions about HIV transmission.

Prevention and Protection from STIs and HIV: Risk of HIV infection can be reduced by limiting exposure to risk factors. Key approaches for HIV prevention include:

- Sexual abstinence or delay the sexual debut till one is prepared to deal with any emotional, social or physical consequences of the same.
- Mutually monogamous relationship where both are non-infected.
- Avoid casual or unplanned sexual contacts.
- Engage in safer sexual behaviours (anal, vaginal or oral sex with a condom).

- Avoid intake of alcohol or drugs before engaging in sexual activity as they may reduce/affect an individual's capacity to decision-making with regard to safer sex measures.
- Early detection and treatment of STIs in case of an existing infection.
- Seek appropriate counselling and testing for HIV if one suspects a possible infection.
- Check if blood, blood products, organs and tissues have been screened for HIV, prior to transfusion or transplant, respectively.
- When visiting a doctor or hospital/pathology laboratory, insist on the usage of disposable/sterilised needles and syringes and surgical instruments.
- Never share syringes/needles and other sharp objects like razors and blades (WHO, 2014a).

Activities

Activity 9.5: Video Discussion on STIs and HIV

Learner Outcome: At the end of this activity, the participants will develop basic knowledge about STIs and HIV.

Procedure: Show the following video films on STIs and HIV/AIDS:

- What is an STI? http://www.youtube.com/watch?v=llnXtPZOazM
- TeachAIDS (Hindi) HIV Prevention Tutorial. http://www.youtube.com/watch?v=anft5mGkihU

Questions for Discussion: Use the following questions to discuss this activity:

- What is an STI?
- What is HIV and how does it spread?
- How can one protect oneself from infection by HIV?
- What is AIDS?

Time Estimate: 45 min

Activity 9.6: Exercise on Myths and Facts About HIV Transmission

Learner Outcome: At the end of this activity, the participants will dispel common myths related to how HIV spreads and how it does not.

Procedure: Use the following procedure to conduct this activity:

1. Conduct a quiz with the participants about HIV. Ask them to sit in pairs. Give each pair a copy of the Exercise on Modes of HIV Transmission, given at the end of the chapter.

2. Allow each pair 10 min to discuss their responses (true or false) and the reason for the same. At the end of 10 min, ask each pair to share their response. Clarify doubts or misconceptions if any. Refer to answer key below for the relevant cues.

No.	Answer key for the facilitator
1.	False: Use of sterilised needles is however a must while pricking the blood donor
2.	True: However, if blood unit being transfused has been checked for HIV and other infectious diseases, then it is safe for use. Screening of all blood samples for HIV has been made mandatory through law for all blood banks
3.	True: Injecting drugs per se does not transmit HIV, but sharing of needles with infected persons puts one at risk of infection. It is strictly advised to use sterilised needles and not to share them with other intravenous drug users
4.	True: Greater the number of one's sexual partners, greater the risk of contracting HIV, because one can never be sure of their sexual behaviours or HIV status
5.	False: HIV does not spread in a married couple if both partners are not infected and continue to remain in a monogamous relationship with each other. However, if any one partner engages in a risky sexual behaviour (intercourse with person whose HIV status is unknown or drug use), then the other marital partner may stand at a risk of infection. Many women in India have been infected within marital relationships
6.	True: Women in sex work have a high prevalence of HIV infection because of the very nature of their work. Hence, the chances of infection are higher if one has engaged in unprotected sexual intercourse. If the sex work is uninfected, then her uninfected client is likely to remain uninfected as well
7.	False: Persons infected with HIV continue to remain and look healthy for most of the initial years of their infection. Therefore, appearing fit and healthy does not negate the possibility of a person being infected
8.	False: The risk of HIV infection is not nil with a known person because knowing a person does not necessarily imply knowing about his/her behaviours
9.	False: HIV does not spread by using public toilets
10.	False: HIV does not spread by these ways since they do not harbour any infectious fluids that are necessary for HIV transmission

11.	False: HIV does not spread by touching or shaking hands with an HIV-infected person
12.	False: Once a mosquito bites an HIV-infected person, the virus fails to survive in its intestine
13.	True: This is because razors and blades have sharp edges that may lead to cuts on skin and deposition of blood. However, the chances of infection by the above behaviour are low
14.	True: If the barber fails to use a clean blade or scissors. Always insist on the use of clean blades/scissors to prevent infection. However, chances of infection are low
15.	True: Skin provides a good barrier against the entry of HIV in the bloodstream. But if the skin has any open wounds or cuts, then touching HIV contaminated blood can expose one to the risk of HIV transmission. In any case, blood should never be touched with bare hands
16.	False: This is because HIV is present in very small or non-infectious quantities in urine and saliva
17.	True: However if a condom tears or is used incorrectly, it may not provide the required protection against HIV
18.	False: The different contraceptive methods (except condoms) do not provide protection against HIV and STIs
19.	True: Having a single sexual partner protects one from HIV provided both are in a mutually faithful relationship with each other
20.	False: HIV does not spread if one has more than one wife, provided all the wives and the husband are not infected and do not engage in sexual intercourse outside the marriage

Questions for Discussion: Use the following questions to discuss this activity:

- What new aspect did you learn about HIV and AIDS?
- Why do myths and misconceptions surround HIV and AIDS?
- How do these myths add to the stigma and discrimination against persons living with HIV?
- Does having the right knowledge help?

Time Estimate: 45 min

Activity 9.7: Video Discussion on Children Affected by AIDS

Learner Outcome: At the end of this activity, the participants will become sensitive to stigma and discrimination of children affected by AIDS.

Procedure: Show the video film:

AIDS Ek Ladki Ki Kahani (Hindi)—Meena Unicef
https://www.youtube.com/watch?v=O6wiDiE_TnQ

Questions for Discussion: Use the following questions to discuss this film:

- Why were Rano's friends teasing or name-calling her? How did this impact her?
- Why did Rano's friends assume that she had AIDS?
- Why were Rano and her family facing stigma and discrimination?
- How did Meena help Rano?
- How can we help children living with AIDS or having family members with AIDS?

Time Estimate: 15 min

Use of Contraceptives

Concepts and Theories

Use of Contraceptives

Adolescents engaging in sexually intimate relations should have access to knowledge about contraception, their advantages and disadvantages along with ways to access them in a confidential and non-threatening manner to protect themselves from early or unwanted pregnancies and other STIs. A good contraceptive is user-friendly and safe.

Range of Contraceptive Methods: In general, with the exception of male and female sterilisation, all methods that are appropriate for healthy adults are also potentially appropriate for healthy, post-pubertal adolescents (WHO, 2004b). A wide range of contraceptive methods are discussed in Summary Chart 9.3 (adapted from Panthaki, 1998 and The Population Council, 2011). No one contraceptive method is perfect, and every method has its own characteristics, advantages and disadvantages. Some methods carry risks of side effects. Only two methods, the male and female condom, protect against HIV (The Population Council, 2011).

Gender Differentials: Most contraceptive methods are for use by females except for the male condom and male sterilisation. The choice would depend on several factors like whether one wants protection from pregnancy or STIs or both or which method more suits one's body. In general, girls and women are expected to be responsible to prevent pregnancy. But, a boy and a man should also share this responsibility by:

- Abstaining from sex without contraception,
- Communicating with his female partner before having sex,
- Educating himself about different contraceptive methods,
- Using condoms correctly and consistently,
- Where appropriate, using other male methods such as withdrawal or vasectomy,
- Supporting his female partner in using her contraceptive method (The Population Council, 2011).

Activities

Activity 9.8: Quiz on Contraceptive Methods

Learner Outcome: At the end of this activity, the participants will develop awareness about the different contraceptive methods with reference to strengths and limitations of each.

Procedure: Use the following procedure to conduct this activity:

1. Ask the participants if they have heard of contraceptives.

   - Have you heard about contraceptives or birth control measures? Which ones?
   - Where did you hear or read about them?
   - Why does one need contraceptives?

2. Discuss the Summary Chart 9.3 on contraceptive methods, or show one of the following video films:

   - What are birth control pills? http://www.youtube.com/watch?v=BbUw417Lcw0
   - Women and Sex: Emergency contraceptive pills and side effects. http://www.youtube.com/watch?v=o5rU9g_7PZc

3. Arrange to show different contraceptives like the oral pills, male and female condoms to explain the mechanism of contraception so that participants get a touch and feel of them.
4. Circulate a copy of the Quiz on Contraceptive Methods (Adapted from the Contraceptive Method Crossword Puzzle, Activity 51, Unit 7 in The Population Council, 2011, p. 164), given at the end of the chapter, to all to read the questions and enter the appropriate answers.
5. Discuss the correct answers: facilitator's answer key: 1—Vasectomy; 2—Female Condom; 3—Implant; 4—Coitus Interruptus; 5—Oral Pills; 6—Diaphragm; 7—Tubal Ligation; 8—IUD; 9—Spermicides; 10—Injectables; 11—Male condoms; 12—Cervical mucus

Questions for Discussion: Use the following questions to discuss this activity:

- How important is it to select the right contraceptive method? How can this be ensured?
- Do you think that the onus of contraception tends to rest only with the girls? If yes, why? If no, why?
- Do you think contraceptive methods empower girls/women to protect themselves from pregnancy?
- How important is it to ensure communication about contraception and protection from STIs in any sexual relationship?

Time Estimate: 45 min

Concluding Activity: Achievement of the Learner Objectives

Learner Outcome: By the end of the concluding activity, the participants will ascertain if they have achieved the learner objectives.

Procedure: Use the following procedure to conduct the concluding activity:

1. Show the power points/a chart on the learner objectives, ask the participants to read them one at a time, and ask the group if they think they have achieved the objective.
2. The participants may be asked to share their responses in their diary with reference to the following questions:

   - What was a new learning for you in this session?
   - What did you like the best in this session and why?
   - Which activity was most effective?
   - What was not clear/confusing?
   - How can you apply what you have learnt?

Time Estimate: 15 min

Appendix: Summary Charts and Exercises

Summary Chart 9.1 Understanding sexual rights
(Adapted from WHO 2006, p. 5)

Sexual rights are the right of all persons, free of coercion, discrimination and violence, to:	The highest attainable standard of sexual health, including access to sexual and reproductive health care services
	Seek, receive and impart information related to sexuality
	Sexuality education
	Respect for bodily integrity
	Choose their partner
	Decide to be sexually active or not
	Consensual sexual relations
	Consensual marriage
	Decide whether or not, and when, to have children
	Pursue a satisfying, safe and pleasurable sexual life

Summary Chart 9.2 Understanding responsibilities in sexual relationships (Adapted from The Population Council 2011)

Factors that contribute to having mutually satisfying, responsible, and safe sexual experiences:	Knowing that you and your partner both have the same rights,and cooperating to ensure mutual respect, consent and responsibility
	Treating each other as equals, and as people, not just as bodies
	Feeling comfortable in communicating what each partner wants or does not want
	Respecting a partner's right not to do anything that feels uncomfortable or unsafe
	Being honest with each other
	Feeling intimacy
	Feeling cared for
	Using safe and effective ways to protect yourself and your partner from unwanted pregnancy and sexually transmitted infections (STIs), including HIV
	Working to protect yourself and your partner from emotional harm
	Being aware of your own desires and comfort level and those of your partner
	Being able to give and to accept pleasure

Summary Chart 9.3 Contraceptive methods
(Adapted from Panthaki (1998) and The Population Council (2011))

Natural Methods		Advantages and/ or disadvantages
Abstinence	Abstinence refers to refraining from vaginal, anal or oral intercourse. Both partners need to consent to express their sexual feelings in non-penetrative ways.	No risk of pregnancy and STIs/ HIV. Preferable for adolescents to practice abstinence until they are mature to handle physical and psychosocial aspects of sexual intercourse.
Coitus Interruptus	Coitus Interruptus refers to withdrawal of penis from the vagina before ejaculation.	Not a very reliable method as semen can escape before ejaculation and does not provide protection from HIV. It requires a great deal of control on part of the male partner to withdraw before ejaculation.
Rhythm method	This involves keeping a track of the ovulation cycle to predict the fertile period in a girl or woman. Abstinence/ correct use of barrier methods during the fertile period can prevent conception.	No health hazards. Recommended for girls and women with regular menstrual cycle. However, it does not offer protection from STIs/ HIV.
Spacing Methods		
Barrier methods: Condoms, Diaphragm and Chemical spermicide	A male condom is a thin rubber sheath rolled on to the erect penis prior to penetration. This prevents the sperms from entering the vagina. It should be properly worn and carefully removed. Should not be reused.	Easily available and main method of protecting oneself against STIs. However, small chances of failure remain as it may slip off or tear if not worn correctly or not removed before penis becomes soft.
	A female condom is a lubricated plastic sheath with two rings. One remains outside the vagina, covering part of the labia, and the other is placed in the vagina, covering the cervix. It forms a pouch that collects the semen.	Prevents conception and STIs/ HIV. A Woman can control its usage. However, it is not very cost effective and not as easily available as the male condom. Also, user has to ensure that the penis enters the female condom and not between the vagina and the condom.

Barrier methods: Condoms, Diaphragm and Chemical spermicide	The diaphragm is a soft rubber cap to be put into the vagina shortly before the intercourse to cover the entrance to the womb, thus stopping the entry of the sperms into the womb. It is more effective when used with a spermicide jelly that inactivates the sperms.	No health risk but a girl or woman may need to be trained to insert and remove the diaphragm.
Hormonal methods: Oral pills, Injectables and Implants	Oral pills consist of the two female sex hormones in small quantities to prevent the release of ovum from the ovary each month.	Needs to be taken regularly and may not work if any tablet is missed. Almost 100 percent effective when taken regularly. Consult doctor prior to taking it
	Injectables are of two types – one that has to be taken once in every three months; and the other once in every two months. They are hormonal contraceptives that work by inhibiting ovulation.	Menstrual cycle may become irregular or may take time to regularise once the injectable is discontinued.
	Implants: Norplant implant consists of six matchstick size rods containing a form of progesterone. Is implanted below the skin of one's upper arm by minor surgery. It works by suppressing ovulation, creating thick cervical mucus preventing the entry of sperms into the cervix and creating a thin endometrial lining.	It lasts for nearly five years after which the capsule can be removed and fertility can be restored. Menstrual cycle may become irregular.
	Emergency Contraception (EC) is a single dose pill that helps to prevent pregnancy after unprotected intercourse (contraceptive failure, breakage of condom or after rape) has occurred.	EC can prevent pregnancy if taken within five days after unprotected sex, but works best when taken as early as possible within this time period. EC should be used as a back-up contraceptive method. It is not an abortion. It provides no protection against STIs.

Intrauterine Devices (IUDs)	They are small devices, commonly shaped like a T, that are placed in the uterus by a health care provider. Some IUDs release progestin (a hormone), while others contain copper, which has antifertility effects. They keep the sperm from reaching the egg.	They are effective for two to five years after which they need to be replaced. Menstrual cycle may get irregular in the first six months of usage.
Permanent Sterilisation Methods		
Vasectomy	It is a permanent surgical method in which the vas deferentia are blocked so that sperms cannot be released into the semen at the time of ejaculation.	The surgery has no effect whatsoever on the man's health, strength or masculinity/ virility.
Tubal Ligation	Tubal ligation is a surgical method in which the fallopian tubes are tied up to prevent the sperms from meeting the ovum.	Should be used only when one is sure about not wanting children any further.
Tubectomy	Tubectomy is a surgical method in which the fallopian tubes are cut and the ends are tied.	

Exercise for Activity 9.1: Myths and Facts about Sexual Behaviours and Gender Normst

No	Attitude to Sexual Behaviours and Gender Norms	Agree/ Disagree
1.	Masturbating frequently is harmful.	
2.	Good girls/ women never masturbate.	
3.	Boys should engage in sexual acts prior to marriage so that they can perform on their first night of marriage.	
4.	Good girls do not see erotic magazines or films.	
5.	Girls who have knowledge about sexual behaviours have a loose character.	
6.	It is natural for boys to touch or push girls in crowded places to feel their bodies.	
7.	If girls do not protest to the above touches by boys, they are enjoying it.	
8.	Girls should actively seek information on sexuality to make informed and responsible sexual decisions.	
9.	Good girls never make the first move in a sexual act. They should be passive recipients.	
10.	A girl friend is the boy friend's property so he owns her body to enjoy as he likes.	
11.	Boys should feel sexually attracted only to girls and girls should feel attracted only to boys.	

Exercise for Activity 9.8: Quiz on Contraceptive Methods

1. A surgical procedure that prevents the male's release of sperm:

   _____

2. A thin sheath or pouch that a woman or girl inserts into her vagina to prevent sperm from   entering her own body (two words)

   _____

3. A small rod inserted into the woman or girl's arm.

   _____

4. Pulling the penis out of the vagina before ejaculation.

   _____

5. A woman or girl takes it d aily to prevent pregnancy (common name, two words). _____

6. A rubber cup that is filled with spermicide and inserted into the vagina, covering the cervix:_____

7. An operation in which a woman's fal lopian tubes are cut or tied to prevent the egg and sperm from meeting (two words):_____

8. Inserted into the uterus, and often shaped like a T (abbreviation):_____

9. Various substances inserted into the vagina to kill sperm (plural):

   _____

10. Shots given to a woman or girl periodically to prevent ovulation and thicken cervical mucus (plural): _____

11. A man or boy wears it on his penis during sex; it prevents pregnancy and protects against STIs/HIV (two words)

   _____

12. A woman or girl can tell when she is fertile based on the amount and consistency of   _____ (two words)

Exercise for Activity 9.6: Myths and Facts about HIV Transmission

No.	Beliefs on Modes of HIV Transmission	Agree/ Disagree
1.	HIV can spread by donating blood.	
2.	HIV can spread by receiving blood transfusion.	
3.	HIV is spread by injecting drugs.	
4.	HIV can spread by having multiple sexual partners.	
5.	Married persons do not become infected by HIV.	
6.	HIV spreads by visiting to women in sex work.	
7.	HIV does not spread by having sexual intercourse with a fit and healthy person.	
8.	HIV does not spread by having sexual intercourse with a known person.	
9.	HIV can spread by using public toilets.	
10.	HIV can spread by sharing spoon, plate, glass, soap and clothes with an HIV infected person.	
11.	HIV can spread by shaking hands or touching an HIV infected person.	
12.	HIV can spread by mosquito bites.	
13.	HIV can spread by sharing razors and blades.	
14.	HIV can spread by going to a barber for shaving and hair cutting.	
15.	HIV can spread by touching blood contaminated with HIV.	
16.	HIV can spread by touching urine or saliva of an HIV infected person.	
17.	Using condoms during penetrative sexual intercourse can prevent HIV.	
18.	Contraceptives provide protection against HIV and STIs.	
19.	Having a single sexual partner protects one from acquiring HIV infection.	
20.	HIV can spread if a person has more than one wife.	

References

Abraham, L. (2002). *Bhai-behen*, true love, time pass: Friendships and sexual partnerships among youth in an Indian Metropolis. *Culture, Health and Sexuality, 4*(3), 337–353.

American Psychological Association. (2008). *Answers to your questions: For a better understanding of sexual orientation and homosexuality.* Washington, D.C.: Author. Retrieved from http://www.apa.org/topics/lgbt/orientation.pdf.

India: Ministry of Health & Family Welfare. (2013). *A strategic approach to reproductive, maternal, newborn, child and adolescent health (RMNCH+A) in India for Healthy Mother and Child.* New Delhi: Author. Retrieved from http://www.unicef.org/india/1._RMNCHAStrategy.pdf.

India: Ministry of Law & Justice. (2013). *The criminal law (amendment) ordinance 2013.* Retrieved from http://lawmin.nic.in/ld/ord_criminal_law.pdf.

International Institute for Population Sciences & ICF. (2017). *National Family Health Survey (NFHS-4), 2015–16: India.* Mumbai: IIPS.

International Institute for Population Sciences & Population Council. (2010). *Youth in India: Situation and needs 2006–2007.* Retrieved from http://iipsindia.org/pdf/India%20Report.pdf.

Jejeebhoy, S. J., & Sebastian, M. P. (2003). *Actions that protect: Promoting sexual and reproductive health and choice among the young in India.* New Delhi: Population Council. Retrieved from http://www.popcouncil.org/uploads/pdfs/wp/seasia/seawp18.pdf.

Kail, R. V., & Cavanaugh, J. C. (2007). *Human development a life span view* (4th ed.). Canada: Thomson Learning Inc.

Mehra, M. (2013). *Taking stock of the new anti rape law.* Retrieved from http://kafila.org/2013/05/05/taking-stock-of-the-new-anti-rape-law-madhu-mehra/.

Panthaki, D. (1998). *Education in human sexuality: A sourcebook for educators.* Mumbai: Family Planning Association of India.

Rathod, A. (2014). *Why Mumbai can't crack safe sex.* Times of India. Retrieved from http://timesofindia.indiatimes.com/life-style/health-fitness/health/Why-Mumbai-cant-crack-safe-sex/articleshow/35058168.cms.

Santhya, K. G., & Jejeebhoy, S. J. (2012). *The sexual and reproductive health and rights of young people in India: A review of the situation.* New Delhi: Population Council. Retrieved from http://www.popcouncil.org/uploads/pdfs/2012PGY_IndiaYouthSRHandRights.pdf.

Sigelman, C. K., & Rider, E. A. (2006). *Life span human development* (5th ed.). China: Thomson Learning Inc.

The Population Council. (2011). *It's all one curriculum: Guidelines and activities for a unified approach to sexuality, gender, HIV, and human rights education.* New York: Author. Retrieved from http://www.popcouncil.org/uploads/pdfs/2011PGY_ItsAllOneGuidelines_en.pdf.

United Nations Population Fund. (2013). *The state of the world population 2013 motherhood in childhood facing the challenge of adolescent pregnancy.* New York: Author. Retrieved from http://www.unfpa.org/webdav/site/global/shared/swp2013/EN-SWOP2013-final.pdf.

World Health Organization. (2004a). *Adolescent pregnancy: Issues in adolescent health and development.* Geneva. Retrieved from http://apps.who.int/iris/bitstream/10665/42903/1/9241591455_eng.pdf.

World Health Organization. (2004b). *Contraception issues in adolescent health and development.* Geneva: Author. Retrieved from http://whqlibdoc.who.int/publications/2004/9241591447_eng.pdf.

World Health Organization. (2006). *Defining sexual health. Report of a technical consultation on sexual health 28–31 January 2002, Geneva.* Retrieved from http://www.who.int/reproductivehealth/publications/sexual_health/defining_sexual_health.pdf.

World Health Organization. (2014a). *HIV/AIDS fact sheet N°360.* Retrieved from http://www.who.int/mediacentre/factsheets/fs360/en/.

World Health Organisation. (2014b). *Sexually transmitted infections (STIs) fact sheet N°110.* Retrieved from http://www.who.int/mediacentre/factsheets/fs110/en/. December 10, 2017.

Module 10
Child Rights to Prevention of Child Marriage

Prerequisite Modules

The prerequisite Modules for this Module are:
From *Sourcebook I on Introduction to Rights-Based Direct Practice with Children*:

- Modules on Life Skills Development

From *Sourcebook II on Child Rights Education for Participation and Development: Primary Prevention*:

- Introduction to Child Rights Education
- Child Rights to Participation and Children's Associations

From *Sourcebook III on Child Rights Education for Inclusion and Protection: Primary Prevention*:

- Child Rights to Family Life Education
- Rights of Girls and Children with Disability to Non-Discrimination and Inclusion
- Child Rights to Prevention of Problems with Sexual Relationships.

Conceptual Framework of Child Marriage

Concepts and Theories

Concept of Child Marriage

According to the United Nations Population Fund (UNFPA, 2012, p. 11), "The term "child marriage" is used to describe a legal or customary union between two people, of whom one or both spouses is below the age of 19. While boys can also be subjected to child marriage, the practice affects girls in greater numbers and with

© Child Rights and You 2018
M. Desai and S. Goel, *Child Rights Education for Inclusion and Protection: Primary Prevention*, Rights-based Direct Practice with Children,
https://doi.org/10.1007/978-981-13-0417-0_10

graver consequences. Child marriage is often referred to as "early" and/or "forced" marriage since children, given their age, are not able to give free, prior and informed consent to their marriage partners or to the timing of their marriage. Many girls, for example, may have little understanding of or exposure to other life options. They may "willingly" accept marriage as their allotted fate. An element of coercion may also be involved if families apply social or emotional pressure or urge marriage for economic reasons, or further advocate marriage in the (misguided) belief that such a union will keep their daughters safe". This definition emphasises child marriage as mainly an issue of girls, forced marriage, without consent, for economic reasons and the misguided rationale of protection of girls.

According to ECPAT and PLAN International (2015), child, early and forced marriage (CEFM) may be a route to systematic, albeit unrecognised, sexual abuse and exploitation of girls. No longer children, not yet adults, child brides tend to be denied fulfilment of their fundamental rights and access to social services otherwise granted to unmarried children and married women. The marginal social roles assigned to married girls discontinue the privileges of childhood, while precluding access to powers granted to adult members of their communities.

Historical Background of Child Marriage

Kapadia (1966) noted that from the time of Dharmasutra (600–300 B.C.), there was a trend in favour of marriage of girls as soon as they reached puberty, though it was not entirely common. He quoted from Boudhayana Dharmasutra, "Let him give his daughter, while she goes still naked, to a man who has not broken the vow of chastity and who possesses good qualities, or even to one destitute of good qualities, let him keep (the maiden) in (his house) after she has reached the age of puberty". Since virginity was regarded as a badge of respectability for a woman, it came to be encouraged as an index of high caste. Consequently, marriage would be desired before any scope for suspicion regarding the virginity of a girl presented itself. The extolling of virginity was a conducive factor in the contemporary Brahmin trend towards pre-puberty marriage, and insistence on it as a requisite qualification of an elite marriage accelerated pre-puberty marriages among the Hindus. And once it became a pattern with the Brahmins, it soon tended to become the norm for the Hindu society as a whole (Kapadia, 1966).

Prevalence of Child Marriage

According to NFHS-4 (IIPS & ICF, 2017), early marriage has been declining over time. The present trends are:

- Twenty-eight percent of women age 18–29 and 17 percent of men age 21–29 marry before reaching the legal minimum age at marriage.

- Urban women marry later than rural women. For women age 25–49, the median age at first marriage is 1.7 years more among urban women than rural women (19.8 years versus 18.1 years).
- Women having 12 or more years of schooling marry much later than other women. The median age at first marriage for women age 25–49 increases from 17.2 years for women with no schooling to 22.7 years for women with 12 or more years of schooling.
- Women in the highest wealth quintile marry much later (20.8 years) than women in other wealth quintiles (17.4–19.0 years).

Thus, child marriage disproportionately and devastatingly impacts girls' rights, to education, health, development and personal relationships. Focusing on "children" seems to diminish the importance of gender inequality in shaping patterns of child marriage (Girls not Brides, n.d.).

Causes of Child Marriages

Causes of child marriage comprise protection of virginity of girls, patriarchal subordination of girls, poverty and financial benefit, family and cultural norms, lower sex ratio due to female foeticide and end of education.

Protection of Virginity of Girls: Protection of virginity of girls is the original cause for child marriages. High value is often placed on the virginity of the girl—it is believed, in many such families, that if a girl is not a virgin when she marries, it brings shame and dishonour upon the family. Unmarried women are often seen as liabilities for family integrity and honour. Sometimes young girls are encouraged to marry older men, due to the perception that an older husband will be able to act as a guardian against behaviour deemed immoral and inappropriate (The Red Elephant Foundation, 2013). Child marriage may be seen by these families as a way of protecting young girls from premarital sex, pregnancy outside of marriage, rape and even prostitution. This justification for child marriage only makes sense where women and girls have no greater value than as repositories for family honour or where girls' potential sexuality is seen as a risk that must be monitored and contained (Equality Now, 2014).

Perception of Girls as Commodities: Child marriage reflects the dominance of patriarchal norms surrounding marriage, which view girls as objects to be "protected" and exchanged as commodities, rather than as bearers of rights. These norms lead to the treatment of daughters as economic burdens whose primary value is their virginity and reproductive capacity. In rural and poor areas, girls are particularly vulnerable to child marriage due to the predominance of these patriarchal views and widespread poverty (The Center for Reproductive Rights, 2013). Early marriage is one way to ensure that a wife is "protected", or placed firmly under male control; that she is submissive to her husband and works hard for her in-laws' household; that the children she bears are "legitimate"; and that bonds of affection between couples do not undermine the family unit (United Nations Children's Fund (UNICEF) Innocenti Research Centre, 2001).

Poverty and Financial Benefit: Poverty is one of the major factors underpinning early marriage. Where poverty is acute, a young girl may be regarded as an economic burden and her marriage to a much older—sometimes even elderly—man, is a family survival strategy, and may even be seen as in her interests (UNICEF Innocenti Research Centre, 2001). Findings of a youth study noted that rural, poorly educated and economically disadvantaged young women and those from scheduled castes and tribes were considerably more likely than other women to have experienced early marriage (Santhya & Jeejebhoy, 2012).

ECPAT International (2006) noted that child marriages are often arranged and negotiated for financial benefit in cash or in kind by a third party and, inasmuch as these arrangements provide access to children as sexual partners, they can be categorised as a form of commercial sexual exploitation of children (CSEC). In many cases, the families are unaware of the financial transactions involved but feel pressured to agree to such marriages due to the high cost of dowries (i.e. the price the girl's parents have to pay the groom's family at the time of marriage, which is much less for younger girls).

Family and Cultural Norms: A rural family is generally characterised by agrarian economy, where collectivism, kinship orientation and patriarchy are functional. Customs surrounding marriage, including the desirable age and the way in which a spouse is selected, depend on a society's view of the family—its role, structure, pattern of life and the individual and collective responsibilities of its members. Child marriage is common in this context where marriages typically take place according to customary rites and remain unregistered (UNICEF Innocenti Research Centre, 2001). Child marriage is perceived to facilitate easy adjustment to the culture and norms of the in-laws' family.

Lower Sex Ratio due to Female Foeticide: ECPAT International reports that, in some Indian states, such as Haryana and Punjab, sharp imbalance in the sex ratio caused by female foeticide has been resulting in trafficking of young girls from the impoverished States like Orissa, Jharkhand, Bihar, Assam and West Bengal for the purpose of marriage (ECPAT & PLAN International, 2015).

End of Education: Gender inequality in education is both a cause and a symptom of child marriage. Girls who drop out of primary school or failed to make the transition to secondary school are more vulnerable to the social, cultural and economic forces that perpetuate child marriage. There is clear evidence that the more education young girls receive the later they marry, especially if they reach secondary school. Compared with women who have either no education or only a primary school education, the median age for marriage among those with a secondary education is higher. Parents may decide to discontinue their daughter's education on the grounds that the costs are unjustified in the light of an impending marriage (Brown, 2012). A large majority (77%) of young women with no education were married before they were 18, compared to just 7% of those with 12 or more years of schooling (Santhya & Jejeebhoy, 2012).

Violation of Girl Child's Rights in Child Marriage

UDHR: Arranging a child marriage first of all violates Article 16(2) of the Universal Declaration of Human Rights (1948) which states that "Marriage shall be entered into only with the free and full consent of the intending spouses". (http://www.un.org/en/documents/udhr/).

UNCRC: In performing a child marriage, the following child rights of the UNCRC (1989) are violated:

- Child's right to education
- Child's right to protection from vulnerability and commercial exploitation.
- Child rights to express views, being heard and being given due weight; to seek, receive and impart information; and to freedom of thought, conscience and religion.

The UNCRC Article 24(3): States Parties shall take all effective and appropriate measures with a view to abolishing traditional practices prejudicial to the health of children. Child marriage is the main such practice in India that needs to be strictly abolished.

Activities

Introductory Activity 10.1: Video Discussion on Child Marriage

Learner Outcome: At the end of this activity, the participants will get introduced to the issue of child marriage.

Procedure: Use the following procedure to conduct this activity:

1. Ask the participants what they mean by child marriage.
2. Discuss the definition and historical background of child marriage.
3. Show one of the following video films:

   Chhoti Si Dulhan (Hindi)—Meena Unicef
   https://www.youtube.com/watch?v=uKsbmLKYmsU

Use the following questions to conduct discussion on the video film:

• Why did the *bania* want his son to marry a young girl?
• What does the girl Rita want to do?
• When should a girl get married?
• What rights of the girl child are violated in child marriage?

My Daughter and I (Nation Against Early Marriage):
https://www.youtube.com/watch?v=wARDb2JYfvw
Use the following questions to conduct discussion on the video film:

• What was the reason for child marriage of this woman?
• What was her experience after marriage?
• What role did her father play in supporting her and other girls?
• What did the former child bride decide to do about her daughter's marriage?

Time Estimate: 30 min

Activity 10.2: Small Group Discussion on Causes and Prevalence of Child Marriage

Learner Outcome: At the end of this activity, the participants will understand the causes of child marriage.

Procedure: Use the following procedure to conduct this activity:

1. Show Summary Chart 10.1 to introduce the causes of child marriage.
2. Form six small groups and allocate a cause to each of them to read the notes and discuss with examples that they may know of:

   (1) Protection of virginity of girls,
   (2) Patriarchal subordination of girls,
   (3) Poverty and financial benefit,
   (4) Family and cultural norms,
   (5) Lower sex ratio due to female foeticide and
   (6) End of education.

3. Ask the small groups to make a presentation of their discussion to the large group for further inputs.
4. Introduce the following units of the module:

   • Effects of Child Marriage and Violation of Child Rights,
   • Policy and Legislation for Prevention of Child Marriages,
   • Strategies for Prevention of Child Marriages.

Time Estimate: 30 min

Effects of Child Marriage and Violation of Child Rights

Concepts and Theories

Effects of Child Marriage

Child marriages lead to end of childhood, end of education, forced and unprotected sexual relationships, early pregnancy, maternal mortality and recycling of malnutrition leading to perinatal, neonatal and infant mortality, gender equality and poverty. It also makes children vulnerable to violence and exploitation, abandonment, early widowhood and slavery.

End of Childhood: The imposition of a marriage partner upon a child means that a girl or boy's childhood is cut short and their fundamental rights are compromised. The assumption is that once a girl is married, she has become a woman even if she is only 12. Equally, where a boy is made to marry, he is now a man and must put away childish things. For both girls and boys, early marriage has profound physical, intellectual, psychological and emotional impacts, cutting off educational opportunity and chances of personal growth (UNICEF Innocenti Research Centre, 2001). Child marriage requires girls to perform heavy amounts of domestic work, demonstrate fertility, and raise children while still children themselves. Married girls and child mothers face constrained decision-making and reduced life choices (UNICEF, 2005). By marrying a girl off early, the risk of uncertainty to her prospects or damage to a family's honour is significantly removed, although not the physical, psychological and other risks to the girl herself (Equality Now, 2014).

End of Education: End of education makes children vulnerable to early marriage and early marriage inevitably denies children of school age their right to the education they need for their personal development, their preparation for adulthood and their effective contribution to the future well-being of their family and society. Indeed, married girls who would like to continue schooling may be both practically excluded from doing so (UNICEF Innocenti Research Centre, 2001).

Forced and Unprotected Sexual Relationships: In the case of girls married before puberty, the normal understanding between families is that there will be no sexual intercourse until first menstruation (UNICEF Innocenti Research Centre, 2001). However, once married, girls are likely to feel, and in many cases are, powerless to refuse sex. They are likely to find it difficult to insist on condom use by their husbands, who commonly are older and more sexually experienced, making the girls especially vulnerable to HIV and other sexually transmitted infections (United Nations Population Fund, 2012). Very few girls in early marriages in developing countries have access to contraception; nor would delayed pregnancy necessarily be acceptable to many husbands and in-laws. Indeed, in many societies, childbearing soon after marriage is integral to a woman's social status (UNICEF Innocenti Research Centre, 2001).

Early Pregnancy: The ill-effects of early pregnancy are already discussed in the earlier module.

Maternal Mortality: Most studies from developing countries have reported that levels of maternal mortality are higher in young adolescents. The main causes of adolescent maternal death are malaria, pregnancy-induced hypertension, puerperal sepsis and septic abortion. However, if education, social status and use of health facilities are taken into account there remains some doubt as to whether or not young maternal age as such is a predictor of likelihood of maternal death. The most important medical problems of adolescent mothers in the postpartum period are anaemia, inadequate nutrition and (in the first days) pre-eclampsia. But some psychosocial problems are even more important (e.g. interruption of education, poverty, disruption of family relations) (World Health Organization (WHO), 2004).

Perinatal, Neonatal and Infant Mortality: Evidence from developed and developing countries is available showing that adolescent pregnant girls are at increased risk for preterm delivery (less than 37 weeks) compared to older pregnant women. Possible etiological and/or associated factors are immaturity of organs (especially in girls with low gynaecological age, i.e. a short interval between menarche and pregnancy), and social factors such as metropolitan residency and low educational attainment. The incidence of low birth weight (less than 2500 g) is higher in adolescents compared to older mothers, chiefly because of the increased incidence of preterm births. Although in some studies the incidence of small for gestational age (SGA) infants was also higher, several epidemiological investigations have showed that young maternal age is not an independent risk factor for SGA infants. In several studies, perinatal or neonatal mortality is higher among infants of adolescent mothers, with the infants of the youngest mothers at greatest risk (WHO, 2004).

Recycling of Gender Inequality: Child marriage reinforces gender inequalities, jeopardises education, is harmful to health and turns millions of girls into second-class citizens, locking them and their children into cycles of poverty (Brown, 2012). Child marriage reinforces a woman's dependence on men for the rest of her life (The Red Elephant Foundation, 2013).

Recycling of Poverty: Child marriage and early pregnancy play a pivotal role in transmitting poverty and disadvantage across generations. The link between education on the one side, and the status of women and the well-being of their children on the other, is well known. Child marriage breaks that link. Since children of young, uneducated mothers are also more likely to be malnourished and less likely to attain higher levels of education, the cycle of poverty perpetuates. Similarly, the poverty that fuels child marriage in turn perpetuates poverty by transmitting diminished life chances to children (Brown, 2012).

Violence and Exploitation: A cross-country statistical analysis carried out by UNICEF (2005) showed that women who married as girls are more likely to experience domestic violence and believe that in some cases a man is justified in beating his wife. After marriage, these girls are often exploited, used as domestic servants and as free or cheap agricultural labour, abused and kept in isolation or even resold to other "buyers" to suffer further sexual abuse and exploitation. Domestic violence was highest, at 67%, among girls who were married before the age of 19. Many such girls flee from their husbands or are subsequently divorced or widowed, becoming extremely vulnerable to commercial sexual exploitation (ECPAT International, 2006).

Abandonment: When girls are given in marriage to men—often older men—in exchange for money, these marriages may be for a few weeks or for several months, after which the girls are abandoned by their husbands and deprived of the rights acquired by marriage. In addition to the psychological trauma suffered, the victims are stigmatised by society and marginalised by their own families (UNICEF Innocenti Research Centre, 2009). Desertion by husbands may have a more devastating effect on girls and women who married young than the premature union itself. Once the link with her parental home has been severed by marriage, as well as the one with her husband's household by separation, the girl no longer belongs to anyone or anywhere. Abandoned married girls normally find it hard to engage gainfully in a profession after having been segregated at home and barred from the opportunity to develop marketable skills. Ostracism is also likely to affect them more than their husbands, reducing further the possibility of building a new life for themselves (ECPAT & PLAN International, 2015).

Widowhood: The child bride who is widowed very young can suffer additional discrimination. Widows suffer loss of status and they, along with their children, are often denied property rights, and a range of other human rights (UNICEF Innocenti Research Centre, 2001).

Slavery: Child marriage is likely to lead to a lifetime of domestic and sexual subservience over which girls have no control (UNICEF Innocenti Research Centre, 2001). According to Turner (2013), determining whether cases of child marriage constitute slavery requires an examination of the extent to which the child, or the adult they become, is effectively "enslaved" through the physical, psychological and/or economic powers of "ownership" and control exercised over them. This can be assessed by looking at how children enter marriage, how they are treated during marriage, and whether they are realistically able to leave or dissolve the marriage should they so wish as discussed below.

Absence of Free, Full and Informed Consent to Marriage: Consent is central both to the right to marry and slavery. Children are in a weaker position to give free, full and informed consent than an adult may be. The unequal power dynamic between adults and children can ensure that this is the case even if a child says that they agree to a marriage, or at least do not express refusal. Children are also less able to be fully informed about the true nature or impact of a marriage or union. The meaningful consent of any child is arguably doubtful, but the younger the child the less able they are to exercise free, full and informed consent.

Treatment in Marriage: Control and Ownership: Upon entering a new house-hold, many children appear to have little or no bargaining power with their spouse and/or in-laws regarding their own movements, belongings or even person. Choices from earning an independent income to consent to sexual relations may not be available to these children. The question of control can be compounded for girls, who are often expected to leave the family home to live with their husband and his wider family once married.

Inability to leave or end a Marriage: Under international law, spouses should have equal rights to the dissolution of marriage. Those subject to slavery or slavery-like practices in child marriage, whether still children or the adults that such children become, are unable to choose to leave their marriage, however difficult their situation may be.

Activities

Activity 10.3: Posters on Effects and Violation of Child Rights in Child Marriage

Learner Outcome: At the end of this activity, the participants will develop awareness on the effects and violation of child rights in child marriage.

Procedure: Use the following procedure to conduct this activity:

1. Show the video film:

   LIKE SISTERS: Award-winning short film on Child Marriage by Childline
   https://www.youtube.com/watch?v=6Zb0tU2e63E.
   Use the following questions to conduct discussion on the video film:

   - Why was Maya married at the age of 13 years?
   - What was Maya's situation after her marriage?
   - What were the reasons for her death?

2. Alternately, discuss the case study of another Maya (The Center for Reproductive Rights, 2013) who is now 50, was married at 10 to Hari Narayan, who is five years older than her. "Today, I wish my parents hadn't married me off so early". "I was turned into someone's wife before I knew what it meant to me", says Maya. When she knew that she would have to leave her home and parents once and for all after marriage, she could not stop crying. "I felt I was discarded and my parents no longer loved me", says she, adding, "All my joy was gone at once". "My mother-in-law expected me to be like a perfect daughter-in-law. She wanted me to do all the work in the kitchen, which I wasn't capable of. When I couldn't perform my duty as a daughter-in-law, she scolded me. I was fearful of her shadow". Maya says her husband, too, was not mature enough to stand by her when she needed his support and sympathy. "Whenever my mother-in-law berated me, I would seek his emotional support", says she. "But he would always

fail me". She says she often felt lonely—already discarded by her parents and yet not fully accepted by her husband as well as the parents-in-law.

By the age of just 15, she had already had her first baby. A few months later, probably as a result of having to deliver the baby at a very early age, she suffered from uterine prolapse, which subjected her to a combination of pain, humiliation and frustration for more than three decades. Two years after her first child was born, Maya gave birth to yet another baby who could not survive a measles outbreak. "I was unable to look after two children at the same time", says she. "In retrospect, I think I could've saved my second child, too, if I was mature by then". I was too shy to consult my husband about using contraceptives", says she. "I used Norplant only after giving birth to five children".

3. Show Summary Chart 10.2 to summarise the effects of child marriages:

   (1) End of childhood,
   (2) End of education,
   (3) Forced and unprotected sexual relationships,
   (4) Early pregnancy and maternal mortality,
   (5) Recycling of malnutrition leading to infant mortality,
   (6) Recycling of gender inequality,
   (7) Recycling of poverty,
   (8) Violence and exploitation,
   (9) Abandonment,
   (10) Early widowhood,

4. Form ten small groups and allocate an effect to each of them to read the notes, discuss and make posters for creating public awareness on effects of child marriage.

Time Estimate: 45 min

Policy and Legislation for Prevention of Child Marriage

Concepts and Theories

Policy for Prevention of Child Marriage

Eradicating early marriage requires community, national, regional and international commitments. UNICEF, UNFPA and UN Women have issued a joint statement calling for urgent action to end the harmful practice of early marriage by:

- Enacting and enforcing legislation to increase the minimum age of marriage for girls to 18 and raise public awareness about child marriage as a violation of children's human rights.
- Mobilising girls, boys, parents and leaders to change discriminatory gender norms and create alternative social, economic and civil opportunities for girls.

- Addressing the root causes of child marriage, including gender discrimination and low value of girls, violence against girls and women, poverty and religious or cultural justifications.
- Improving access to good quality primary and secondary education, ensuring that gender gaps in schooling are eliminated (World Vision, 2013).

Ending child marriage requires action by multiple actors at many levels:

- Empowering girls with information about their rights and the skills to exercise them will be crucial.
- Encouraging families and communities to question child marriage and to envision other options for their daughters.
- Services such as schools, health centres and others must be tailored to the needs of adolescent girls (Girls not Brides, n.d.).

The National Policy for the Empowerment of Women (2001) has a section on Rights of the Girl Child that states that "All forms of discrimination against the girl child and violation of her rights shall be eliminated by undertaking strong measures both preventive and punitive within and outside the family. These would relate specifically to strict enforcement of laws against prenatal sex selection and the practices of female foeticide, female infanticide, child marriage, child abuse and child prostitution etc".

The overall goal of the National Strategy for Prevention of Child Marriage (India: Ministry of Women and Child Development, 2013) is to accelerate the decline in the incidence of child marriage in the next decade. More broadly, the strategy has the following objectives:

1. To promote a sustainable and long-term shift in mindset and social norms that perpetrate child marriage.
2. To promote an enabling environment and strengthen protection mechanisms, including the enforcement of the CMPA (The Prohibition of Child Marriage Act, discussed below.

The National Strategy Document for Prevention of Child Marriage (2013) suggests the following strategic directions:

- Law enforcement
- Access to quality education and other opportunities,
- Changing mindsets and social norms,
- Empowerment of adolescents.

The Prohibition of Child Marriage Act

According to the Prohibition of Child Marriage Act, enacted in 2006 ((India: Ministry of Law and Justice, 2007), every child marriage, whether solemnised before or after the commencement of this Act, shall be voidable at the option of the contracting party who was a child at the time of the marriage. The core provisions of the Act are as follows:

Section 2(a): … "child" means a person who, if a male, has not completed twenty-one years of age, and if a female, has not completed eighteen years of age.

Section 3: Child marriages to be voidable at the option of contracting party being a child:

(1) Every child marriage, whether solemnised before or after the commencement of this Act, shall be voidable at the option of the contracting party who was a child at the time of the marriage: Provided that a petition for annulling a child marriage by a decree of nullity may be filed in the district court only by a contracting party to the marriage who was a child at the time of the marriage.

(2) If at the time of filing a petition, the petitioner is a minor, the petition may be filed through his or her guardian or next friend along with the Child Marriage Prohibition Officer.

(3) The petition under this section may be filed at any time but before the child filing the petition completes two years of attaining majority.

Section 9: Punishment for male adult marrying a child: Whoever, being a male adult above eighteen years of age, contracts a child marriage shall be punishable with rigorous imprisonment which may extend to two years or with fine which may extend to one lakh rupees or with both.

Section 10: Punishment for solemnising a child marriage: Whoever performs, conducts, directs or abets any child marriage shall be punishable with rigorous imprisonment which may extend to two years and shall be liable to fine which may extend to one lakh rupees unless he proves that he had reasons to believe that the marriage was not a child marriage.

Section 11(1): Punishment for promoting or permitting solemnisation of child marriages: Where a child contracts a child marriage, any person having charge of the child, whether as parent or guardian or any other person or in any other capacity, lawful or unlawful, including any member of an organisation or association of persons who does any act to promote the marriage or permits it to be solemnised, or negligently fails to prevent it from being solemnised, including attending or participating in a child marriage, shall be punishable with rigorous imprisonment which may extend to two years and shall also be liable to fine which may extend up to one lakh rupees: Provided that no woman shall be punishable with imprisonment.

Section 12: Marriage of a minor child to be void in certain circumstances: Where a child, being a minor:

(a) is taken or enticed out of the keeping of the lawful guardian; or

(b) by force compelled, or by any deceitful means induced to go from any place; or

(c) is sold for the purpose of marriage; and made to go through a form of marriage or if the minor is married after which the minor is sold or trafficked or used for immoral purposes, such marriage shall be null and void.

Section 13(1): Power of court to issue injunction prohibiting child marriages: If a Judicial Magistrate of the first class or a Metropolitan Magistrate is satisfied that a child marriage in contravention of this Act has been arranged or is about to be solemnised, such Magistrate shall issue an injunction against any person including a member of an organisation or an association of persons prohibiting such marriage.

Section 16: Child Marriage Prohibition Officers:

(1) The State Government shall, by notification in the Official Gazette, appoint for the whole State, or such part thereof as may be specified in that notification, an officer or officers to be known as the Child Marriage Prohibition Officer having jurisdiction over the area or areas specified in the notification.
(2) The State Government may also request a respectable member of the locality with a record of social service or an officer of the Gram Panchayat or Municipality or an officer of the Government or any public sector undertaking or an office bearer of any nongovernmental organisation to assist the Child Marriage Prohibition Officer and such member, officer or office bearer, as the case may be, shall be bound to act accordingly.
(3) It shall be the duty of the Child Marriage Prohibition Officer:

(a) to prevent solemnisation of child marriages by taking such action as he may deem fit,
(b) to collect evidence for the effective prosecution of persons contravening the provisions of this Act,
(c) to advise either individual cases or counsel the residents of the locality generally not to indulge in promoting, helping, aiding or allowing the solemnisation of child marriages,
(d) to create awareness of the evil which results from child marriages,
(e) to sensitise the community on the issue of child marriages and so on.

CEDAW

According to Article 16(2) of the Convention on the Elimination of all forms of Discrimination against Women (CEDAW) (United Nations, 1979), "The betrothal and the marriage of a child shall have no legal effect, and all necessary action, including legislation, shall be taken to specify a minimum age for marriage and to make the registration of marriages in an official registry compulsory".

(http://www.un.org/womenwatch/daw/cedaw/text/econvention.htm#article16).

The Compulsory Registration of Marriages Bill

Child marriages are rampant in many parts of India in spite of this legislation. One reason is that this law does not consider child marriages illegal, only voidable. Moreover, registration of marriages in India is a weak system. The National Commission for Women has prepared a Draft on The Compulsory Registration of Marriages Bill, 2005, mainly to prevent child marriages and to ensure minimum age of marriage, among other reasons (The National Commission for Women, 2005).

Legislation that sets 18 as the minimum age for marriage is not enough; loopholes—related to customary laws must be removed, and related laws must be in place which protect women and girls' rights, including property rights, access to remedies, support for those wishing to leave a marriage, protection from violence, access to health services. (Girls not Brides, n.d.).

Activities

Activity 10.4: Small Group Discussion on Review of Child Marriage Legislation in India

Learner Outcome: At the end of this activity, the participants will develop awareness on the child marriage law in India.

Procedure: Use the following procedure to conduct this activity:

1. Form four small groups and allocate the following sections of the law to them to read and review with examples that they know of:

   (a) Sections 2(a) and 3,
   (b) Sections 9, 10 and 11,
   (c) Sections 12 and 13,
   (d) Section 16,

2. Ask the small groups to make a presentation of their reviews to the large group.

Questions for Discussion: Use the following questions to discuss this activity:

- What are the advantages of the law?
- What are the limitations of the law?
- What are your recommendations for a more effective law to prohibit child marriage in India?

Time Estimate: 30 min

Strategies for Prevention of Child Marriage

Concepts and Theories

Strategies for prevention of child marriages comprise empowerment of girls and boys, mobilisation of families and communities, promoting girls' education, financial support to girls and their families, etc.

Empowerment of Girls and Boys

Among the successful programmes are those that empower girls at risk of child marriage through, life skills training, provision of safe spaces for girls to discuss their futures, the provision of information about their options, and the development of support networks. Such interventions can equip girls with knowledge and skills in areas relevant to their lives, including sexual and reproductive health, nutrition and their rights under the law. Girls are empowered when and if they are able to learn skills that help them to develop a livelihood, help them to better communicate, to negotiate and make decisions that directly affect their lives. Safe spaces and the support they offer help girls overcome their social isolation, interact with peers and mentors and assess alternatives to marriage. As the girls develop their abilities and self-confidence, parents and community members come to regard them differently, which can help to reshape long-held views and customary assumptions (United Nations Population Fund, 2012). Thus workshops on life skill development and child rights education for girls and boys are essential for prevention of child marriages.

Mobilisation of Families and Communities

Traditionally the family and elders of the community make the decision whether, when and whom a girl will marry. Working with parents and other community stakeholders is therefore vital in changing the attitudes and social norms that perpetuate harmful practices such as child marriage. A primary goal is to create an environment in which delayed marriage becomes more socially acceptable than child marriage. At the same time, girls must be able to pursue an education or other alternatives to marriage without the fear of criticism or ridicule. Interventions that spark attitudinal change have included community dialogue, information and education sessions; efforts involving men and husbands; along with mass media messages that spread the word about the dangers of child marriage, the alternatives, and the rights of girls. A review of the evidence suggests that community mobilisation is most effective in shifting norms when it is used in conjunction with the other interventions (United Nations Population Fund, 2012). Thus workshops on life skill development and child rights education for parents and public awareness development are also essential for prevention of child marriages.

Promoting Girls' Education

The more education a girl receives, the less likely she is to marry as a child. Improving access to education for both girls and boys and eliminating gender gaps in education are important strategies in ending the practice of child marriage. This can be achieved through:

- Legislative, programmatic and advocacy efforts to make education free and compulsory, as well as to expand Education for All programming beyond the primary level.
- It is also important to capitalise on the window of opportunity created by the increasing gap in time between the onset of puberty and the time of marriage by providing substantive skills enhancing programmes and opportunities.
- There is a need to develop methods to protect girls at risk of child marriage and to address the concerns of girls and women who are already married by ensuring the fulfilment of their right to a full education and providing them with training to ensure that they can earn a livelihood (UNICEF, 2005).

Secondary education specifically emerges as the strongest factor associated with lower rates of child marriage. For preventing the marriage of young girls at the "tipping point" age—the age at which child marriage prevalence in a country starts to increase markedly (usually 13 or 14), keeping girls in primary school is the most important factor. The best programme approach would be to promote all levels of education to ensure girls reach 18 before they marry (United States Agency for International Development, 2007).

Education policies need to include:

- Cutting direct and indirect school fees to keep girls in primary education.
- Building classrooms close to communities in rural areas with high early marriage rates, thereby reducing the distance that girls have to travel to school.
- Providing support for girls in primary education, including grants for uniforms and textbooks.
- Targeting incentives such as stipends and bursaries for girls' education at critical points, including the transition from primary to secondary school.
- Offsetting the financial pressures on families to marry daughters at an early age through social protection and cash transfers that are conditional on girls being kept in school.
- Designing programmes that promote all levels of education to ensure that girls reach the age of 18 before they marry (Brown, 2012).

The Right to Education Act of 2009 provides for most of these supports except that the Act covers children only till 14 years of age. It needs to be extended up to 18 years of age.

Financial Support for Girls and Their Families

Given that child marriage is linked to poverty, incentive-based programmes have been used to encourage and enable families to postpone the marriage of their daughters and to keep them in school through post-primary and secondary level. Incentives may include loans, scholarships, subsidies and conditional cash transfers. Employment opportunities for girls, such as those supported by microfinance schemes or opened up through vocational training, can generate viable alternatives to child marriage, especially for girls unable to continue their formal schooling. Improving girls' economic standing can also give them a higher status in their families and on this basis, greater control over their lives. For families themselves, direct cash transfers and income-generating activities for their daughters can help to alleviate the economic and social pressures in favour of early marriage (United Nations Population Fund, 2012).

India has a scheme "Incentives to Girls for Secondary Education" to establish an enabling environment to reduce the number of school dropouts and to promote the enrolment of girl child belonging to SC/ST communities in secondary schools and ensure their retention up to the 18 years of age. The scheme further intends to retain such girl child up to class XII. The Scheme covers (i) all SC/ST girls who pass class VIII and (ii) girls, who pass class VIII examination from Kasturba Gandhi Balika Vidhyalayas (irrespective of whether they belong to Scheduled Castes or Tribes) and enrol for class IX in State/UT Government, Government-aided or local body schools. A sum of Rs. 3,000 is deposited in her name, and she would be entitled to withdraw it on reaching 18 years of age. To be eligible for the benefit under the scheme the girl should be unmarried and should be below 16 years of age (as on 31 March) on joining class IX.

Activities

Activity 10.5: Video Discussion on Community Mobilisation for Preventing Child Marriages

Learner Outcome: At the end of this activity, the participants will develop awareness on the strategy of community mobilisation for prevention of child marriages.

Procedure: Show a Video Film on Come Together Preventing Child Marriage in India:

https://www.youtube.com/watch?v=8DIqdNsdLTk.

Questions for Discussion: Use the following questions to discuss this activity:

• Who all were involved in preventing the child marriage?
• Could each of them have done it by themselves?
• What are the advantages of community mobilisation for prevention of child marriage?

Time Estimate: 15 min

Activity 10.6: Street Plays on Strategies for Prevention of Child Marriages

Learner Outcome: At the end of this activity, the participants will develop awareness on the strategies for prevention of child marriages.

Procedure: Use the following procedure to conduct this activity:

1. Show Summary Chart 10.3 to introduce the strategies for prevention of child marriages.
2. Form four small groups and allocate a strategy to each of them to read and discuss with examples.
3. Ask the small groups to prepare street plays to promote their respective strategy and present to the large group for further inputs.

Time Estimate: 45 min

Concluding Activity: Achievement of the Learner Objectives

Learner Outcome: By the end of the concluding activity, the participants will ascertain if they have achieved the learner objectives.

Procedure: Use the following procedure to conduct the concluding activity:

1. Show the power points/a chart on the learner objectives, ask the participants to read them one at a time and ask the group if they think they have achieved the objective.
2. The participants may be asked to share their responses in their diary with reference to the following questions:

   - What was a new learning for you in this session?
   - What did you like the best in this session and why?
   - Which activity was most effective?
   - What was not clear/confusing?
   - How can you apply what you have learnt?

Time Estimate: 15 min

Appendix: Summary Charts

Summary Chart 10.1   Causes of child marriage

Summary Chart 10.2 Effects of child marriages

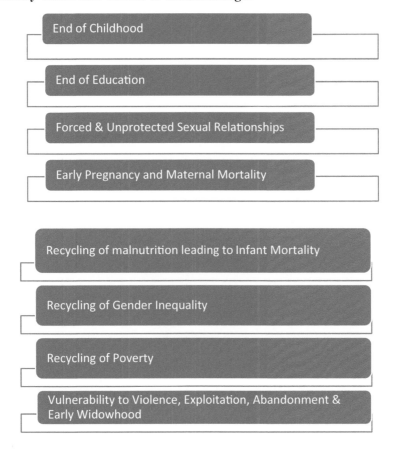

Summary Chart 10.3 Strategies for prevention of child marriages

References

Brown, G. (2012). *Out of wedlock, into school: Combating child marriage through education.* Retrieved from http://educationenvoy.org/wp-content/uploads/2013/09/Child-Marriage.pdf.

ECPAT International (2006). *Global monitoring report on the status of action against commercial sexual exploitation of children: India.* http://www.ecpat.net/sites/default/files/India%201st.pdf.

ECPAT & PLAN International (2015). Unrecognised sexual abuse and exploitation of children in child, early and forced marriage. Bangkok. Retrieved from http://www.ecpat.org/wp-content/uploads/legacy/Child%20Marriage_ENG.pdf.

Equality Now (2014). *Protecting the girl child.* Retrieved from http://www.equalitynow.org/sites/default/files/Protecting_the_Girl_Child.pdf.

Girls not Brides (n.d.). *A theory of change for child marriage.* Retrieved from https://consultations.worldbank.org/Data/hub/files/a_theory_of_change_on_child_marriage_-_girls_not_brides.pdf.

India: Ministry of Law and Justice (2007). The Prohibition of Child Marriage Act, 2006. Retrieved from http://www.hsph.harvard.edu/population/trafficking/india.childmar.07.pdf.

India: Ministry of Women and Child Development (2013). National strategy document on prevention of child marriage. Retrieved from http://wcd.nic.in/childwelfare/Strategychild marrige.pdf.

International Institute for Population Sciences & ICF. (2017). *National Family Health Survey (NFHS-4),* 2015–16: India. Mumbai: IIPS.

Kapadia, K. M. (1966). *Marriage and family in India.* Bombay: Oxford University Press.

Santhya, K. G. & Jejeebhoy, S. J. (2012). The sexual and reproductive health and rights of young people in India: A review of the situation. New Delhi: Population Council. Retrieved from http://www.popcouncil.org/uploads/pdfs/2012PGY_IndiaYouthSRHandRights.pdf.

The Center for Reproductive Rights (2013). *Child marriage in South Asia: Briefing paper.* New York. Retrieved from http://www.reproductiverights.org/sites/crr.civicactions.net/files/documents/ChildMarriage_BriefingPaper_Web.pdf.

The National Commission for Women (2005). Draft on the compulsory registration of marriages bill, 2005. Retrieved from http://ncw.nic.in/pdffiles/compmarriagebill.pdf.

The Red Elephant Foundation (2013). *Child marriages in India: An insight into law and policy.* Retrieved from http://www.ohchr.org/Documents/Issues/Women/WRGS/ForcedMarriage/NGO/TheRedElephantFoundation.pdf.

The United States Agency for International Development (2007). *New insights on preventing child marriage: A global analysis of factors and programmes.* Retrieved from https://www.icrw.org/files/publications/New-Insights-on-Preventing-Child-Marriage.pdf.

Turner, C. (2013). *Out of the shadows: Child marriage and slavery.* Anti-Slavery International. Retrieved from http://www.antislavery.org/includes/documents/cm_docs/2013/c/child_marriage_final.pdf.

United Nations (1979). Convention on the elimination of all forms of discrimination against women. Retrieved from http://www.ohchr.org/en/ProfessionalInterest/pages/cedaw.aspx.

United Nations (1989). Convention on the rights of the child. Retrieved from http://www.ohchr.org/english/law/pdf/crc.pdf.

United Nations Children's Fund (2005). *Early marriage: A harmful traditional practice: A statistical exploration.*

United Nations Children's Fund Innocenti Research Centre (2001). *Early marriage: Child spouses.* Retrieved from http://www.unicef-irc.org/publications/pdf/digest7e.pdf.

United Nations Children's Fund Innocenti Research Centre. (2009). *Handbook on the optional protocol on the sale of children, child prostitution and child pornography.* Retrieved from http://www.unicef-irc.org/publications/pdf/optional_protocol_eng.pdf.

United Nations Population Fund (2012). *Marrying too young: End child marriage.* New York. Retrieved from http://www.unfpa.org/sites/default/files/pub-pdf/MarryingTooYoung.pdf.

World Health Organization (2004). *Adolescent pregnancy: Issues in adolescent health and development.* Geneva. Retrieved from http://apps.who.int/iris/bitstream/10665/42903/1/9241591455_eng.pdf.

World Vision (2013). *Untying the knot: Exploring early marriage in fragile states: Research report.* Retrieved from http://www.worldvision.org/resources.nsf/main/press-reports/$file/Untying-the-Knot_report.pdf.

Relevant Child Rights and You Reports and Articles

Child Rights and You. (2017). *Economic Impact of Child Marriage.* Retrieve from https://www.cry.org/blog/the-economic-impact-of-child-marriage.

Child Rights and You. (2017). *Impact of Girl Child Marriage.* Retrieve from https://www.cry.org/blog/impact-of-girl-child-marriage.

Module 11
Child Rights to Prevention of Conflict With Law

Prerequisite Modules

The prerequisite Modules for this Module are:
From *Sourcebook I on Introduction to Rights-Based Direct Practice with Children*:

- Modules on Life Skills Development

From *Sourcebook II on Child Rights Education for Participation and Development: Primary Prevention*:

- Introduction to Child Rights Education
- Child Rights to Participation and Children's Associations

Conceptual Framework of Conflict with Law in Childhood

Concepts and Theories

Concepts

Juvenile Delinquents: "Juvenile" is a term used to describe a child under the age of majority. This term "juvenile" has, over time, come to have criminal connotations as it is linked to the term "delinquency". Delinquency means criminal or antisocial behaviour or acts committed by children (UNICEF, 2011a). Thus "juvenile delinquent" has become a term that labels a child. In labelling theory, it is important to differentiate between primary deviance and secondary deviance. Primary deviance is the initial criminal act and secondary deviance is accepting the criminal label and consequently committing other crimes like a self-fulfilling prophecy (Hess & Drowns, 2004). The United Nations Convention on the Rights of the Child (UNCRC) does not use the term "juvenile delinquency"; however, it does not mention a right to protection from labelling language. According to the United

Nations (UN) Guidelines for the Prevention of Juvenile Delinquency (The Riyadh Guidelines) (1990), "… labelling a young person as 'deviant', 'delinquent' or 'pre-delinquent' often contributes to the development of a consistent pattern of undesirable behaviour by young persons". It is therefore important to restrict the labelling to specific behaviours rather than the person (Hess & Drowns, 2004).

According to Goldson (2002), research and practice showed that most juvenile offending was petty, opportunistic and transitory and that the majority of children grow out of it. However, he observed that entry of these children into the juvenile justice system results in application of criminal labels that stigmatise them, trigger negative social reaction to them and compound the likelihood of further delinquency. Thus the goal should be to prevent children from entering the juvenile justice system as far as possible.

Children in Conflict with Law: The UN Office on Drugs and Crime (UNODC, 2013) uses the term "Child in conflict with the law" and defines it as a child alleged as, accused of, or recognised as having infringed the criminal law. "Children in conflict with law" describes the situation in which the child is rather than labelling the child as a "juvenile delinquent". According to the Juvenile Justice (Care and Protection of Children) Act, 2015 (henceforth called the JJ Act), "child in conflict with law" means a child who is alleged or found to have committed an offence and who has not completed eighteen years of age on the date of commission of such offence. However, the title of the Act uses the term "juvenile", which tends to perpetuate the label "juvenile delinquent". The Act needs to use the word 'child' rather than 'juvenile'.

Type of Conflict with Law in Childhood: Conflict with law in childhood includes status offences, petty/property offences and violent offences (Desai, 2010, p. 382):

- **Status Offences**: Status offenders are children who commit an act that violates a law or ordinance designed to regulate his or her behaviour because of his or her age or status. Status offences are solely based on the offender's age and are unique to juveniles (children). Anyone above the legal age who engages in the same behaviours would not be committing an offence (Hess & Drowns, 2004). A common example of status offences is truancy.
- **Petty/Property Offences**: Save the Children (2005) states that the overwhelming majority of children in conflict with the law (over 90%) are petty offenders, who mainly commit offences against property and four out of five children who commit an offence only commit once in their lifetime. The JJ Act (2015) defines petty offences as offences for which the maximum punishment under the Indian Penal Code or any other law for the time being in force is imprisonment up to three years. According to the Indian Government report on *Children in India 2012: A Statistical Appraisal* (India: Ministry of Statistics and Programme Implementation, 2012), in 2011, the major crimes by children were committed under "theft" (21.17%), hurt (16.3%) and burglary (10.38%).
- **Violent Offences**: Murder, sexual offences, school bullying and juvenile gangs are manifestations of violent offences.

Causes of Conflict with Law in Childhood

Children's lives, choices and opportunities are affected to a great extent by the social, economic and political realities in which they live. These include communities increasingly fragmented through urbanisation, chronic poverty, social and interpersonal violence, and increased pressure from commercialisation and materialism. Yet, somehow we expect children to remain outside of all this and be better (Save the Children, 2005). Besides labelling children as "juvenile delinquents", the causes of conflict with law in childhood comprise of the following:

- Scientific Construction of "Normal" Childhood and Adolescence
- Testing of Boundaries in Adolescence
- Poverty, Neglect and Abuse
- Learning Disabilities
- Mental Health Disorders

Scientific Construction of "Normal" Childhood and Adolescence: The Western sciences of developmental psychology and child development have developed norms of "normal" childhood development, based on the Western, white, middle class, male constructs of normality. These are based on adultist notions of childhood as a basically biologically driven "natural" phenomenon in which children are distinguished from adults by specific physical and mental (as opposed to social) characteristics. Children are seen as separated from the world of work and devoting their time to learning and play and thus economically worthless, apolitical and asexual (White, 2003). Since childhood is constructed as a time of innocence, of purity and lack of responsibility, when children do not live up to these expectations, our societies respond with particular vindictiveness, as if in shock that the image we created, the childhood we want to believe in, does not exist (Save the Children, 2005). These mythical norms of childhood are being transferred to the world's children, a majority of whom are growing up in poverty groups of the developing nations. The transfer of these "normal" norms to them makes their life seem deviant, inferior or pathological (White, 2003).

Testing of Boundaries in Adolescence: James and James (2012) note that it is no accident that "delinquency" is most commonly a term associated with youth as adolescence may involve testing the established conventions of adulthood. UNICEF (2011b) notes that risk-taking in adolescence is fuelled by a psychological need to explore boundaries as part of the development of individual identity. It leads many adolescents to experiment with alcohol and drugs without sufficient understanding of the potential damage to health or of other long-term consequences of dependency. Adolescents experiment with sexual behaviour, sometimes making informed decisions about protection from pregnancy and sexually transmittable infections (STIs) and at other times without such planning or consent (Sigelman & Rider, 2006, p. 344). Usually, the earlier the transition into sexual activity and intercourse, the more likely the act is to be part of a profile of high-risk behaviours like alcohol or drug use or delinquent activity (Newman & Newman, 2006, p. 343).

Poverty, Neglect and Abuse: Large numbers of children in conflict with law are socio-economic victims, denied their rights to education, health, shelter, care and protection. Many of them have had little or no access to education; many are working children. Some children leave their homes and take to the streets to escape from violence and abuse at the hands of their families. Some are forced to make a living on the streets, in order to survive. Others are abandoned by their families and left to fend for themselves and sometimes for younger siblings. These children, who are abandoned and destitute, are at high risk of sexual exploitation, trafficking and becoming involved in substance abuse and the drug trade through peer influence or the influence of adult criminals (Save the Children, 2004). These children coming into conflict with the law are children who are criminalised for simply trying to survive (Downs, Moore, & McFadden, 2009).

According to the Indian Government report (India: Ministry of Statistics and Programme Implementation, 2012), of the total of 33,887 children who were apprehended during 2011, a large chunk (57%) belonged to the poor families whose annual income was up to Rs. 25,000/. The share of children from families with income between 25,000/- and 50,000/- was 27%. This confirms that poverty is a major driving factor for children to come into conflict with the law.

Save the Children (2005) notes that most of the children who come into conflict with the law are children who are facing challenges in their care and protection and in their relationships with their families, communities and society. Children, who originally come to the attention of the child welfare system because of neglect or abuse, later appear in the system for committing offences. This reappearance suggests that the earlier interventions of the child welfare system were not successful (Downs et al., 2009).

Learning Disabilities and Mental Health Disorders: Learning disabilities such as dyslexia and attention deficit disorder do not cause delinquency, but in the absence of understanding by the society, these disabilities place children/youth at greater risk of conflict with law. School failure, poorly developed social skills, and inadequate school and community supports are associated with the over-representation of youth with disabilities at all stages of the juvenile justice system (The National Center on Education, Disability and Juvenile Justice, n.d.). According to the National Mental Health Association (2004), youth who are involved in the juvenile justice system have substantially higher rates of mental health disorders (60%) than children in the general population (22%).

Prevention of Conflict with Law in Childhood

The section on causes for children in conflict with law shows that conflict with law has its roots in labelling, scientific construction of "normal" childhood, social construction of adolescence and tendency to test boundaries in this stage, neglect and abuse, poverty, and learning disabilities and other mental health problems. If so, the prevention of conflict with law in childhood should comprise the following:

- Replacing the Labelling Language of "Juvenile Delinquency" with "Children in Conflict with Law",
- Deconstruction and Contextualisation of "Normal" Childhood and Adolescence,
- Decriminalisation of Status Offences,
- Alleviation of Poverty,
- Prevention of Neglect and Abuse,
- Use of Alternative Educational Strategies for the Learning Disabled,
- Life Skills Development,
- Gender and Sex Education.

Save the Children (2005) emphasises that children should be prevented from coming into conflict with law in the first place by properly addressing the care and protection challenges they face. Prevention strategies should be prioritised by developing support services for children within their families, communities and societies, with the participation of children themselves. Rose and Fatout (2003) note that social programmes designed to keep children from turning to crime include positive after-school, weekend and holiday activities; positive role models and mentors; school-based community services; and so on. The expression of aggression can be constructively utilised within athletic and other physical activities.

Activities

Introductory Activity 11.1: Case Discussion on Causes and Prevention of Conflict with Law in Childhood

Learner Outcome: At the end of this activity, the participants will develop awareness on causes of conflict with law in childhood and strategies needed to prevent it.

Procedure: Use the following procedure to conduct this activity:

1. Ask the participants the following questions:

   - What they understand by the term "juvenile delinquents"?
   - If this term is replaced by "children in conflict with law" what would it mean?
   - What is the difference between the two terms? Which one do you prefer and why?
   - What are the causes of children being in such situations?

2. Form six small groups and allocate the following cases of conflict with law in childhood among them:

Case 1: Ten-year-old Manu lives and works on the street by doing odd jobs. The police always picks on him and his friends whenever there is a robbery in that area.

Case 2: Seventeen-year-old Meera is an only child of upper middle-class parents who are busy with their careers. Instead of going to college, she solicits as a call girl, to experience the excitement.

Case 3: Three-year-old Ibrahim and his 12-year-old sister Rehana live in a slum with their widowed mother who is bedridden as she is suffering from TB. Rehana earns a living by pickpocketing and making Ibrahim beg.

Case 4: Eight-year-old Prakash was regularly beaten up by his alcoholic father. One day, he ran away to join a friend who lived on the street. Both earn their living by pedalling drugs.

Case 5: Fifteen-year-old Dev is a dyslexic and has not been able to pass his eighth standard for last two years. He bunks school and has got sexually involved with a 16-year-old girl who is a school dropout. He is charged for rape.

Case 6: Seventeen-year-old Munna came to Delhi from a small town looking for a job. He was staying with his cousin and doing odd jobs. With a lot of spare time, he would watch a lot of pornographic movies with his friends. Once they found a lone girl while travelling in a bus and gang-raped her.

3. Ask the small groups to discuss (1) the causes of conflict with law in childhood, (2) responsibilities to prevent the cause by children, parents and the State.
4. Ask the small groups to make a presentation to the large group for further discussion.
5. Show Summary Chart 11.1 to summarise the Concept, Causes and Prevention of Conflict with Law in Childhood.
6. Introduce the following units of the module:

  • Rights of Children Accused of Conflict with Law
  • Juvenile Justice Act in India for Children Accused of Conflict with Law

Time Estimate: 45 min

Rights of Children Accused of Conflict with Law

Concepts and Theories

According to UNICEF (2011a), a child "accused of infringing the penal law" is a term used to refer to children who have been charged with a criminal offence but have not yet been tried before a court.

United Nations Convention on the Rights of the Child

Article 40 of the UNCRC states the following:

1. States Parties recognise the right of every child alleged as, accused of, or recognised as having infringed the penal law to be treated in a manner consistent

with the promotion of the child's sense of dignity and worth, which reinforces the child's respect for the human rights and fundamental freedoms of others and which takes into account the child's age and the desirability of promoting the child's reintegration and the child's assuming a constructive role in society.

2. To this end, and having regard to the relevant provisions of international instruments, States Parties shall, in particular, ensure that:

(a) No child shall be alleged as, be accused of, or recognised as having infringed the penal law by reason of acts or omissions that were not prohibited by national or international law at the time they were committed;

(b) Every child alleged as or accused of having infringed the penal law has at least the following guarantees;

(i) To be presumed innocent until proven guilty according to law;

(ii) To be informed promptly and directly of the charges against him or her, and, if appropriate, through his or her parents or legal guardians, and to have legal or other appropriate assistance in the preparation and presentation of his or her defence;

(iii) To have the matter determined without delay by a competent, independent and impartial authority or judicial body in a fair hearing according to law;

(iv) Not to be compelled to give testimony or to confess guilt; to examine or have examined adverse witnesses; and to obtain the participation and examination of witnesses on his or her behalf under conditions of equality.

(v) If considered to have infringed the penal law, to have this decision and any measures imposed in consequence thereof reviewed by a higher competent, independent and impartial authority or judicial body according to law;

(vi) To have the free assistance of an interpreter if the child cannot understand or speak the language used;

(vii) To have his or her privacy fully respected at all stages of the proceedings.

Detention Pending Trial

According to the United Nations Standard Minimum Rules for the Administration of Juvenile Justice (1985):

- Detention pending trial shall be used only as a last resort and for the shortest possible period of time.
- When possible, detention pending trial shall be replaced by alternative measures, such as close supervision or placement with a family.
- Juveniles under detention pending trial shall be kept separate from adults.

Rights During Trial

The UNODC (2013) recommends the following rights of the child during the trial:

*   Right to legal assistance,
*   Right to fair and speedy trial,
*   Right to information prior to trial,
*   Restrictions on the use of handcuffs and other restraints,
*   Right to presence of parents or legal guardian during trial,
*   Right to legal aid and consular assistance during trial,
*   Right to participation during trial,
*   Right to hear evidence during trial.

Activities

Activity 11.2: Video Discussion on Violation of Rights of Children Accused of Conflict with Law

Learner Outcome: At the end of this activity, the participants will get an exposure to violation of rights of children accused of conflict with law.

Procedure: Use the following procedure to conduct this activity:

1. Show the video film: Save the Children. Raju (right of children in conflict with law)
   http://www.youtube.com/watch?v=KuXIIUnhaac&list=PL38322753F73B5A71
2. Use the following questions to discuss this activity:

   *   Why was Raju accused of theft?
   *   How did the police behave with him?
   *   What child rights were violated?

3. Show Summary Chart 11.2 and discuss the Rights of Children Accused of Conflict with Law. Then ask the following questions about the video on Raju:

   *   Was Raju presumed innocent until proven guilty?
   *   Was he informed promptly and directly of the charges against him?
   *   Were his parents or legal guardians informed?
   *   Was he provided legal or other appropriate assistance in the preparation and presentation of his or her defence?
   *   Was he compelled to give testimony or to confess guilt?
   *   Was his privacy fully respected?

Time Estimate: 30 min

Juvenile Justice Act in India for Children Accused of Conflict with Law

Concepts and Theories

The JJ Act (2015) aims to consolidate and amend the earlier law relating to children alleged and found to be in conflict with law and children in need of care and protection by catering to their basic needs through proper care, protection, development, treatment, social reintegration, by adopting a child-friendly approach in the adjudication and disposal of matters in the best interest of children and for their rehabilitation through processes provided, and institutions and bodies established.

Role of the Police

Police Violence: Save the Children (2005) noted that children's experiences of coming into conflict with the law tend to begin with their first encounters with police or local security officers, and these are often brutal. From immediate violence upon arrest, attempted extortion in exchange for promises of release, torture to extract a confession, regular beatings and further violence, including sexual abuse, are common when in police custody. The continuum of violence that many children experience at the hands of law enforcement agencies means that the agencies are "all powerful" as far as these children are concerned. Usually isolated from the protection of families, who in some cases even view the use of violence by the police as part of "teaching a lesson" to the child, often with no other adults to intervene on their behalf, these children are particularly vulnerable to violent and corrupt police officers. In addition to violence, rampant corruption within some police forces, often compounded by low levels of salaries, leave children at the mercy of unscrupulous officers who use the round-ups, curfews and other restrictions on children's use of public spaces as an easy means of supplementing their meagre incomes.

Recommendations: According to the Council of Europe (2010):

- Police should respect the personal rights and dignity of all children and have regard to their vulnerability, i.e. take account of their age and maturity and any special needs of those who may be under a physical or mental disability or have communication difficulties.
- Whenever a child is apprehended by the police, the child should be informed in a manner and in language that is appropriate to his or her age and level of understanding of the reason for which he or she has been taken into custody. Children should be provided with access to a lawyer and be given the opportunity to contact their parents or a person whom they trust.
- Save in exceptional circumstances, the parent(s) should be informed of the child's presence in the police station, given details of the reason why the child has been taken into custody and be asked to come to the station.

- A child who has been taken into custody should not be questioned in respect of criminal behaviour, or asked to make or sign a statement concerning such involvement, except in the presence of a lawyer or one of the child's parents or, if no parent is available, another person whom the child trusts.
- Police should ensure that, as far as possible, no child in their custody is detained together with adults.
- Authorities should ensure that children in police custody are kept in conditions that are safe and appropriate to their needs.
- Prosecutors should ensure that child-friendly approaches are used throughout the investigation process.

Child Welfare Police Officer and Special Juvenile Police Unit: The UNODC (2013) recommends that specialised police units shall be established in each police station, where only designated and specially trained child police officers shall work. Where there are no specialised police units for children, specialised police officers shall be nominated to deal exclusively with child offenders. The UNODC also recommends that specialised child prosecution offices shall be established by law in each court district. Where there is no specialised child prosecution office, a specialised child prosecutor shall be nominated to deal exclusively with child offenders.

According to Section 107 of the JJ Act (2015):

(1) In every police station, at least one officer, not below the rank of assistant sub-inspector, with aptitude, appropriate training and orientation may be designated as the Child Welfare Police Officer to exclusively deal with children either as victims or perpetrators, in coordination with the police, voluntary and non-governmental organisations.
(2) To coordinate all functions of police related to children, the State Government shall constitute Special Juvenile Police Units in each district and city, headed by a police officer not below the rank of a Deputy Superintendent of Police or above and consisting of all police officers designated under sub-section (1) and two social workers having experience of working in the field of child welfare, of whom one shall be a woman.
(3) All police officers of the Special Juvenile Police Units shall be provided special training, especially at induction as Child Welfare Police Officer, to enable them to perform their functions more effectively.
(4) Special Juvenile Police Unit also includes Railway Police dealing with children.

Role of the Juvenile Justice Board

The State Government is required to constitute for every district one or more Juvenile Justice Boards for exercising the powers and discharging its functions relating to children in conflict with law under the JJ Act (2015). The Board shall consist of a Metropolitan Magistrate or a Judicial Magistrate of First Class not being Chief Metropolitan Magistrate or Chief Judicial Magistrate with at least three years of experience and two social workers, of whom at least one shall be a woman.

According to Section 14(5) of the JJ Act (2015), "The Board shall take the following steps to ensure fair and speedy inquiry, namely:

(a) At the time of initiating the inquiry, the Board shall satisfy itself that the child in conflict with law has not been subjected to any ill-treatment by the police or by any other person, including a lawyer or probation officer and take corrective steps in case of such ill-treatment;

(b) In all cases under the Act, the proceedings shall be conducted in simple manner as possible and care shall be taken to ensure that the child, against whom the proceedings have been instituted, is given child-friendly atmosphere during the proceedings;

(c) Every child brought before the Board shall be given the opportunity of being heard and participate in the inquiry;

Activities

Activity 11.3: Visit to a Police Station

Learner Outcome: At the end of this activity, the participants will get an exposure to working of a police station with reference to protecting children.

Procedure: Plan a visit to the nearby police station to understand the structure and procedure of the police station when protection is requested for a child being commercially exploited.
Children can plan to ask the following questions:

• When can the police help children?
• How does the police help children?
• When can children get into conflict with the police?
• Have they heard of the rights of the child?
• What is the role of the police with the children accused of conflict with law?
• Does this police station have a Special Juvenile Police Unit or a Child Welfare Police Officer required by the JJ Act?
• Do they inform the parents?
• Where do they detain the child? At the police station?
• How can children's conflict with law be prevented?

Time Estimate: 2 h

Activity 11.4: Role of the Juvenile Justice Board with Reference
to Children Accused of Conflict with Law

Learner Outcome: At the end of this activity, the participants will learn about the role of the JJB with reference to children accused of conflict with law.

Procedure: Invite a member of the local Juvenile Justice Board to talk about its functioning. Participants can use the following questions to understand their role with reference to children accused of conflict with law:

- When are children arrested under this law?
- How is the JJB constituted?
- What is the role of the JJB?
- How does it deal with children accused of conflict with law?
- Does it use the restorative justice approach?
- What are the advantages of this system?
- What are the limitations of this system?

Time Estimate: 60 min

Concluding Activity: Achievement of the Learner Objectives

Learner Outcome: By the end of the concluding activity, the participants will ascertain if they have achieved the learner objectives.

Procedure: Use the following procedure to conduct the concluding activity:

1. Show the power points/a chart on the learner objectives, ask the participants to read them one at a time and ask the group if they think they have achieved the objective.
2. The participants may be asked to share their responses in their diary with reference to the following questions:

   - What was a new learning for you in this session?
   - What did you like the best in this session and why?
   - Which activity was most effective?
   - What was not clear/confusing?
   - How can you apply what you have learnt?

Time Estimate: 15 min

Appendix: Summary Charts

Summary Chart 11.1 Concept, causes and prevention of conflict with law in childhood

Causes						
Labelling Children as 'Juvenile Delinquents'	Scientific Construction of 'Normal' Childhood and Adolescence	Poverty	Neglect and Abuse	Learning Disabilities	Testing of Boundaries	Mental Health Disorders

↓

Children in Conflict with Law

Children below 18 years of age who are
alleged or found to have committed any of the following types of offences

↑

Prevention Strategies						
Replacing the Labelling Language of 'Juvenile Delinquency' with 'Children in Conflict with Law'	Deconstruction and Contextualisation of 'Normal' Childhood and Adolescence & Decriminalisation of Status Offences	Alleviation of Poverty	Prevention of Children's Neglect and Abuse by Life Skills Development & Child Rights Education for Primary Duty Bearers	Use of Inclusive Approach & Alternative Educational Strategies for the Learning Disabled	Life Skills Development	Mental Health Treatment

Summary Chart 11.2 Rights of children accused of conflict with law

- To be presumed innocent until proven guilty according to law.
- To be informed promptly and directly of the charges against him or her, and, if appropriate, through his or her parents or legal guardians, and to have legal or other appropriate assistance in the preparation and presentation of his or her defence.
- To have the matter determined without delay by a competent, independent and impartial authority or judicial body in a fair hearing according to law.
- Not to be compelled to give testimony or to confess guilt; to examine or have examined adverse witnesses and to obtain the participation and examination of witnesses on his or her behalf under conditions of equality.
- If considered to have infringed the penal law, to have this decision and any measures imposed in consequence thereof reviewed by a higher competent, independent and impartial authority or judicial body according to law.
- To have the free assistance of an interpreter if the child cannot understand or speak the language used.
- To have his or her privacy fully respected at all stages of the proceedings.

Child Rights regarding Detention Pending Trial

- Detention pending trial shall be used only as a last resort and for the shortest possible period of time.
- When possible, detention pending trial shall be replaced by alternative measures, such as close supervision or placement with a family.
- Juveniles under detention pending trial shall be kept separate from adults.

Child Rights during Trial

- Right to legal assistance
- Right to fair and speedy trial
- Right to information prior to trial
- Restrictions on the use of handcuffs and other restraints
- Right to presence of parents or legal guardian during trial
- Right to legal aid and consular assistance during trial
- Right to participation during trial
- Right to hear evidence during trial

Acknowledgements This chapter is partly adapted from the following chapter by the author: Desai, M. (2010). Chapters 19: Conflict with Law in Childhood and Tertiary Prevention. In *A Rights-Based Preventative Approach for Psychosocial Well-Being in Childhood*. Heidelberg: Springer, Series on Children's Well-Being: Indicators and Research.

References

Council of Europe. (2010). *Guidelines of the Committee of Ministers of the Council of Europe on child friendly justice*. Retrieved from https://wcd.coe.int/ViewDoc.jsp?Ref=CM/Del/Dec (2010)1098/10.2abc&Language=lanEnglish&Ver=app6&Site=CM&BackColorInternet= DBDCF2&BackColorIntranet=FDC864&BackColorLogged=FDC864.

Desai, M. (2010). *A rights-based preventative approach for psychosocial well-being in childhood*. Series on Children's Well-Being: Indicators and Research. Heidelberg: Springer.

Downs, S. W., Moore, E., & McFadden, E. J. (2009). *Child welfare and family services: Policies and practice* (8th ed.). Boston: Pearson A and B.

Goldson, B. (2002). Children, crime and the state. In B. Goldson, M. Lavalette, & J. McKechnie (Eds.), *Children, welfare and the state* (pp. 120–135). London: Sage Publications.

Hess, K. M., & Drowns, R. W. (2004). *Juvenile justice*. Australia: Thomson Wadsworth.

India: Ministry of Law and Justice. (2015). *Juvenile Justice (Care and Protection of Children) Amendment Act, 2015*. New Delhi. Retrieved from http://wcd.nic.in/sites/default/files/JJ% 20Act,%202015%20_0.pdf.

India: Ministry of Statistics and Programme Implementation. (2012). *Children in India 2012: A statistical appraisal*. Retrieved from http://mospi.nic.in/mospi_new/upload/Children_in_India_ 2012.pdf.

James, A., & James, A. (2012). *Key concepts in childhood studies* (2nd ed.). London: Sage Publications.

National Mental Health Association. (2004). *Mental health treatment for youth in the Juvenile justice system: A compendium of promising practices*. Retrieved from www.nmha.org/children/ JJCompendiumofBestPractices.pdf.

Newman, B. M., & Newman, P. R. (2006). *Development through life: A psychosocial approach* (10th ed.). Belmont: Brooks/Cole.

Rose, S. R., & Fatout, M. F. (2003). *Social work practice with children and adolescents*. Boston: Allyn and Bacon.

Save the Children. (2004). *Juvenile justice: Modern concepts of working with children in conflict with the law*. Retrieved from http://www.crin.org/docs/save_jj_modern_concepts.pdf.

Save the Children. (2005). *The right not to lose hope: Children in conflict with the law*. London: Author. Retrieved from http://www.crin.org/docs/The_Right_not_to_LR.pdf.

Sigelman, C. K., & Rider, E. A. (2006). *Life-span human development* (5th ed.). Australia: Thomson.

The National Center on Education, Disability and Juvenile Justice. (n.d.). *Resources on prevention of delinquency*. Retrieved from http://www.edjj.org/focus/prevention/. Accessed 27 November 2007.

United Nations. (1985). *Standard minimum rules for the administration of Juvenile justice*. Retrieved from https://www.ncjrs.gov/pdffiles1/Digitization/145271NCJRS.pdf.

United Nations. (1989). *Convention on the rights of the child*. Retrieved from http://www.ohchr. org/english/law/pdf/crc.pdf.

United Nations. (1990). *Guidelines for the prevention of Juvenile delinquency (The Riyadh Guidelines)*. Retrieved from http://www.crin.org/docs/resources/publications/hrbap/IHCRC/ UnitedNationsGuidelinesforthePreventionofJuvenileDelinquency.pdf.

United Nations Children's Fund. (2011a). *Guidance for legislative reform on Juvenile justice*. New York: Author. Retrieved from http://www.unicef.org/policyanalysis/files/Juvenile_justice_ 16052011_final.pdf.

United Nations Children's Fund. (2011b). *The state of the world's children 2011: Adolescence: An age of opportunity*. New York: Author. Retrieved from http://www.unicef.org/sowc2011/pdfs/ SOWC-2011-Main-Report_EN_02092011.pdf.

United Nations Office on Drugs and Crime. (2013). *Justice in matters involving children in conflict with the law: Model law on Juvenile justice and related commentary*. Vienna. Retrieved from http://www.unodc.org/documents/justice-and-prison-reform/Justice_Matters_Involving-Web_ version.pdf.

White, B. (2003). *A world fit for children? Dies Natalis address delivered on the occasion of the 51st anniversary of the Institute of Social Studies*, The Hague, The Netherlands. Retrieved from http://lcms.eur.nl/iss/diesnatalis2003_WhiteOCR.pdf.

Relevant Child Rights and You Reports and Articles

Child Rights and You. (2013). *Age Does Matter*. Retrieve from https://www.cry.org/blog/age-does-matter_24.

Child Rights and You. (2014). *CRY's Response to the Draft Juvenile Justice Bill 2014 circulated by the Ministry of Women and Child Development*. Retrieve from https://www.slideshare.net/ HAQCRCIndia/crys-response-to-the-draft-juvenile-justice-bill-2014-circulated-by-ministry-of-women-child-development.

Ganotra, K. (2014). *Will amendments to the Juvenile Justice Act actually serve their purpose?* Retrieve from http://www.thealternative.in/society/will-amendments-to-the-juvenile-justice-act-actually-serve-their-purpose/.

Kashyap, A. & Menon, P. (2007). *Demystifying the Best Interests Principle in India, CRY National Child Rights Research Fellowship*. Retrieve from https://www.cry.org/resources/pdf/NCRRF/ Aruna_&_Pratibha_2007_Report.pdf.

English–Hindi Glossary

अंग्रेजी-हिंदी शब्दावली

English	Hindi
• Abortion	गर्भपात
• Abuse	दुर्व्यवहार
• Acceptance	स्वीकार
• Accused	मुल्जिम
• Activity	गतिविधि
• Activity time	गतिविधि का समय
• Adaptability	अनुकूलनशीलता
• Adolescence	किशोरावस्था
• Art work/posters	कलाकृति
• Asset building	संपत्ति निर्माण
• Awareness	जागरूकता
• Best interest of the child	बच्चों के सर्वोत्तम हित
• Bullying	बदमाशी
• Care and protection of children	बच्चों की देखरेख और सुरक्षा
• Child abuse	बच्चों से दुर्व्यवहार
• Child labour	बाल मजदूर/श्रमिक
• Child marriage	बाल विवाह
• Child prostitution	बाल वेश्यावृत्ति
• Child protection	बाल संरक्षण
• Child sex tourism	बच्चों के यौन शोषण के लिए पर्यटन

© Child Rights and You 2018
M. Desai and S. Goel, *Child Rights Education for Inclusion and Protection:
Primary Prevention*, Rights-based Direct Practice with Children,
https://doi.org/10.1007/978-981-13-0417-0

• Child sexual abuse	बाल यौन दुर्व्यवहार
• Child Welfare Committee	बाल कल्याण समिति
• Children in conflict with law	विधि विरुद्ध/अपराध में लिप्त बच्चे
• Children in need of care and protection	देखभाल और संरक्षण की आवश्यकता वाले बच्चे
• Commercial exploitation of children	बच्चों का वाणिज्यिक शोषण
• Commercial sexual exploitation of children	बच्चो का वाणिज्यिक यौन शोषण
• Community mobilisation	समुदाय जुटाव
• Consent	सहमति
• Contraceptive	गर्भनिरोधक
• Corporal punishment	शारीरिक दंड
• Crime	गुनाह/अपराध
• Case study discussion	केस अध्यायन चर्चा
• Child citizenship	बाल नागरिकता
• Child responsibility	बच्चे की ज़िम्मेदारी
• Child rights	बाल अधिकार
• Child rights education	बाल अधिकार का शिक्षण
• Childhood	बचपन
• Children	बच्चे
• Children's associations	बच्चों के संघटन
• Children's empowerment	बच्चों के सशक्तिकरण
• Children with disability	विकलंग बचाई
• Committee	समिति
• Concept	संकल्पना
• Confidentiality	गोपनीयता
• Constitutional rights	संवैधानिक अधिकार
• Consumer	ग्राहक/उपभोक्ता
• Consumer rights and responsibilities	ग्राहक/उपभोक्ता के अधिकार और जिम्मेदारियां
• Cooperation	सहयोग
• Criticism	आलोचना
• Culture	संस्कृति
• Cultural diversity	सांस्कृतिक विविधता
• Cultural life	सांस्कृतिक जीवन
• Cultural rights	सांस्कृतिक अधिकार
• Cycle	चक्र
• Democratic	लोकतान्त्रिक
• Democratisation	जनतंत्रीकरण
• Development	विकास
• Dignity	गौरव
• Direct practice with children	बच्चों के साथ प्रत्यक्ष कार्य
• Discrimination	भेदभाव

• Discussion	चर्चा
• Displacement	विस्थापन
• Diversity	विविधता
• Domestic child labour	घरेलू बाल मजदूर/श्रमिक
• Emotional/psychological/verbal abuse	भावनात्मक/मनोवैज्ञानिक/मौखिक दुर्व्यवहार
• Economic citizenship	आर्थिक नागरिकता
• Education	शिक्षा
• Emotional abuse	भाविक दुर्व्यवहार
• Empathy	सहानुभूति
• Empowerment workshops	सशक्तिकरण कार्यशाला
• Environment	वातावरण
• Evaluation	मूल्यांकन
• Exclusion	हिष्कार
• Exercise	व्यायाम
• Expected outcome	अनुमानित परिणाम
• Experiential method	अनुभवी विधि
• Facilitating	अभिनंदन करना
• Family	परिवार
• Family forms	परिवार के प्रकार
• Family internal dynamics	पारिवारिक आंतरिक गतिशीलता
• Family interactions with its environment	परिवार और पर्यावरण का सम्बन्ध
• Family life	पारिवारिक जीवन
• Family rights	पारिवारिक अधिकार
• Family structure	परिवार संरचना
• Family well-being	पारिवारिक कल्याण
• Financial education	आर्थिक/वित्तीय शिक्षा
• Financial planning	आर्थिक आयोजन
• Foeticide	भ्रूण हत्या
• Fun	मज़ा
• Game	खेल
• Gender	लिंगभाव
• Girls	लड़कियाँ
• Group	समूह
• Identity	पहचान
• Ideology	विचारधारा
• Inclusion	समावेश
• Inclusive	सम्मिलित
• The Indian constitution	भारतीय संविधान
• Individual	व्यक्ति/व्यक्तिगत
• Interaction	पारस्परिक व्यवहार

• Intercultural harmony	अंतर सांस्कृतिक सद्भावना
• Juvenile Justice Act	बाल न्याय अधिनियम
• Juvenile Justice Board	बाल न्याय परिषद्
• Kidnapping	अपहरण
• Legal rights	कानूनी अधिकार
• Literacy	साक्षरता
• Local self-governance	स्थानीय स्वशासन
• Marketing	विपणन
• Mass media	व्यापक माध्यम
• Method	पद्धति
• Methodology	पद्धतिशास्त्र
• Mock	दिखावटी
• Money	पैसे
• Observation home	निरिक्षण गृह
• Older persons	वृद्ध
• Other backward classes	अन्य पिछड़ा वर्ग
• Paedophilia	बड़ों का छोटों के प्रति यौन आकर्षण
• Participant	प्रतिभागी
• Participation	भागीदारी
• Physical abuse	शारीरिक दुर्व्यवहार
• Plan	योजना
• Planning	आयोजन करना
• Play	खेल
• Plurality	अधिकता
• Policy of reservations	आरक्षण की नीति
• Prejudice	पूर्वधारणा
• Prevention	निवारण
• Primary duty-bearers of children	बच्चों के प्राथमिक कर्तव्यों
• Principles of child rights	बाल अधिकारों के सिद्धांत
• Procedure	प्रक्रिया
• Protection	संरक्षण
• Psychological abuse	मानसिक दुर्व्यवहार
• Questions for discussion	चर्चा के लिए प्रश्न
• Quiz	चर्चा के लिए प्रश्न
• Recreation	मनोरंजन
• Regional language rights	प्रादेशिक/क्षेत्रीय भाषा अधिकार
• Regulation	नियमीकरण
• Rehabilitation	पुनर्वास
• Religious conflicts	धार्मिक संघर्ष
• Religious rights	धार्मिक अधिकार

• Reservation	आरक्षण
• Respect	आदर करना
• Response	प्रतिक्रिया
• Right to information	सूचना का अधिकार
• Role-plays	भूमिका निभाते हैं
• Safe	सुरक्षित
• Sale of children	बच्चों की बिक्री
• Savings Accounts	बचत खाते
• Saving systems	बचत प्रणाली
• Sexual relationship	लैंगिक सम्बन्ध
• Sexually transmitted infections	यौन रोग
• Scheduled castes	अनुसूचित जाति
• Scheduled Tribes	अनुसूचित जनजाति
• Self-assessment	आत्म मूल्यांकन
• Skills	कौशल
• small group discussion	छोटे समूह चर्चा
• social justice	सामाजिक न्याय
• Society	समाज
• Stereotyping	रूढ़िबद्धता
• Story	कहानी
• Street plays	सड़क नाटकों
• Survivor	उत्तरजीवी
• Sustainable consumption	उपभोक्ता का सातत्य
• Teamwork	सामूहिक कार्य
• Teenage pregnancy	युवा अवस्था में गर्भ धारण
• Touch	स्पर्श
• Theory	सिद्धांत
• Tools	साधन
• Trafficking of children	बच्चो का अवैध व्यापार
• Tribal children	आदिवासी बच्चे
• Unsafe	असुरक्षित
• Untouchability	अस्पृश्यता
• Verbal abuse	मौखिक दुरुपयोग
• Victim	पीड़ित
• Violation	उल्लंघन
• Violence	हिंसा
• Vocational guidance	व्यावसायिक मार्गदर्शन
• Wealth	समृद्धि